James Croston

Nooks and corners of Lancashire and Cheshire

James Croston

Nooks and corners of Lancashire and Cheshire

ISBN/EAN: 9783337150266

Printed in Europe, USA, Canada, Australia, Japan

Cover: Foto ©Andreas Hilbeck / pixelio.de

More available books at **www.hansebooks.com**

NOOKS AND CORNERS

OF

𝕷ancashire and 𝕮heshire.

A WAYFARER'S NOTES IN THE PALATINE COUNTIES,

HISTORICAL, LEGENDARY, GENEALOGICAL,

AND DESCRIPTIVE.

BY

JAMES CROSTON, F.S.A.

Fellow of the Royal Historical Society of Great Britain; Member of the Architectural,
Archæological and Historic Society of Chester; Member of the
Council of the Record Society.

Author of "On Foot through the Peak," "A History of Samlesbury," "Historical Memorials
of the Church in Prestbury," "Old Manchester and its Worthies,"
etc., etc.

JOHN HEYWOOD,
DEANSGATE, AND RIDGEFIELD, MANCHESTER;
AND 11, PATERNOSTER BUILDINGS,
LONDON.
1882.

JOHN HEYWOOD, PRINTER, HULME HALL ROAD,
MANCHESTER.

PREFACE.

THIS volume is not put forth as professedly a history of the places described, the Author's aim having been rather to seize upon and group from such accredited sources of information as were available, the leading facts and incidents relating to special localities, and to present the scenes of human life and action in a readable and attractive form by divesting, in some degree, the tame and uninviting facts of archæology of their deadly dulness; to bring into prominent relief the remarkable occurrences and romantic incidents of former days, and, by combining with the graver and more substantial matters of history an animated description of the physical features and scenic attractions of the localities in which those incidents occurred, to render them more interesting to the general reader.

A popular writer—the Authoress of "Our Village"—has said that she cared less for any reputation she might have gained as a writer of romance, than she did for the credit to be derived from the less ambitious but more useful office of faithfully uniting and preserving those fragments of tradition, experience, and biography, which give to history its living interest. In the same spirit the following pages have been written. There are within the Palatine Counties of Lancaster and Chester many objects and places, many halls and manor-houses that possess an abiding interest from the position they occupy in "our rough island story," and from their being associated, if not with events of the highest historic import, yet at least with many of those subordinate scenes and occurrences—

those romantic incidents and half-forgotten facts that illustrate the inner life and character of bygone generations. These lingering memorials of a period the most chivalrous and the most romantic in our country's annals may occasionally have received the notice of the precise topographer and the matter-of-fact antiquary, but, though possessing in themselves much that is picturesque and attractive, they have rarely been placed before the reader in any other guise than that in which the soberest narrative could invest them. In them the romance of centuries seems to be epitomised, and to the "seeing eye" they are the types and emblems of the changing life of our great nation; legend and tradition gather round, and weird stories and scraps of family history are associated with them that bring vividly before the mind's eye the domestic life and manners of those who have gone before, and show in how large a degree the Past may be made a guide for the Present and the Future.

It only remains for the Author to acknowledge his obligations to those friends who, by information communicated, and in other ways, have aided him in his design. His thanks are due to JOHN EGLINGTON BAILEY, Esq., F.S.A., of Stretford; JOHN OLDFIELD CHADWICK, Esq., F.S.S., F.G.S., of London; Dr. SAMUEL CROMPTON, of Cranleigh, Surrey; Lieutenant-Colonel FISHWICK, F.S.A., of Rochdale; and THOMAS HELSBY, Esq., of the Inner Temple. He is also indebted to the kindness of GILBERT J. FRENCH, Esq., of Bolton, for the loan of the several engravings which add interest to the story of Samuel Crompton.

UPTON HALL, PRESTBURY, CHESHIRE,
DECEMBER, 1881.

CONTENTS.

CHAPTER VII.

CHAPTER VIII.

CHAPTER IX.

CHAPTER X.

ILLUSTRATIONS.

B

SUBSCRIBERS.

ADSHEAD, G. H., Esq., Fern Villas, Bolton Road, Pendleton, nr. M'chester.
ANDREW, FRANK, Esq., Ashton-under-Lyne.
ARDERN, L., Jun., Esq., Hazel Grove, Cheshire.
ARMITAGE, ELKANAH, Esq., The Rookery, Pendleton, Manchester.
ARMSTRONG, THOMAS, Esq., F.R.M.S., Highfield Bank, Urmston.
ARNOLD, HENRY, Esq., Blackley, near Manchester.
ASHTON, J. T., Esq., Wellington Road South, Stockport.
ASHWORTH, CHARLES E., Esq., Fairfield, Manchester.
ASHWORTH, GEORGE, Esq., 3, Charlotte Street, Manchester.
ASCROFT, W. T., Esq., 3, Stamford Street, Altrincham.
ASPLAND, L. M., Esq., 47, Linden Gardens, South Kensington, London, S.W.
ASQUITH, D., Esq., Lancashire & Yorkshire Railway Offices, Manchester.
ATKINSON, GEORGE, Esq., Stockport.
ATHERTON, W. H., Esq., Southbank Road, Southport.
ATHENÆUM, The, Manchester.
ATTOCK, F., Esq., Somerset House, Newton Heath.

BAILEY, J. EGLINTON, F.S.A., Egerton Villa, Stretford.
BARLOW, J. R., Esq., Edgeworth, near Bolton.
BARNES, ALFRED, Esq., Farnworth.
BARNES, THOMAS, Esq., Farnworth.
BARTON, RICHARD, Esq., West Leigh Lodge, West Leigh, Lancashire.
BAYLEY, WILLIAM, Esq., Craybrow, Lymm, Warrington.
BAZLEY, Sir THOS., Bart., Eyford Park, Stow-on-the-Wold, Gloucestershire.
BEAMAN, Mrs., Haydock Lodge, Ashton-in-Makerfield, Lancashire.
BEALES, ROBERT, Esq., M.D., J.P. (Mayor), Congleton.
BELLIS, THOMAS, Esq., Northenden, near Manchester.
BERRY, JAMES, Esq., Jun., Palatine Square, Burnley.
BESWICK, JOHN, Esq., Victoria Hotel, Strangeways, Manchester (2 copies).
BIBBY, W. H., Esq., Levenshulme.
BIRCH, HERBERT, Esq., The Vicarage, Blackburn.

BIRLEY, HUGH, Esq., M.P., Moorland, Withington.

BIRLEY, J. SHEPHERD, Esq., Moss Lee, Bolton-le-Moors.

BLEASDELL, The Rev. J., Henry Square, Ashton-under-Lyne.

BODDINGTON, HENRY, Jun., Esq., Strangeways Brewery, Manchester.

BOLGER, Miss SARAH, Atherton, Bournemouth, Hants.

BOLTON, JOHN, Esq., Southfield, Blackburn.

BONE, John W., Esq., F.S.A., 26, Bedford Place, Russell Square, London.

BOOTH, AARON, Jun., Esq., 4, South Street, Albert Square, Manchester.

BOOTH, JAMES, Esq., 52, Todmorden Road, Burnley.

BOOTE, DANIEL, Esq., Oakfield, Ashton-on-Mersey.

BOURNE, Sir JAMES, Heathfield, Liverpool.

BOWDLER, WILLIAM HENRY, Esq., J.P., Kirkham, Lancashire.

BOWES, Dr. JOHN, The Blue Coat School, Warrington.

BOWKER, S. J. Esq., 42, Great Ancoats Street, Manchester.

BOULTON, ISAAC WATT, Esq., J.P., Stamford House, Ashton-under-Lyne (2 copies).

BRADSHAW, CHRISTOPHER, Esq., Kenwood, Ellesmere Park, Eccles.

BRADSHAWE, GEORGE PARIS, Esq., 30, Gloucester Street, Warwick Square, London.

BRADSHAWE-ISHERWOOD, Mrs., Marple Hall, Stockport.

BRADSHAW, S., Esq., 241, Broad Street, Pendleton.

BRADWELL, DENNIS, Esq., J. P. Higher Daisy Bank, Congleton.

BRAMWELL, ROBERT, Esq., 5, Green Street, Ardwick Green.

BRAGG, HARRY, Esq., The Mount, Blackburn.

BRANSBY, WILLIAM, Esq., 46, Deansgate, Manchester.

BROWN, Rev. Canon, M.A., Staley Vicarage, Stalybridge.

BROWNHILL, JOHN, Esq., Alderley, Cheshire.

BRIDGEMAN, Rev. The Honble. G. T. O., Wigan Hall, Wigan.

BROADBENT, GEO. HARRY, Esq., L.K.Q.C.P.I. and L.M., Ashton-under-Lyne.

BROADBENT, EDWIN, Esq., Reddish, near Stockport.

BROCKBANK, W., Esq., Pall Mall, Manchester.

BUCKLEY, Mr., Strangeways Brewery.

BUDD, Mrs. M., Cedar Villa, Wilbraham Road, Fallowfield, Manchester.

BULTEEL, S. W., Esq., Victoria Park, Manchester.

BURGESS, SAMUEL, Esq., Lancashire and Yorkshire Railway Offices, Manchester.

BURTON, ALFRED, Esq., 37, Cross Street, Manchester.

BURGHOPE, WILLIAM, Esq., Albert Villa, near Malvern.

BURTON, JOSEPH, Esq., Lyme View, Bramhall, Cheshire.

BURTON, J. H., Esq., F.R.H.S., 5, Trafalgar Square, Ashton-under-Lyne.

BURTON, Mrs. LINGEN, Abbey House, Shrewsbury.

BUSTARD, J., Esq., Summer Lane, Barnsley.

CALDERBANK, Captain, Stockport.

CAMERON, JOHN D., Esq., The Grove, Sale, Cheshire.

CARRINGTON, H. H. SMITH, Esq., Whaley Bridge, near Stockport.

CARVER, Mrs. J., Sunnyside, Whalley Range, Manchester.

CARR, JOHN, Esq., 2, McDonald's Lane, Manchester.

CASSON, E., Esq., Raper Lodge, Bramhall Park, Cheshire.

CHADWICK, T., Esq., The Grove, Urmston, near Manchester.

CHETHAM'S LIBRARY, Manchester.

CHORLTON, THOMAS, Esq., 32, Brasenose Street, Manchester.

CHORLTON, WILLIAM, Esq., Fairfield, near Manchester.

CHORLTON, THOMAS, Esq., 32, Brazenose Street, Manchester.

CHRISTY, RICHARD, Esq., Poynton Towers, Cheshire.

CLARE, CHARLES LEIGH, Esq., Park Lane, Higher Broughton, Manchester.

COATES, The Misses, Sunnyside, Crawshawbooth, Lancashire.

COLLINS, JAMES, Esq., Ada Villa, Old Trafford, Manchester.

COOMBES, The Rev. G. F., B.A., Portwood, Stockport.

COOPER, EDWARD, Esq., 10, Downing Street, Manchester.

COOPER, THOMAS, Esq., Mossley House, Congleton.

COULTATE, WILLIAM MILLER, Esq., F.R.C.S., J.P., 1, Yorke Street, Burnley.

COWIE, Very Rev. B. MORGAN, D.D., Dean of Manchester, The Deanery, Manchester.

CRAIG, ANDREW L., Esq., 148, Cheapside, London.

CRAVEN, JAMES, Esq., Woodland House, Whalley Range, Manchester.

CREEKE, Major A. B., Monkholm, near Burnley.

CRONKESHAW, JOHN, Esq., White Bull Hotel, Blackburn.

CROSS, JOHN, Esq., Cambridge Villa, Heaton Norris.

CROSS, The Right Hon. Sir R. A., M.P., Eccle Riggs, Broughton-in-Furness.

CROMPTON, SAMUEL, Esq., M.D., Cranleigh, Surrey.

CUNLIFF, JOHN, Esq., Lomber Hey, near Stockport.

CURZON, N. C, Esq., Lockington Hall, Derby.

CUFF, JAMES HENRY, Esq., Millington, near Altrincham.

CUNLIFFE, EDWARD THOMAS, Esq., Handforth.

DALE, THOMAS, Esq., J.P., Bank House, Park Road, Southport.

DAVENPORT, E. H., Esq., Davenport, Bridgnorth, Shropshire.

DAY, Mr. T. J., Heaton Moor, Stockport.

DEVONSHIRE, His Grace the Duke of, Chatsworth, Chesterfield.

DILLON, Rev. GODFREY, Radcliffe (2 copies).

DOBSON, MATTHEW, Esq., Cheadle.

DORRINGTON, JAMES T., Esq., Bonishall, near Macclesfield.

DOWNING, WILLIAM, Esq., Springfield Olton, Acock Green, Birmingham.

DYER, A. C., Esq., National Provincial Bank of England, Manchester.

EARWAKER, J. P., Esq., M.A., F.S.A., Pensarn, Abergele.
EASTWOOD, J. A., Esq., 49, Princess Street, Manchester.
EATON, C. Esq., 3, St. Edward Street, Leek.
ECKERSLEY, C., Esq., Tyldesley, Lancashire.
EDGAR, ROBERT A., Esq., Seymour Lodge, Heaton Chapel.
EDGE, J. BROUGHTON, Esq., Broad Oak Park, Worsley.
EILBECK, H., Esq., Ashton-upon-Mersey, Cheshire.
ELLISON, JOHN, Esq., Stockport Road, Ashton-under-Lyne.
ELWEN, GEORGE, Esq., 11, Knott Street, Higher Broughton, Manchester.
ENION, J. C., Esq., Piccadilly, Manchester.
EQUITABLE CO-OPERATIVE SOCIETY, Greenacres Hill, Oldham.
EVANS, Miss LYDIA, The Heys, near St. Helens, Lancashire.
EVANS, JOHN, Esq., 1, Mitton Street, Greenheys.
EYRE, The Rev. W. H., Stonyhurst College, near Blackburn *(5 copies)*.

FAIRBROTHER, HENRY, Esq., 106, Albert Square, Manchester.
FEATHER, The Rev. GEORGE, The Vicarage, Glazebury, Leigh, Lancashire.
FIELDEN, JOHN, Esq., Dobroyd Castle, Todmorden *(2 copies)*.
FLETCHER, J. SHEPHERD, Esq., M.D., 75, Lever Street, Manchester.
FLETCHER, THOMAS, Esq., Lever House, near Bolton-le-Moors.
FOLLY, THOMAS, Esq., Warrington.
FOYSTER, J. ASHER, Esq, 5, Norfolk Street, Manchester.
FRANKLAND, GEO., Esq., *Express* Office, Burnley.
FRESTON, T. W., Esq., 8, Watling Street, Manchester.
FRY, JOSEPH, Esq., Manchester.

GAMBLE, Colonel, Windlehurst, St. Helens.
GARTSIDE, R. A., Esq., Dacres, Greenfield, near Manchester.
GASKELL, A. E., Esq., 255, Moss Lane, East, Manchester.
GASKELL, JOSIAH, Esq., Burgrave Lodge, Ashton-in-Makerfield
GEE, CHARLES, Esq., Gorton, Manchester.
GERARD, Major, Aspull House, Wigan.
GIBBONS, BENJAMIN, Esq., London Road, Manchester.
GILL, RICHARD, Esq., 7, Pall Mall, Manchester.
GILBODY, A. H., Esq., Edge Lane, Chorlton-on-Medlock.
GOODMAN, DAVENPORT, Esq., Eccles House, Chapel-en-le-Frith.
GRAHAM, JOSEPH, Esq., Carlton Road, Burnley.
GRAHAM, Rev. PHILIP, Turncroft, Darwen.
GRANTHAM, JOHN, Esq., 2, Rothsay Place, Old Trafford, Manchester.
GRAY, ROBERT, Esq., Greenfield House, Hyde.
GRADWELL, SAMUEL, Esq., Holmes Chapel, Cheshire.
GRATRIX, SAMUEL, Esq., J.P., West Point, Whalley Range, Manchester.

GREAVES, GEORGE, Esq., Hayfield.
GREENALL, Sir GILBERT, Bart., Walton Hall, Warrington.
GREENALL, Colonel, Lingholme, Keswick.
GREENALL, Major, The Old Rectory, Grappenhall.
GREENE, Mrs. TURNER, Southworth House, Wigan.
GREENHALGH, JOSEPH DODSON, Esq., Gladstone Cottage, Bolton.
GREENWAY, C., Esq., J.P., Darwen Bank, Darwen.
GREENWOOD, Charles, Esq., 26, Aked's Road, Halifax.
GROVES, G. H., Esq., Kent Villa, Urmston, near Manchester.
GRUNDY, ALFRED, Esq., Whitefield, near Manchester.
GUEST, W. H., Esq., 78, Cross Street, Manchester.

HADFIELD, GEORGE, Esq., 110, King Street, Manchester.
HAGUE, JOHN SCHOLES, Esq., White Hall, Chinley, Derbyshire.
HALL, JOSHUA, Esq., Kingston House, Hyde.
HALL, JOHN, Esq., The Grange, Hale, Cheshire.
HALL, ROBERT, Esq., Anes House, Hyde.
HALSTEAD, LOUIS, Esq., Redwaterfoot, Corneholme.
HAMPSON, WILLIAM, Esq., Rose Hill, Marple, Cheshire.
HAMPSON, J. R. Esq., Old Trafford.
HAMPSON, J. T., Esq., Solicitor, Ashton-under-Lyne.
HARLOW, Miss, Heaton Norris, Stockport.
HARTLEY, WILLIAM, Esq., Greek Street, Stockport.
HARTLEY, Mrs., Brierfield House, near Burnley.
. HARTLEY, JOB W., Esq., Westgate, Burnley.
HARDWICK, C., Esq., 72, Talbot Street, Moss Side, Manchester.
HARWOOD, Alderman JOHN J., Northumberland Street, Higher Broughton.
HAWORTH, The Rev. J. G., Tunsteads Vicarage, Stacksteads.
HAWORTH, S. E., Esq., Holyrood, Prestwich.
HAWORTH, RICHARD, Esq., J.P., 28, High Street, Manchester.
HEGINBOTTOM, THOMAS, Esq., J.P., (Mayor), Stamford House, Ashton-under-Lyne.
HELSBY, THOMAS, Esq., Lincoln's Inn, London.
HIBBERT, HENRY, Esq., Broughton Grove, Grange-over-Sands.
HICKS, JOHN, Esq., Mytton Hall, Whalley, Lancashire.
HIGGINS, ARTHUR, Esq., King Street, Salford.
HIGGINS, JAMES, Esq., Woodhey, Kersal, Manchester.
HIGSON, THOMAS, Esq., Red Cliffe, Alderley Edge, Cheshire.
HILL, T. D., Esq., Fairfield.
HINDLEY, THOMAS, Esq., Stockport.
HIRST, JOHN, Esq., Ladcastle, Dobcross.
HODGSON, T., Esq., Cravenholme, Didsbury.

HOOLEY, SAMUEL J., Esq., Manchester and Liverpool District Bank Limited, Tunstall.

HOWE, JAMES, Esq., Bellfield House, Ashton-under-Lyne, near Manchester.

HODGKINSON, JAMES B., Esq., Green Bank, Sale, Cheshire.

HODGKINSON, S., Esq., Marple, Cheshire.

HOLDEN, THOMAS, Esq., Bolton.

HOLMES, JAMES, Esq., Egerton Road, Fallowfield, Manchester.

HORNBY, JAMES, Esq., Wigan.

HYDE, WALTER, Esq., Cromwell House, Heaton Chapel.

INGHAM, B., Esq., York Chambers, Brasenose Street, Manchester.

JACKSON, ALFRED, Esq., Burnley Lane, Burnley.

JACKSON, B., Esq., Heathfield, Ashton-upon-Mersey.

JACKSON, HARTLEY, Esq., Pickup Terrace, Burnley.

JACKSON, H. J., Esq., Ashton-under-Lyne *(2 copies).*

JOHNSON, J. A., Esq., 73, Albert Road, Southport.

JOHNSON, J. H., Esq., F.S.A., 73, Albert Road, Southport.

JONES, JOHN JOSEPH, Esq., Abberley Hall, Stourport.

KAY, JACOB, Esq., 5, Booth Street, Manchester.

KEENE, R. Esq., Irongate, Derby.

KETTLE, A. J., Esq., Addiscombe, Prestwich Park, near Manchester.

KETTLE, W. C., Esq., Addiscombe, Prestwich Park.

KENDERDINE, FREDERICK, Esq., Morningside, Old Trafford.

KNOTT, JAMES, Esq., 55, Higher Ardwick, Manchester.

KNOTT, JOHN, Esq., Dartmouth House, Hurst, Cheshire.

LANCASTER, ALF, Esq., Manchester Road, Burnley.

LAWTON, JAMES KINDER, Esq., Hazel Grove, near Stockport.

LEEDHAM, F. H., Esq., Burnage Lane, near Manchester.

LEECE, JOSEPH, Esq., Mansfield Villa, Urmston, near Manchester.

LEES, EDWARD B., Esq., Kelbarrow, Grasmere.

LEIGH, JAMES, Esq., 66, Deansgate, Manchester.

LEVER, ELLIS, Esq., Culcheth Hall, Bowdon.

LEES, SAMUEL, Esq., Park Bridge, Ashton-under-Lyne.

LEIGH, JOHN, Esq., The Manor House, Hale, Cheshire.

LEIGH, CHARLES, Esq., Bank Terrace, Wigan.

LEYLAND, JOHN, Esq., The Grange, Hindley, near Wigan.

LIBRARIES, FREE PUBLIC, Manchester.

LIBRARY, FREE PUBLIC, Town Hall, Rochdale.

LIBRARY, FREE, Peel Park, Salford.

LIBRARY, FREE, The Stockport.

LIBRARY, FREE, The Wigan.
LIBRARY, FREE, The Heywood, near Manchester.
LIBRARY, FREE, The Bolton-le-Moors.
LINFOOT, JOSEPH, Esq., Cannon Street, Manchester.
LINGARD-MONK, RICHARD, B. M., Esq., Fulshaw Hall, Wilmslow.
LLOYD, THOMAS, Esq., Brooklands House, Brooklands, Cheshire.
LONG, JOHN F., Esq., 135, Great Ancoats Street, Manchester.
LONGDEN, A. W., Esq., Marple, Cheshire.
LONGWORTH, SOLOMON, Esq., Whalley, Lancashire.
LONGSHAW, Mrs., Beech Priory, Southport.
LONGTON, EDWARD JOHN, Esq., M.D., The Priory, Southport.
LORD, HENRY, Esq., 42, John Dalton Street, Manchester.
LUPTON, ARTHUR, Esq., 136, Manchester Road, Burnley.
LUPTON, BENJAMIN, Esq., Cumberland Place, Burnley.
LUPTON, JOSEPH TOWNEND, Esq., 28, Manchester Road, Burnley.
LOWE, J. W., Esq., St. James's Square, Manchester.

MARSDEN, Rev. Canon, Great Oakley, Harwich, Essex.
MARSDEN, The Rev. W., Fullarton House, Upper Brook Street, M'chester.
MARSHALL, E. W., Esq., 38, Barton Arcade, Manchester.
MARSON, GERVASE, Esq., Thorncliffe House, Higher Broughton, Manchester.
MARSON, JAMES, Esq., High Cliffe, Warrington.
MASSEY, JOHN, Esq., J.P., Hawk's House, near Burnley *(2 copies)*.
MAYOR'S LIBRARY, The, Manchester, per Alderman Patteson.
McQUHAE, WILLIAM, Esq., 5, Stamford Street, Brooks's Bar, Manchester.
McKENNA, BERNARD, Esq., Lea Grange, White Moss, Blackley, nr. M'chester.
McKERROW, Alderman JOHN B., J.P., Norcliffe, Broughton Park.
METCALF, WILLIAM, Esq., 2, Vernon Avenue, Eccles.
MIDDLETON, THOMAS, Esq., Springfield, Adlington, Lancashire.
MIDWOOD, G. H., 55, Faulkner Street, Manchester.
MILLS, WILLIAM, Esq., 12, New Brown Street, Manchester.
MILNER, GEORGE, Esq., 57A, Mosley Street, Manchester.
MITCHELL, WILLIAM, Esq., Brook Villa, Golbourne.
MOORE, D., Esq., Woodville, Bramhall, Cheshire.
MOORHOUSE, CHRISTOPHER, Esq., 4, St. Paul's Road, Kersal, Manchester.
MORTON, WILLIAM, Esq., 12, Brown Street, Manchester.
MOTHERSILL, EDWARD, Esq., Dane House, Sale, Cheshire.
MOULTON, GEORGE, Esq., Hall's Crescent, Collyhurst.
MUIRHEAD, THOMAS S., Esq., Ash Lodge, Halliwell Lane, Cheetham.
MURRAY, Alderman (the late), Apsley House, Hyde Road, Manchester.
MYERS, HENRY, Esq., 140, Newcastle Street, Stretford Road, Manchester.

C

Napier, George W., Esq., Merchistoun, Alderley Edge.
Neal, William, Esq., Ashton-under-Lyne.
Newton, Walter, Esq., 69, Bridge Street, Manchester.
New, Philip N., Esq., 15, Baillie Street, Rochdale.
Norreys, Miss, Davyhulme Hall, Lancashire.
Northcott, James B., Esq., King Street, Manchester.

Owen, William, Esq., Palmyra Square, Warrington.
Park, Rev. R., M.A., 3, The Crescent, Salford.
Parker, Edward, Esq., Browsholme Hall, Yorkshire.
Patteson, Alderman, J.P., Victoria Park, Manchester.
Peacock, Richard, Esq., Gorton Hall, near Manchester.
Perkins, Stanhope, Esq., 6, Healey Terrace, Fairfield, near Manchester.
Phillips, John William, Esq., Brown Hill, Burnley.
Phillips, Miss, Welcombe, Stratford-on-Avon.
Piccles, Thomas L., Esq., Rock Cottage, New Mills, Derbyshire.
Pilkington, James, Esq., Swinithwaite Hall, Bedale, Yorkshire.
Pink, Wm. Duncombe, Esq., Leigh.
Pooley, C. J., Esq., Knutsford.
Pollitt, James, Esq., Guide House, Ashton-under-Lyne.
Pooley, W. Ormsby, Esq., J.P., Knutsford.
Portico Library, The, Mosley Street, Manchester.
Potter, Rupert, Esq., 2, Bolton Gardens, South Kensington, London, S.W.
Potts, Arthur, Esq., Hoole Hall, Chester.
Preston, Thomas, Esq., 92, Manchester Road, Burnley.

Raby, William, Esq., 78, Cross Street, Manchester.
Ralphs, Samuel, Esq., 56, Sandy Lane, Stockport.
Ramsbottom, G. H., Esq., Altham Hall, near Accrington.
Ramsbotham, John, Esq., 22, Arbour Street, Southport (2 copies).
Rawsthorne, H., Esq., East Street, Preston.
Redhead, R. Milne, Esq., Springfield, Seedley, Manchester (2 copies).
Richmond, T. G., Esq., Ford House, Prestbury.
Richmond, Fred, Esq., 163, Radnor Street, Hulme, Manchester.
Richmond, James, Esq., Mosely House, Burnley.
Rickards, Charles H., Esq., J.P., Seymour Grove, Old Trafford, Manchester.
Rigby, S., Esq.
Robinson, William, Esq., The Hollies, Talbot Road, Old Trafford.
Robson, Thomas W., Esq., 18, Aytoun Street, Manchester.
Rooke, George, Esq., Moorside, Sale.
Roundell, C. J., Esq., M.P., Osborne, Fernhurst, Hazlemere.

ROYLE, JOHN, Esq., 53, Port Street, Manchester.

ROYLANCE, E. W., Esq., Brookfield, Bury Old Rd., Cheetham Hill, M'chester.

RUMNEY, THOMAS, Esq., Hallcroft Cottage, Carnforth.

RUSHTON, THOMAS LEVER, Esq., Moor Platt, Horwich, near Bolton.

RYDER, T. D., Esq., St. James's Square, Manchester.

RYLANDS, J. PAUL, Esq., F.S.A., Highfields, Thelwall.

RYLANDS, W. HARRY, Esq., F.S.A., Biblical Archæological Society, 11, Hart Street, Bloomsbury, London.

SCHUNCE, J. EDGAR, Esq., Wicken Hall, near Rochdale.

SEVERS, FRED, Esq., 1, Dalton Terrace, Clayton St., Chorlton Rd., M'chester.

SCOTT, JOHN OLDRED, Esq., 31, Spring Gardens, London, S.W.

SCHOFIELD, THOMAS, Esq., J.P., Thornfield, Old Trafford.

SHAW, GILES, Esq., 72, Manchester Road, Oldham.

SHIERS, GEORGE ALFRED, Esq., Tyntesfield, Ashton-upon-Mersey.

SHIERS, RICHARD, Jun., Esq., Earlscliffe, Bowdon, Cheshire.

SIDEBOTHAM, JOSEPH, Esq., F.R.A.S., F.L.S., F.S.A., Erlesden, Bowdon, Cheshire.

SITWELL, R., Esq., Morley, Derby.

SLARK, J. and A., Esqrs., 41, Fishergate, Preston.

SMEAL, A., Esq., Ravensla, Whalley Road, Whalley Range, Manchester.

SMITH, ASTON W., Esq., The Old Hall, Bootle.

SMITH, BRYCE, Esq., 16, Nicholas Street, Manchester.

SMITH, GEORGE J. W., Esq., Savings Bank, Stockport.

SMITH, JAMES, Esq., Highfield, Edge Lane, Chorlton-cum-Hardy.

SMITH, Rev. J. FINCH, M.A., F.S.A., Aldridge Rectory, Walsall.

SMITH, J., Jun., Esq., Legh Street, Warrington.

SMITH, ROBERT McDOWELL, Esq., Crumpsall, near Manchester.

SMITH, WILLIAM, Esq., Adswood Grove, Stockport.

SMITH, J. J., Esq., King Street, Manchester.

SOWLER, Lieut.-Colonel, Oak Bank, Victoria Park, Manchester.

STANLEY, C. J., Esq., Halscote, Grange-over-Sands.

STANTON, HENRY, Esq., Greenfield, Thelwall.

STEVENS, James, Esq., F.R.I.B.A., Lime Tree House, Macclesfield.

STEINTHAL, H. M., Esq., The Hollies, Fallowfield, near Manchester.

STUBS, PETER, Esq., Statham Lodge, Warrington.

STANYER, The Rev. W., 41, Corporation Street, Manchester.

STARKEY, Miss, Northwich, Cheshire.

STEVENS, EDWARD, Esq., Alderley Edge, Cheshire.

STRANGEWAY, WILLIAM N., Esq., 59, Westmoreland Rd., Newcastle-on-Tyne.

STANNING, Rev. J. H., The Vicarage, Leigh.

SUTCLIFFE, FRED, Esq., Ash Street, Bacup.

SYDDALL, JAMES, Esq., Chadkirk, Romily, Cheshire.

TAYLOR, THOMAS, Esq., 33, St. James Street, Burnley.

THOMPSON, Alderman Jos., J.P., Riversdale, Wilmslow.

THORLEY, WILLIAM, Esq., Lancashire and Yorkshire Railway Offices, Manchester.

TOLLEY, Thomas, Esq., Warrington,

TOPP, ALFRED, Esq., J.P., Farnworth.

TOULMIN, GEORGE, Esq , *Guardian* Office, Preston.

TURNER, W., Esq., Rusholme

TURNER, JOHN, Esq., Woodville, Lytham.

TWEEDALE, CHARLES LAKEMAN, Esq., Holmefield House, Crawshawbooth.

UNDERDOWN, R. G., Esq., M. S. & L. Railway Company, Manchester.

WADDINGTON, WILLIAM, Esq., Market Superintendent, Burnley.

WADDINGTON, WM. ANGELO, Esq., 5, Carlton Road, Burnley.

WALKDEN, — Esq., 16, Nicholas Street, Manchester.

WALKER, THOMAS, Esq., Oldfield, Cheshire.

WALMESLEY, OSWALD, Esq,, Shevington Hall, near Wigan.

WALSH, Dr. JOHN, Stonyhurst, near Whalley, Lancashire.

WALTERS, CHARLES, Esq., Clegg Street, Oldham.

WARNIRGTON, the Museum and Library.

WATTERSON, WM. CRAVEN, Esq., Hill Carr, Bowdon, Cheshire

WAINWRIGHT, JOHN, Esq., Carlton Lodge, Stretford.

WARBURTON, JOHN, Esq., Fairlie Villas, Raspberry Road, Fallowfield.

WARBURTON, SAMUEL, Esq., Sunnyhill, Crumpsall, Manchester.

WARBURTON, HENRY, Esq., The Elms, Hendham Vale, Manchester.

WATERS, — Esq., Manchester.

WATTS, JAMES, Esq., Portland Street, Manchester.

WATTS, JOHN, Esq., 23, Cross Street, Manchester.

WEBB, F. W., Esq., Chester Place, Crewe.

WEBSTER, WILLIAM, Esq., Abbotsfield,. St. Helens.

WHITE, CHARLES, Esq., Holly Villa, Warrington.

WHITTAKER, W. WILKINSON, Esq., Cornbrook Park, Manchester.

WHITEHEAD, EDWIN, Esq., The Hurst, Taunton Road, Ashton-under-Lyne.

WHITTAKER, ROBERT, Esq., Birch House, Lees, near Manchester.

WILD, ROBERT, Esq., 134, St. James's Street, Burnley.

WILKINSON, A., Esq., Westbourne Grove, Harpurhey, Manchester.

WILKINSON, T. R., Esq., The Polygon, Ardwick, Manchester.

WILKINSON, JOHN, Esq.,.25, Manor Street, Ardwick, Manchester.

WILKINSON, WILLIAM, Esq., M.A., Middlewood, Clitheroe.

WILSON, WILLIAM, Esq., Savings Bank, Stockport.

WILSON, C. M., Esq., Lancaster Villa, Broughton Park, Manchester.

WINTERBOTHAM, HENRY, Esq., F.R.C.S., Bury New Road, Manchester

WOLSTENHOLME, CHARLES, Esq., Richmond Hill, Bowdon, Cheshire.

WOOD, JOHN, Esq., J.P., Arden, near Stockport,

WOOD, RICHARD, Esq., J.P., Plimpton Hall, Heywood, near Manchester

WOOD, WILLIAM, Esq., Woodville, Bramhall, Cheshire.

WOOD, W. C., Esq., Brimscall Hall, Chorley, Lancashire,

WORTHINGTON, ED., Esq., Appley Bridge, near Wigan,

WOODHOUSE, GEORGE, Esq., Heath Bank, Chorley New Road, Bolton.

WOOD, ROBERT, Esq., Drywood Hall, Worsley.

WORTHINGTON, Alderman T., 33, Church Street, Manchester,

WRIGHT, E. ABBOTT, Esq., Castle Park, Frodsham, Cheshire.

YATES, J. W., Esq., Ashton-upon-Mersey.

YEOMAN, JOHN, Esq., 30, Union Street, Ardwick, Manchester.

BOOKSELLERS.

Bemrose & Sons, Derby.
Brown & Sons, Macclesfield.
Butler, S., Altrincham.
Burghope & Strange, Burnley.
Burgess, Henry, Northwich.

Cooke, Stretford Road, Manchester.
Cornish, J. E., Piccadilly and St. Ann's Square, Manchester.

Dodgson, J., Leeds.
Day, T. J., Market Street, Manchester.
Dooley, Henry, Stockport.

Galt, J. & Co., Corporation Street, Manchester.
Gray, Henry, Topographical Bookseller, 25, Cathedral Yard, Manchester.
Grundy, 68, Woodhouse Lane, Wigan.

Howell, E., Liverpool.
Holden, Adam, 48, Church Street, Liverpool.
Heywood, Abel & Son, Oldham Street, Manchester.

Kenyon, W., Newton Heath, Manchester.

Littlewood, James, Ashton-under-Lyne.
Lupton, J. & A., Burnley.

Minshull & Hughes, Chester.

Pearse, J. C., Southport.
Pearse, Percival, Warrington.
Phillipson & Golder, Chester.
Platt, Richard, Wigan.

RIDER, Leek.

ROWORTH, St. Ann's Square, Manchester.

ROBINSON, Preston.

SMITH, W. H. & SON, 1, New Brown Street, Manchester.

SMITH, W. H. & SON, L. & N.W. Railway and M.S. & L. Railway Book-
stalls, London Road Station, Manchester.

STOCK, ELLIOT, 62, Paternoster Row, London, E.C.

TUBBS & BROOK, Market Street, Manchester.

TRÜBNER & Co., London.

WALMSLEY, G. G., 50, Lord Street, Liverpool.

YABSLEY & Co., Sale, Cheshire.

NOOKS AND CORNERS

OF

LANCASHIRE AND CHESHIRE.

CHAPTER I.

A RAILWAY RAMBLE—THE ROMAN CITY ON THE RIBBLE
A DAY-DREAM AT RIBCHESTER.

N a bright morning in the exuberant summer time,
ere the country had lost the freshness of its earlier
beauty, or the forest trees had begun to bend
beneath the weight of their blushing burdens, we
found ourselves on the platform of the Victoria
Station with a friend, the companion of many a
pleasant wandering, equipped for a journey to the fair country
which skirts the base of Pendle Hill. We were both in high
spirits, and the beauty of the opening day added to our
enjoyment. The morning was cool and clear, and radiant with
the early sunshine—one of those genial days when, as Washington
Irving says, we seem to draw in pleasure with the very air we
breathe, and to feel happy we know not why—the invigorating
freshness of the atmosphere giving a pleasant impulse to the
spirits. There had been a slight fall of rain during the night,

I

but the breeze which followed had dried up the roadways, and now all was bright and clear, and the unclouded sun poured down a flood of brilliance that added to the charms of the early morn, imparting a gladdening influence which even the sparrows seemed to share as they flitted to and fro about the eaves with unceasing twitter.

For some distance the railway is carried over the house-tops, and as the train speeds along we can look down upon the dreary web of streets, the labyrinth of dwellings, the groves of chimneys, the mills, workshops, and brick-kilns, and the strange admixture of squalor, wretchedness, and impurity that go to make up the royal borough of Salford. Soon we reach the outskirts, where the country still struggles to maintain its greenness; then, after a short stoppage at Pendleton, we enter upon the pleasant vale of Clifton, where we are enabled to breathe the balmy atmosphere and drink in the fresh fragrance of the flower-bespangled meads. Pleasant is it to escape from the gloomy hives of brick, with their busy human throng, and to look abroad upon the expanse of country reposing in the summer sunshine. The gentle showers of the night seem to have refreshed the thirsty soil, and to have given an invigorating aspect to the landscape, imparting to the turf a brighter hue, and to the trees which clothe the folding bluffs a brighter tinge of colouring, whilst the sunlight gleams upon the fields and on the already ripening grain, and sparkles upon the lingering rain-drops that hang like strings of pearls from every bush and twig. On the left the quaint old hall of Agecroft, with its picturesque black and white gables, twinkles through the wind-shaken leaves; the Irwell meanders pleasantly through the fertile meadows on the right; and beyond, the grey embattled tower of Prestwich Church may be seen rising prominently above the umbraged slopes that bound the opposite side of the valley.

On, on we go with a screech and a roar, rattling over viaducts, rumbling through rocky cuttings, rushing along steep embankments; then rolling rapidly again over the level country, from whence we can look back upon the dingy town of Bolton, memorable in the annals of the great civil war as the place where the martyr Earl of Derby sealed his loyalty with his life. The changing aspect of the country now becomes manifest. Every mile brings a fresh picture, and the variety itself adds to the interest of the journey. The land is prettily featured—green and undulating, with well-wooded cloughs and shady dingles, backed by lofty gritstone ridges, which here and there soften into slopes of fertile beauty that form an admirable relief to the pale blue hills which stretch away to the furthest point of distance. Just before

reaching the station at Chapeltown we get sight of Turton Tower, a fine old relic of bygone days, once the home of Manchester's most noted "worthy"—Humphrey Chetham—and for a time, as tradition tells us, the abode of Oliver Cromwell; and close by is a picturesque gabled summer-house, surmounting a gentle eminence, that forms a conspicuous object for miles around. Still onward, past scattered hamlets, past mills, bleachworks, and collieries; past farms, cottages, and old-fashioned timber-built dwellings that more or less merit the appellation of "hall" applied to them; past meadows, fields, and pastures, where the hedge-rows and trees seem to revolve in a never-ending reel, while the telegraph wires that stretch from post to post rise and fall in a succession of graceful genuflexions. On, on! Small streams are crossed, bridges are shot through, and then the "express" thunders past with a deafening roar, almost terrifying the life out of a nervous old lady who sits opposite to us, and who, on recovering her breath, feels instinctively inside her left-hand glove to make sure that her ticket has not been spirited away by the fiery iron monster. Darwen—cold, stony-looking Darwen—is passed, and presently Blackburn is reached, where a few minutes is considerately allowed to stretch our legs and look about us. The prospect, however, is not altogether lovely, and the people are as little prepossessing in appearance as the place itself, so that we are not sorry when our brief respite is brought to an abrupt termination by the sharp "Now then, gentlemen," of the guard, when, resuming our seats, the carriage door is slammed to by that energetic official.

A few puffs, a whistle, and a screech, and we are moving swiftly over the green landscape again. The meadows widen, and the trees and hedges fly past as if driven by the whirlwind. Onwards, on and on, until we reach the little roadside station that forms the terminus of our railway journey.

Ribchester, for that is the name of the station, is Ribchester station only by courtesy*—the old Roman town whose name has been somewhat unceremoniously appropriated being a good three miles away; so that we shall have to lengthen our walk considerably before we reach the Roman *Rigodunum*. On leaving the station we turn to the left, and then, crossing the railway bridge, follow an ascending path that leads past a few squalid-looking cottages which stand irregularly along the edge of a tract of common land—the grazing ground of an impassive donkey and of a flock of geese that begin to sibilate and crane their necks

---

* Wilpshire is the name now given to the station.

spitefully as we go by. A little brick chapel with a bell-cot at one end stands on the further side of the green, and close by is the village school. Leaving this uninviting spot, we continue our walk past a few waste-looking fields and across the level summit of an eminence the verdant slopes of which stretch away on either side. Presently the road descends, winding hither and thither between pleasant hedgerows and embossed banks, garlanded with the gaily-coloured flowers of the exuberant summer time, " the jewels of earth's diadem," speaking of Him

> Whose hand hath shed wild flowers
> In clefts o' the rock, and clothed green knolls with grass,
> And clover, and sweet herbs and honey dews,
> Shed in the starlight bells, where the brown bees
> Draw sweets.

At every turn we get pretty snatches of scenery, with glimpses of cattle-dappled pastures and green fields, where the black, glossy rooks are hovering about and cawing loudly to each other as if discussing the result of their recent entomological researches. Looking across the country the high downs are seen with their broad green cloud-mottled shoulders, half-hiding the undulating hills that stretch away along the dim blue line of the horizon. By-and-by Ribblesdale, one of the prettiest vales in the kingdom, opens upon us. Below, the river winds its snake-like course through the meadows, its ample bosom gleaming in the sun like molten silver. On the right, lying low among the tall ash-trees, is Salesbury Hall, a quaint half-timbered mansion, once the abode of a branch of the great family of the Talbots, one of whom aided in the capture of the unfortunate Henry VI., and previously the home successively of the Salesburys, the Cliderhows, and the Mauleverers. Conspicuous on the further side of the valley are seen the stately towers of Stonyhurst crowning a wooded slope, that swells gradually up from the margin of the Hodder, forming one of the spurs of Longridge Fell. Looking up the valley, the eye takes in the long-backed slopes of Pendle Hill, the abrupt elevation on which stands the ruined keep of Clitheroe Castle, the

wooded heights of Wiswell and Whalley, the dark-hued moorlands
that extend to the ancient forests of Bowland, with Bleasdale
Moor, Waddington Fell, and the screen of hills that sweep round
in an irregular circle to meet the huge form of Longridge Fell
lying upon the landscape like a monster couchant.

A quaint relic of the olden time stands by the wayside on the
left. A gabled mansion of the time of the Second Charles, now
occupied by a farmer, but still bearing the name of New Hall,
though, as the date (1665) testifies, the storms of more than
two hundred winters have broken upon it since George Talbot,
a younger son of Sir John of that name, placed his initials
and the crest of his family above the doorway. At this point
the road diverges to the right, and a few paces bring us to the
margin of the Ribble, when a charming prospect meets the eye,
a prospect that would have delighted the heart of Cuyp had he
had the opportunity of sketching it. There was no stir or fret—
no excitement. All was calm, placid, and serene. The swift and
shallow Ribble lay before us, sparkling and glistening all over,
save on the further side, where a row of trees that fringed the
roadway flung the broad shadows of their spreading branches
upon its placid bosom. There was a Sabbath-like peace in the air,
and the stillness of a summer day lay profoundly as a trance
upon the scene. An old-fashioned punt, moored to the side, lazily
dragged its creaking chain, and now and then chafed itself against
the bank as the motion of the water gently swayed it to and fro.
Before us Ribchester Bridge lay bestriding the stream—its broad
circular arches reflected in the water with a distinct vividness that
was interrupted only at intervals when their image was broken into
a quivering indistinctness as a passing gust rippled the mirrored
bosom of the water. As we stood gazing upon the scene, a boat
borne by the current slowly glided down the river, looking like a
bird suspended in the blue of heaven. The oars were poised in
the rowlocks, and the water, dripping from their flashing blades,
fell upon the glassy surface, and spread out in widening silver
rings that floated slowly onwards.

CHICHESTER BRIDGE.

Crossing the bridge, at the foot of which stands a comfortable inn—the De Tabley Arms—we wound away to the left, following the bold sweep of the Ribble, and a few moments later entered the "Aunciente Towne" of Ribchester. Ribchester! What visions of antiquity float before the imagination as the stranger enters this little unpretending village, for town it can now hardly be called. What memories of the past are awakened at the mere mention of the name. The old distich, which the inhabitants still take pride in repeating, tells us that

> It is written upon a wall in Rome
> Ribchester was as rich as any toune in Christendome.*

The first glimpse, even were we unsupported by tradition, would lead us to believe that this part of the valley of the Ribble was even in earliest times a place of some importance, for, admirably protected by Nature, and adapted as it must then have been to the requirements of an untamed and uncivilised race, it was hardly likely to have escaped the searching eye of our Celtic forefathers, being then protected by naked marshes, and flanked on each side by lofty eminences, with a wide river between on which their slim coracles might float ; whilst adjacent was the great forest of Bowland, the haunt of the wolf, the boar, and other wild animals, whose skins would supply clothing, and their flesh sustenance, to the hardy hunter. Whether the primeval Britons established a colony here or not, certain it is that when the more refined subjects of the Cæsars had established themselves as conquerors of the country, Ribchester attained to a high degree of eminence, and became one of the richest and most important stations in the newly-acquired territory. For the greater protection and security of the conquered lands in the North, Agricola constructed a chain of forts from one extremity of Lancashire to the other, and occupying the sites now held by Lancaster, Ribchester, Walton, Blackrod, Manchester, Overborough, and Colne. The most

---

* Camden's Britannia, Ed. 1586, p. 431.

2

important of these stations, as evidenced by the richness and variety of the remains that have at different times been discovered, was the one at Ribchester. The place lost its pre-eminence after the fall of the Roman government in Britain, but the foundation of its buildings long defied the ravages of time, though now the searching eye can scarce discover the faintest relic of their former existence. Leland, the old topographer, who visited the place in the early part of the 16th century, says : " Ribchester is now a poore thing ; it hath beene an Auncient Towne. Great squared stones, voultes, and antique coynes be found ther : and ther is a place wher that the people fable wher that the Jues had a temple."* No doubt the temple existed, for the remains of it have been traced in later times, but it was Pagan and not Jewish, and was dedicated, as Dr. Whitaker supposed from an inscription found upon the site, by an empress or princess of the Imperial Roman family to the goddess Minerva. Ribchester has been prolific in remains of Roman art, and many of the altars, statues, bronzes, and " antique coynes " that have been dug up have been carried away to enrich the archæological museums of other parts of the country, or have found their way into those of private collectors, where they are practically lost to the student of antiquity, for, unfortunately, there is hardly a town in Lancashire which possesses a museum worthy of the name where such exhumed treasures might find a fitting resting-place. Pennant mentions having seen a sculpture, discovered on digging a grave in the churchyard, representing a Roman soldier carrying a *labarum*, or standard of cavalry ; but perhaps the most remarkable relic is the elaborately ornamented bronze helmet found in 1796, familiar to antiquaries by the engravings which have appeared in the *Vetusta Monumenta*, and in the histories of Whitaker and Baines. So lately as the beginning of the present century a Roman house and hypocaust were brought to light whilst excavating the foundations for a building on the

* Itinerary IV., fol. 39.

banks of the river; altars dedicated to various divinities have on different occasions been unearthed, with other memorial stones, coins, pottery, glass, articles of personal adornment, ampullæ, fibulæ, &c.; and even in recent times, though less frequently than of yore, when the earth is removed to any considerable depth relics are turned up which help to illustrate the habits and customs of the Roman settlers, and prove the wide diffusion of the elegant and luxurious modes of life it was their aim to introduce.

It requires no great stretch of the imagination to picture the Ribchester of those far-off days. The picture, it is true, may be only shadowy and indistinct seen through the long distance which intervenes; but, carrying the mind back to those remote times, let us contemplate the scene presented to our fancied gaze. It is Britain—Britain in the darkest period of its history, the Britain of Caractacus and Boadicea—but how great the contrast from the Britain of to-day! A broad flowing river separates us from the opposite land, the tide flows up, and the wavelets break monotonously upon the shore. Before us and on each side rise gently swelling hills clothed with dense forests of oak—primeval monarchs that have budded and flourished and shed their leaves through long centuries of silent solitude. There are no towns or villages, no fertile meadows and rich pasture fields; not a sign of a habitation can we discern save here and there where the dark woods have been thinned, and a solitary hut, rudely constructed of wood and wattles, bears evidence of man's existence. Looking more closely into the picture, we can discover the naked and painted forms of human beings—men eager, impetuous, brave, armed with javelin and spear, and ready to engage with any chance foe that may cross their path whilst seeking for their prey among the wild beasts of their native woods.

Gradually the view dissolves. Softly, slowly. it fades away, and darkness overspreads the scene. Hark! The sound of distant strife breaks faintly upon the ear; there is a rumble of war chariots and the hollow tramp of legionaries; then a fire blazes on the top of Longridge Fell, lighting up the heavens with a ruddy glare; the signal is answered by successive flashes from Pendle Hill and from beacons more remote. In a moment the scene is alive with the forms of men armed with spear and shield, hurrying to and fro, brandishing their javelins with impatient haste, eager to meet the coming foe. Meanwhile the conquering eagles of imperial Rome are seen advancing. Cohort follows cohort, and legion succeeds to legion. With measured pace and steady tread they come. There is the shock of mortal combat; the valley echoes with the clang of arms and the fell shout of war; and Briton and Roman are struggling together for conquest and for life.

> The hardy Briton struggled with his foe,
>   Dared him to battle on the neighb'ring height;
> And dusky streamlets reddened with the flow
>   From heroes dying for their country's right.
>
> Their simple weapons 'gainst the serried ranks,
>   Full disciplined in war, were hurled in vain;
> Well greaved and helmeted, the firm phalanx
>   Received their fierce attack in proud disdain.

It is over. Undisciplined valour yields to superior military skill, and the heroic Britons, defeated but not subdued, are driven for refuge within the fastnesses of their native woods, leaving those green slopes crimsoned with the life-blood of a people who, if they knew not how to fight, knew at least how valiant men should die.

Another tableau of history succeeds. Order arises out of disorder. After many struggles, in which her greatest generals have taken part, Rome, by her obstinate bravery, has succeeded in carrying her eagles northward as far as the banks of the Tay. The line of conquest is marked by a chain of forts erected with masterly judgment to keep in check the more disaffected of the northern tribes, and these strongholds are connected by a network of military ways, the course of which, after a lapse of eighteen centuries, may still be discerned—a proof that the Roman road makers were no despicable engineers.

One of these military ways—the one from *Mancunium* (Manchester)—led through Ribchester, and, passing Stoneygate, climbed the rugged slopes of Longridge Fell and along the tops of the hills, whence, taking an easterly direction, it traversed the Forest ot Bowland, and thence continued to *Eboracum* (York). Though their levels were chosen on different principles, the lines they followed were indicated by the great features of nature, and were pretty much the same as those adopted by the makers of our modern iron roads. Long centuries after the Roman had taken his departure these military roads formed the great highways of traffic. The tracks traversed by Agricola and his victorious legionaries have since been trodden in succession by Pict and Scot, by Plantagenet and Tudor, by Cavalier and Roundhead, by the hapless followers of the ill-fated Stuart, and by the ruthless soldiery of the Hanoverian King, and in later and more peaceful times by long lines of pack-horses, laden with the products of the Lancashire looms.

Agricola, having now satisfied his thirst for military glory, has become a pacificator and law-giver in the newly-acquired provinces. The subjugated natives, attracted by the fame of the illustrious Roman, steal from their hiding places in the woods, and learn the manners and customs of civilisation, and with them, it is to be feared, vices which before they knew not of.

Turn we again. Another picture dawns upon us, dimly and obscurely enough at first, but becoming more distinctly visible as the darkness fades away. The appearance of the people is changed, and the aspect of the country has changed with them. Time has passed on—the river that we before gazed upon still flows on as of yore, though somewhat narrowed in its proportions. The woods now ring with the war clarion of the invincible auxiliaries; the wattled huts have disappeared; and in the assart space they occupied a flourishing city is seen, with halls and porticoes and statues, in humble imitation of the then magnificence of the city that crowns the seven hills. Where the oaks grew thick, and the wild bull, the wolf, and the boar reigned in undisputed possession, a military fortification has been built, with ramparts and towers and turrets, and close by, to celebrate the subjugation of the brave Brigantes, a pagan temple has been reared in honour of Minerva, for the sound of glad tidings has not yet come across the sea. The scene is one of bustle and organisation. Here, on the quay, merchants are congregated with traders from Gaul and Phœnicia, and adventurers from more distant lands, bartering earthenware, implements of agriculture, and other commodities which those colonists of the old world have brought with them, for the treasures of the soil. There a gang of labouring captives, sullen and unwilling, are toiling under the eye of their relentless taskmasters. Strange-looking vessels are borne upon the bosom of the stream, unwieldy in form, with long lines of oars shooting out from each side, and prows resplendent with paint and gilding, standing high up out of the water. Now and then a gaily-decorated galley floats past, freighted with fair Olympias, or bearing, per-chance, some tender Sistuntian maid, whose loving heart, flinging aside the trammels of religion and race, has cast her lot with the conquerors of the land. Under the shadow of that wall a sentinel, in classic garb, with helmet and sandal, paces his measured round, and, pausing now and then, leans upon his spear, and muses upon the scenery of his own German home. Within the garrison all is gaiety and enthusiasm ; there are marchings and countermarchings, and transmissions of signals, and relievings of guard. How the lances glitter in the light, and the brazen helmets reflect the glory of the midday sun. Here are gathered fighting men from all parts of Europe—Dalmatians, Thracians, and Batavians—who are talking over the victories of the past, and thinking, perhaps, of those timorous eyes that beamed tenderly upon them, and wept their departure from their distant homes—Moors of swarthy hue from the shores of Africa, whose dark skins have flashed terror into the souls of the pale Northern tribes ; stern-visaged Frisians from the marshes of Holland ; and stalwart Asturians, with veteran warriors who have fought through many a campaign and earned for them-selves the proud title of conquerors of the world.

The conquerors of the world! Time has passed rapidly on, and Rome, the vaunted mistress of the world, with difficulty grasps her own. Pierced by barbarian hordes, torn by intestine wars, weakened at heart and tottering to her ruin, her last legions have been recalled for her own defence, and the fair provinces of the West are abandoned to the Northern savages, who come, as Gildas relates, "like hungry and ravening wolves rushing with greedy jaws upon the fold."

> Yet once again, a change—and lo!
> The Roman even himself must go;
> While Dane and Saxon scatter wide
> Each remnant of his power and pride.

Enfeebled by long submission to the Roman yoke, deprived of the protection of the forces of the empire, the flower of her youth drafted away to swell the armies of the Emperors Maximus and Constantine, Britain is left in a state of utter defencelessness, and speedily becomes a prey to those warlike hordes that come pouring in from the maritime provinces of Germany, Norway, and Sweden. The period that follows is one of anarchy and confusion, of Saxon conquest and Danish spoliation.

But we pass on. Another picture is shadowed forth, and what is this that meets the gaze? The scene of fierce war and angry passions, of conquest and oppression, of barbaric rudeness and pagan splendour, is now a desolate and deserted waste, where the frail creations of man are blended with the ever-enduring works of God. The relentless foot of Time has pressed heavily upon these wrecks of human greatness—a few straggling walls, a ruined temple, pavements worn down by the tread of many a Roman foot, broken columns, with fragments of masonry, are all the vestiges that remain to denote the ancient importance of the Roman *Rigodunum*—all the signs that are left to point out where merchants gathered and where warriors prepared for conquest and for fame.

The departure of the Roman legionaries inflicted a heavy blow on the fortunes of the city. The period of Saxon conquest was

followed by the descent of the wild Scandinavian marauders—the
Jarls and sea-kings of the North, who, with their piratical hordes,
swept the country, leaving the red mark of death and desolation in
their wake.

> What time the Raven flapped his gory wing,
>   And scoured the White Horse o'er this harried realm ;
> His crowded galley brought the dread Viking.
>   Lust at his prow, and rapine at the helm.

The splendour of Ribchester must have waned rapidly, for after
the overthrow of Harold on the red field of Hastings, when the
victorious Norman made his great survey of the conquered
country, it had become so insignificant as to be accounted a mere
village dependent upon Preston, then rising into note.   Yet it did
not escape the fury of the invading Scot, whose footsteps were
everywhere marked with blood and destruction, for in one of those
frequent incursions after the defeat at Bannockburn—when, as old
Hollinshead tells us, the victorious Bruce marched his army
through Cumberland, Westmoreland, and Lancaster to Preston—
the miserable inhabitants were driven from their homes, and the
place burned to the ground.   Subsequently its fortunes revived,
and for a time it could boast of having no less than three fairs, an
evidence of its increased importance.   In the unhappy struggle
between Charles the First and his Parliament it was the scene of
an encounter (April, 1643) between the Royalist forces, led by the
Earl of Derby, and the Parliamentarian levies, commanded by
Colonel Shuttleworth, resulting in a victory for the latter; and
tradition says that five years later (August, 1648) Cromwell slept
at the old white house, opposite the Strand, on the night before
the memorable battle of Ribblesdale, and there, with Major-
General Ashton, matured the plan of those operations which ere
the next setting of the sun had proved fatal to the Duke of
Hamilton, and tinged the flowing river with the blood of his
Scottish followers as deeply as their ancestors had dyed it with
English blood three centuries before.   In more peaceful times,

when the cotton trade was yet in its infancy, hand-loom weaving flourished, and formed the staple industry ; but the day of prosperity has passed, and the place has now dwindled down to the condition of a mean and insignificant country village, old-fashioned in aspect and quiet enough for the grass to grow in the narrow and painfully-ill-paved streets that struggle on towards the river. So lifeless looking is it that were it not for a few loiterers standing about the doorway of the "Bull," and that we now and then hear the clack of the shuttle, it would seem

> Like one vast city of the dead,
> Or place where all are dumb.

After long centuries of vicissitude and change, except the shadowy memories of the past, the ancient parish church is almost the only object that remains to arrest the steps of the inquiring wayfarer, and this well deserves examination. Tradition hovers about the place, and tells us that after the conversion of King Edwin, the great missionary Paulinus here proclaimed the glad tidings of salvation, in commemoration of which event the symbol of the Christian's faith—the cross—was planted, contemporaneously with those in the neighbouring churchyard of Whalley ; and that the first "modest house of prayer" was erected on the spot once occupied by the temple of Minerva. The late Canon Raines believed the church at Ribchester was coeval in antiquity with that at Whalley. It is the work of many hands and many separate eras, and, as may be supposed, exhibits many different styles of architecture. The oldest part is undoubtedly the chancel, the windows of which are, for the most part, of the narrow lancet style, showing that it must have been built about the year 1220. Portions of the nave and the north aisle exhibit the rich detail of the Decorated period, and the tower bears evidence that it is of later date, the main features being of Perpendicular character. In the south wall of the chancel is an ancient arched sedilia, with a piscina and credence table attached, and on the north side is a solid block of stone, whereon are carved three heraldic shields bearing the arms

3

of the Hoghtons and some of their alliances. This stone is commonly supposed to be a tomb, but it is more probable that it was intended as a seat in times when only the patron and some of his more influential neighbours were so accommodated, the general body of worshippers standing or kneeling during the services of the Church. The Hoghtons, whose arms it bears, were for generations lords of Ribchester, and one of them, Sir Richard Hoghton, in 1405, founded and endowed the chantry on the north side known as the "Lady Chapel," in which are still preserved the remains of the ancient altar and piscina.

Our story is told, and we now draw the veil over these grass-grown by-ways of the past. Eighteen centuries have rolled by since Agricola planted his eagles on the northern shores of the Ribble ; for 400 years the Roman wrought and ruled ; Saxon and Dane and Norman have followed in his wake, and each successive race has left its distinctive peculiarities stamped upon the institutions of the country. In that time kingdoms and empires have risen and passed away, generation after generation has come and gone. The old hills still lift their heads to the breezes of heaven, the stream flows on as of yore, and the sun shines with the same splendour as it shone in those ancient days—but where are they who peopled the busy scene?

> They are vanished
> Into the air, and what seemed corporal melted.

With Cassius we might exclaim,—

> They are fled away and gone,
> And in their stead the ravens, crows, and kites
> Fly o'er our heads.

The splendid civilisation which the Roman colonists brought with them did not long outlive their departure. The strongholds they built, the palaces they reared, have disappeared. Where once gleamed the spears of the Imperial soldiery the plough now passes and the harvest smiles. The Roman has passed away, and the glory of Ribchester has passed away with him, scarcely a stone now remaining to tell the story of its former greatness.

MARPLE HALL.

CHAPTER II.

MARPLE HALL—THE BRADSHAWS—COLONEL HENRY BRADSHAW
THE STORY OF THE REGICIDE.

HESHIRE abounds with ancient houses, but few, if any, of them are more interesting from their historical or traditional associations than Marple Hall, the home of Colonel Henry Bradshaw, the noted Cromwellian soldier, and the place where his younger brother, "Judge" Bradshaw," passed the earlier years of his eventful life. It is one of the few old mansions of the county that have remained to the descendants of the earlier possessors, and though located in close proximity to a district singularly at variance with associations awakened by the time-honoured memorials of bygone days, is yet surrounded by much that is picturesque and attractive.

The house, which stands a mile or more away from the straggling village from which it takes its name, is within the compass of a pleasant walk from Stockport or Hazel Grove, but it is more readily approached from the Rose Hill Station of the Macclesfield and Bollington Railway. It cannot be seen from the highway, but an antiquated and somewhat stately looking gateway, a few yards from the station, gives admission to a tree-shaded drive that leads across the park, at the further end of which the quaint old pile comes in view, standing upon a natural platform or terrace, with a lichened and moss-grown wall on the further side, all grey and weather-worn, that extends along the edge of the precipice on which it is built. The shelving slopes below are clothed with shrubs and trees that furnish a pleasant shade in the summer time; wild flowers in abundance peep out from the clefts and crevices; and were our visit made in the earlier months of the year, while the white fringe of nature's weaving yet lingers upon the skirts of winter's mantle, we should find the acclivities plentifully besprinkled with the pale and delicate blossoms of the snowdrop—the firstling of the year awakening from its lengthened sleep to proclaim the reanimation of the vegetable world. At the foot of the cliff is a sequestered dingle with a still pool, the remains, possibly, of a former moat or mere,* that gleams in the green depths, and a tiny rivulet that looks up through the overhanging verdure as it wanders on in pastoral and picturesque seclusion. The well-wooded heights of Thorncliffe shut in this bosky dell from the valley of the Goyt, across which, from the terraced heights, there is a delightful view in the direction of Werneth Low, the Arnfield and Woodhead Moors, and the range of green uplands and dusky eminences which stretch away in long succession to the pale blue hills that in the remote distance bound the landscape. There this interesting memorial of the stormiest period of England's history stands in peaceful serenity, lifting its dark stone front above the surrounding offices and out-buildings, with its high-peaked gables draped with a luxurious mantle of ivy that softens the sterner outlines into beauty, its long, low, mullioned windows, and its entrance tower and balcony above, now protected by a latticed railing, so as to form a kind of observatory, and which once had the addition of a cupola.

> High on a craggy steep it stands,
> Near Marple's fertile vale,
> An ancient ivy-covered house
> That overlooks the dale.

---

* The name, anciently written Mer-pull, seems to be a corruption of Mere-pool. A little lower down the river is Otters-pool, and these two point to the conclusion that the Goyt had at one time a much greater breadth here than it has now.

And lofty woods of elm and oak
That ancient house enclose,
And on the walls a neighb'ring yew
It sombre shadow throws.

A many-gabled house it is,
With antique turret crowned,
And many a quaint device, designed
In carvings rude, is found.

So says Mr. Leigh, in one of his " Legendary Ballads of Cheshire."
The first glimpse gives evidence of the fact that it has been
erected at different periods, additions having been made from
time to time as the convenience or requirements of successive
occupants have dictated ; but none of these are of modern date,
or in any way detract from its venerable aspect. On the south a
lofty wall encloses the garden and a court that occupies the entire
front of the house. Tall pillars of the Carolinian period,
supporting a pair of gates of metal-work, forming the principal
entrance, give admission to this court ; and if the wayfarer is
fortunate enough to be provided with an introduction, or if with a
taste for antiquarian investigation he unites the manners of a
gentleman, he may rely upon a courteous reception.

The time of our visit is a pleasant autumn afternoon. The
trees and hedges are in the fulness of their summer verdure ;
but the waning of the year is evidenced by the lengthened
shadows, the warm golden hue that is deepening upon the landscape, and the russet, purple, and yellow with which the woods,
though green in the main, are touched. Turning suddenly to the
right, we quit the highway, and saunter leisurely along the broad
gravelled path. As we approach the gates we become conscious
that something unusual is astir. Pedestrians are wending their way
towards the hall ; occasionally a carriage rattles past ; and then,
as we draw near, the sounds of mirth and minstrelsy break upon
the ear. Passing through the old gateway leading to the court,
we find groups of people on the lawn, and the lady of the house
is flitting to and fro with a pleasant word and a kindly greeting

for every one. A *fête champêtre* is being held in the grounds, and
a fancy fair is going on in one of the outbuildings, which has been
smartened up and decorated for the occasion, the proceeds of
the sale, we are told, going towards the rebuilding of

> The decent church that tops the neighbouring hill,

or rather the building of a new one by its side, which, when
finished, is to supersede it. A "steeple-house," forsooth! At the
very mention of the name a host of memories are conjured up.
For a moment the mind wanders back along the dim avenues of
the past to the stormy days of Cavalier and Roundhead, and we
think of the mighty change the whirligig of time has brought
about since Bradshaw's fanatical soldiery bivouacked here, ready
to plunder and profane the sanctuary, and to destroy, root and
branch, hip and thigh, the "sons of Belial" who sought solace
within its walls, or, as Hudibras has it :—

> Reduce the Church to Gospel order,
> By rapine, sacrilege, and murder.

Happily, fate has not ordained that we should sleep here this
night; for Marple, be it remembered, has its ghost chamber—
what ancient house with any pretensions to importance has
not?—and if the shades of the departed can at the "silent,
solemn hour, when night and morning meet," revisit this lower
world, those of the stern old Puritan colonel and the grim-
visaged "Lord President" would assuredly disturb our slumber.

But let us quit the shadowy realms of legend and romance,
and betake ourselves to that of sober, historic fact. After the
overthrow of Harold on the fatal field of Hastings, Marple
passed into the hands of Norman grantees, and in the days of
the earlier Plantagenet Kings formed part of the possessions of
the barons of Stockport, being held by them under the Earl of
Chester on the condition of finding one forester for the Earl's
forest of Macclesfield. The lands, with those of Wyberslegh, in
the same township, were, some time between the years 1209

and 1229, given by Robert de Stockport as a marriage portion to his sister Margaret on her marriage with William de Vernon, afterwards Chief Justice of Chester, a younger son of the Baron of Shipbrooke, who through his mother had acquired the lands of Haddon, in Derbyshire ; and from that time Marple formed part of the patrimony of the lords of Haddon until the death of Sir George Vernon, the renowned "King of the Peak," in 1567, a period of three centuries and a half, the esta·es being then divided between his two daughters, Haddon with other property in Derbyshire devolving upon Dorothy Vernon, the heroine of the romantic elopement with Sir John Manners, the ancestor of the Dukes of Rutland, whilst Marple and Wyberslegh fell to the lot of Margaret, the wife of Sir Thomas Stanley of Winwick, the second son of Edward Earl of Derby—that Earl of whom Camden says that " with his death the glory of hospitality seemed to fall asleep." Their son, Sir Edward Stanley, of Tonge Castle, in Shropshire, having no issue, sold the manor and lands of Marple in small lots to Thomas Hibbert,* chaplain to Lord Keeper Bridgman, who married Elizabeth, daughter of Henry Bradshaw, of Marple, and who was the grandfather of the celebrated divine, Henry Hibbert.

Some time about the year 1560 the Henry Bradshaw here named, who was a younger son of William Bradshaw, of Bradshaw Hall, near Chapel-en-le-Frith, the representative of an old Lancashire family of Saxon origin, seated at Bradshaw, near Bolton, from a time anterior to the Conquest, and which had been dispossessed and repossessed of its estates by the Norman invaders, married Dorothy, one of the daughters and co-heirs of George Bagshawe, of the Ridge, in the parish of Chapel-en-le-Frith, a family that in a later generation numbered amongst its members the eminent Nonconformist divine, William Bagshawe, better known as the "Apostle of the Peak," and became tenant of a

---

* Thomas Hibbert was the direct ancestor of the Hibberts of Birtles, and (until recently) of Hare Hill, near Alderley.

house in Marple called The Place, still existing, and forming part of the Marple estate. By this marriage he had a son bearing his own baptismal name, and, in addition, two daughters, Elizabeth, who became the wife of Thomas Hibbert as already stated, and Sarah, who is said by some genealogists—though on what authority is not clear—to have been the wife of John Milton, the wealthy scrivener, of Bread Street, London, and the mother of England's great epic poet, whom John Bradshaw in his will spoke of as his "kinsman John Milton."

In 1606, as appears by a deed among the Marple muniments, dated 7th July, 4 James, Henry Bradshaw the elder, therein styled a "yoman," purchased from Sir Edward Stanley, for the sum of £270, certain premises in Marple and Wyberslegh, comprising a messuage and tenement, with its appurtenances, another tenement situate in Marple or Wibersley, and a close commonly called The Place, the said premises being at the time, as is stated, partly occupied by Henry Bradshaw the elder and partly by Henry Bradshaw the younger, his son and heir-apparent. The estate at that time must have been comparatively small. Two years later (30th June, 1608), as appears by the Calendar of Recognizance Rolls of the Palatinate of Chester, now deposited in the Record Office, London, Henry Bradshaw, to further secure his title, obtained an enrolment of the charter of Randal Earl of Chester, granting in free-forestry Merple and Wibreslega, as they are there called, with lands in Upton and Macclesfield, to Robert, son of Robert de Stockport; and another enrolment of the charter of Robert de Stockport, granting to William Vernon, and Margery his wife, the lands of Marple and Wybersley, from which William and Margery the property passed, as we have said, by successive descents to Sir Edward Stanley, from whom Bradshaw acquired it.

Henry Bradshaw the younger, following the example of his father, also married an heiress, thus further adding to the territorial possessions, as well as to the social status, of his house, his wife being Catherine, the younger of the two daughters and co-heirs of Ralph Winnington, the last male representative of a family seated for seven generations at Offerton Hall, a building still standing near the highroad midway between Stockport and Marple, though now shorn of much of its former dignity. The registers of Stockport show that they were married there on the 4th February, 1593. To them were born four sons and two daughters. William, the eldest, died in infancy. With Henry, born in 1600, and John, born in 1602, we are more immediately concerned, for it is round them that the interest and the associations of Marple chiefly gather.

The elder Bradshaw, the founder of the Marple line, died in 1619-20, when Henry, his son, who had then been a widower sixteen years, succeeded to the family estates. No records of his private life have been preserved, but it may not be unreasonably assumed that, after the death of his wife, and as he did not re-marry, he lived in comparative retirement, leading the life of an unostentatious country gentleman, improving his estate, and super-vising the education of his children. Two years after he had entered upon the possession of his inheritance, that important functionary the Herald made his official visitation of Cheshire, when the gentlemen and esquires of the county were called upon to register their descents and show their claim to the arms they severally bore ; and it is worthy of note, as indicating his indiffer-ence to, or disdain of, the " noble science," that though, as we have seen, of ancient and honourable lineage and entitled to bear arms, Henry Bradshaw did not obey the Herald's summons,* probably "feeling assured," as Macaulay said of the old Puritan, "that if his name was not found in the Registers of Heralds, it was

---

* Whilst the head of the Cheshire Bradshaws risked the displeasure of the Herald by neglecting his summons, his kinsmen in Lancashire, who were steady and decided Royalists, with more regard for constituted authority, attended the Court, entered their descents, and, in further proof of his right to the honourable distinction of arms, John Bradshaw, of Bradshaw, produced a precious letter from Henry Percy, the first Earl of Northumberland, K.G., the father of Hotspur, to his " well-beloved friende" John Bradshaw, a progenitor who had probably served and fought at Chevy Chase and elsewhere in the reign of the second Richard.

recorded in the Book of Life ; and hence originated his contempt for territorial distinctions, accomplishments, and dignities."

Surrounded by home affections, Bradshaw appears to have taken little interest in public affairs ; though, as a strict Calvinist and stern moralist, he could not but have looked with disfavour on the republication of the " Book of Sports," and the revival of the Sunday wakes and festivals, in which religion and pleasure were so strangely blended ; nor, as an Englishman, could he have been an indifferent spectator of the breach which was gradually widening between the King and his people.

A cloud was then gathering which presaged a great religious and political tempest. The year in which Bradshaw lost his wife was that which closed the long and brilliant reign of the last of the Tudor sovereigns. James of Scotland succeeded—a King who reigned like a woman after a woman who had reigned like a man. The Puritans in Elizabeth's time were comparatively insignificant in numbers, but the strictness of the Queen's ecclesiastical rule acted upon their stubborn nature, and those who were averse to Episcopacy, and impatient of uniformity in rites and ceremonies and the decorous adjuncts of a National Church, grew formidable under James, and turbulent and aggressive after the accession of Charles. The policy of Elizabeth gave a political standing ground to Puritanism, and Puritanism gave to the political war in which the nation became involved a relentless character that was all its own. In 1634 was issued the writ for the levying of Ship-money— "that word of lasting sound in the memory of this kingdom," as Clarendon calls it—a word which lit the torch of revolution, and for a period of eleven years kept the country in almost uninterrupted strife. The occasion was eagerly availed of by the discontented; pulpits were perverted by religious fanatics, and violent appeals made to the passions of the populace, who were preached into rebellion; while more thoughtful, yet brave and strong-minded men, impressed with a stern, unflinching love of justice, and a determination to maintain those liberties they held to be their birthright, contended to the death against "imposts"

and " levies " and " compositions," and against the worse mockery
of " loans " which no man was free to refuse, as well as the
despotism that more than threatened their common country. It
was a fatal time for England. Dignified by some high virtues,
possessing many excellent endowments both of head and heart,
Charles yet lacked sincerity, forethought, and decision, and the
capacity required for the wise conduct of affairs. The blame for the
strifes and contentions which arose does not, however, attach wholly
to the sovereign, nor yet to his subjects. The absolutism of the
Tudors was, in a measure, the cause of the sins of the Stuarts, and
the sins of the Stuarts brought about the miseries of the Rebellion,
just as in turn the despotic rule and grinding social tyranny of the
Commonwealth period led to the excesses of the Restoration.
Charles was born out of season, and lived too much in a world of
his own ideas to comprehend the significance of events that were
passing around him. The twining of the Red and White Roses
upon the ensanguined field of Bosworth was followed by the
break-up of the feudal system, and the effacement of many of the
old landmarks of English society ; a new class of landowners had
sprung into existence, eager for the acquirement of political
freedom, and the king was unable or unwilling to recognise the
changed condition of things. He inherited from his father
inordinate notions of kingly power, and he resolutely shut his eyes
to the fact that he had to deal with an entirely different state of
public opinion. The power of the sovereign had waned, but
that of the people had increased ; Parliament, while bent upon
abridging the ancient constitutional prerogative of the Crown, was
equally resolute in the extension of its own. The King persisted
in his determination to reign and govern by " divine right "—he
refused to yield anything—and in the fierce struggle which he
provoked he fell. Moderation was no longer thought of ; the time
for compromise was past ; the seeds of strife were sown and
nurtured both by King and Parliament, who, distrusting and
wearied of each other, no longer cared for peace. At length the
storm burst. At Manchester, on the 15th July, 1642—a month

before the unfurling of the Royal standard at Nottingham—very nearly upon the spot where now stands the statue of Cromwell, the first shot was fired and the first blood shed in that great conflict which drenched the country in civil slaughter.

When the first shot was fired which proclaimed to anxious England that the differences between the King and the Parliament were only to be settled by an appeal to arms, the two sons of Henry Bradshaw had attained to the fulness of manhood, Henry, the eldest, having then lately completed his forty-second year, while John was his junior only by two years.

Henry Bradshaw, the third of the name, who resided at Marple, was born, as previously stated, in 1600, and baptised at the old church at Stockport on the 23rd June in the same year. Following with admirable consistency the practice of his progenitors, he further added to the territorial possessions of his house by marrying a rich heiress—Mary, the eldest of the two daughters and co-heirs of Bernard Wells,* of Holme, in the parish of Bakewell. The marriage settlement bears date 30 Sep., 6 Charles I. (1631), and Mr. Ormerod, the historian of Cheshire, says that he had bestowed upon him by his father-in-law the hall of Wyberslegh, but this is evidently an error, for, as we have previously seen, his father and grandfather between them purchased Wyberslegh, along with Marple, from Sir Edward Stanley, a quarter of a century previously, and the hall continued, as it had been from time immemorial, appendant to that of Marple. It is more than probable, however, that he took his young bride to Wyberslegh, and resided there during his father's lifetime, so that it would appear that the first of the Bradshaws settled at Marple lived at The Place, where he died in 1611, after which it ceased to be occupied as the family residence. Henry, his son, resided at the hall, and the youngest of the three occupied Wyberslegh until he succeeded to the family estate. Mary Wells, by whom he had a son who succeeded as

---

* This marriage is recorded on a brass to the memory of Bernard Wells, affixed to the north wall of the chancel in Bakewell Church.

heir, and two daughters, predeceased him, and he again entered
the marriage state, his second wife being Anne, daughter of George
Bowdon, of Bowdon, in Cheshire, by whom he had five sons and
one or more daughters. Though by no means insensible to the
advantages accruing from the possession of worldly wealth, it
does not appear that he added materially to his temporal estate by
his second marriage. The Bowdons were a family of ancient rank,
who at one time owned one-fourth part of Bowdon, but their
estates had gradually dwindled away, and were finally alienated by
sale to the Booths of Dunham, in the early part of Elizabeth's
reign.

Inheriting from his father the Puritan sentiments of the age,
Henry Bradshaw carried those feelings with him into a more active
arena. Living in close neighbourship with Colonel Dukenfield,
Edward Hyde, of Norbury, Ralph Arderne, of Harden, Ralph
Holland, of Denton, and holding intimate relations with the Booths
of Dunham, the Breretons of Handforth, the Stanleys of Alderley,
and other influential Presbyterian families, their friendship doubtless helped to shape the part he took in public affairs. When the
storm which had been long gathering burst, he took his stand with
the Parliament against the King, and became one of the most
active officers on the side of the Commonwealth. He served as
sergeant-major in the regiment commanded by his neighbour,
Robert Dukenfield, and would, therefore, in all probability, take
part in the lengthened siege of " Mr. Tatton's house of Whitten-
shaw (Wythenshawe)," in the winter of 1643-4, as well as in the
fruitless attempt, a few months later, to defend Stockport Bridge
against Rupert and his Cavaliers, who were hastening to the relief
of Lathom House, in Lancashire, where the heroic Countess of
Derby was bravely defending her husband's home against greatly
superior forces. Though a Cheshire man, he held a lieutenant-
colonel's commission in Assheton's Lancashire regiment, and subsequently was appointed to the command of the entire militia within
the Macclesfield hundred, in his own county. He was present also
with the Cheshire men at the final overthrow of the Royalist army—

the "crowning mercy," as Cromwell phrased it—at Worcester, Sept. 3, 1651, where it was said he was wounded, but if so the injury must have been only slight, for before the end of the month he was acting as one of the members of the court-martial appointed under a commission from Cromwell for the trial of the Earl of Derby. After the disaster at Worcester, the Earl had accompanied the King in his flight, until he was safe in the care of the Pendrells, when, with Lord Lauderdale, Lord Talbot, and about 40 troopers, he started northwards, in the hope of overtaking the remnant of the Scotch army, but when near Nantwich the fugitives fell into the hands of Oliver Edge,* a captain in the Manchester regiment, also returning from Worcester. Quarter having been given by his captor, the Earl naturally believed that he would be entitled to the immunities of a prisoner of war, but he soon found himself under close confinement in Chester Castle, of which Colonel Dukenfield was at the time governor. Cromwell, having got his most formidable foe in his power, resolved to get for ever rid of him by the shortest process that time and circumstances admitted. The Earl was therefore at once brought for trial before Bradshaw and the other members appointed on the court-martial, on the charge of high treason in contravening an Act of Parliament passed only a few weeks before, and of which, as his accusers were well aware, he could have no knowledge, and, in defiance of the recognised laws of war and the conditions on which he had surrendered, was pronounced guilty and sentenced to be beheaded at Bolton. Dr. Halley, in his history of "Lancashire Puritanism and Nonconformity," says that Colonel Bradshaw, notwithstanding that he had voted for the rejection of the Earl's plea, "earnestly entreated his

---

* Oliver Edge, to whom Lord Derby surrendered, resided at Birch Hall Houses, in Rusholme. To his credit it should be said that, whilst strictly faithful to his oath, he treated his illustrious captive with the respect due to fallen greatness when conducting him and his friends as prisoners to Chester. In one of his letters to his Countess, the Earl speaks of Captain Edge as "one that was so civil to me that I, and all that love me, are beholden to him."

brother, the Lord President, to obtain a commutation of the punishment," but, if he did, his efforts were unsuccessful. Seacombe attributed the execution of the Earl to the "inveterate malice" of (President) Bradshaw, Rigby, and Birch, which originated, he says, as to Bradshaw, because of the Earl's refusing him the Vice-Chamberlainship of Chester ;* Rigby, because of his ill-success at Lathom ; and Birch, in his lordship having trailed him under a hay cart at Manchester on the occasion of the outbreak in July, 1642, by which he got, even among his own party, the epithet of "Lord Derby's Carter." He adds that, "Cromwell and Bradshaw had so ordered the matter that when they saw the major part of the House inclined to allow the Earl's plea, as the Speaker was putting the question, eight or nine of them quitted the House, and those left in it being under the number of forty, no question could be put." The latter statement, however, is hardly borne out by the *Commons Journal,*† which, under date "14 October, 1651," makes this brief mention of the reception of the Earl's petition :—

Mr. Speaker, by way of report, acquaints the House with a letter which he had received from the Earl of Derby ; and the question being put — That the said letter be now read, the House was divided. The yeas went forth, Sir William Brereton and Mr. Ellis tellers for the yeas, with the yeas, 22 ; Mr. Bond and Major-General Harrison, tellers for the noes, with the noes, 16, so it passed in the affirmative. A letter from the Earl of Derby, of the 11th of October, 1651, with a petition therein enclosed, entitled, "The Humble Petition of the Earl of Derby," was this day read.

In the administration of affairs in his own county, Colonel Bradshaw took an active part. He was one of the commissioners for the Macclesfield hundred for the sequestration of the estates of those who retained Royalist opinions, or who refused to take the

* If so, this must have been in 1640, when the Earl, who was at that time Chamberlain, gave the appointment (27 July, 14 Car. I.) to Orlando Bridgeman, son of the Bishop of Chester, in succession to Roger Downes, of Wardley Hall, near Manchester.

† vii.—27.

national covenant, and his name appears first among the signataries to the famous Lancashire and Cheshire petition to the Parliament, praying for the establishment of the Presbyterian religion, and urging that "the frequenters of separate conventicles might be discountenanced and punished." The petitioners who had previously pleaded conscience having gained the ascendancy were now anxious to stifle freedom of thought, and to exercise a tyranny over their fellow-men, justifying the remark of Fuller, that "those who desired most ease and liberty for their sides when bound with Episcopacy, now girt their own garments closest about the consciences of others." In those troublous times marriage as a religious ceremony was forbidden, and became merely a civil contract entered into before a justice of the peace, after three "publications" at the "meeting place," or in the "market

place," the statute declaring that "no other marriage whatsoever shall be held or accounted a marriage according to the laws of England." Bradshaw, as a county justice, officiated at many of these civil marriages, and his neat and carefully-written autograph frequently appears in the church books of the period, with his heraldic seal affixed (for, however he might affect to contemn such vanities, he was yet careful to display the armorial ensigns of his house when acting officially with his more aristocratic neighbours), sometimes as appointing parish registrars, and at others ordering the levying of church rates and sanctioning the parish accounts, which at the time could not be passed without magisterial confirmation.

Colonel Bradshaw lived to see the fall of the Commonwealth,

and the overthrow of that form of government he had done so much to establish, but he did not long survive the restoration of monarchy. After that event had taken place, he was brought before the Lords Committee to answer for the part he had taken in the court-martial on Lord Derby, and committed to the custody of the Messenger of Black Rod. He appears, however, to have been leniently dealt with, for, after submitting to what reads very like an apology for his conduct, he was set at liberty, and permitted to pass the remainder of his days in peace. Those days were but few: the anxiety consequent upon the changed aspect of affairs was too much for him—his spirit was broken, and he died at Marple a few months after (11th March, 1661-2). On the 15th March, 1661-2, in accordance with his previously-expressed desire, his remains were laid beside those of his father and grandfather in the little chapel belonging to his family, then standing on the south side of the chancel of Stockport Church.

It does not appear that a copy of his will, which was proved at Chester, by the executor, 27th February, 1662, has at any time been published, but the following abstract, made by Mr. J. Fred. Beever, and contributed by him to "Local Gleanings," appeared in the *Manchester Courier* of October 15, 1875 :—

2 July 12 Car. II (1660) I Henry Bradshaw of Marple co. Chester doe . . . buried in my father's grave in Marple Quire in the par. Churche of Stockport if I depart this life in Cheshire . . . my sonne John Bradshawe . . . all my lands in Bowden Medlarie (Bowdon Edge ?) and Mellor in the county of Darbie . . . my sonne William Bradshawe . . . my lands in Chapel-le-Frith and Briggeworth (Bugsworth ?) co. Derby . . . Godfrey Bradshawe, Francis Bradshawe and Joseph Bradshawe, my three youngest sonnes . . . all my lands in Torkington co. Chester . . . Anne my lovinge wife . . . she having a jointure out of my lands in Cheshire and Wibersley . . . my sonne and heire Henery Bradshawe . . . all my bookes . . . my twoe daughters Barbara and Catharine, they being by their grandfather Wells and his wife well provided for. To my daughter Dorothy . . . £400, to my daughter Rachel . . . £500, to my youngest daughter Anne . . . £400 . . . my said sonne Henery Bradshawe . . . (the residuary legatee and executor) . . . my good friend Edward Warren, of Poynton esq. . . . (overseer).

Bradshaw was wont to lament that he had "a small estate and eleven children." The whole eleven, as well as his second wife survived him. Among the family portraits at Marple was (and may be still) one of a young maiden, said to be a daughter of the colonel. Round this lady the glamour of romance has been cast, and a tradition tells the story of her unhappy fate. In those times, when not unfrequently members of the same family took opposite sides, when father contended with son, and brother met brother in mortal conflict, Miss Bradshaw, with scant regard for the religious and political principles of her house, had formed an attachment for a young officer in the Royalist army, whose family had in happier days been on terms of intimacy with her own. Though he had espoused the cause of his sovereign, the Puritan colonel, in consideration of former friendships, treated him with personal kindness and welcomed him to his house. On one occasion, when entrusted with the conveyance of despatches to the King, who was then with his army at Chester, having occasion to pass near Marple, the young cavalier halted and stayed the night with the family of his betrothed. Mistress Bradshaw, with a woman's intuitiveness, suspecting the nature of his mission, and fearing the letters he was commissioned to deliver might bode no good to her husband's house, resolved, with the help of a trusty waiting-maid, to secretly ascertain their contents. Having done this, and found that her worst fears were realised, her next thought was how to prevent their reaching the King's hands without awakening the suspicions of their bearer. Summoning to her councils an old servitor of the family, it was decided to partially sever the straps by which the saddle-bags containing the dreaded missives were attached, so that the attendant, when guiding their bearer across the ford, might detach and sink them in the Goyt, when they would be lost for ever. On the early morrow the gay young soldier, having taken leave of his lady-love, hastened upon his mission ; the old retainer, who was nothing loth to speed the parting guest, accompanying him towards the river, but, giving a somewhat free interpretation to his instructions, concluded that if it was desirable to get rid of the letters it might be equally desirable to get rid of their bearer, and so, instead of conducting him to the ford, he led him to the deepest part of the river, which had become swollen with the storm of the previous night. The young cavalier plunged into the stream, and in an instant both horse and rider were swept away by the surging flood. Miss Bradshaw witnessed the act of treachery from the window of her chamber, but was powerless to prevent the catastrophe. She saw the fatal plunge, gave one long piercing shriek, and fell senseless to the ground. Reason had for ever left her.

Such is the legend that has floated down through successive generations, and still obtains credence with many of the neighbouring villagers, who, with a fondness for the supernatural, delight to tell how the shade of the hapless maid of Marple is sometimes seen lingering at nightfall about the broad staircases and corridors of what was once her home, or, as the pale cold moon sheds her silvery radiance on wood and sward, wandering along the grassy margin of the river and by the deep dark pool where her lover lost his life. Mr. Leigh has made the incidents of this tradition the basis of one of the most pathetic of his recently-published Cheshire ballads. Another writer on Marple has, however, given a different version. He says the lady was Miss Esther Bradshaw, and that her lover was "Colonel Sydenham, the Royalist commander," whom she ultimately married. It is a pity to spoil so pretty a story, but strict regard for prosaic fact compels us to avow our disbelief in it, and that for a twofold reason—(1) that Colonel Sydenham was not a "Royalist," but had been an active officer during the war on the Parliament side; and (2) that Colonel Bradshaw never had a daughter Esther. The story so circumstantially related rests, we believe, on no better foundation than the once popular though now almost forgotten romance of "The Cavalier," written under the *nom de plume* of Lee Gibbons, by Mr. Bennett, of Chapel-en-le-Frith, some sixty years ago.

Henry Bradshaw, the Parliamentarian soldier, as the eldest surviving son, inherited the family estates, while John, his younger brother, was left to push his fortunes as best he could. Possessing much natural shrewdness and ability, with no lack of energy and self-confidence, he was content with the position, strong in the belief that

> The world's mine oyster,

and in the bitter struggle between monarchy and democracy he was quick to avail himself of the opportunities which tended to his own wealth and aggrandisement.

He first saw the light in 1602, but the exact p'ace of his birth has not been ascertained. In an article in Britton and Brayley's "Beauties of England and Wales," believed to have been written by Watson, the historian of the Earls of Warren, it is stated that he was born at Wyberslegh; but Mr. Ormerod, in his "History of Cheshire," doubts the probability of this, "inasmuch," he says, "as the family only became possessed of that seat by the marriage of his elder brother Henry with the daughter of Mr. Wells," but this, if we may venture to differ from so deservedly high an authority, must be an error, for Wyberslegh, which had for many generations been appendant to the hall of Marple, was in the occupation of his father or grandfather when the Marple property was purchased by them in 1606; it is not unlikely, therefore, that the younger Bradshaw was residing at Wyberslegh at the time of his son John's birth. His baptism is thus recorded in the Stockport register :—

1602. Dec. 10. John, the sonne of Henrye Bradshawe, of Marple, baptized.

At a later date some zealous Royalist has written in the margin the word "traitor." It has been said that his mother died in giving him birth. This, however, is not strictly correct, though her death occurred a few weeks after that event, the register of Stockport showing that she was buried there January 24, 1603-4, and her son Francis, who would seem to have been a twin with John, was baptised at the same place three days later.

Of the early life and habits of the future Lord President nothing positively is known. From his will we learn that he received his early classical education at Bunbury, of which school that staunch Puritan, Edward Burghall, afterwards Vicar of Acton, was at the time master; subsequently he was sent to Queen Elizabeth's Free School at Middleton, in Lancashire, then lately remodelled and endowed by Nowell, Dean of St. Paul's, and, "as part of his thankful acknowledgment," he at his death bequeathed to each of these institutions £500 for "amending the wages of the master and usher." There is a very general opinion that he was at King Edward's Grammar School in Macclesfield also for a time; though there is no evidence of the fact, this is by no means improbable. Macclesfield was conveniently near to his home, and the school had at that time obtained a high reputation from the ability and scholarly attainments of at least two of its masters, John Brownswerd, "a schoolmaster of great fame for learning," as Webb says, "who living many years brought up most of the gentry of this shire," and Thomas Newton, one of the most distinguished Latin poets of the Elizabethan era; and some countenance is given to this supposition by the phrase in his will, "I had *part* of my educa'con" at Middleton and Bunbury. The Macclesfield school at that time abutted upon the churchyard, and there is a tradition that young Bradshaw, while with some of his playmates, and in a boyish freak, wrote the following prophetic lines upon a gravestone there:—

> My brother Henry must heir the land,
> My brother Frank must be at his command,
> Whilst I, poor Jack, will do that
> That all the world shall wonder at.

The authenticity of this production may very well be questioned, for, however ambitious his mind, we can hardly suppose that this young son of a quiet, unostentatious country gentleman could have had the faintest glimmering of his future destiny any more than that his muse was moved by prophetic inspiration.

He served his clerkship with an attorney at Congleton, whence he proceeded to London, and studied for some time at Gray's Inn, of which learned society he entered as a student for the bar in 1622, and with such assiduity did he apply himself to his studies that in later years Whitelock, in his "Memorials," bore willing testimony that he was "a man learned in his profession." Having completed his studies, he returned to Congleton, where he practised for some years, and, taking an active part in the town's affairs, was elected an alderman of the borough—the house in which he resided, a quaint black and white structure, having been in existence until recent years. In 1637 he was named Attorney-General for Cheshire and Flintshire, as appears by the following entry on the Calendar of Recognizances Rolls for the Palatinate of Chester : " 13 Car. I., June 7. "Appointment of John Bradshawe as one of the Earl's attorneys-at-law in the counties of Chester and Flint, during pleasure, with the same fees as Robert Blundell, late attorney there, received." In the same year he was chosen Mayor of Congleton, an office he is said to have discharged with ability and satisfaction, being, as a local chronicler records, " a vigilant and intelligent magistrate, and well qualified to administer justice." He certainly cannot be charged with indifference or lack of zeal while filling this position, for the corporation books show that he left his mark in the shape of " certain orders, laws, and ordinances," he set down " for the better regiment and government of the inhabitants, and the preservation of peace and order." These regulations, which were of a somewhat stringent character, imposed fines upon the aldermen and other dignitaries who neglected to provide themselves with halberds, and to don their civic gowns and other official bravery, when attending upon their chief, while the " freemen" of the borough were left with little freedom to boast of. It is evident that, Calvinist and Republican though he was, and a Puritan of the most "advanced " school, Bradshaw, even at that early period of his public career, had little liking for the severe simplicity affected by his political and religious associates, the regulations he laid down indicating a fondness for histrionic display and a love for the trappings and pageantry of office. As might be supposed, a small country town, the merry-hearted inhabitants of which were proverbial for their love of bear-baiting and their fondness for cakes and sack, was not a likely place to afford scope for the exercise of the talents of so resplendent a genius, so, seeking a more active sphere, he betook himself to the metropolis, where he continued to follow his profession. The year in which Cromwell gained his great victory at Marston Moor was that in which we find him for the first time employed in the service of the Parliament, being joined (Oct., 1644) with Mr. Newdegate and the notorious Prynne in the prosecution of the Irish rebels, Lords Macguire and Macmahon, before the Commissioners of Oyer and Terminer, which resulted in the rebel lords being condemned and executed.

It is not unlikely that Bradshaw had made the acquaintance of Prynne before he left Congleton, for the year of his mayoralty there was one in which that "pestilent breeder of sedition," as he was called, after standing in the pillory with Bastwick and Burton, and having his ears clipped, passed through Cheshire on his way to the prison at Carnarvon, making what reads very like a triumphal progress, and creating no small stir among the disaffected Puritans in the county, who regarded the victim of a harsh and unwise persecution as a sufferer for the cause of the true Gospel. His conductors treated him with much leniency—indeed, on the whole, they seem to have had rather a pleasant outing, stopping for two or three days at a time at the principal halting-places, and enjoying themselves when and where they could. At Tarporley, Tarvin, and Chester the offender was admitted to the houses of his friends, and received visits from some of the more notable of the anti-Royalist faction in the city and county, a procedure which drew down upon him the episcopal wrath—Bridgeman, the Bishop, being greatly scandalised at the idea of the "twice-censured lawyer and stigmatised monster," as he called him, being entertained in his own cathedral city "by a set of sour factious citizens." The complaint, it must be admitted, was not without cause, for it seems the

6

mayor and corporation began to waver in their orthodoxy, and became slack in going to hear sermons at the cathedral, so that the energetic prelate "could not have his eye upon their behaviour" as he desired. Whether this was due to the pleasant and moving discourses of Prynne, or that the sermons at the cathedral were too dry and lifeless to suit the tastes of the Cestrians, is not clear, but to remedy the evil Bridgeman had a bran new pulpit erected in the choir, capacious enough for all the canons to preach in at one time, had they been so minded ; and, further, ordered all other preachers in the city to end their discourses before those at the cathedral began, in order that the civic authorities might have no excuse for negligence in their attendance on sound doctrine, as delivered within its walls.

The manner in which Bradshaw conducted the prosecution of the Irish rebels evidently gave satisfaction to his employers, and paved the way to his future advancement ; certain it is that, after this time, he is frequently found engaged upon the business of the Parliament. When so employed he was not a pleasant person to encounter, as poor old Edmund Shallcross, the rector of Stockport— the parish in which his boyhood was spent—had good reason to know. For the particulars of this little incident in the life of the future judge, affording, as it does, an interesting side glance of the state of religious feeling in Marple when the Bradshaws were all-powerful, we are indebted to the researches of that indefatigable antiquary, Mr. J. P. Earwaker. It seems there had been a dispute of long standing between the Bradshaws and Shallcross on the vexed question of the tithes of Marple, a circumstance that in itself would no doubt be sufficient to satisfy the rector's Presbyterian neighbours when in authority that he was "scandalous" and "delinquent." Be that as it may, on the breaking out of the war Shallcross was turned out of his living, and his property, which included an extensive library, was confiscated. He appealed to the Commissioners of Sequestrations, and among the State papers which Mr. Earwaker has lately unearthed is an interesting series of interrogatories relating to persons in Cheshire suspected of delinquency, the following being the answer to those concerning the parson of Stockport :—

Edward Hill, of Stopforth (Stockport), glazier, knew Mr. Shallcrosse, formerly minister at Stopforth, who about the yeare 1641 refused to lett to farme the tythes of Marple to the townsmen of Marple att their own rates, but offered them the same at such rates as was conceived they might well gaine att. And that aboute two yeares after Articles were exhibited against the said Mr. Shallcrosse for delinquency, who thereupon appealed to the Committee of Lords and Commons for sequestracons, and went severall times to London about the same busines, and was once goeing to have the same heard, and had a convoy of horse of the Parliament's partye, and some of the King's partye came forth of Dudley Castle, and (he) then was by them slayne. And this deponent further saith that he was servaunt to the said Mr. Shallcrosse for seaven yeares before his death, whoe did acquaint this examinante that hee had found much opposition by Sergeant Bradshawe, whoe then was solicitor for the Commonwealth.

He also saith that the tythes of Stopforth are reputed to be worth 400li. by the yeare or thereabouts, and saith that hee hath heard generally reported that Sir William Brereton had a power invested in him to place or displace such ministers as were scandalous or delinquents. And he further saith that hee believed if the said Mr. Shallcrosse had complied with the desires of the said Mr. Bradshawe and his father and brother, that the said Mr. Shallcrosse would not have been sequestrated.

Bradshaw's next step in advancement was in 1646, when, on the 6th October, the House of Commons appointed him, in conjunction with Sir Rowland Wandesford and Sir Thomas Bedingfield, Commissioners of the Great Seal for six months, an appointment that was, however, overruled by the House of Lords. From this time his rise was rapid, honours and emoluments seeming to crowd upon him. On the 22nd February following both Houses voted him to the office of Chief Justice of Chester, an appointment that would amply compensate for the disappointment he had experienced in Lord Derby's previous refusal to bestow on him the vice-chamberlainship of the city. On being relieved of his office as one of the Commissioners of the Great Seal, he was named (March 18, 1647) as one of the judges for Wales, an office he appears to have held conjointly with his post at Chester. Three months later we find him again associated with Prynne, the two, with Serjeant

Jermyn and Mr. Solicitor St. John, being appointed by the Parliament to conduct the proceedings against the intrepid Judge Jenkins, who, when impeached of treason before the Commons, not only refused to kneel at the bar of the House, but had the temerity to call the place "a den of thieves."

On the 12th October, 1648, as we learn from Whitelocke, Parliament, in accordance with a recommendation of the Commissioners of the Seal, ordered a new call of serjeants-at-law, and Bradshaw's name is found among those then voted to receive the coif.

It has been suggested by a local writer that, in this, Parliament had an ulterior object in view, the purpose of Bradshaw's promotion being to secure an efficient instrument for conducting the proceedings against the Sovereign, which were then contemplated. This, however, is extremely improbable, for Parliament, it should be remembered, was averse to any extreme measure, and was, in fact, anxious to come to terms with the beaten King, its agents being at the very time engaged in negotiating with him the abortive treaty of Newport. But Cromwell had determined that Charles's life should be sacrificed, and the will of the army and its guiding genius had become paramount, for a military despotism was already usurping the powers of the State. The breach between the army and Parliament was widening daily, and the great struggle which was to decide the future destinies of England was at hand. The army, flushed with victory, had returned from the destruction of its enemies; conscious of its own power, it demanded vengeance on the "chief delinquent," as the King was called, and sent an expedition to the Isle of Wight to seize his person, and convey him to Hurst Castle. Meanwhile, the Commons had discussed the concessions made by Charles, and by a majority of 140 to 104 had decided that they "were sufficient grounds for settling the peace of the kingdom." Scarcely had the vote been recorded when a decisive blow was struck by the army at the independence of Parliament, for on the following morning, Colonel Pride, at the head of his regiment of foot, and accompanied with a regiment of horse, blockaded the doors leading to the House of Commons, and seized in the passage all those members who had been previously marked on a list as hostile or doubtful, and placed them in confinement, none being allowed to enter the House but the most furious and determined of the known friends to "the cause."* The obnoxious element having been thus effectually got rid of, the sword waved openly over the legislative benches, and the army in effect constituted the government. The next day this remnant of the House—the " Rump," as it was thereafter designated— rescinded the obnoxious vote, and appointed a day of humiliation, selecting Hugh Peters, Caryl, and Marshall to perform the service. The "purge" of the Commons had secured the certainty of concurrence in the wishes of the army, and accordingly, on the 23rd December, a committee was appointed to prepare charges for the impeachment of the King, and on the 28th an ordinance for his trial was read. In order to give their designs some resemblance to the form and principle of law, the House on the 1st January voted "that by the fundamental law of the land, it is treason for the King of England to levy war against the Parliament and kingdom." This vote, when sent up to the Lords for their concurrence, was rejected without a single dissentient voice, a procedure that led the remnant of the Commons a few weeks later to declare that "the House of Peers was useless and dangerous, and ought to be abolished." On the 4th January an ordinance was presented for erecting a new High Court of Justice for the trial of the King, which was read the first, second, and third time, assented to, and passed the same day. The Commissioners named in it included all the great officers of the army, four peers, the Speaker, and principal members of the expurgated House of Commons. The twelve judges unanimously refused to be of the commission, declaring its purpose and constitution to be contrary to the principles of English law; Whitelocke, who had received the coif at the same time as

---

* This extraordinary outrage, perpetrated in the name of freedom and justice, has ever since been familiarly known as " Pride's Purge."

Bradshaw and his colleague Widdrington, two of the most eminent lawyers of the time, also refused to sit on the tribunal. The Commissioners met on the 10th, and appointed Bradshaw, who was absent, their president. It would seem to have been originally intended that he should only take a subordinate part in the business, for on the 3rd January the committee had decreed that Serjeants Bradshaw and Nichols, with Mr. Steel, should be " assistants." Steel acted as Attorney-General, but Nichols could not be prevailed upon to give attendance.

It is not known with certainty whether Bradshaw was aware of the intention to elect him president of the commission for the trial of the King, but it is more than probable he had been informed of what was contemplated, and he certainly cannot be said to have been averse to the office, for undoubtedly he had resolution and courage enough to decline it had he felt so disposed. He attended the court in obedience to the summons on the 12th, and, when called to take the place of president, after asking to be excused, submitted to the order and took his place, whereupon it was ordered, " that John Bradshaw, serjeant-at-law, who is appointed president of this court, should be called by the name and have the title of Lord President, and that as well without as within the said court, during the commission and sitting of the said court." Clarendon says that " when he was first nominated he seemed much surprised, and very resolute to refuse it ; which he did in such a manner, and so much enlarging upon his own want of abilities to undergo so important a charge, that it was very evident he expected to be put to that apology. And when he was pressed with more importunity than could have been used by chance, he required time to consider of it, and said 'he would then give his final answer,' which he did the next day, and with great humility accepted the office, which he administered with all the pride, impudence, and superciliousness imaginable."

Clarendon was evidently of opinion that he had been previously informed of the position he would be asked to fill, and the " pride " spoken of in the administration of the office was only in accord

with that fondness for display to which allusion has already been
made. Suddenly raised to a position of pre-eminence as the head
of a tribunal wholly unprecedented in the extent and nature of its
assumed authority, he was not the man to dispense with any of
those outward manifestations which might give dignity and impres-
siveness to his dread office. He had 20 officers or other gentlemen
appointed to attend him as a guard going and returning from
Westminster Hall; lodgings were provided for him in New Palace
Yard during the sittings of the court ; and Sir Henry Mildmay, Mr.

PRESIDENT BRADSHAW.

Holland, and Mr. Edwards were deputed to see that everything
necessary was provided for him. A sword and mace were carried
before him by two gentlemen, 21 gentlemen that were near carried
each a partizan, and he had in the court 200 soldiers as an
additional guard. A chair of crimson velvet was placed for him in
the middle of the court, and a desk on which was laid a velvet
cushion ; many of the commissioners, as Whitelocke says, donned
"their best habits," and the President himself appeared in a scarlet

robe, and wearing his celebrated peaked hat, remaining covered when the King was brought before him, though he expressed himself as greatly offended that his Sovereign did not remove his hat while in his presence.

Into the particulars of the trial we do not desire to enter—they are matters which history has made known; nor do we wish to dwell upon the incidents attendant upon it—the calm and dignified demeanour of the ill-starred King; his denial of the authority of the court, and consistent refusal to recognise a power founded on usurpation; the ill-concealed vanity of the judge; the imposing pomp and glitter of the regicidal court; the intrepid loyalty of Lady Fairfax, who startled the commission by her vehement protest when the charge was made, and the scarcely less courageous conduct of her companion, Mrs. Nelson; the rancorous hatred displayed by the King's accusers; the mockery of proof; the refusal to hear the fallen monarch's appeal; the revilings of the excited soldiery; the expressions of sympathy of the people; or the brutal blow bestowed upon the poor soldier who ventured to implore a blessing on his Sovereign's head—all these are recorded and are embalmed in the hearts of the English people. The bloody episode which will for ever darken our national annals was an event without precedent in the world's history. For the constitution of the court no authority could be found in English law, it was illegal, unconstitutional, and, in its immediate results, dangerous to liberty. Whatever might be the faults of Charles— and they were many—his death was not a political necessity, nor can it be justly said to have been the act of the nation, for the voice of public opinion had never been heard, and therefore the country must be exonerated of any participation by approval or otherwise in the criminality of that unfortunate deed—it was the act of a faction in the House of Commons, acting under the influence of a faction in the army. In this momentous business Bradshaw may have persuaded himself that he was performing a solemn act of duty to his country, but, looked at in the light of after history, that act can only be pronounced a criminal blunder.

Tradition says that the warrant for the King's execution was signed in Bradshaw's house* at Walton-on-Thames, a building still standing near Church Street in that pleasant little town, though now subdivided into several small tenements, and shorn of much of its ancient splendour—his own signature, of course, appearing first on that well-known document.

Now, after a lapse of more than two centuries, and when the welfare of the throne and the people are identical, we can afford to look back upon the great tragedy in which Bradshaw played so profound a part calmly and without bitterness of spirit. From the anarchy, the foulness of the tyranny of those times, the nation, the Church, and the people have emerged with a firm hold on better things. Prelacy, which had been trampled under foot, and Presbyterianism, which became to Independency much what

Prelacy had been to Presbyterianism, have reappeared, but the severe asceticism and religious fervour of the Puritan, and the catholicity and breadth of view of the Churchman have commingled and become elements of the national life, fruitful for good by reason that they no longer come into violent collision with each other.

When Bradshaw had brought his Sovereign to the block, he may be said to have fulfilled the prediction of his early youth, for assuredly he had

. Done that
Which all the world did wonder at.

---

* Though now closed in by humbler dwellings, the house must have been in Bradshaw's time far away from any other building of equal size and pretensions. There is a common belief in the neighbourhood that an underground passage led from it to Ashley Park, where Cromwell, it is said, at that time resided.

7

He had accepted an office which sounder lawyers shrank from
undertaking, and had entitled himself to the gratitude of those
who, by compassing the death of the King, sought to accomplish
their own ambitious ends ; and it must be admitted that those who
benefited by his daring were neither slow nor niggardly in
rewarding him for his services to the "cause," for never was a
royal favourite so suddenly raised to a position of power, and
wealth, and consequence, and never was monarch more lavish in
the favours bestowed upon a courtier than was the newly-appointed
Government in doing honour to and enriching its legal chief. The
Deanery House at Westminster was given as a residence to him
and his heirs, and a sum of £5,000 allowed to procure an equipage
suitable to his new sphere of life, and such as the dignity of his
office demanded. "The Lord President of the High Court of
Justice," writes Clarendon, "seemed to be the greatest magistrate
in England. And, though it was not thought seasonable to make
any such declaration, yet some of those whose opinion grew quickly
into ordinances, upon several occasions declared that they believed
that office was not to be looked upon as necessary *pro hac vice*
only, but for continuance, and that he who executed it deserved
to have an ample and liberal estate conferred upon him for
ever."

As his office did not expire with the King's trial, Parliament on
the 6th February allowed him to appoint a deputy to supply his
place at Guildhall, where he had sat as judge, and on the 14th of
the same month, when Parliament made provision for the exercise
of the executive authority by the appointment of a Council of
State, he was selected by the House as one of the thirty-eight
members. Of this body Bradshaw was chosen president, and his
kinsman, John Milton, Latin secretary. At the first meeting
(March 10), if we are to believe our old friend Whitelocke, he
seemed "but little versed in such business," and spent much of the
time in making long speeches. Two days afterwards he was
appointed Chief Justice of Wales, but he did not go there immediately, for on the 20th of the same month he sat again as Lord

President of the Council, at whose discussions it would seem he was not disposed to remain a mere passive instrument, for, as Whitelocke remarks, he "spent much of their time in urging his own long arguments, which are inconvenient in State matters." "His part," as he adds, "was only to have gathered the sense of the council, and to state the question, not to deliver his own opinion."

Whatever may have been his demeanour in the council, outside, at least, the duties of his office were discharged with firmness and energy, as the townsmen of Manchester had cause to know. When, in 1642, the town was threatened with an attack by Lord Derby, the Presbyterians had entrusted its defence to Colonel Rosworm, a German engineer, who had been trained in the wars of the Low Countries, and who had agreed to give his services for six months for the modest sum of £30. A faithful and valuable servant he proved, though a provokingly ill-tempered one, for he never ceased to bewail the beggarly remuneration he had agreed to accept, or to rail at the "despicable earthworms," as he termed those who had offered it. As he refused to sign the national covenant, that not being included in the contract, and being, as he thought, no part of a soldier's duty, his employers took an irreconcileable hatred against him, and, when the danger was past, repudiated their share of the bargain. Unable to obtain the pittance for which he had risked his life, he left the town in disgust, and repaired to London to lay his grievances before the Government, and implore their interference. As a consequence, the following peremptory letter was addressed to the town by Bradshaw, which no doubt had a salutory effect on the "despicable earthworms," whom the angry old soldier had charged with being "matchless in their treachery, and setting the devil himself an example of villainy" :—

For the town of Manchester, and particularly for those who contracted with Lieut.-Colonell Roseworme, these are.

Gentlemen,—The condition of the bearer being fully made known, and his former merit attested to us by honourable testimony, and very well known to yourselves, himself also being by birth a stranger, and unable to present his complaints in the ordinary legall forme, give us just occasion to recommend him to you for a thorough performance of what, by your contract and promise, is become due unto him for his speciall service done to your town and country, whereto we conceive there is good cause for you to make an addition, and that there can be no cause at all for your backwardness to pay him what is his due.

As touching that which is otherwise due to him from the State, after some other greater businesses are over, he may expect to be put in a way to receive all just satisfaction. In the meane time we committ him and the premises to your consideration for his speedy relief, and we doe require you to give us notice of your resolutions and doings herein, within one month after the receipt thereof.

Signed in the name and by order of the Council of State appointed by authority of Parliament.

Jo. BRADSHAWE, Pr. Sedt.

Whitehall, 7th July, 1649.

It must be confessed that the President, with all his "rare modesty" and patriotism, was not so self-denying but that he looked sharply after the main chance. On the 19th June, 1649, Parliament voted him a sum of £1,000, and on the same day ordered that it should be referred to a committee to consider how he was to be put into possession of the value of £2,000 a year, to be settled as an inheritance upon him and his heirs for ever.

Wealth and honours were literally showered upon him, and for a time the history of the Government was little else than a history of Bradshaw. On the 30th June he was re-appointed to the office of Chief Justice of Chester, Humphrey Macworth, of Shrewsbury, who afterwards acted as President of the court-martial which tried Lord Derby, being named as his deputy. On the 15th July a Bill passed through Parliament settling £2,000 a year on him and his heirs, and nine days later (July 24th) another £2,000 per annum was granted to him and them out of the sequestrated estates of the Earl of St. Albans at Somerhill, in Kent, and those of Lord Cottington in Wiltshire, the latter including the famous Fonthill. This last-named grant was in all probability the one referred to in the order of June 19, when a committee was ordered to consider how an annual payment of that amount could be settled.

Four days after these grants were made, an Act was passed constituting him Chancellor of the Duchy of Lancaster, an office t' at subsequently, when others were abolished, was on his account specially retained, and on the 2nd April, 1652, secured to him. His name appears on the list of Justices of the Peace for his native county in 1650; in the same year he was again named of the Council of State, and retained his office of President. The following letter, extracted from the State papers, is interesting as showing the relations existing between Bradshaw and Cromwell, and the estimation in which he was held by the Lord General :—

My Lord,—I return you my humble and heartie thanks for your late noble and friendly letter, whereby I have the comfort and assurance of your lordship's faire interpretation of my past, and (so I dare call them) well ment actions, which I shall not desyre to account for or justify to any man lyving so soon as to yourself ; of whome I shall ever have that esteeme as becomes me to have of one who daylie approves himself religion's and his countrey's best friend, and who may justly challenge a tribute of observance from all that syncerely wysh them well, in which number I shall hope ever to be found.

My Lord, I have ('tis true) taken the boldness to write some few letters to you since your late departure hence, and I have satisfaction enough that they were receyved, and are not dyspleasing to you. Your applycation to the gentleman, named in yours, who is of so knowne fytnesse and abylytie to procure you effectuall returnes, was an act, in my apprehension, savouring of your usuall prudence, and tending to the advantage of the publique affayres committed to your trust and care; neither can any wyse man justifie any charge of seeming neglect of others in that respect. I am sorry your lordship hath bene put to any expense of your so pretious tyme, for removing any such doubts; but these my over carefull fryends, who have created your lordship this trouble, have, I must confess, occasyonally contrybuted to my desyred contentment, which is, and ever hath been, synce I had the honour to be knowne unto you, to understand myself to be reteyned and preserved in your good opinion. And if my faithfull endeavours for the publique, and respects unto your lordship in everything wherein I may serve you, may deserve a contynuance thereof, I may not doubt still to find that happiness; and this is all the trouble I shall give your lordship as to that matter.

We are now beginning with a new councell another yeare. I might have hoped, either for love or something els, to have been spared from the charge, but I could not obtaine that favour ; and I dare not but submyt, where it is cleare to me that God gives the call. He also will, I hope, give

His poore creature some power to act according to His mynd, and to serve Him in all uprightness and syncerytie, in the way wherein He hath placed me to walk.

My Lord, I have no more, but to recommend you and all your great affaires to the guydance, mercy, and goodness of our good God, and to subscrybe myself, in all truth of affection,

Your lordship's ever to be disposed of

Jo. Bradshawe.

Whytehall, 18 Feb., 1650.

The customer who wronged Sir James Lidod is ordered to restore and satisfie, and to come up to answer his charge, which, probably, will fall heavy upon him.

For his Excellency the Lord General Cromwell, These.

Bradshaw acted as President of the Council of State in 1651, and again in the year following. So far his success had been uninterrupted, and as the supreme magistrate his power and influence was second only to that of Cromwell himself. His authority was almost absolute. The amiable Evelyn, in his diary, records that he could not witness the burial of Dorislaus, "the villain," as he writes, "who manag'd the trial against his sacred Majesty," until "I got a passe from the rebell Bradshaw, then in great power;" and again, when he went to Paris with only "an antiquated passe, it being so difficult to procure one of the rebells without entering into oathes, which I never would do," and he had to bribe the officials at Dover, he found "money to the searchers and officers was as authentiq as the hand and seale of Bradshawe himselfe," "where," he adds, "I had not so much as my trunk open'd."

The very rapidity with which Bradshaw had attained to power made him a formidable competitor with, if not indeed a dangerous rival to, the man in whose goodwill he had said it was his "desyred contentment" "to be reteyned and preserved;" and there can be little doubt that his boldness and unflinching adherence to the principles he had espoused brought about his own undoing, for it was not long before an incident occurred which for ever alienated Cromwell's friendship from him. The occasion was one memorable in the annals of England—the dissolution of the Long Parliament, on the 20th April, 1653. Finding the action of the "Rump," as it was called, inimical to his designs, Cromwell, who seems to have begun to think that government by a single person was desirable, went down to Westminster with a force of 300 men, broke up the House, expelled the members, and, pointing to the mace, directed Col. Worsley—Manchester's first Parliamentary representative—to " take away that bauble," which having been done, he ordered the doors to be locked, and then returned to his lodgings at Whitehall. And so, without a struggle or a groan, unpitied and unregretted, the Long Parliament, which for 12 years had under a variety of forms alternately defended and invaded the liberties of the nation, fell by the parricidal hands of its own children.

Bradshaw, refusing to submit in silence to such a daring infringe- ment of the liberties of Parliament, resolved upon taking his place as head of the Council of State the same afternoon, thinking, probably, that his presence might deter Cromwell from committing any further acts of violence ; but the Lord General was not to be so easily diverted from his purpose. Taking Lambert and Major- General Harrison with him, he proceeded to the Council, and expelled its members in the same abrupt and arbitrary manner that he had dismissed the Commons. Addressing Bradshaw and those assembled with him, he said,—

Gentlemen, if you are met here as private persons, you shall not be disturbed ; but if as a Council of State, this is no place for you ; and, since you cannot but know what was done at the House in the morning, so take notice that the Parliament is dissolved.

To which Bradshaw replied,—

Sir, we have heard what you did at the House in the morning, and before many hours all England will hear. But, sir, you are mistaken to think that Parliament is dissolved, for no power under heaven can dissolve them but themselves ; therefore, take you notice of that.

The President's spirited reply cost him Cromwell's friendship, who, though he continued to treat him with the outward manifesta- tions of respect, ever afterwards regarded him with feelings of distrust. Exasperated though he was, Cromwell must have felt the justice of the rebuke, for in a conference afterwards with his brother-in-law, Desborough, he remarked that his work in clearing the House was not complete until he had got rid of the Council of State, which, he said, " I did in spite of the objection of honest Bradshaw, the President."

The Republican leaders, indignant at the forcible expulsion of the Rump Parliament, denounced it as an illegal act, wh'ch undoubtedly it was, but Cromwell was not the man to be bound by the ordinary laws of constitutional liberty. The miserable remnant of the Parliament, it must be admitted, had become a reproach ; it had become supreme through similar unconstitutional violence, and was itself violating its own contract in refusing to vote its own dissolution. The spirit manifested by Bradshaw has been likened to that of an ancient Roman ; but whether in the resistance he offered he was influenced by purely patriotic and disinterested motives may be very well questioned, for it must not be forgotten that he had looked with complacency on the illegal and high-handed proceeding which had laid the Parliament at the feet of the army, when that sharp medicine, " Pride's Purge," was administered—an act of daring violence by virtue of which alone he held his office and had acquired his wealth.

Up to this time, as we have said, his career had been characterised by uninterrupted success ; but the uniform good luck which had hitherto shown what daring could accomplish when upheld by an intelligent head and dauntless heart, now forsook him. Cromwell, who was aiming at arbitrary government in his own person, could not, on finding his authority thus openly disputed by the President of the Council, but have had misgivings that the man who had sufficient resolution to pass sentence of death upon the King might not be unwilling, should occasion arise, to perform the same office upon himself. It became necessary, therefore, for the accomplishment of his plans that Bradshaw's power should be abridged ; and though Parliament, on the 16th September, 1653, enacted that the continuance of the palatinate power of Lancaster should be vested in him, and he was also named one of the interim Council of State that was to meet relative to a settlement of the Government, he was no longer permitted to occupy an office of actual power and authority.

On the 16th December, 1653, Cromwell was inaugurated Lord Protector of the Commonwealth. Bradshaw, who was a thorough Republican, and who certainly had the courage of his convictions, was equally opposed to unlimited power, whether exercised by the King or by the Protector, at once set himself to counteract the authority of his former patron. In the first Parliament of the Protectorate he sat for his native county, but it was only for a very brief period, for scarcely had the representatives of the people assembled than they fell to questioning the Protector's authority, when Cromwell, after surrounding the House with his guards, administered a corrective in the shape of a declaration promising allegiance to himself, which he required every member to sign, shortly after which he dismissed them unceremoniously to their homes.

For a year and nine months England was left without a Parliament, the supreme power being exercised by the Protector, and every one holding office was required to take out a commission from him. This Bradshaw refused to do, alleging that he held his office of Chief Justice of Chester by a grant from the Parliament of England to continue *quamdiu se bene gesserint*, and should therefore retain it, though willing to submit to a verdict of twelve Englishmen as to whether he had carried himself with that integrity which his commission exacted; and shortly after this protest he set out on the circuit without any further attempt being made to hinder him. His daring and firmness, as might be expected, widened the breach and still further provoked the anger of Cromwell, who wrote a letter to Major-General Bridge, at Middlewich, requesting that he might be opposed by every means at the approaching election at Chester. By some accident this letter fell into the hands of Bradshaw's friends, and was publicly read in the city. In spite of this opposition he succeeded in securing his election, but, there being a double return, neither representative took his seat. The Protector had not only used his power against Bradshaw

8

at Chester, but he also succeeded in preventing his election for London, a position he had aspired to.

Cromwell and his Independents had gone beyond the Puritan Republicans, who, joining with the Anabaptists, Fifth Monarchy. men, and other fanatics, protested against any earthly sovereignty. Plots for restoring the Commonwealth were rife, and there is good reason to believe that in some of these Bradshaw was implicated ; certain it is that he was in correspondence with Okey and Goodgroom, whom he assured that " the Long Parliament, though under a force, was the supreme authority in England."

The feeling of jealousy and distrust entertained by Cromwell and Bradshaw for each other, though not openly avowed, became evident to all, and Whitelocke says that in November, 1657, " the dislike between them was perceived to increase." These mutual jealousies were not, however, to be of long continuance, for in less than a year the grave had closed over the object of Bradshaw's distrust. On the 3rd September, 1658, the anniversary of his victories over the Scots at Dunbar, and the Royalists at Wor-cester—his " Fortunate Day " as he was wont to call it, Cromwell passed away, and his son and successor, even had he been so disposed, was too weak to continue any very energetic resistance.

On Richard Cromwell's accession, a new Parliament was called, when Bradshaw was again returned to the House of Commons for Chester. Though he did not scruple to take the oath of fidelity to the new Protector, he, nevertheless, entered into active co-operation with Haslerig, Vane, and other Republicans, in their opposition to the Government. This Parliament came to an end on the 22nd April, 1659, the dissolution having been forced by the officers of the army, and with it Richard Cromwell's power and authority were gone, and the Protectorate was at an end.

It is about this time that we discover the first indications of Bradshaw's health failing him. At the Easter assizes, in 1659, he was lying sick in London, and unable to attend the Welsh circuit ; and as Thomas Fell, who had been associated with him—the Judge Fell, of Swarthmoor in Furness, whose widow George Fox, the founder of the Society of Friends, afterwards married—had died in September of the previous year, John Ratcliffe, Recorder of Chester, was appointed to act as his deputy *pro hac vice tantum.* That anomalous authority, the "Rump," which the elder Cromwell had so ignominiously expelled from the House of Commons, was, on the 17th May, restored by the same power of the army that, six years previously, it had been dismissed. Six days after, a Council of State was appointed, in which Bradshaw obtained a seat, and was elected president; and on the 3rd June following he was named, with Serjeants Fountain and Tyrrel, a Commissioner of the Great Seal. His health, however, had now seriously given way, and as he had been for some months suffering from "aguish dystemper," he asked to be relieved of the duties of the office. For the following copy of a letter written at this time, while he was lying sick at Fonthill—one of the few of Bradshaw's which have escaped destruction—the author is indebted to the courtesy of that industrious labourer in the field of literature, the late Mr. John Timbs, F.S.A., by whom it was transcribed from the original in the possession of Mr. F. Kyffin-Lenthall, a descendant of "Speaker" Lenthall, to whom it was addressed :—

Honourable Sir,—I have, by Mr. Love, a member of this happie P'liament, receyved the Howse's pleasure touching myself in relation to ye Great Seale, wherein, as I desire wth all humble thankfulnes to acknowledge ye respect and favour done me in honouring me with such a trust, so I should reckon it a great happiness if I were able immediately to answer ye call and personallie attend ye service wch at present I am not, laboring under an aguish dystemper of about 8 months' continuance ; for removing whereof (after much Physicke in vaine) according to advyce on all hands, I have betaken myself to the fresh ayre, and hope (though my fitts have not yet left me) to receive benefit and advantage thereby. And for this I humbly begge ye Parliamts leave and permission, if upon this just occasion they shall not in their wysdome think fit otherwise to dyspence with me. In ye meane time it hath been and is noe small addition to my other afflictions that for want of health it hath not bene in my power according to my Heart's earnest desire to be serviceable in my poor measure to the publiq. But by ye helpe of God when through his goodnes my strength shal be restored (of wch I despayre not) I shal be most free and willing to serve ye Parliment and Commonwealth in anie capacity and that through dyvine assistance wth all diligence, constancy and faithfulness, and to ye utmost of my power.

Sir, I judged it my dutie to give this account of myself to ye House, and humbly desyre by your hand it may be tendered to them ; for whom I daylie praye that God would blesse all their counsels and consultations, and succeede all their unwearyed endevors for ye happie setling and establishment of this latelie languyshing and now revived Commonwealth upon sure and lasting foundations.

Sir, I rest and am
Your humble Servant
Jo. BRADSHAWE.

(Fonthi) "ll in Wyltshire

.... in 1659

.... scentis Respublica. Primo.

(Read June 9, 1659)
For the Right Honble William Lenthall, Speaker
of ye Parliament of the Commonwealth
of England. These.

Consider what it is we ask, and consider whether it be not the same thing we have asserted with our lives and fortunes—*a Free Parliament.* And what a slavery is it to our understandings, that these men that now call themselves a Parliament, should declare it an act of illegality and violence in the late aspiring General Cromwell to dissolve their body in 1653, and not make it the like in the garbling of the whole body of the Parliament from four hundred to forty in 1648 ? What is this but to act what they condemn in others ? *A new free Parliament !* This is our cry.

On the 1st of August, Sir George Booth appeared in arms, and in a few days was at the head of several thousand men. Through the influence of Mr. Cook, a Presbyterian minister in Chester, he and his troops gained admission to the city. Colonel Lambert, with a well-disciplined force, was sent by the Parliament after them, and an engagement took place at Winnington Bridge, near North-wich, when Sir George and his army—which Adam Martindale likened to "Mahomet's Angellical Cockes, made up of fire and snow"—were completely routed.

On the return of the victorious army to London a schism broke out between the officers and the Parliament, which was followed by one of those outrages upon the liberties of the Parliament with which the country had become only too painfully familiar. Lambert and his troops surrounded the House, which Lenthall, the

Speaker, and the other members were prevented by the soldiery from entering. Bradshaw felt the insult, and, anticipating that the break-up of the House would be followed by the dissolution of the Council of State, went the same day, ill as he was, to the meeting, in the hope that he might serve the cause of the Republic, and when Colonel Sydenham, the member for Dorsetshire, and one of the Committee of Safety, in attempting to justify the arbitrary act of the army by affirming, in the canting phraseology of the day, that "a particular call of the Divine Providence" had necessitated its having recourse to this last remedy, Bradshaw, says Ludlow, "weak and attenuated as he was, yet animated by his ardent zeal and constant affection to the common cause, stood up, and, interrupting him, declared his abhorrence of that detestable action, and told the Council that, being now going to his God, he had not patience to sit there to hear His great name so openly blasphemed."

This was his last public act—the last office he was permitted to render to the Commonwealth he had so long served, as he said, "with all diligence," for he passed out of the world a few days after, his death occurring on the 22nd November, 1659, in his 57th year. His remains were deposited with great pomp in the Sanctuary of Kings, from which, however, they were soon to be ignominiously ejected. His funeral sermon was preached by Mr. Row, who took for his text Isaiah lvii., 1. His Republican spirit animated him to the last, for Whitelocke says that, so little did he repent of his conduct towards his Sovereign, that "he declared a little before he left the world, that if the King were to be tried and condemned again, he would be the first man that should do it."

John Bradshaw married Mary, the daughter of Thomas Marbury, of Marbury, Cheshire, by his first wife Eleanor, daughter of Peter Warburton, of Arley, and he thus connected himself with some of the best families in the county. This lady, who was some years his senior, predeceased him without having borne any issue ; and when the President died he had not a child to continue his

name or inherit the vast wealth he had accumulated. The closing
years of his life were for the most part spent at his pleasant retreat
at Walton-on-Thames, of which mention has already been made;
and there is very little doubt but that within the wainscotted rooms
of that quaint old mansion many and frequent were the consultations touching the fate of England. A popular writer, who visited
the house some years ago, in describing it, says that an aged
woman, who then occupied a portion of the building, summed up
her account of it with the remark that "it was a great house once,
but full of wickedness; and no wonder the spirits of its inhabitants
troubled the earth to this day." Though we are not of those
who "see visions and dream dreams," and hold familiar converse
with visitants from the world of shadows, we may yet echo the
remark of the writer referred to: "It is trite enough to say what
tales these walls could tell, but it is impossible to look into them
without wishing 'these walls had tongues.'"

The character of Bradshaw has been variously estimated and
depicted in every hue, though it would seem to have been little
understood, for his admirers have refused to see any defects in
him, while those who abhor his principles have denounced him as
a "monster of men." It does not come within our province to
offer any critical opinion on his life and actions—to pronounce
upon the purity of his motives or the sincerity of his doings. His
cousin Milton, who, however, can hardly be accepted as an
impartial witness, has written his eulogy in an eloquent passage
in the "Second Defence of the People of England;" and
Godwin, in his "History of the Commonwealth," thus speaks of
him :—

An individual who was rising into eminence at this time was John
Bradshaw, the kinsman of Milton. He was bred to the profession of the
law, and his eloquence is praised by Lilburn. Milton, who seems to have
known him thoroughly, speaks of him in the highest terms, as at once a
professed lawyer and an admirable speaker, an uncorrupt patriot, a man
of firm and entrepid cast of temper, a pleasant companion, most hospitable to his friends, most generous to all who were in need, most
peaceable to such as repented of their errors.

The same writer adds : " In December, 1644, he was appointed high sheriff of his native county of Lancashire." This last statement is an error which has gained currency by frequent repetition. Bradshaw was not a Lancashire man ; and his namesake, who held the shrievalty of that county by virtue of the ordinance of the 10th February, 1644, when Parliament, exercising the Royal functions, assumed the powers of the Duke of Lancaster, and who, in contravention of the Act of 28 Edward III., retained it for four successive years, was the head of the line of Bradshaw, in the parish of Bolton, and, therefore, only remotely connected with the Marple stock.

After the Restoration both Houses of Parliament decreed (4th December, 1660) that his body, with those of Cromwell and Ireton, should be exhumed and drawn to the gallows at Tyburn, and there hanged and buried beneath it. Evelyn, in his " Diary," thus describes the revolting spectacle he saw on the 30th January, the anniversary of the King's execution, and the " first solemn fast and day of humiliation to deplore the sinns which so long had provok'd God against His afflicted Church and people " :—

> This day (O the stupendous and inscrutable judgments of God !) were the carcases of those arch rebells Cromwell, Bradshaw the Judge who condemned his Majestie, and Ireton, sonn-in-law to the Usurper, dragg'd out of their superb tombs in Westminster among the Kings, to Tyburne, and hang'd on the gallows there from nine in the morning till six at night, and then buried under that fatal and ignominious monument in a deepe pitt ; thousands of people who had seene them in all their pride being spectators. Looke back at Nov. 22, 1658 (Cromwell's funeral) and be astonish'd ! and feare God and honour the King ; but meddle not with them who are given to change.

It has been asserted, though without any apparent authority, that Bradshaw was buried at Annapolis, in America, and Mr. St. John says the following inscription was engraved on a cannon placed at the head of his supposed grave :—

> Stranger ! ere thou pass, contemplate this cannon, nor regardless behold that near its base lies deposited the dust of John Bradshaw, who,

nobly superior to selfish regards, despising alike the pageantry of courtly splendour, the blast of calumny, and the terror of regal vengeance, presided in the illustrious band of heroes and patriots who firmly and openly adjudged Charles Stuart, tyrant of England, to a public and exemplary death, thereby presenting to the amazed world, and transmitting down to applauding ages, the most glorious example of unshaken virtue, love of freedom, and impartial justice ever exhibited in the blood-stained theatre of human action. Oh! reader, pass not on till thou hast blessed his memory, and never, never forget that rebellion to tyrants is obedience to God!

The heads of the three regicides were undoubtedly placed upon Westminster Hall, and Bradshaw's and Cromwell's remained fixed on the spikes in 1684, when Sir Thomas Armstrong's* was placed between them.

Among the papers still preserved at Marple is the probate copy of the President's will, a lengthy abstract of which has been given by Ormerod in his "History of Cheshire." It bears date March 22, 1653, and there are two codicils appended, dated respectively March 23, 1653, and September 10, 1655. By it he bequeaths to his wife, Mary Bradshaw, all his manors, lands, and hereditaments in Kent and Middlesex for her life, as jointure in lieu of dower; and devises to her, and her executors in case of her decease, his manors, &c., in Kent, for the term of five years, to commence immediately after her decease, with liberty in her lifetime to dispark the park at Somerhill, for her subsistence, and for making provision for her kindred, "God not havinge vouchsafed me issue." He further devises his manors, &c., in the counties of Berks, Southampton, Wilts, and Somerset, with his reversions in Middlesex, in trust to his friend Peter Brereton, his nephew Peter Newton (the son of his sister Dorothy), and his trustie servant, Thomas Parnell, and their heirs, for the payment of his debts, &c., for the payment of £100 per annum, for ten years after his decease, to his nephew Henry Bradshaw, and £20 per annum to his cousin Katherine

---

* Sir Thomas Armstrong, who had taken part in the Duke of Monmouth's rebellion, was executed on the judgment of the notorious Jefferies, as an outlaw without trial, though his year had not expired.

Leigh, for life, with further trust to pay £300 per annum to his brother Henry Bradshaw, until the estates settled by the will descend to him; and also to expend £700 in purchasing an annuity for "manteyning a free schoole in Marple, in Cheshire; £500 for increasing the wages of the master and usher of Bunbury schoole; and £500 for amending the wages of the schoolmaster and usher of Midleton schoole, in Lanc'r (in which twoe schooles of Bunb'rie and Midleton I had part of my educac'on, and return this as part of my thanfull acknowledgement for the same). These two sums of £500 to be laid out in purchaseing annuities." Then follow a number of small bequests—an annuity of £40 for seven years to Samuel Roe, his secretary, for maintaining him at Gray's Inn, and remunerating his assistance to his executors; £250 to the poor of Fonthill, Stopp, Westminster, and Feltham; a bequest of the impropriation of Feltham, for the use of a proper minister to be established there; an annuity of £20 for providing a minister at Hatch, in Wiltshire, charged on his estate there; legacies to his chaplain, Mr. Parr, Mr. Strong, the preacher at the Abbey, and Mr. Clyve, a Scottish minister; his houses and lodgings at Westminster to the governors of the almshouses and school there; and the residue of the estate to his brother Henry, excepting £100 to his niece Meverell and her sister of the whole blood. The first codicil directs his executors to sell the Hampshire estates and to fell timber not exceeding the value of £2,000 on his estates in the county of Kent for payment of his debts; and the sum of £50 "to my cozen Kath. Leigh who now liveth with me;" and he further bequeaths all his law books, and such divinity, history, and other books as his wife shall judge fit, "to his nephew Harrie Bradshawe." It may be mentioned that the library thus bequeathed remained at Marple until the close of the last century, when, after having been augmented by later generations of the family, it was sold to Mr. Edwards, of Halifax. Subsequently it was offered for sale by Messrs. Edwards, of Pall Mall, being then catalogued with the library of Mr. N. Wilson, of Pontefract, and those of two deceased antiquaries, the entire

9

collection, according to a writer in the *Gentleman's Magazine* (v. lxxxvi., part 1), being more splendid and truly valuable than any which had been previously presented to the curious, and such as "astonished not only the opulent purchasers, but the most experienced and intelligent booksellers of the metropolis." The second codicil gives to his wife's assignees seven years' interest in his Kentish estates after her death, confirms her right to dispark Somerhill, dispose of the deer, and convert the same to the uses of husbandry. It further confirms the Middlesex estates to her for life, and gives her his house at Westminster, held on lease from the governors of the school there, and directs that £1,000 due from the State on account of his office of Chancellor of the Duchy of Lancaster, and Chief Justice of Chester, Flint, Denbigh, and Montgomery, be applied to discharge his debts. It annuls several legacies, and bequeaths others, among them one of £10 to John Milton; appoints a legacy of £5 each to all his servants living at the time of his decease; and makes several additional legal provisions. The will was proved in London, December 16, 1659, by Henry Bradshaw, the nephew—Mary Bradshaw, the late wife and sole executrix of the testator, being then dead, and Henry Bradshaw, the brother, having renounced execution.

The will is interesting, as showing the extent to which the Lord President had contrived to enrich himself out of the sequestrated estates of obnoxious Royalists during the period of the usurpation. Shortly before the Restoration his nephew Henry was ejected from Fonthill by the heir of Lord Cottington, who recovered possession of his ancestral home; and though he managed to secure a large proportion of the property bequeathed by the will, the benevolent intentions of the testator were in a great measure frustrated by the changes made in the disposition of the estate after the return of Charles II. through the operation of the Act of Confiscation.

Bradshaw makes allusion in his will to the fact that "God had not vouchsafed him issue." Though no children were born to him by his wife, he is said to have had "an illegitimate son, whose last descendant, Sarah Bradshaw, married, in 1757, Sir Henry Cavendish, ancestor of Lord Waterpark." In the absence, however, of any substantial evidence, the accuracy of this statement may well be questioned, for we can hardly suppose the testator would have bequeathed so large a property to his nephew, and have made no provision for his own offspring, while permitting him to bear and perpetuate his name. Though the bar sinister was the reverse of an honourable augmentation, the stigma of illegitimacy did not attach so much in those days as now. Sir Henry Cavendish, the ancestor of Lord Waterpark, who was himself descended from an illegitimate son of Henry, the eldest son of Sir William Cavendish, of Chatsworth, by his third wife, the renowned "Bess of Hardwick," married, August 5, 1757, Sarah (or, according to some authorities, Mary) only child and heiress of Richard Bradshaw, who, during her husband's lifetime, was, in her own right, created (15th June, 1792) Baroness Waterpark, of Waterpark, in Ireland; and the supposition that John Bradshaw left an illegitimate son seems to rest upon the statement made by Playfair, in his "British Family Antiquities," and reiterated by Burke, and still more recently in the "Peerage" of Forster, that this lady was "lineally descended from the Lord President Bradshaw."

Another member of the family employed in the public service during the Commonwealth period was Richard Bradshaw. His name does not appear in any of the pedigrees of the Marple line, nor has his identity been established, though it is very probable he was a nephew of the Lord President's, and he was certainly present as one of the mourners at his funeral. He held the office for some time of Receiver of the Crown Revenues in Cheshire and North Wales, and was subsequently appointed to the post of English Resident at Hamburg, whence he was transferred to Russia, and other of the northern Courts. A great number of his letters are given in Thurloe's "State Papers," and they are especially interesting as showing the care taken to watch the movements of Charles II., and the actions of the European Powers likely to render him assistance in any attempt to recover the throne. In one of these letters addressed on his return to England to Secretary Thurloe, and dated from Axeyard, 1st November, 1658, requesting that the sum of £2,188 0s. 9d. then due to him from the Government might be paid, some curious circumstances are related in connection with his previous official life. He says :—

I am necessitated to acquaint your lordship, that in the yeare 1648, I beinge then receiver of the crowne-revenue in North-wales and Cheshire for the state, and cominge to London to passe accomts, and pay in some money to Mr. Fauconberg the receiver generall, my lodgings in Kinge Street, Westminster, was broake into by theeves the very same day the apprentises riss in London and came down to Whitehall ; and £430 was taken fourthe of a trunke in the chamber where I lay. Though it was a tyme of great distraction, yet I used such meanes with the warrants and assistants of Mr. Fauconbridge, as that I found out and apprehended the fellows the next day, in which the messenger, Captain Compton, was assistinge to me, whoe were tryed and condemned at the sessions in the Old Bailey as Compton very well knowes, being the sonnes of persons of note in Covent Garden. The prosecution of them cost me above £100, besides the greatest trouble that ever I had in my life aboute any businesse. But before my accompte could be declared by the commissioners for the revenue, whereon I expected allowance for that money, I was commanded to Hamburg ; and now being to settle these accompts in the exchequer, to have out my ultimate discharge thence, I am told that it is not in the power of the lords commissioners for the treasury to give allowance thereof in the way of the exchequer, without a privy seale to pardon that sume. Therefore I humbly request that the £430 so taken may be included in the privy seal with the £3,461 5s. 1?d., and then the whole will be £3,891 5s. 10d., which, if your lordship be satisfyed with the accompts, I pray that Mr. Milbey or Mr. Moreland may have your lordship's order to make ready for the seale.

The riot referred to was no doubt that of the 9th of April, when, in disregard of the strict Puritan orders in relation to religious observances, the apprentices were found playing at bowls in Moorfields during church time. They were ordered by the militia guard to disperse, but refused, fought the guard, and held their ground. Being soon after routed by cavalry, they raised the cry of "clubs," when they were joined by the watermen. The fight lasted through the night, and in the morning they had got possession of Ludgate and Newgate, and had stretched chains across all the great thoroughfares, their cry being "God and King Charles." The tumult lasted for forty hours, and was not put an end to until they were ridden down by a body of cavalry from Westminster.

In his petition to the Council of State, praying to be paid the full sum of £2,188 11s. 4d., Richard Bradshaw states that he had " suffered the loss of £5,000 in the late wars of this nation, without any reparation for the same, and for above seventeen years freely exposed his life at home and abroad in the service of the State ; that the same was disbursed out of his affection to his country, whilst he resided as public minister in foreign parts, and, if not paid, he should be now, at his return, rent from his small estate, it being more than he hath got in the service of the Commonwealth.

On the 9th March, 1659-60, the Council directed the amount to be paid, and on the 12th his accounts were ordered for that purpose to be laid before Parliament. It does not appear, however, to have been received, for on the 23rd and 31st he is again found petitioning Thurloe on the matter, and in the changes that were then taking place it is doubtful if he ever got anything. Whether, as he feared, he was " rent from his small estate " or not is not recorded, but it is evident that in a pecuniary sense he was not so successful as his kinsman, the Lord President ; yet he was a man of much energy and ability. and his letters give an interesting account of the political affairs of foreign Courts at the time. He appears to have been continually short of money through the Government remaining indebted to him, and this fact rather suggests the idea that Cromwell, who had already broken with John Bradshaw, desired to hold him as a kind of hostage, and keep him wherever he chose to place him.

With a portion of the wealth acquired under John Bradshaw's will, Henry, his nephew, in 1693, purchased Bradshaw Hall, in Lancashire, which, as previously stated, had for many generations been the residence of another branch of the family, that had then become extinct in the male line. It is a singular fact that

within a comparatively short period, nearly all, if not all, the
branches of the Bradshaw family became extinct in the male line —
the Bradshaws of Haigh, of Bradshaw, and of Aspull, in Lancashire; of Bradshaw Edge, and of Barton, in Derbyshire; and
finally, as we shall see, of Marple, in Cheshire, the latter by the
death of the Lord President's grand-nephew in 1743.

The subsequent history of the Bradshaws is soon told.
Henry, who inherited the patrimonial estates as well as the
bulk of his uncle's property, married Elizabeth (erroneously
called Magdalene in Ormerod's, Forster's, and Burke's pedigrees), one of the daughters and co-heirs of Thomas Barcroft,
by whom, on the death of her father in 1688, he acquired
the demesne of Barcroft, in Whalley parish, Lancashire, with
the hall, an ancient mansion dating from the time of Henry
VIII. This Henry made considerable additions to Marple,
and erected a great portion of the outbuildings, as evidenced
by the frequent repetitions of his and his wife's initials

B

H E

1669

upon the hall and the stables. By his marriage he had three
sons, Henry, High Sheriff of Derbyshire in 1701, who had to
wife Elizabeth, daughter of Richard Legh, of the East Hall,
in High Legh, and died in 1724, without issue ; Thomas,
who died unmarried in 1743; and John, who predeceased
his brother, being also issueless ; the estates, on the death of
Thomas, devolving upon the only daughter, Mary, who married
William Pimlot, and by him had two sons, the eldest of whom,
John, succeeded to the estates under a settlement made by his
uncle, Thomas Bradshaw, and had issue a daughter and only
child, Elizabeth, married to Lindon Evelyn, of Keynsham Court,
county Hereford, Esq., M.P. for Dundalk, whose only daughter
and heir, Elizabeth, married, December 29th, 1838, Randall
Edward Plunkett, Baron Dunsany, elder brother of the present
holder of that title.

Mary Pimlot, surviving her husband, again entered the marriage state, her second husband being Nathaniel Isherwood, of Bolton, by whom she had two sons, Nathaniel, who, under his uncle's settlement, succeeded as heir to the Marple and Bradshaw estates on the death of John Pimlot. He married Elizabeth, daughter and heiress of Henry Brabin, of Brabin's Hall, in Marple, but died without issue in 1765, when the property passed to his younger brother, Thomas Isherwood, who married Elizabeth, daughter of Thomas Attercroft, of Gillibrand House, near Blackburn, and by her had a son, who died in infancy, and six daughters. She predeceased her husband; when he married for his second wife Mary, daughter and heir of Thomas Orrell, of Saltersley, in Cheshire. This lady, who died 18th May, 1797, bore him four sons and five daughters. Thomas Bradshaw-Isherwood, the eldest son, succeeded, but died unmarried 5th January, 1791, when the estates passed to Henry Bradshaw-Isherwood, the second son, who also died unmarried January 26, 1801, the Marple and Bradshaw properties then devolving upon his younger brother, John Bradshaw-Isherwood, born 19th June, 1776, who married, at Bolton, October 19, 1812, Elizabeth, eldest daughter and co-heir of the Rev. Thomas Bancroft, M.A., vicar of Bolton. In 1815 he filled the office of Sheriff of Cheshire, and by his wife, who survived him and died 1st April, 1856, he left, in addition to six daughters, a son, Thomas Bradshaw-Isherwood, Esq., the present owner of Marple and Bradshaw, born 10th February, 1820. Mr. Bradshaw-Isherwood, who is a J.P. and D.L. for Cheshire, married 22nd July, 1840, Mary Ellen, eldest surviving daughter of the late Rev. Henry Bellairs, M.A., rector of Bedworth, in Warwickshire, and Hon. Canon of Worcester, one of the heroes of Trafalgar, by his wife Dorothy Parker, daughter and coheir (with Mary, first wife of John, Earl of Strafford, distinguished for his brilliant services in the battles of the Peninsula and at Waterloo, and Sarah, wife of Captain Carmichael) of Peter Mackenzie, of Grove House, Middlesex, descended from the Mackenzies, barons of Kintail. The issue of this marriage is

two sons, John Henry Bradshaw-Isherwood, born 27th August,
1841, who married, in 1864, Elizabeth, daughter of Thomas Luce,
Esq., formerly member for Malmesbury, and Arthur Salusbury
Bradshaw-Isherwood, born 21st May, 1843.

We have said sufficient to establish the claim of Marple to rank
among the most interesting of the historic homes of the Palatinate.
The building, which is a good example of the early Jacobean
period, with considerable additions of late seventeenth century
work, has undergone comparatively few changes, having happily
escaped those coarse assaults to which so many of our old
mansions have been subjected by modern renovators. So little
is it altered that it would require no great effort of the imagination
to picture the momentous conferences of the chiefs of Cheshire
Nonconformity that were held within its walls, or to re-people its
sombre apartments with the buff-jerkined, jack-booted, and heavily-
accoutred troopers who followed Henry Bradshaw to the field;
indeed, we might almost fancy that the very chairs and tables have
remained undisturbed during the whole two centuries and more
that have elapsed since those eventful days. Of modern furniture
there is comparatively little, almost everything the house contains
being of an age gone by, and in keeping with its ancient character.

As anything like a detailed description of the interior is beyond
the purpose and the limits of this sketch, we shall content ourselves
with pointing out the principal apartments and some of the more
notable objects they contain. The principal front is on the south
side, from which a porch, supported by stone columns, forming the
central projection from the house, gives admission to the entrance
hall, an apartment 40 feet long and 20 feet wide, lighted at each
end by long low mullioned windows. The floor is laid with
alternate squares of white stone and black marble, and the ceiling,
which is flat, is crossed by massive oaken beams. The want of
elevation gives a somewhat gloomy and depressing effect, and this
is heightened by the coloured glass in the windows, which further
subdues the light. The furniture is of black oak, bright with the
rubbings of many generations; and against the walls are disposed

suits of mail, morions, corslets, and implements of war that
have no doubt done duty in many a well-fought field. On the
left of the entrance, leading from the hall, is the library, twenty
feet square, lighted on the south side by a mullioned window,
filled with stained glass, and having the armorial ensigns of the
Bradshaws and their alliances carved upon the wainscot. On
the same floor, and adjoining the library, is the dining-room,
a spacious apartment, thirty feet by twenty feet, with an oriel
window at the north end, commanding an extensive view of the
valley of the Goyt and the surrounding country. The walls of this
room are hung with portraits, and include several that are said to
have been brought from Harden Hall, and to have once belonged
to the Alvanley family. Among them is one of Queen Elizabeth,
and others representing the Earls of Essex and Leicester, Lord
Keeper Coventry, Sir Roger Ascham, and General Monk; there is
also a portrait of one of the Dones of Utkinton, hereditary chief
foresters of Delamere, and of his wife, who stands by his side.
Close by the door, on the right of the entrance hall, is a broad
oaken staircase, with decorated balustrades, leading to the upper
chambers. The walls are hung with portraits, views, &c., and in
one corner we noticed an antique spinning-wheel, the property
apparently of some former spinster of the house. The first
chamber we enter is a small ante-room, wainscotted, with a fireplace composed of ancient Dutch tiles, above which is a shield,
with the arms of the Bradshaws carved in relief, with the date
1665. A flight of circular steps leads from this chamber to the
drawing-room, which is immediately over the dining-room, and
corresponding with it in dimensions. The walls of this apartment are hung with tapestry of Gobelins manufacture, the subjects
being Diana and her Nymphs, and Time and Pleasure. On the
same floor is another chamber, now occupied as a bedroom, which
is interesting from the circumstance that the black and white
timber gable, the only fragment apparently of the original structure
remaining, is exposed to view, showing where the projecting bay
has been added when the house was enlarged by Henry Bradshaw,

10

the Lord President's nephew, shortly after the Restoration. Opposite the wainscotted ante-room before referred to is a small tapestried bed-chamber, where tradition says the Lord President first saw the light; and here is the very bed on which, according to the same reputable authority, he slept—an antiquated four-poster, very substantial and very elaborately ornamented, with a cornice round the top, with the following admonitory sentences,* in raised capitals, carved on three sides of it, though it is to be feared the Lord President did not study them with much advantage :—

> HE THAT IS UNMERCIFUL, MERCY SHALL MISS;
> BUT HE SHALL HAVE MERCY THAT MERCIFUL IS.

And on the inside :—

> LOVE GOD AND NOT GOLD,
> SLEEP NOT UNTIL U CONSIDER HOW U HAVE SPENT THE TIME;
> IF WELL, THANK GOD ; IF NOT, REPENT.

There were formerly in this room, and may be now, a helmet, breastplate, and pair of spurs that were supposed to have belonged to John Bradshaw, but which are more likely to have been worn by his elder brother Henry, the Parliamentarian soldier. On the window of the same chamber is inscribed the well-known pro-phetic lines that John is said to have written when a lad attending the Macclesfield Grammar SchooL On the right of the entrance hall are two small chambers, of comparatively little interest; and adjoining them is the servants' hall, the most noticeable feature in which is a moulding in stucco, and here also

---

* At Bradshaw Hall, in Chapel-en-le-Frith, the ancient patrimonial seat of the stock from which the Marple Bradshaws sprang, there is on the landing of one of the staircases a similar inscription :—

> Love God and not gould.

> He that loves not mercy
> Of mercy shall miss ;
> But he shall have mercy
> That merciful is.

is repeated the family arms—argent, two bendlets sable, between
as many martlets of the second ; with the crest, a stag at gaze
under a vine tree fructed ppr., and the motto, " *Bona Benemerenti
Benedictio.*" A passage in the rear of the house communicates
with a door on the north or terrace front, on the lintel of which is
carved the date 1658. The outbuildings are extensive. They are
partly of stone and partly of brick, and with their quaint gables,
pinnacles, and clock tower form a very picturesque grouping.
They are commonly supposed to have been erected by "Colonel"
Henry Bradshaw, for the accommodation of his Roundhead
troopers ; but the idea is dispelled by the initials

B
H E

and the date, 1669, which may still be discerned—an evidence
that they were erected in more peaceable times by Henry, the
Colonel's son and successor, who, as we have seen, married
Elizabeth Barcroft, and became heir to much of his uncle's
wealth. Altogether, the old place is a deeply-interesting memorial of times now happily gone by. Its history is especially
instructive, and it is impossible to wander through its antiquated
chambers without recalling some of the momentous scenes and
incidents in the country's annals. Happily, evil hands have not
fallen upon it. It is preserved with jealous care ; and from the
few changes it has undergone we gather the idea—always a
pleasant one—that here antiquity is reverenced for its worth.

CHAPTER III.

N that sequestered tract of country that stretches away
from the mountain to the main—from the mouth of
the Kent to where the Duddon flows down to join the
sea, and extending from the majestic barrier of the
Lake country to the silvery shores of Morecambe
Bay—the wide estuary that divides the Hundred of
Lonsdale and separates the districts of Cartmel and Furness from
the other parts of Lancashire—there is a wealth of natural beauty
and many an interesting nook undreamt of by the ordinary tourist,
who, following in the steps of imitative sight-seers, rushes along the
great iron highway to the North, forgetting that the fairest spots in
the world are reserved for those who have the wisdom to seek out
and earn their pleasures for themselves. In that pleasant corner of
Lancashire, mountain and valley, moor and fell, blend together in
happy relationship, presenting a panorama of swelling hills, wood-
clad knolls, and quiet secluded hamlets within the bright setting of
the shimmering sea. It is, as poor John Critchley Prince was wont
to sing :—

> A realm of mountain, forest-haunt, and fell,
>   And fertile valleys beautifully lone,
> Where fresh and far romantic waters roam,
> Singing a song of peace by many a cottage home.

And where—

> Only the sound of the distant sea,
> As a far-off voice in a dream may be,
> Mingles its tale with the woodland tones,
> As the sea waves wash o'er the tidal stones.

But it is not for the lover of the picturesque alone that the district offers more than ordinary attractions. There are few localities so rich in records of the past, or surrounded by so many traditional associations. In addition to the magnificent ruins of Furness, there is the scarcely less interesting pile of Cartmel, one of the few priory ;

churches that England now possesses, and which only escaped destruction in the stormy times of the Reformation by the inhabitants literally buying off the King's Commissioners. On Swarthmoor, "the German baron, bold Martin Swart," mustered "his merry men" when Lambert Simnel, the pretender to the Crown, landed at Piel, in 1486, an escapade in which we fear "Our Lady of Furness" was not altogether free from implication. Here, too, is Swarthmoor Hall, once the home of Judge Fell ; and close by is the modest Quakers' Chapel, the first built by George Fox, the founder of the Society of Friends. Holker Hall has been for a century and more the home of the Cavendishes, as it was previously of the Lowthers and the Prestons. The little hamlet of Lindale has been made the scene of one of the most charming of Mrs. Gaskell's stories, and almost within bow-shot is Buck Crag, sheltering beneath which is the humble dwelling that for many a long year was the abode of Edmund Law, the curate and schoolmaster of Staveley, the spot where the younger Edmund Law, Bishop of Carlisle, and father of Lord Ellenborough, first saw the light.

Before the enterprise and skill of Brogden and Brunlees had bridged the estuaries of the Kent and the Leven, and carried the railway from Carnforth to Ulverston, the journey to Whitehaven and the western lakes had to be made across the broad expanse of sand left by each receding tide, and a perilous journey it was. In bygone days the monks of Cartmel maintained a guide, paid him out of "Peter's Pence," and, in addition, gave him the benefit of their prayers, which in truth he often needed ; and when their house was dissolved, "Bluff King Hal" charged the expenses of the office upon the revenues of the Duchy of Lancaster, so that the "Carter," as he is now called, is an old-established institution. There is no beaten pathway "Over Sands," for every tide removes the traces of those who have gone before, and the channels are so constantly shifting that what yesterday might be firm and solid to the tread, to-day may be only soft and treacherous pulp. The locality has been oftentimes the scene of mourning and sorrow, and many are the tales that are told of the "hair-breadth 'scapes" of those who have been overtaken by the "cruel crawling tide" while journeying over the perilous waste. The old adage tells us that

> The Kent and the Keer
> Have parted many a good man and his meear (mare).

And the registers of Cartmel bear testimony to the fact that, of those who now sleep peacefully in its "God's Acre," a hundred and twenty or more have met their fate while crossing the shifty channels of this treacherous shore. The poet Gray, writing in

GRANGE-OVER-SANDS.

1767 to Dr. Wharton, relates a pathetic story of a family who were overtaken by a mist when half way across and lost their way; and Edwin Waugh, in his pleasant, gossiping way, tells how an ancient mariner, when asked if the guides were ever lost on the sands, answered with grim *naïveté*: "I never knew any lost. There's one or two drowned now and then, but they're generally found somewhere i'th bed when th' tide goes out." When the subjects of the Cæsars had established themselves here, the old Roman General Agricola made a journey "Over Sands," and the difficulties he encountered are related by Tacitus the historian. Mrs. Hemans braved the dangers, for in one of her letters she says: "I must not omit to tell you that Mr. Wordsworth not only admired our exploit in crossing the Ulverston Sands as a deed of 'derring do,' but as a decided proof of taste. The Lake scenery, he says, is never seen to such advantage as after the passage of what he calls its 'majestic barrier.'" In the old coaching days the journey began at Hest Bank, about three miles from Lancaster, where the guide was usually in waiting to conduct the travellers across, when a mixed cavalcade of horsemen, pedestrians, and vehicles of various kinds was formed, which, following the coach, and headed by the browned and weather-beaten "Carter," slowly traversed the trackless waste, the incongruous grouping suggesting the idea of an Eastern caravan on its passage across the desert. If nothing else, the journey had the charm of novelty and adventure, which in some degree compensated for the hazard incurred; and the scenes of danger and disaster witnessed have furnished the theme for more than one exciting story, as "Carlyon's Year" and the "Sexton's Hero" bear witness. But the romance of the sands is fast passing away. The guides have now comparatively little to do, the perilous path is traversed less and less frequently every year, so that ere long we shall probably only hear of it as a traditional feature of the times when the name of Stephenson was unknown and railways were only in the womb of time.

On the western side of the Milnthorpe Sands, nestling at the foot of the green slopes of Yewbarrow, with its whitened dwellings

11

peeping from their garniture of leaves, and its rock-strewn beach
lipped by the capricious sea, is the slowly-rising village of Grange,
with its sands and its sea, its pleasant walks and cheerful drives,
all sheltered from the north winds by the great Cartmel fells
clustering at its back. A place that lures you by the peaceful
quietude that prevails, for here Ethiopian serenaders and blind
bag-pipers are unknown, and youthful lazzaroni with white mice
and pink-eyed guinea pigs are beings the people wot not of. It is
not "dressy," nor is it fashionable in the sense that Scarborough
is, so that you can take your ease in your inn without risk of being
chilled by the freezing presence of Lord Shingleton or my Lady
Marina. The wandering creature who calls himself a tourist,
and is always in search of some new sensation, passes it by as
slow and unexciting, and the herd of holiday-makers who delight
to perform aquatic *poses plastiques* once a year prefer to do so in
such over-crammed places as Southport, or that marine Babylon—
Blackpool. Nevertheless, it is a pleasant place to stay at when
you have nothing to do, and all the day to do it in ; a retreat
where you can shake off those fancies associated with every-
day life that cloud the brow and spoil the digestion, and get rid
of that

> Army of phantoms vast and wan
> That beleaguer the human soul.

But our present purpose is not to write a description of Grange,
for though it is a pleasant place to stay at it is also a pleasant
place to go away from—a convenient spot from whence little
excursions can be made to neighbouring places of interest and
attraction, and this time it is Wraysholme Tower, the ruined home
of the once powerful Harringtons, and the rocky promontory of
Humphrey Head, where tradition says the last wolf "in England's
spacious realm" was hunted down, that attracts our wandering
steps.

As we slowly wend our way towards the upper end of the village,
pausing now and then to gaze across the broad expanse of More-

cambe Bay to the wooded shores on the Lancaster side, and the great fells that stretch away in rear to join the pale blue hills of Yorkshire, we get sight of an antiquated building with mullioned windows, now half buried in the ground, which in former times served as a granary for the storage of the rich harvests gathered by the fraternity of Cartmel, and hence the name of "Grange" which has been given to the place. At an angle of the road, near the higher end, is the church, erected some twenty years ago through the persevering efforts of a lady resident. Keeping along the level way, we come presently to a cross-road, and, turning sharply to the left, pass the farmhouse where, for generations, the "Carters" have resided. A few minutes' walk along the railway line brings us to a pleasant indentation in the shore, where Kent's Bank, a tiny watering place, with a trim hotel and cosy-looking villas, bright with flowers and creeping plants, is striving to rival its more famous neighbour. In a green nook by the sea is a pleasant mansion that occupies the site of a more ancient structure, Abbot Hall, once the abode, as tradition affirms, of the abbots of Cartmel, but, as there were no "abbots" of that house, it is more likely to have belonged to the fraternity of Furness, who, as we know, had lands here granted to them as far back as 1135. Mr. Stockdale, in his *Annales Caermoelensis*, suggests that it was built for the convenience of the abbot when journeying from Furness to his possessions in Yorkshire. He says :—

No doubt the puisne monarch (the abbot) and his cavalcade would travel, in making these journeys, in a stately, lordly, and ostentatious way, and would pass along the narrow tracks from the (Furness) Abbey to the Red Lane end, at Conishead Bank, with more or less difficulty, and then, entering upon the sea sands, would, in a short time, reach "the Chapel Island," where, in the little homely chapel, prayers would be earnestly offered up for the safe passage of the remainder of the dangerous, though much the smaller, Morecambe estuary. This needful duty having been performed, the long cavalcade would slowly wend its way over the creeks, gullies, and quicksands, till the opposite bank of the estuary was gained, and then by the old Roman road called now the Back Lane, to the town of Flookborough, and from thence to Allithwaite, and by the very old road up and over the precipitous hill to the abbot's own comfortable and well-sheltered residence, Abbot Hall. . . . As there has always been a tradition that there was a chapel near Kirkhead and Abbot Hall—some remains of which, even graves, it is said, existed in the last century—there can but be little doubt that the abbot and his numerous suite would, after their night's rest at Abbot Hall, resort to this chapel and again pray for a safe passage over the wild and dangerous Lancaster estuary, eight or nine miles in width, not passed at this day, even in the presence of a guide, with entire safety.*

A pleasant rural lane leads up from the station at Kent's Bank to Allithwaite, a little straggling village, the inhabitants of which contrive to earn a scanty livelihood by fishing and "cockling" upon the sands. Steep banks rise on each side, festooned with plumy ferns and wild flowers, crested with spiked thorn-bushes, scrubby hazels, and spreading ash-trees, that wave their shadowy branches overhead. The honeysuckle spreads its delicious perfume around, and as we saunter leisurely along the sunlight glints through the leafy openings, shooting down long arrowy rays, that here brighten with golden touches the gnarled and knotted stem of a sturdy oak, and there light up a churlish bramble, like a woman's radiant smile reflecting its cheeriness upon some worthless Caliban. On the left is Kirkhead, a lofty knoll, crowned with a prospect tower—Barrow's summer-house, as it is called—from the summit of which there is a view that well repays the labour of ascent. Wraysholme's ruined tower, whither we are wending our way, is but a short mile distant, and as we have a long summer afternoon before us, we may wander at our will. Having mounted the breezy hill, we lie down on a cushion of soft grass at the foot of the building to gaze upon the scene, listening the while to the wild bird's song and the hoarse melody of the fitful sea.

---

* Upon the Abbot Hall estate are some lands which still bear the name of Chapel Fields, in which, at three feet from the surface, human skeletons have been exhumed. The spot may therefore with much probability be assumed to have been the site of an oratory, where a monk of the abbey officiated in offering up prayers for the safety of such as crossed the sands, Kent's Bank being the point from which they would start upon their journey towards Lancaster.

The wide expanse of Morecambe Bay lies before us like an out-stretched panorama, in which every jutting headland, every indentation, and every crease in the green hills can be distinctly traced. Far below us a long stretch of shore runs out ; an old boat lies upon its side, chained to a miniature anchor ; children are disporting themselves round it, and a few bare-legged fishermen are busy arranging their long nets, for the tide is not yet in, though we can see where the crafty silent sea comes stealing up from the south, each delicate wavelet, as it breaks upon the yellow sand in a white line of surge, creeping nearer and nearer to the beach. The softest of summer breezes plays upon the water, breaking it into innumerable ripples that dance and glitter in the mellow light. Here and there a few cloud shadows fleck the surface. A soft summer haze, like an ocean of white mist, hangs in mid distance, and where it lifts, shows little patches of the blue of heaven beyond. A broad streak of light marks the line of the horizon where sea and sky blend together. A solitary white sail glints in the blaze of sunlight, one or two fishing boats with red-brown sails spot the sea with colour, and far away a long line of black smoke shows where a steamer is rapidly ploughing its way towards the Irish coast. Sheltering in quiet beauty in the little cove below is Kent's Bank, its buildings, dwarfed by the intervening space, looking like a group of children's toys. Grange is hidden behind the projecting ridge of rock ; but Holme Island, with its pretty little marine temple, stands well out from the shore, like an emerald gem in the flashing waters. Sheltering it from the northern blasts, a range of rugged limestone rocks, all channelled and weather-worn, and fringed with over-lapping trees, is seen ; and there, where a few puffs of white smoke gleam brightly against the deep blue of space, a train is bearing its living freight across the broad Milnthorpe Sands. Arnside Knott, with its shady back-ground of wood, thrusts up its huge form as a foil to quiet Silverdale, reposing by its side ; then, sweeping round in an irregular circle towards the east, we have an ever-varying shore and an amphitheatre of intersecting hills, now dark with shadow and

now gay with the tints of the many-hued vegetation, with Ingleborough and the great Dent Fells far, far beyond, yet, in the pure
atmosphere, seeming so near and so clear that we may almost
fancy we can see the purple heather blooming upon their sides.
Further south, bathed in a flood of sunshine, the battlemented keep
of Lancaster Castle comes full in sight, with its frowning gate-
tower, through which many an ill-starred wretch has doubtless
trembled as he passed, and where, upon its threshold, may be said
yet to linger the solemn footprints of mingled innocence and guilt—
a stony relic that calls to remembrance "Old John o' Gaunt,
time-honoured Lancaster," and turns back the pages of the
Book of Time to the turbulent days which witnessed the fierce
forays of the Northern hordes and the still fiercer struggles of
the rival Roses ; and beyond the Castle, the green knolls rising
above the water-line in the direction of Heysham and Sunder-
land—Cape Famine, as the people call it—looking like so many
islands in a sea of silver.

Carrying the eye round to the west, a picture scarcely less
beautiful meets the gaze. The low-lying plain on the right—the
Wyke,* as it is called—has, within living memory, been reclaimed
from the hungry sea ; and where was once old ocean's bed there
are now lush pastures, and fields of waving grain that give promise
of an abundant harvest. Below us, peeping up from a clump of
trees, are seen the ruined walls of Wraysholme Tower, where the
lordly Harringtons held sway, and with which we shall make more
intimate acquaintance by-and-by ; and near thereto Humphrey
Head, looking like a monster couchant, thrusts its huge form far
out from the shore. The little village beyond is Flookborough,
and within half a mile is Cark, contiguous to which, half hidden
among the umbraged woods, is Holker, the favourite seat of the

---

* "Wyke" signifies a bay with a low shore; and the now fertile plain,
which includes some hundreds of acres, protected with deep embankments
and valve gates for the land streams, was reclaimed many years ago through
the enterprise of Mr. Towers, of Dudden Grove, and the late Mr. Stockdale,
of Cark.

Duke of Devonshire. Across the Leven sands we get a glimpse of Chapel Island, a little sea girt solitude, with the crumbling ruins of its ancient sanctuary peeping through the gloom of the over-shadowing trees, where, in days of yore, the monks of Furness "their orisons and vespers sung," and offered prayers "for the safety of the souls of such as crossed the sands with the morning tide." Almost within bow-shot are the rich woods and glades of Conishead; and further on, the old town of Ulverston can be discerned, with the great rounded hill—the Hoad—in the rear, on which the monument to the memory of its distinguished son, the late Sir John Barrow, stands—

> On the gusty down,
> Far seen across the sea-paths which he loved,
> A beacon to the steersman.

At the extreme corner of the Furness shore, where the tall chimneys shoot up and the thick smoke hangs like a pall, is Barrow, which by the magic power of iron has been suddenly transformed from an obscure fishing village into a busy and populous town, and the seat of industrial and commercial activity. Reaching far out into the sea is lonely wave-girt Walney, with its ruined castle—the pile of Fouldrey—built on the foundation of the Vikings' stronghold by the monks of Furness as a defence against the marauding Scots—looming darkly against the flashing waters. Black Comb, stern, bleak, and wild, its gleaming summit breaking through the clouds, lifts its huge form with frowning majesty above the dreary moors and storm-worn hills; and, rear-ward, the eye wanders over the Coniston range to the Old Man, and thence to Bowfell, the twin pikes of Langdale, and round towards Skiddaw, where a succession of mighty headlands—the silent companions of the mist and cloud—crowd one upon another until the dim outlines of their giant peaks are lost in the blue infinity of space.

Apart from its natural beauty and the pleasant prospect it com-mands, Kirkhead is not without attractions for those who delight in investigating the memorials of prehistoric times. On the steep acclivities on the south side of the hill, mantled with ferns and coarse weeds, and well-nigh hidden with trees and brushwood, is the entrance to a natural opening or cavern in the limestone rock, 40 or 50 feet in length and about 20 feet high, which in the dim and shadowy past has evidently been the abode of some primeval Briton. You can get down to it by an inconvenient track from the top, but the better way is by a path that winds round the base of the hill, through the scrub, and along the edge of the meadow until you reach a heap of soil and *débris* left from previous explorations, when the entrance is seen just above. In the excavations that have been made a skull and other human remains have been discovered, with fragments of rude pottery, implements of stone, and the bones of the red deer, wild boar, fox, and other animals. Near the surface was also found a coin of the reign of the Emperor Domitian (A.D. 84)—strong presumptive evidence that there have been a succession of tenants, and some of them during the period of Roman occupation. Repeated examinations have been made of this primitive abode, and an account of its hidden mysteries will be found in Dr. Barber's " Prehistoric Remains."

Descending from our lofty eyrie, we pass through the little village of Allithwaite, and then strike into a pleasant leafy lane on the left, bordered with tall trees—oak, and ash, and beech—that look as green and luxurious as if they were buried in some inland combe instead of having had the sea breezes sweeping over them for many a long winter past. A little rindle keeps us in pleasant companionship, sparkling here and there in the deep shadow, and now and then we get glimpses of the level waste of silver sand and the sea beyond, shining through the summer haze. A few minutes' walking and we come in sight of the crumbling remains of Wraysholme Tower, the object of our present pilgrimage, standing a little way back on the left of the road. A bright-eyed youngster holds the gate open for us, with expectant glances, as we pass through into the farmyard, in which the old weather-worn relic stands, and the gladsome looks with which our modest *largesse* is received assure us that it is not unworthily bestowed.

The embattled tower or peel is all that now remains, and whatever of other buildings there may have been have long since disappeared. Built for defence, and as a place of refuge for men and cattle against the incursions of Scottish marauders and enemies approaching from the Irish Sea, it formed the strongest and most

WRAYSHOLME TOWER.

important feature of the original structure ; and even now, though dismantled and forlorn, and applied to "base uses" its founders little dreamt of, with its thick walls, its small jealous windows, and its gloomy apartments, it gives evidence of purposed resistance to sudden intrusion, and shows that security rather than convenience

12

was the object of its builders—a lingering memorial of those grim
and stern old times ere order had spread and law had superseded
might, when even power could only feel secure when protected by
strongly-fortified walls, a

> Monument of rudest times,
> When science slept entombed, and o'er the waste,
> The heath-grown crag, and quivering moss of old
> Stalk'd unremitted war.

The tower in general form is a parallelogram, measuring about forty-
five feet by thirty ; the strongly-grouted walls are surmounted by
an overhanging parapet, with a watch-turret projecting from each
angle, giving it the character cf a fortalice—as, indeed, it was in
the troublous times when watch and ward and beacon lights were
necessary safeguards against sudden assaults.   In an angle of the
thick walls is a spiral stone staircase, communicating with the
upper chambers and the roof—the latter, in its original state,
having been flat and covered with lead.   The masonry, though of
great strength, is plain and of the simplest character, the only
carved work being the small square-headed windows in the upper
stories, which have foliated lights, divided by a mullion, and are
apparently of later date than the main structure, having probably
been inserted about the close of the long reign of Edward III.   In
one of these windows the arms and crests of the Harringtons and
Stanleys were formerly to be seen, but they were some years ago
removed for safety, and are now placed in a window of the adjacent
farmhouse.   One of the small diamond panes has the well-known
Stanley crest—an eagle, with wings endorsed, preying upon an
infant in its cradle, with the addition of the fret or Harrington
knot—*nodo firmo*—at each angle.   On another pane are the letters
Q (the equivalent of W) H, with the fret above and below—the
initials being probably those of Sir William Harrington, who,
according to Dr. Whitaker, fell mortally wounded on the plains of
Agincourt, on that memorable St. Crispin's Day in 1415*.   A third

---

* This is an error on the part of the learned historian, for Sir William
Harrington's death did not occur until 1450.

pane has depicted upon it an eagle's claw, a cognizance of the Stanleys, with a fleur de lis on each side.

It is not known with certainty when Wraysholme was erected; but probably it was not long after William Mareschal, Earl of Pembroke, founded the Priory of Cartmel (1188); and it may have been intended as a protection for the fraternity of that house, in the same way that Piel Castle was for the security of the monks of Furness; but, if so, the brotherhood did not enjoy a very lengthened tenure, for a little more than a century after, it is found in the possession of the great feudal family of the Harringtons of Aldingham, descended from the Haveringtons or Harringtons of Haverington, near Whitehaven. Sir Robert Harrington, the first

of the name settled at Aldingham, which he had acquired in right of his wife, had two sons, the younger of whom, Michael Harrington had—8 Edward II. (1314-15)—a grant of free-warren in Alinthwaite (Allithwaite), in which township Wraysholme is situated, but the property eventually passed to the descendants of the elder brother, Sir John, a great-grandson of whom, Sir William Harrington, Knight of the Garter, was standard-bearer at the battle of Agincourt, where he is erroneously said to have lost his life. This Sir William married Margaret, daughter and heir of Sir Robert Neville, of Hornby Castle, and by her had a son, Sir Thomas Harrington.

In the fierce struggles of the Red and White Roses the Harringtons ranged themselves on the side of the Yorkists, and

suffered severely in that internecine conflict. Sir Thomas Harrington, who married a daughter of the house of Dacre, and
succeeded to the Hornby estates in right of his mother, fell
fighting under the standard of the White Rose at Wakefield Green,
and his only son, Sir John Harrington, received his death-blow
while fighting by his side on that memorable day (December 31,
1460), a day fatal to the House of York, and scarcely less fatal to
the victorious Lancastrians; for the cruelties there perpetrated by
the Black-faced Clifford were repaid with ten-fold vengeance at
Towton a few months later. Drayton, in his "Queen Margaret,"
recounts the butcher-work that Clifford did at Wakefield when the
brave Richard Plantagenet, Duke of York, and his son, the Earl of
Rutland, fell together—when

> York himself before his castle gate,
> Mangled with wounds, on his own earth lay dead;
> Upon whose body Clifford down him sate,
> Stabbing the corpse, and cutting off the head,
> Crowned it with paper, and to wreak his teene,
> Presents it so to his victorious queene,

and the "victorious queene," the haughty Margaret of Anjou, in
the insolence of her short-lived triumph, gave the order,—

> Off with his head, and set it on York gates,
> So York may overlook the town of York,

Dr. Whitaker tells us that when the news reached Hornby that
Sir Thomas and Sir John Harrington, father and son, with their
kinsman, Sir William Harrington, Lord Bonville of Aldingham,
were slain, the widow of Sir Thomas withdrew to her daughter
for consolation, but her son's widow, Matilda, a sister of the
Black-faced Clifford, partaking, as it would seem, of her brother's
hard nature, remained, and "was at leisure to attend to
business."

With Sir John's death the male line of this branch of the
Harringtons terminated.   He left two daughters, Anne and
Elizabeth, his co-heirs, then aged respectively nine and eight years.

Their paternal uncle, Sir James Harrington, took forcible possession of the estates and claimed them as his own, but on an appeal to the Court of Chancery, he was dispossessed and committed to the Fleet, when the wardship of the two young heiresses and the custody of their inheritance were granted to Thomas Lord Stanley, who considerately married the eldest, Anne, to his third son, Sir Edward Stanley, the hero of Flodden Field, and the youngest to his nephew, John Stanley, of Melling, the son of his brother, the first Sir John Stanley* of Alderley, in Cheshire.

Sir Edward Stanley, who eventually became the possessor of both Wraysholme and Hornby, the former, as it would seem, having been forfeited to the Crown by the attainder of his wife's uncle, Sir James Harrington, who, with his brother, Sir Robert, fought on the side of Richard III. at Bosworth Field, had been a soldier from his youth up. "The camp," it is said, "was his school, and his learning the pike and sword." The lords of Wraysholme, with their retainers, had many a time and oft set out to repel the Scots in their plundering raids across the Border, but now they were called upon to meet the Scottish King himself, who had entered England with a powerful army, and laid waste some of the Border strongholds. Summoning his followers, the valiant Stanley prepared himself for the field, when, as the old ballad tells us, —

> Sir Edward Stanley, stiff in stour,†
> He is the man on whom I mean,
> With him did pass a mighty pow'r,
> Of soldiers seemly to be seen.
>
> Most lively lads in Lonsdale bred,
> With weapons of unwieldy weight,
> All such as Tatham Fells had fed,
> Went under Stanley's streamer bright.
>
> *   *   *   *   *

---

* By a curious error, which has been repeated in many of the published pedigrees, this Sir John Stanley is represented as a base son of James Stanley, Warden of Manchester, and afterwards Bishop of Ely. Bishop Stanley's son, who was also distinguished for his valour on the field of Flodden, was Sir John Stanley, of Honford (Handforth), in Cheadle parish, Cheshire.

† Stour, *i.e.*, fight.

From Silverdale to Kent sand side,
Whose soil is sown with cockle shells,
From Cartmel eke and Connyside,
With fellows fierce from Furness Fells.

He and his brave men marched forward until they came to
" Flodden's fatal field," when Stanley was entrusted with the
command of the rear of the English army, which he led so
valiantly, and made such a sudden and unexpected onslaught with
his bowmen, that the Scots were put to flight, leaving their King
dead upon the field. Scott has enshrined Stanley's deeds at
Flodden in imperishable verse, and few couplets are more
frequently quoted than that which tells us—

" Victory !—
Charge, Chester, charge! On, Stanley, on ! "
Were the last words of Marmion.

Doubtless it was a gay day at Wraysholme when the stout
Lancashire lads, with their brave leader, returned to tell the tale
of victory. Henry VIII., keeping his Christmas at Eltham, the
following year (1514), commanded that Sir Edward Stanley, as a
reward for his services in having won the hill and vanquished
those opposed to him, as also that his ancestors bore the eagle as
their crest, should there be proclaimed Lord Monteagle, which was
accordingly done, and by that title he had summons to Parliament, and was made a Knight of the Garter.

Sir Edward Stanley, Lord Monteagle, died in 1584, and about
this time the old peel of Wraysholme passed to the Dicconsons, a
branch of the family of that name seated at Wrightington, in
Eccleston parish, for in the following year " Richd. Dicconson, of
Raisholme," appears among the *liberi tenentes* in Cartmel parish,
and the place continued in the possession of this family for a
century or more. In 1756 it was purchased by John Carter, of
Cart Lane, and given by him, in 1790, to his daughter Dorothy,
the wife of John Harrison, from whom it has descended through
the female line to the present possessor—Thomas Newby Wilson,
of Landing, Newby Bridge.

The gloomy-looking old tower, in which the chivalrous and intrepid Harringtons so long held sway, now only exhibits the melancholy aspects of desertion and decay. It is used as an out-building to the neighbouring farmhouse, and, though much dilapidated, tells more of time, and time's slow wasting hand, than of the ruinous havoc of ruthless war.

The glory has long passed away, for two centuries and more have rolled by since it was in the heyday of its prosperity. It is now tenantless and forlorn, its battlements are broken, its rooms are desolated, and the wind whistles through the narrow case-ments that once were storied with the heraldic achievements of its knightly owners. Old time has pressed heavily upon it—may no ruder hand hasten its destruction !

A little more than half a mile from Wraysholme Tower is Humphrey Head, a huge mass of carboniferous limestone that thrusts its gaunt form far out into the bay, dividing the Milnthorpe from the Ulverston Sands. To the north it rises abruptly from the plain, here grim and grey and lifeless-looking, and there decked with a rich embroidery of lichens, moss, and trailing ivy, while the ledges of the rock are covered with a thick vegetation of ash and hazel, the bright greenery of which is in places relieved by the darker foliage of the yew that here thrives luxuriously. Round towards the sea the steep acclivities are all broken, channelled, and weather-worn, with scarcely a sign of vegetation to relieve their general sterility ; and huge heaps that have been brought down by successive storms lie strewn about the shore in picturesque confusion. The rocky cliff which rears its naked front almost perpendicularly to a considerable elevation is not without its tale of sorrow, as we gather from the following warning, inscribed upon a block of limestone :—

> Beware how you these rocks ascend,
> Here William Pedder met his end,
> August 22nd, 1857. Aged 10 years.

Near the top of the cliff is the Fairies' Cave—a large cavernous opening or recess formed by the shrinkage of the limestone; and at the base is the Holy Well, a mineral spring famed for its curative properties in Camden's time, and which even within memory was resorted to by the Cumberland miners, who came in large numbers to drink its health-inspiring waters. The spring issues through a fissure in the rock within a few feet of the ground, the flow being at the rate of about a gallon a minute, continuing without variation through the different seasons of the year. The water is perfectly clear and colourless, and effervesces slightly on agitation—an indication of the presence of free carbonic acid. Dr. Barber, who has written an account of the spa, tells us the principal ingredients are the chlorides of sodium and magnesium, and the sulphates of lime and soda; and that in its chief characteristics it most resembles the waters at Wiesbaden and the Ragoczy spring at Kissingen. Its celebrity would seem to have arisen as much from its diluent powers as from its medicinal virtues; and probably recent analyses, which have disclosed the fact that it contains but a small proportion of solid ingredients, have broken the charm with which traditional piety had surrounded it, and caused the health-seeking pilgrims who formerly believed in its virtues to seek elsewhere the refreshing and restorative draughts which nature provides. The spring is now virtually abandoned; the cottage close by, in which the high-priestess formerly resided, is tenantless and falling to decay; but the key of the spring can be had from the neighbouring farmhouse.

Tradition gathers round this little corner of Lancashire, and the shaping power of imagination has clothed it with the weird drapery of romance—that

> Dubious light
> That hovers 'twixt the day and night,
> Dazzling alternately and dim.

When the Harringtons established themselves here the wolf and the wild boar roamed at large through the thick forests of Cartmel, and among the legends and scraps of family history that have floated down through successive generations is the story that

on the eminence to the north of Wraysholme the last wild boar
was hunted down; from which circumstance the hill has ever since
borne the name of Boar Bank.   It is said, too, that, far back in the
mist of ages, it was from Wraysholme Tower a gallant company
rode forth to hunt the last wolf " in England's spacious realm ; "
and that, after a long and weary chase, the savage beast was
tracked to its lair on the wooded heights of Humphrey Head, and
there transfixed by the spear of a Harrington. Tradition has been
well described as the nursing-mother of the Muses, and these bits
of legendary lore, which have been deeply rooted in the memories,
and for many a generation have delighted the firesides, of the
Cartmel cottagers, have inspired the pen of a local poet, who has
told the story of "The Last Wolf" in spirit-stirring verse. This
interesting ballad, though varying considerably from the current
tradition, is yet a valuable contribution to our Palatine anthology.
Its great length—seventy-five verses—prevents our giving it entire,
but the following passages will give an idea of the salient features
of the story :—

> The sun hath set on Wraysholme's Tower,
>   And o'er broad Morecambe Bay ;
> The moon from out her eastern bower
>   Pursues the track of day.

> On Wraysholme's grey and massive walls,
>   On rocky Humphrey Head,
> On wood and field her silver falls,
>   Her silent charms are shed.

> No sound through all yon sleeping plain
>   Now breaks upon the ear,
> Save murmurs from the distant main,
>   Or evening breezes near.

>   •   •   •   •   •   •   •

> Within those walls may now be seen
>   The festive board displayed,
> And round it many a knight, I ween,
>   And many a comely maid.

13

> For know that on the morrow's dawn,
> With all who list to ride,
> Sir Edgar Harrington hath sworn
> To hunt the country-side.

> A wolf, the last, as rumour saith,
> In England's spacious realm,
> Is doomed that day to meet its death,
> And grace the conqueror's helm.

> And he hath sworn an oath beside,
> Whoe'er that wolf shall quell
> Shall have his fair niece for a bride,
> And half his land as well.

The "fair niece" is the orphan Lady Adela—

> For beauty famous far and wide,

whose heart has previously been given to Sir Edgar's son ; but the course of true love has been characterised by the proverbial absence of smoothness, and the young knight, to escape his father's wrath, has betaken himself to the wars in Eastern lands.

The night's carousal draws to a close, and at break of day the huntsman's horn wakes the sleepers to a glorious chase, when

> Full threescore riders mount with speed,

chief among whom, and the competitors for the fair Adela's hand, are the two knights, Laybourne and Delisle—the latter the long-lost son of Sir Edgar, who has returned from the Crusades, and appears in disguise and under an assumed name, though the old retainers, as they view the stranger knight, know that

> The long-lost wanderer meets their sight,
> Whate'er his name be now.

The wolf, scared from his covert on Humphrey Head, leads the hunters a long and exciting chase over Kirkhead, past Holker and Newby, and across "the Leven's brawling flood," to the Old Man of Coniston. The dogs are again upon the track, and the grisly beast is away through "Easthwaite's lonely deep," through wood-

land, brake, and forest hoar, "through Sawrey's pass," and on to
the shores of Windermere, where,

> With one bold plunge, the mere he takes,
> And, favoured by the wind,
> The flabbing scent abruptly breaks,
> And leaves his foes behind.

But the "tireless bloodhounds" are once more upon the scent, the
rival knights follow in hot pursuit, and

> Away along the wooded shore
> The chase betakes him now,
> Beneath the friendly shade of Tower
> And craggy Gummerhow.

> Then turn aside to Witherslack,
> Where Winster's waters range,
> And thence to shingly Eggerslack,
> And sand-surveying Grange.

Then, with the instinct of despair, the brute makes for his old
haunt on Humphrey Head, as "evening shades appear." Reaching
a deep chasm in the rock, wolf and hounds rush headlong to their
destruction. Laybourne's horse rears at the "giddy brink," but the
"bold Delisle" rushes madly on, crying—

> Adela! I'll win thee now!
> Or ne'er wend forth again.

Delisle and his "Arab white" pursue their headlong course down
the rocky gulf—

> Awhile from side to side it leapt,
> That steed of mettle true,
> Then swiftly to destruction swept,
> Like flashing lightning flew.

> The shingle in its headlong course,
> With rattling din gave way;
> The hazels snap beneath its force,
> The mountain savins sway.

By chance the Lady Adela happens to be riding by at the moment, upon her "palfrey white"—

> When, lo! the wild wolf bursts in sight,
> And bares his glistening teeth!

> Her eyes are closed in mortal dread,
> And ere a look they steal,
> The wolf and Arab both lie dead,
> And scatheless stands Delisle!

The Red Cross knight now reveals himself as the lost son of Sir Edgar. The father welcomes the wanderer, and in fulfilment of his promise, bestows "his fair niece for a bride." The result may be anticipated. The Prior of Cartmel, happening opportunely to be passing, "to drink the Holy Well"—

> Sir Edgar straight the priest besought
> To tarry for awhile;
> Who, when the lady's eye he caught,
> Assented with a smile.

The "Fairies' Cave," on Humphrey Head, served for the nonce as a chapel, for

> The monk he had a mellow heart,
> And, scrambling to the spot,
> Full blithely there he played his part,
> And tied the nuptial knot.

> And hence that cave on Humphrey Hill,
> Where these fair deeds befel,
> Is called Sir Edgar's chapel still,
> As hunters wot full well.

> And still the holy fount is there
> To which the prior came;
> And still it boasts its virtues rare,
> And bears its ancient name.

> And long on Wraysholme's lattice light,
> A wolf's head might be traced,
> In record of the Red Cross Knight,
> Who bore it for his crest.

> In Cartmel church his grave is shown,
> And o'er it, side by side,
> All graved in stone, lies brave Sir John
> And Adela his bride.

Such is "The Legend of the Last Wolf." The supposed monument, "all graved in stone," still adorns the choir of Cartmel church. Beneath the ponderous canopy the recumbent figures of the knight and his lady, lying side by side, may still be seen, looking the very types of chivalrous honour and conjugal felicity; and there for certainty is the sculptured figure of the veritable wolf, reposing quietly at their feet—confirmations strong as proofs of holy writ, although prosaic antiquaries, disdaining the faint glimmerings of truth that only steal through the haze of tradition, tell us, with irreverent disregard for the poetry of romance, that the story is apocryphal; and further try to shake our faith by affirming that the figures are those of the valiant Harrington, who fell fighting for the White Rose at Wakefield, and his wife, a daughter of the lordly house of Dacre. But we will not discuss the identity of the departed knights, or the merits of their respective claims to the battered effigies that have failed to perpetuate their names—monuments that

> Themselves memorials need.

High up on Humphrey Head the cave in which the nuptial knot was tied still remains; and there, at the foot, is the Holy Well, the waters of which flow as freely as they did in days of yore, though now only imbibed when a chance wayfarer finds his way to this lonely seaside nook, and quaffs a goblet to the memories of the

> Brave Sir John,
> And Adela his bride,

and the holy friar who made them one.

CHAPTER IV.

F any reader wishes to obtain a brief respite from the busy life of the "unclean city," to get away from the noise of looms and spindles, the smoke of factories and the smell of dyes, and to find within easy distance of the great manufacturing metropolis a place of perfect quiet and repose where he may feel that for all practical purposes he is "at the world's end," let him by all means spend a summer afternoon in that quaint little out-of-the-way nook, Gawsworth, and he will return to the crowded mart with little inclination to cry out with the Roman Emperor, "*Perdidi diem.*" Yet how few there are who have made acquaintance with this *beau-ideal* of a quiet rural retreat. The places which it is the proper thing to visit, or "do," as the phrase is, are all carefully mapped out for our convenience ; but the literary finger-posts afford but little guidance to the true rambler, who knows that the fairest spots are those which are oftenest overlooked. Gawsworth may be easily reached from Alderley or Chelford ; but perhaps the most convenient starting point is Macclesfield, from which it is distant a short four miles.

Macclesfield does not present a particularly prepossessing appearance, though it possesses much that is historically interesting, and you may here and there see relics of mediæval times; but the long centuries have wrought many changes in its condition, and those changes can hardly be said to be from grave to gay. Its forest was once the hunting-ground of kings. A royal palace occupied a site very near to the present Park Lane, and in the Fourth Edward's reign Humphrey, Duke of Buckingham, had a princely residence there. The town itself was walled, and though there is not now a single stone remaining, the recollection of its fortifications is preserved in the streets—Chestergate, Church Wallgate, and Jordangate—which form the principal outlets from it. Notwithstanding that it once boasted a royal owner, it now presents but a dingy and uninviting aspect, so that we are little loth to leave its steep and tortuous streets, and what Nathaniel Hawthorne would call its ugliness of brick, and betake ourselves to the open country.

On getting clear of the town, we enter upon a pleasant rural highway that rises and falls in gentle undulations. Tall trees border the wayside, which, as we advance, grow thicker, until we reach a double line of spreading beeches that meet in an entanglement overhead, and form a long shady avenue, through which a pleasant vista is obtained. Now and then we meet a chance wayfarer and occasionally a sleepy-looking carter with his team, but the road is comparatively little frequented, and we almost wonder that with the limited traffic it does not become grass-grown. Though it is quiet now-a-days, it was lively enough in the old coaching times, when the "Red Rover" and the "Defiance" were in the zenith of their popularity, and the tootling of the guard's bugle daily awoke the echoes to the inspiring notes of the "British Grenadiers," for it was then the great highway between Manchester and the metropolis. But those days are changed, and our dream of the past is rudely dispelled by the shrill whistle of the "express" as it shoots along the edge of the Moss, leaving a long white pennon of steam in its wake.

As we journey on we get agreeable glimpses of the country, and the varied character of the scenery adds to the charm. Below us on the left stretches a broad expanse of bog—Danes Moss, as it is called—commemorating some long-forgotten incursion of the wild Scandinavian hordes—

> When Denmark's raven soared on high.

On the outskirts of the town is an old farmstead, called Cophurst, on the site of which, as tradition sayeth, Raphael Hollinshead, the chronicler, resided three hundred years ago. Close by is Sutton, once the home of another Cheshire worthy—Sir Richard Sutton—"that ever famous knight and great patron of learning," as King, in his "Vale Royal," calls him, "one of the founders of Brazenose, in Oxford, where by his bounty many of Cheshire youth receive most worthy education." The foreground is broken into picturesque inequalities, and in the rear rises a succession of swelling hills, part of the great Kerridge range—the stony barriers of the Peak country. Where the steep crags cut sharply against the eastern sky is Teg's Nose, famed for its gritstone quarries. Further on, Shutling's Low rears its cone-shaped peak to a height of 1,660 feet, and behind we catch sight of the breezy moor, on the summit of which stands that lonely hostelry, the Cat and Fiddle, the highest public-house, it is said, to be found in the kingdom. The great hill-slopes, though now almost bare of wood, once formed part of the great forest of Macclesfield, in which for generations the Davenports, as chief foresters, held the power of life and death over the robber bands who in the old times infested it, as well as the punishment of those who made free with the Earl's venison; and they not only held but exercised their rights, as the long "Robber Roll" at Capesthorne still testifies. Though it has long been completely disafforested, the memory of it still lingers. Forest Chapel, away up in the very heart of this mountain wilderness, perpetuates the name, and Wildboa. Clough—Wilbor Clough, as the Macclesfieldians persist in calling it—Hoglegh, and Wolfscote remind us of the former denizens of these moorland wastes. Beyond Teg's Nose a great gap opens in the hills, and then Cloud End rears its rugged form—dark, wild, and forbidding. From the

GAWSWORTH OLD HALL.

14

summit, had we time to climb it, a charming view might be obtained of the picturesquely varied country—

> Of farms remote and far apart, with intervening space
> Of black'ning rock and barren down, and pasture's pleasant face ;
> And white and winding roads that creep through village, vale, and glen,
> And o'er the dreary moorlands, far beyond the homes of men.

On the right the scenery is of a more pastoral character. Lawns and meadows stretch away, and the eye ranges over the broad fertile plain of Cheshire—over quaint sequestered nooks and quiet homesteads, and old-fashioned villages, with here and there a grey church tower rising in their midst ; over well-tilled fields and daisied pastures, and league upon league of cultivated greenness, where the thick hedgerows cross and recross each other in a network of verdant beauty. The crumbling ruins of Beeston Castle crowning the edge of a bold outlier of rock, may be dimly discerned, with Peckforton rising close by its side, and beyond, where a shadowy form reaches like a cloud across the horizon, we can trace the broken outline of the Welsh hills, with Moel Fammau towering above them all.

Presently the battlemented towers of Gawsworth Church are seen peering above the umbrage ; then we come to a cross road, and, turning sharply to the left, continue along a green old bosky lane, and past the village school, close to which is a weather-worn memorial of bygone days—the old wayside cross standing beneath a clump of trees, erected, as old writers tell us, to " guide and guard the way to church," and the sight of which, with the surroundings, calls to remembrance Hood's lines on the symbol of the Christian's faith :—

> Say, was it to my spirit's gain or loss,
>   One bright and balmy morning, as I went
>   From Liège's lonely environs to Ghent,
> If hard by the way-side I found a cross,
> That made me breathe a pray'r upon the spot—
>   While Nature of herself, as if to trace
>   The emblem's use, had trail'd around its base
> The blue significant Forget-me-not ?

Methought, the claims of Charity to urge
    More forcibly, along with Faith and Hope,
The pious choice had pitched upon the verge
    Of a delicious slope,
    Giving the eye much variegated scope;—
" Look round," it whisper'd, "on that prospect rare,
    Those vales so verdant, and those hills so blue;
Enjoy the sunny world, so fresh and fair,
    But (how the simple legend pierced me thro'!)—
        " Priez pour les Malheureux."

For a short distance the road now descends, and near the bottom
a bank rises abruptly on the right, crowned with a plantation of
oak and larch—the " sylvan shade "—beneath which reposes the
" breathless clay " of the eccentric poet, wit, and player—Samuel
Johnson—known by his generation as " Lord Flame," of whom we
may have something to say anon.   A few yards further on is the
new hall, or " New Buildings," as it is sometimes called, a plain
brick house, the south wing only of which has been completed,
built in Queen Anne's reign by that Lord Mohun who brought the
noted Cheshire will case to a sanguinary end, when he and his
adversary, the Duke of Hamilton, fell together in a duel in Hyde
Park, Nov. 15, 1712.   At this point the view of Gawsworth opens
upon us, presenting one of the fairest pictures of quiet rural
beauty that Cheshire possesses.   There is a dreamy old-world
character about the place, a sweet fragrance of the olden time, and
a peaceful tranquillity of the present ; and the ancient church, the
picturesque half-timbered rectory, and the stately old hall, with the
broad grass-bordered road, the wide-spreading sycamores, and the
old-fashioned fish ponds, in the weed-grown depths of which every
object, with the overarching sky and the white clouds sailing
therein are given back with distinct vividness, impart an air of
venerable and undisturbed respectability.   The place belongs so
entirely to the past, and there seems such a remoteness between
the hoar antiquity of a scene so thoroughly old English and the
busy world from which we have just emerged, that we almost
hesitate to advance.

There is no village, so to speak, the church, the parsonage, and the two halls, with a cottage or two adjoining the church steps, being all the buildings we can see; there is not even that usual and supposed to be indispensable adjunct of an old English country village, the village inn, the nearest hostelry being the Harrington Arms, an old coaching house on the London road, a quarter of a mile or more away. The church, a grey and venerable pile, with a remarkably well proportioned tower, which exhibits some good architectural details of the perpendicular period, stands in its graveyard, a little to the south of a broad

GAWSWORTH CROSS.

grass-grown road, upon a gentle eminence encompassed by a grey stone fence that looks as ancient as the building itself. Tall trees overshadow it—larch and fir—that rear their lofty spines from near the water's edge, and, yielding to the northern blasts, bend in graceful curves towards the ancient fane. You can mount the steps and pass through the little wicket into the quiet "God's-acre," and surely a spot more suggestive of calm and serious thought is rarely witnessed. Move slowly through the tall grass and round the green graves where

> The rude forefathers of the hamlet sleep.

Tread lightly upon the weather-stained and moss-grown stones that loving hands have set up to keep alive the memories of those who sleep beneath. Near the porch is the chamfered shaft of an ancient cross, and close by two or three venerable yews cast their funereal shade. One of them, an aged torso, is garlanded with ivy, and buttressed on one side by a short flight of steps that have been built against it. Its gigantic roots grasp the earth with a tenacity that time cannot relax. It has lived through long centuries, and seen generation after generation christened, married, and buried, and, though now hollowed and decayed, the trunk still preserves some of that vitality that was in its fulness when the valorous Fittons were in the heyday of their power.

Separating the churchyard from the road is an artificial lake or ‑ fish-pond, one of a series of three or four, through each of which the water flows in succession, and where, in the chivalrous days of the knightly owners of Gawsworth, the water jousts and other aquatic games took place. But those times of pomp and pageantry have passed away, and the surface is now seldom ruffled save when occasionally a fish rises, or a stately swan glides gracefully through the warm sunshine. In its smooth mirror you can see the old grey tower, the projecting buttresses, the traceried windows, and the embattled parapets of the church, with their pleasant environment of green all clearly reflected, presenting the appearance of an inverted picture ; while the old patrician trees that border the wayside bend over the glassy surface, creating in places a vernal shade that Undine might delight in.

On the opposite side is the Rectory, a picturesque old structure of black and white timber work, "magpie" as the people call it hereabouts, with quaint overhanging gables, grotesque carvings, and mullioned windows, with small diamond panes—one of them, that lighting the hall, a spacious apartment with an open timber roof, containing fragments of heraldic glass that would seem to have formerly belonged to the church. There is a wide entrance porch in the centre of the building, and over the door, between two shields of arms, this inscription—" Syr Edward Fytton, Knight, with my lady Mare ffyton, hys wyffe "—from which it has been commonly assumed that the house was built by Sir Edward Fitton, who married Mary, the daughter and co-heir of Guicciard Harbottle, of Northumberland, and so would fix the time of erection in the reign of Henry VIII. But this inscription originally belonged to another building of later date than the Rectory, which, as we learn from some verses preserved in Ashmole's "Church Notes," taken *circa* 1654, was erected by George Baguley, who was rector of Gawsworth from 1470 to 1497.

The "old" Hall, the ancestral home of the Fittons, now occupied by Lord Petersham, stands a short distance east of the church. Like the Rectory, it is half-timbered and of the Elizabethan period, but the building is now incomplete, a part having been taken down some seventy years ago, though the original quadrangular form may still be traced. In the rear, in what has been originally the courtyard, is a curious octagonal oriel of three stories, each story overhanging the one immediately below in a sort of telescope fashion. The windows are filled with leaded panes arranged in a variety of shapes and patterns. The principal front, which faces the road, has been rebuilt and painted in imitation of timber-work. Over the principal entrance is a shield of sixteen quarterings, representing the arms of the Fittons and their several alliances, surrounded by a garter, on which is inscribed the motto, " *Fit onus leve* "—a play upon the family name. There is also the following inscription beneath—

> Hec scvlptvra finita fvit apvd
> Villam Galviæ in Hibernia per
> Richardvm Rany. Edwardo Fyton
> Milite primo dño presidente totius
> Provinciæ Conatiæ et Thomoniæ.
> Anno Domini 1570.

In front of the hall is a grove of walnut trees, very patriarchs of their kind; and adjoining is a large grassy amphitheatre, which Ormerod, the Cheshire historian, has described as "a deserted pleasure ground;" but, after careful examination, and with some show of probability, pronounced by Mr. Mayer to be an ancient

tilting ground, where in times past the warlike Fittons amused
themselves and their Cheshire neighbours with displays of martial
skill and bravery.

Before we enter the church or view the hall, it may be well to
glance briefly at the earlier history of the place. Gawsworth,
though now an independent parish, was formerly included within
the limits of the great parish of Prestbury ; and even at the
present day the whole of the townships which surround it—
Macclesfield, Sutton, Bosley, North Rode, Marton, Siddington,
and Henbury—all owe ecclesiastical allegiance to the mother
church of that widespread parish. The original name, as we learn
from the Domesday survey, was *Gouersurde.* After the Conquest
it formed part of the possessions of the Norman Earls of Chester ;
one of whom, Randle de Meschines, in the twelfth century, gave
it to his trusty follower, Hugh, son of Bigod, with the right of
holding his own courts, without pleading before the prefects at
Macclesfield, in consideration of his rendering to the earl annually
a caparisoned horse ; and this Hugh, in accordance with the
fashion of the age, adopted the name of Gawsworth. Subsequently the manor seems to have passed to Richard Aldford,
whose daughter, Lucy, brought it in marriage to the Orrebies, who
held it free from all service save furnishing one man in time of war
to assist in the defence of Aldford Castle. They retained
possession until the reign of Edward I., when Richard, son of
Thomas de Orreby, dying without male issue, his only sister,
Isabel, who succeeded to the inheritance, and who had previously
married in succession Roger de Macclesfeld and Sir John de
Grindon, Knight, both of whom she survived, conveyed it on her
marriage in 1316-17 to her third husband, Thomas Fytton, a
younger son of Edmund Fytton, of Bolyn (Wilmslow) ; and thus
Gawsworth became closely associated with a family noted for their
chivalrous exploits, and famous in the annals of the county.

Of the early history of this distinguished family—" Knights of a
long-continued Race and of great worth," as Webb styles them—
who for so many generations held sway and practised a splendid

hospitality in Gawsworth, but few memorials have been preserved beyond the dry details embodied in their *Inquisitiones post mortem* in the Public Record Office, and the inscriptions which still remain upon the sumptuous monuments erected to their memory in the church which their pious munificence reared.

Thomas Fitton, who acquired the manor of Gawsworth by his marriage with the heiress of Orreby, had a son also named Thomas, who married Margaret, a daughter and co-heir of Peter Legh, of Bechton, and added to the patrimonial estate half of the manor of Bechton and lands in Lostock-Gralam, which he obtained in right of his wife. It was during the lifetime of this Thomas that we find the first attempt made to erect the chapelry of Gawsworth, which was then dependent upon Prestbury, into a separate parish. At that time the Abbot of St. Werburg's, Chester, held the rectory of Prestbury, and in the chartulary of his house it is recorded that in April, 1382, he conceded to John Caxton, rector of Gawsworth, the privilege of burying his parishioners on paying a moiety of the dues within ten days after each burial, and with a proviso that any parishioner of Gawsworth might be interred at Prestbury without any claim on the part of the rector of Gawsworth.

In explanation of the granting of this privilege it may be mentioned that in those times, on the formation of a parish, the inhabitants were required to perform their parochial rites at the mother church, the "ealdan mynstre" of the parish. But as many parishes were of considerable territorial extent, those resident in the remote hamlets found it inconvenient to resort on all occasions to the mother church. To provide for the spiritual requirements of the people in such districts, private chapels or oratories, founded by the lords of the soil, were allowed to be licensed in convenient situations. They were frequently attached or immediately adjacent to the lord's mansion, and were designed more especially for his own accommodation and that of his dependents; and Gawsworth, which is distant nearly six miles from Prestbury, was of this class. To prevent such foundations trenching upon the rights of the mother church, they were merely licensed for preaching and

15

praying, the ministration of the sacrament of baptism and the performance of the right of burial being strictly prohibited. These latter were the true parochial rites, and the grant of them to a chapel or oratory severed its connection with the parish church, and converted it into a parochial chapel, or, more strictly speaking, into an independent church.

But who was John Caxton, the parson of Gawsworth? The name is not very frequently met with, and the thought suggests itself that he may have been, and probably was, a kinsman of that William Caxton who, a century later, set up his press in the precincts of Westminster Abbey, and revolutionised the world by practising the art which Gutenberg had invented.

In 1391 Thomas Fitton was appointed one of a number of influential persons in Cheshire who were constituted a commission to levy a subsidy of 3,000 marks (£2,000) in the city of Chester, on account of the King's confirmation of the old charters belonging to that city. He died in 1397, and was succeeded by his son, Sir Lawrence Fitton, then aged 22, who married Agnes Hesketh, a daughter of the house of Rufford, in Lancashire. This Sir Lawrence, who held the lordship for the long period of 60 years, fills no inconsiderable space in the annals of the county. He was frequently one of the forest justices in eyre, the assizes being then held in Macclesfield, and took an active part in the stirring events of his time. When, in 1399, Richard the Second went over to Ireland to avenge the death of Roger Mortimer, by chastising the Irish chieftains who had risen in insurrection, he, in order to increase the strength of his Cheshire guard by a fresh levy, issued his orders to Sir Lawrence Fitton and others commanding them to summon the best archers in the Macclesfield hundred between 16 and 60, and to select a number to go to Ireland in his train, who were to be at Chester on the morrow of the Ascension of our Lord for inspection by the King's officers. The King did not actually sail till the 4th of June, when he was joined by Sir Lawrence Fitton, who, as appears by an entry on the Recognizance Rolls of the palatinate, had protection granted him on his departure ;

and at this time, under date June 5, we find a licence to
William Prydyn, parson of Gawswerth, Robert de Tounley,
John Tryket, and Matthew del Mere to act as his attorneys and
to look after his affairs while absent in Ireland on the King's
service.

" When the shepherd is absent with his dog the wolf easily leaps
into the fold." So says the proverb, and Richard had unpleasant
experience of the truthfulness of it, for scarcely had he loosed his
sails before some of the more discontented of his nobles at home
were plotting for his overthrow.

Within a month of his departure Henry Bolingbroke, Duke of
Hereford, the only son of old John of Gaunt, who had been
banished the kingdom, landed at Ravenspur, near Hull—as
Shakspere writes—

> The banish'd Bolingbroke repeats himself,
> And with uplifted arms is safe arrived
> At Ravenspurg,

and before the end of July was at the head of a large army in the
wolds of Worcestershire. It was not until towns and castles had
been yielded to the invader that the King received intelligence of
the insurrection, for the winds had been contrary, and by the time
he landed at Milford the revolution was virtually accomplished. Il
news does not always travel apace, and in these days, when the
trembling wire speeds the message through air and sea, it seems
difficult to realise the thought of a rebellion stalking through
England unchecked for weeks without the news reaching in the
sister isle him whom it most immediately concerned. On reaching
England, Richard started for Chester, where he had many friends
and his power was strongest. At Flint he was delivered by the
perfidious Percy into the hands of Bolingbroke, thence he was
taken to Chester, and afterwards conveyed to London and lodged
in the Tower, when, after having resigned the crown, he was formally
deposed—an act that was followed by his removal to Pontefract,
where, according to common report, he was murdered by Sir Piers

Exton and his assistants, though it is more likely he was allowed to perish of starvation.

Whether Fitton was one of those who hastened to pay court to the usurper, and in a bad game elected to adhere to the winning side, is not clear, but he must have quickly accommodated himself to the changed state of affairs, and to have gained the confidence of Bolingbroke—"King Henry of that name the Fourth."

Scarcely was Richard dead when a great revulsion in public feeling occurred, old hatreds and jealousies were revived, and those who had clamoured most for his death now exclaimed—

> Oh, earth, yield us that King again,
> And take thou this;

and the usurping Henry, who had dreamed only of the throne as a bed of roses, found himself between the fell spectres conscience and insatiate treason. In Wales, where Richard had possessed a strong attachment, Owen Glendower raised the standard of revolt, renounced allegiance to the King, and claimed to be the rightful Prince of Wales, when he was joined by young Harry Percy, the Hotspur of the famous ballad of *Chevy Chase.* To meet this new danger, Prince Henry, Falstaff's Prince Hal—" the nimble-footed mad-cap Harry, Prince of Wales," who was also Earl of Chester, and lived much in the county, joined his forces to those of his father, and on the 11th January, 1403-4, we find him directing a writ to Sir Lawrence Fitton, requiring him to repair "to his possessions on the marches of Wales, there to make defence against the coming of Owen Glendower, according to an order in Council enacting that, on the occasion of the war being moved against the King, all those holding possessions on the marches should reside on the same for the defence of the realm," and the Recognizance Rolls show that a few days later the Lord of Gawsworth was appointed on a commission "to inquire touching those who spread false rumours to the disquiet of the people of the county of Chester, and disturbance of the peace therein, also to array all the fencible men of the hundred of Macclesfield."

In 1416, when, after the victory at Agincourt, Henry V. was preparing for his second expedition to France, with the design of claiming the crown, Sir Lawrence Fitton, with Sir John Savage, Knight, Robert de Hyde, Robert de Dokenfield, and John, the son of Peter de Legh, was appointed collector of the subsidy in the Macclesfield hundred, part of the 3,000 marks granted to the King by the county of Chester; and in 1428, with other influential Cheshire knights and gentry, he was summoned to the King's Council at Chester, with regard to the granting of a subsidy to the King (Henry VI.) His death occurred on the 16th March, 1457, when he must have been over 80 years of age, and his inquisition was taken 37 Henry VI. (1459), when his grandson Thomas, then aged 26, was found to be his next heir. As previously stated, he had to wife Agnes Hesketh. This lady died in 1422, and he would appear to have re-married, for in the inquisition taken after his death mention is made of "Clemencia, his wife," who is said to be then alive.

During his long life a movement was taking place in the Church which brought about a great change in religious thought and action, and in which Wycliffe, the rector of Lutterworth, may be said to have been the chief actor. The rapacity of the monks was securing or had secured for themselves the larger portion of the livings of the country, the parishes being handed over to the spiritual care of vicars, with the small tithes as a miserable stipend. In this manner the rich rectory of Prestbury had been appropriated to the Abbey of St. Werburg, Chester; and possibly it was this circumstance, as much as his own personal convenience, which induced Caxton, acting under the influence of his patron, the father of Sir Lawrence Fitton, to seek to detach the chapel of Gawsworth from the mother church of Prestbury. Having accomplished this, Sir Lawrence Fitton would seem to have set about the erection of a building more suited to its increased importance as a parish church, and an examination of the building points to the conclusion that the greater portion of the fabric was erected during his lifetime, as evidenced by the architectural details of the building, as well as by the shields of arms displayed on different parts of the tower, representing the alliances of the family, the latest impalement being the coat of Mainwaring, intended to commemorate the marriage of his son Thomas with Ellen, daughter of Randle Mainwaring, of Over Peover, which would seem to fix the date between the years 1420 and 1430, and not in the reign of Edward III., as generally supposed. In the Cheshire Church Notes, taken in 1592, there is preserved an account of a window to the memory of Sir Lawrence Fitton and his wife, which formerly existed in the church at Gawsworth. He is represented as in armour, and kneeling with his wife before desks in the attitude of devotion; on his surcoat were displayed the arms of Fitton, and on the lady's mantle those of Hesketh; behind the knight were eight sons, and in rear of the lady four daughters, and underneath the inscription, "*Orate pro bono statu Laurencii ffitton milit' et Agnet' uxor ejus cum pueris suis.*"

By his wife Agnes Sir Lawrence Fitton had a son Thomas, who, as stated, married Ellen, daughter of Randle Mainwaring, of Over Peover, and their names were in like manner commemorated by a window, which has now disappeared, comprising three panes, one representing Sir Randle Mainwaring and his wife Margery, daughter of Hugh Venables, Baron of Kinderton, kneeling before desks; the second, Thomas Fitton and seven sons; and the third, his wife and six daughters, all kneeling, and the inscription, "*Orate pro a'iabus Thomæ ffitton, filii Laurencii ffitton, et Elene ux' ejus, et om' puerorum suorum, qui istam fenestram fieri fecerunt.*"

Thomas Fitton pre-deceased his father, leaving a son, also named Thomas, who succeeded as heir on the death of his grandfather in 1457, he being then 25 years of age. This Thomas inherited the martial spirit of his ancestors, and took his share in the fierce struggle of the White and Red Roses, which destroyed the flower of the English nobility, and impoverished and well-nigh exhausted the country—"that purple testament of bleeding war"—

> When, like a matron butcher'd of her sons,
> And cast aside some common way, a spectacle
> Of horror and affright to passers by,
> Our bleeding country bled at every vein !

He was present in the sanguinary encounter at Bloreheath, near Drayton, on that fatal 23rd July, 1459—St. Tecla's Day—when Lord . Audley and the Lancastrians were defeated, and was knighted on the field ; and there is on the Cheshire Recognizance Rolls, under date April 29th, 38-9 Henry VI. (1460), the record of a general pardon granted to Thomas Fitton and Richard Fitton, late of Gawsworth ; William, son of Lawrence Fitton, late of Gawsworth ; Edward, brother of Thomas Fitton, late of Gaws-worth ; some of their kinsmen of the Pownall stock, and other Cheshire gentry, with a long list of residents in Gawsworth, the retainers of the Fittons—names that are still familiar in the neighbourhood —" in consideration," as it states, "of the good service of the said Thomas Fitton, Knight, and his adherents at Blore-heth." His name also occurs under date June 10, 1463, with those of John de Davenport, of Bramhall ; Hugh Davenport, of Henbury ; and Christopher Davenport, of Woodford, in the appointment of collectors of a subsidy for the King (Edward IV.) in the Macclesfield Hundred. He married Ellen, daughter of Sir Peter Legh, of Lyme, but this lady, who predeceased him, bore him no issue. He died April 27, 1494, when the estates devolved upon his brother and next heir, Edward Fitton, then aged 60 years. This Edward, by his marriage with Emmota, the daughter and sole heiress of Robert Siddington, had at that time acquired possession of two parts of the manor of Siddington, which had been held by his wife's family for many generations on the tenure of rendering a red rose yearly, and thus he added materially to the territorial wealth and influence of the Gawsworth house. Though there is no absolute evidence of the fact, there is yet good reason to believe that the south porch of Gawsworth Church was added or rebuilt by this Edward Fitton, one of the carved decorations being a rose, in the leaves of which may be discerned two heads, evidently intended to represent Henry VII. and his Queen, who, by their marriage, had united the rival houses of York and Lan-caster, and so terminated the long and bitter War of the Roses.

Edward Fitton died 15th February, 1510-11, leaving, with other issue, a son John, who succeeded as heir, and who, as appears by the inquisition taken after his father's death, was then 40 years of age. He had married, in 1498, Ellen, daughter of Sir Andrew Brereton, the representative of a family that had been seated at Brereton from the time of William Rufus. By her he had, with other issue, a son Edward, who succeeded at his death, which occurred on the Sunday after St. Valentine's Day, 1525. In the Cheshire Church Notes already referred to, mention is made of a memorial window formerly existing on the south side of Gawsworth Church, containing the arms of Fitton quartering those of Sid-dington and Bechton, with the inscription underneath : "*Orate pro a'iabus Edwardi ffitton et Emmotæ uxis suæ, et pro a'iabus Johannis ffitton, et Elene ux' sue . . . . . et Roberti Sadyngton et Elene uxoris sue ;*" and there was also formerly in one of the windows of the south aisle of Wilmslow Church, as we learn from Mr. Earwaker's "East Cheshire," a representation of John Fitton and his wife. The drawing made by Randle Holmes shows the figure of a knight kneeling on a cushion and wearing a tabard of arms, the coat being that of Fitton of Gawsworth ; and lower down is a knight kneeling, with his tabard of arms quarterly— (1) Orreby, (2) Siddington, (3) Bechton, and (4) Fitton. Behind him kneel eight sons ; opposite, also kneeling, is his wife, wearing an heraldic mantle representing the arms of Brereton, with a shield containing the same coat above her head ; and behind her, kneeling, six daughters. The inscription had then disappeared, but it is clear that the first figure was intended for Edward Fitton of Gawsworth, whilst the other represented his son John, and his wife, Ellen Brereton, and their children.

On the death of John Fitton, in 1525, the family estates devolved upon his eldest son Edward, who received the honour of knighthood, and in the 35th Henry VIII. (1543-4) held the shrievalty of the county. He married Mary, the younger daughter and co-heir of Sir Guiscard Harbottle, a Northumberland knight, and by her had five sons and six daughters. He died on February 17, 1548, and on his inquisition, which was taken the same year,

Edward Fitton, his son, then aged 21 years, was found to be his heir.

Edward Fitton, who succeeded to the Gawsworth estates on the death of his father, in 1548, was born 31st March, 1527 ; and when only 12 years of age had been united in marriage with Anne, one of the daughters of Sir Peter Warburton, of Warburton and Arley, the lady being a month younger than himself. He was one of the foresters of Macclesfield, and was exempted from serving upon juries and at the assizes, in accordance with the terms of a writ dated 29th March, 5 and 6 Edw. VI. (1532), addressed to the sheriff of the county. Eight years after his coming in possession of the patrimonial lands, as appears by letters patent bearing date 3 and 4 Philip and Mary (1556-7), he, in conjunction with William Tatton, of Wythenshawe, who in 1552 had espoused his eldest sister, Mary, obtained a grant from the Crown of Etchells, part of the confiscated estates of Sir William Brereton, together with Aldford and Alderley, the property being subsequently partitioned ; Aldford and Alderley remaining with Sir Edward, whilst Etchells passed to his son-in-law, William Tatton.

Subsequently his name occurs in the palatine records, with those of William Davenport, Knt., and William Dokenfield and Jasper Worth, Esquires, as collectors of a mise in Macclesfield, in 1559-60.

The influential position which the Fittons held in their own county was due, as we have seen, not less to their martial bearing than to their successful marriages, and it was this chivalrous spirit which was ever a characteristic of the stock that led to their being frequently employed in the public service. In the person of Sir Edward Fitton the ancient fame of the family was well sustained. In 1569, the year in which Shane O'Neill, the representative of the royal race of Ulster, was attainted in Parliament—that daring chief of a valorous line, whose

> Kings with standard of green unfurl'd,
> Led the Red-branch knights to danger :
> Ere the emerald gem of the western world
> Was set in the crown of a stranger—

16

when Ireland was in a state of anarchy and confusion—when the
Desmonds and the Tyrones were trying the chances of insurrection rather than abdicate their unlicensed but ancient chieftainship,
and the half-civilised people were encouraged in their disobedience
to the law by the mischievous activity of the Catholic clergy, who
had been forcibly dispossessed of their benefices, and therefore
wished to free themselves from the English yoke—Sir Edward
Fitton was sent over to Ireland by Queen Elizabeth to fill the
difficult and responsible post of first Lord President of the Council
within the Province of Munster and Thomond—an office he held
for a period of over three years. His position can hardly be said
to have been an enviable one, for the country at that time had
become so wasted by war and military executions, and famine and
pestilence, that two years previously Sir Henry Sidney, the viceroy,
in his letters to Elizabeth, described the southern and western
counties as "an unmeasurable tract, now waste and uninhabited,
which of late years was well tilled and pastured." He adds,—

A more pleasant nor a more desolate land I never saw than from Youghall
to Limerick. . . . So far hath that policy, or rather lack of policy, in
keeping dissension among them prevailed, as now, albeit all that are alive
would become honest and live in quiet, yet are there not left alive in those
two provinces the twentieth person necessary to inhabit the same.

And the description is confirmed by a contemporary writer—a
Cheshire man, by the way, whose early life was spent in the neighbourhood of Gawsworth (Hollinshead)—who thus expresses the
truth with hyperbolical energy :—

The land itself, which before those wars was populous, well inhabited,
and rich in all the good blessings of God, being plenteous of corn, full of
cattle, well stored with fruits and sundry other good commodities, is now
become waste and barren, yielding no fruits, the pastures no cattle, the
fields no corn, the air no birds, the seas, though full of fish, yet to them
yielding nothing. Finally, every way, the curse of God was so great, and
the land so barren, both of man and beast, that whosoever did travel from
one end unto the other he should not meet any man, woman, or child,
saving in towns and cities ; nor yet see any beast but they were wolves, the
foxes, and other like ravenous beasts.

On the dissolution of the Council in September, 1572, Sir Edward Fitton returned to England; but remained only a few months, when he was appointed (March, 1573) Treasurer for the War and Vice-Treasurer and Receiver-General in Ireland. He appears to have taken up his abode in Dublin, where in January of the following year he lost his wife. She was buried in St. Patrick's Cathedral, in that city, January, 1573-4; and in the MSS. of Bishop Sterne there is preserved the following curious account of the ceremonial observed on the occasion of her funeral :—

The order in the presyding for buriall of the worshypful Lady Fitton, on Sonday, bein the 17 day of January, Anno 1573.

First, serteyne youmen to goo before the penon with the armes of Syr Edwarde Fytton, and his wyfe's dessessed; and next after them the penon, borne by Mr. Rycharde Fytton, second son to Syr Edw. Fytton and Lady, his wyfe dessessed; and sarten gentillmen servants to the sayd Syr Edw. Fytton; then the gentill-hossher and the chapplens, and then Ulster Kyng of Armes of Ierland, weyring his mornyng goune and hod, with hys cote of the armes of Ynglande. And then the corpes of the sayd Lady Fytton, and next after the corps the lady Brabason, who was the principal morner, bein lyd and assysted by Sir Rafe Egerton, knyght, and Mr. Fran. Fytton, Esq., brother to the said Syr Edwarde, and next after her, Mistress Agarde, wyfe to Mr. Fran. Agarde; then Mrs. Chalenor, wyfe to Mr. John Chalenor; then Mrs. Dyllon; then Mrs. Bruerton, being the other III murners. Then Syr Edward Fytton goying bytwene the Archebysshoppe of Dublin and the Bishop of Methe; then Sir John Plunkett, Chefe Justice of Ireland; then Master Dyllon, beying the Chefe Baron; then Mr. Fran. Agard and Mr. John Chalenor, wyth other men to the number of XIII gentylmen; then sarten other gentyllwomen and maydens, morners, to the nomber of VIII; and then the Mayor of Dublyn, wyth his brytherne, the Schyreffes and Aldermen; and the poure folks VI men on the one syde of the corse and VI women on the other syde. And so coming to the cherche of St. Patryke, where was a herse prepared, and when they cam to the herse, the yomen stode, halfe on the one side and halfe on the other, the penon berer stood at the fette of the corps; then the corps was layd upon a payer of trestels within the herse, and then the III morners were brought to their places by Ulster Kyng of Armes aforesaid, and the cheffe morner was brought to her place at the hede of the corps, and so the herse was closd; and the tow assystants set uppon tow stowles without the rayles, and then sarvyce was begon by the Bysshope of Methe, and after sarvyce there was a sermon made, and the sermon endyd, the company went home to the house of the sayd Sir Edw. Fytton; and the corpse was buryed by the reverent father, the Bysshop of Methe, and when the corpse was buryed, the clothe was layd again upon the trestylls wythin the herse, which was deckyed with scochyens of armes in pale of hys and her armes, and on the morow the herse was sett over the grave and the penon sett in the wall over the grave. And Ulster Kyng of Armes had V yardes of fyne blake clothe for his lyvery, and 50s. sterling for hys fee, and the herse with the cloth that was on the corse wyth all the furnyture there of the herse."

It may be mentioned that the claim of Ulster King of Arms to the costly materials of which the hearse was composed was disputed by the Vicars Choral of St. Patrick's, and the matter was not settled until 1578, when a decision was given in favour of the former by the Lord Deputy of the Council. Sir Edward Fitton died July 3, 1579, and his remains were interred by the side of those of his wife, the memory of both being perpetuated in an inscription on a sepulchral brass still remaining in St. Patrick's Cathedral, Dublin, on which is engraved the figure of a man with nine children behind him, and, opposite, a woman with six children behind her, all kneeling. The inscription which is below is as follows :—

> Glorify thy name, hasten thy
> Kingdome; Comforte thy flock;
> Confound thy adversaries ;
> Ser Edward ffitton, of Gausworth, in the counte of Chester, in Eng-
> lande, knight, was sent into Ireland by Quene Elizabeth, to serve as the
> first L. President of her highnes Counsell within the province of Connaght
> and Thomonde, who landing in Ireland on the Ascension day, 1569, Ao. R.
> R. Elizabeth XI. lyued there in the rome aforesaid till Mighellmas, 1572,
> Ao. Elizabeth XIIII°. ; and then, that Counsell being dissolued, and he
> repayring into England, was sent over againe in March next following as
> Threasaurer at Warres, Vice-treasaurer, and general receyvor within the
> realme of Ireland, and hath here buried the wyef of his youth, Anne, the
> seconnd daughter of Sir Peter Warburton, of Areley, in the county of
> Chester, knight, who were born both in one yere, viz., he ye last of Marche,
> 1527, and she the first of May in the same yeare; and were maried on
> Sonday next after Hillaries daye, 1539, being ye 19 daye of Januarie, in
> the 12 yere of their age, and lyued together in true and lawfull matry-
> monie just 34 yeres; for the same Sonday of ye yere wherein they were
> maried, ye same Sondaie 34 yeres following was she buried, though she
> faithfully departed this lyef 9 daies before, viz., on the Saturdaie, ye 9 daie
> of Januarie, 1573; in which time God gave them 15 children, viz., 9

sonnes and six daughters ; and now her body slepeth under this Stone, and her soul is retourned to God yt gave yt, and there remayneth in kepinge of Christe Jesus, her onely Saviour. And the said Ser Edward departed this lyef the thirde daie of July. Ao. Dni. 1579. and was buried the xxi daie of September next folowing ; whose fleshe also resteth under the same stone, in assured hope of full and perfect resurrection to eternall lyef in ioye, through Christe his onely Saviour ; and the said Ser Edward was revoked home into England, and left this land the   day of   Anno Domini being the   yere of his age.

At the east end of the north side of Gawsworth Church there is a replica of this inscription, with the figures of Sir Edward and Lady Fitton, and their fifteen children.

A younger brother of Sir Edward was Francis Fitton, who in 1588 married Katherine, the Countess Dowager of Northumberland, one of the four daughters and co-heirs of John Neville Lord Latimer. His portrait was formerly to be seen in the "new" hall at Gawsworth, with a long and curious inscription surrounding it, recording some of the alliances of the family.

Sir Edward Fitton, as stated, died July 3, 1579. His inquisition was taken the following year, when his son, Sir Edward Fitton, Knight, then aged 30, was found to be his heir. He was probably at the time in Ireland, for it was not until April 24, 25 Elizabeth (1583), that he had livery of his lands. In 1602, as appears by an indenture dated June 20 in that year, he sold the manor of Nether Alderley, which had been acquired by his father, to Thomas Stanley, ancestor of the present Lord Stanley of Alderley. Sir Edward filled the office of President of Munster, in Ireland, and died in 1606, leaving, by his wife Alice, daughter and sole heir of John Holcroft, of Holcroft, in Lancashire, with other issue, a son, Sir Edward Fitton, born 29th November, 1572, who was created a Baronet in 1617. He died May 10, 1619, being then aged 47, and was buried at Gawsworth, where a sumptuous monument was erected to his memory by his wife, "the Lady Ann Fytton," daughter and co-heir of James Barratt, of Tenby, in Pembrokeshire, Esq., with the following extravagant effusion inscribed on a panel below :—

Least tongves to fvtvre ages shovld be dvmb,
The very stones thvs speak abovt ovr tomb.
Loe, two made one, whence sprang these many more,
Of whom a King once prophecy'd before.
Here's the blest man, his wife the frvitfvl vine,
The children th' olive plants, a gracefvll line,
Whose sovle's and body's beavties sentence them
Fitt-ons to weare a heavenly Diadem.

Lady Ann Fitton survived her husband many years. Her will
bears date January 31, 1643-4, but the date of probate has not
been ascertained. In it she bequeaths several small legacies to her
grandchildren and others, appoints her daughter, Mrs. Lettice Cole,
sole executrix, and her two grandchildren, William, Lord Brereton,
and Charles Gerard, supervisors. She died 26th March, 1644, and
was buried at Gawsworth.

On the death of Sir Edward the family estates passed to his son,
also named Edward, who was baptised at Gawsworth, August 24th,
1603, and must, therefore, have been under age on his accession to
the property. In October, 1622, he married Jane, daughter of Sir
John Trevor, of Plâs Teg, in Denbighshire, by whom he had a
daughter, Margaret, who died in infancy. Lady Fitton died June,
1638, and was buried at Gawsworth, when Sir Edward again
entered the marriage state, his second wife being Felicia, daughter
of Ralph Sneyd, of Keel, in Staffordshire. Concerning this second
marriage there is the following curious entry in the Corporation
books of the borough of Congleton :—

1638. Paid for an entertainment for Sir Edwd. Fitton, of Gawsworth,
his bride, father, and mother-in-law, on their first coming through the
town, and divers other gentlemen who accompanied him and his bride, on
their going to Gawsworth to bring his lady.   He sent his barber two days
before to the mayor and aldermen, and the rest, to entreat them to bid
them welcome .... 12s. 4d.

The civic authorities of Congleton were noted for their hospitality, and we may therefore assume that little "entreaty" was
required on the part of the "barber" to secure a cordial welcome
for the Baronet and his bride. We are not told what the entertainment consisted of, but no doubt the cakes and sack for which the

old borough had even then long been famous entered largely into the festivities, though the amount charged does not suggest the idea of any very extravagant convivialities.

Sir Edward was soon called by the stern duties of the times from the enjoyment of domestic life. Clouds were gathering upon the political horizon which heralded a tempest ; the seeds of civil war had been sown, and soon King and Commons were arrayed against each other, neither caring for peace, for if the olive branch was held out it was stripped of its leaves, and appeared only as a dry and sapless twig. In the great struggle between Charles and the Parliament the owner of Gawsworth espoused the cause of his Sovereign, and distinguished himself in several military engagements. He raised a regiment of infantry for the King's service from among his own tenantry and dependents, of which he had the command ; and the good people of Congleton, not wishing to have the tranquillity of their town disturbed by the quartering of his troops in it, in the hope of avoiding the inconvenience proferred him their hospitality, as one of the entries in the Corporation accounts shows :—

1642. Wine gave to Colonel Fitton, not to quarter 500 soldiers on the town .. .. 3s. 4d.

Colonel Fitton fought in the battle at Edgehill, where the two armies were first put in array against each other, and was also present with the King at the taking of Banbury, as well as in the operations at Brentford and Reading. He afterwards took part with Prince Rupert in the storming of Bristol, and when that city— exceeded only by London in population and wealth—was, after a terrible slaughter, surrendered (July 27, 1643) by Nathaniel Fiennes to the arms of its sovereign, he was left in charge of the garrison, and died there of consumption in the following month, at the early age of 40. His body was removed to Gawsworth for interment, and the occasion of its passing through the town of Congleton is thus referred to in the accounts :—

Paid for carrying Sir Edwd. Fitton through the town, and for repairing Rood-lane for the occasion .. .. 4s. 0d.

In the south-east angle of Gawsworth Church there is a large monument to the memory of Sir Edward, his first wife, and their infant daughter, placed there by his second wife, who survived him, and afterwards re-married Sir Charles Adderley. It consists of an arch resting upon pillars, beneath which is an altar-tomb supporting the effigies of Sir Edward and his wife, and that of their infant daughter. A tablet containing a long Latin inscription, formerly affixed to the south wall, beneath the canopy, has in recent years been removed to the east wall of the chancel.

Sir Edward left no surviving issue, a circumstance which gave rise to almost endless contentions between the kinsmen of his name and their cousins—the Gerards. Lawsuit followed lawsuit; long and rancorous were the proceedings in the "Great Cheshire Will Case," as it was called; and the fierce struggle, which began in one century with forgery, followed by seduction and divorce, was ended in the next, when the husbands of the two ladies who claimed to be heiresses were slain by each other in a murderous duel in Hyde Park. Immediately after the death of Sir Edward Fitton, Penelope, Anne, Jane, and Frances, his four sisters— married respectively to Sir Charles Gerard, Knight; Sir John Brereton, Knight; Thomas Minshull, Esquire; and Henry Mainwaring, Esquire—entered upon possession of the estates; but, after long litigation, they were ejected by William Fitton, son of Alexander, second surviving son of Sir Edward Fitton, Treasurer of Ireland, who claimed under a deed alleged to have been executed by Sir Edward, settling the estates upon himself, with remainder in succession to his sons, Edward and Alexander, the latter of whom succeeded him in the possession, and he obtained three verdicts in his favour. One of the sisters of Sir Edward Fitton—Penelope—had married Sir Charles Gerard, of Halsall, in Lancashire, and by him had a son, Sir Charles Gerard, created Lord Brandon in 1645, and Earl of Macclesfield in 1679. Lord Brandon was one of the notable gallants at the profligate Court of Charles II. He held the office of Gentleman of the Bedchamber, and was also Captain of the Guards—the latter a commission which he relinquished for a douceur of £12,000 when the King wanted to bestow the dignity upon his illegitimate son, the Duke of Monmouth. He kept up a large establishment in London, surrounded by trim gardens, the remembrance of which is perpetuated in the names of the streets that now occupy the site—Gerard Street and Macclesfield Street, in Soho. His wife, a French lady, brought herself into disfavour at Court through indulging in the feminine propensity of allowing her tongue to wag too freely in disparagement of the notorious courtesan, Lady Castlemaine, as we learn from an entry in " Pepys's Diary " :—

1662-3. Creed told me how, for some words of my Lady Gerard's against my Lady Castlemaine to the Queene, the King did the other day apprehend her in going out to a dance with her at a ball, when she desired it as the ladies do, and is since forbid attending the Queen by the King; which is much talked of, my lord her husband being a great favourite.

On the restoration of the King, nineteen years after the death of Sir Edward Fitton, and thirty after the entail had been confirmed, as alleged by a deed-poll, Lord Gerard produced a will which would be looked for in vain in the Ecclesiastical Court at Chester, purporting to have been made in his favour by his mother's brother, Sir Edward Fitton. Hot, fierce, and anxious was the litigation that followed, and in 1663 a small volume was printed at the Hague, entitled, " A True Narrative of the Proceedings in the several Suits-in-law that have been between the Right Honourable Charles, Lord Brandon, and Alexander Fitton, Esqr., published for general satisfaction, by a Lover of Truth." Fitton pleaded the deed-poll, but Gerard brought forward one Abraham Grainger, then confined in the Gate House, who made oath that he had forged the name of Sir Edward to the deed under a threat of mortal violence, whereupon the Court of Chancery directed a trial to determine whether the deed-poll was genuine or not. The forgery was admitted by Grainger, and corroborated by other witnesses, who deposed that they had heard Fitton confess that Grainger had forged a deed for him, for which he had paid him £40. The judgment of the Court was given in favour of Gerard, and the deed declared to be a forgery. The strangest part of the story remains. Grainger, impelled

17

either by remorse or the desire to escape a heavy penalty by acknowledging the smaller offence, made a written confession setting forth that he had perjured himself when he swore that he had forged the name of Sir Edward, and had been compelled to do so by the threats of Lord Gerard. Pepys, who had a strong dislike to Lord Gerard, refers to the circumstance in his " Diary " : —

My cosen, Roger Pepys, he says, showed me Grainger's written confession of his being forced by imprisonment, &c., by my Lord Gerard, most barbarously to confess his forging of a deed in behalf of Fitton, in the great case between him and my Lord Gerard; which business is under examination, and is the foulest against my Lord Gerard that ever anything in the world was, and will, all do believe, ruine him ; and I shall be glad of it.

The anticipations of the gossiping diarist were not, however, realised. The confession, being unsupported by evidence, was discredited, and Fitton, who was adjudged to be the real offender, was fined £500 and committed to the King's Bench.

Alexander Fitton, who was thus dispossessed of the property, lingered in prison until the accession of James II., when, having embraced the Romish faith, he was released from confinement and taken into favour by the King, who made him Chancellor of Ireland, and subsequently conferred upon him the honour of knighthood and created him Lord Gawsworth. He sat in the Irish Parliament of 1689, where he appears to have been actively employed in passing Acts of forfeiture of Protestant property, and attainder of Protestant personages. On the abdication of James he accompanied him into exile, where he remained, and, dying, left descendants who, it is to be feared, benefited little from the tutelar dignities his sovereign had conferred upon him.

The whimsical *finesse* of the law, which wrested from Alexander Fitton the lands owned for so many generations by his progenitors and bestowed them upon the Gerards, though it added wealth, did not convey peace or contentment to the successful litigants. Their history during the brief period they owned the Gawsworth estates partakes much of the character of a romance in real life, but it is one that is by no means pleasant to contemplate. Charles Gerard, on whom the barony of Brandon and the earldom of Macclesfield had been successively conferred, died in January, 1693-4, when the titles and estates devolved upon his eldest son, who bore the same baptismal name. Charles, the second earl, was the husband of the lady who, by her adulterous connection with Richard Savage, Earl Rivers, and as the heroine of the famous law case that followed upon the birth of the celebrated but unfortunate poet, Richard Savage, acquired an unenviable notoriety even in that age, when profligacy formed such a prominent characteristic of society.

The Countess of Macclesfield, under the name of Madame Smith, and wearing a mask, was delivered of a male child in Fox Court, near Brook Street, Holborn, by Mrs. Wright, a midwife, on Saturday, the 16th January, 1697-8. The earl denied the paternity, and satisfactorily proved the impossibility of his being the father of the son borne by his countess; who, on her side, narrated a stratagem she had devised, whereby the disputed paternity could not be denied. The stratagem was not unknown in the licentious comedies of the time, but no credit was given to it in this case; and thus the honour of Gerard was saved from being tainted by the bastard of Savage. A divorce was granted in 1698; but the law deemed the earl to be accountable, through his own profligacy, for the malpractices of his wife, and decreed that he should repay the portion he had received with her in marriage. With this amount she married Colonel Brett, the friend of Colley Cibber, by whom she had a daughter, Ann Brett, the impudent mistress of George I., her illegitimate offspring by Lord Rivers—Richard Savage, whom she disowned—being educated at the cost of her mother, Lady Mason. It has been alleged that Savage was an impostor, and this opinion was held by Boswell, the biographer of Dr. Johnson, who says: "In order to induce a belief that the Earl Rivers, on account of a criminal connection with whom Lady Macclesfield is said to have been divorced from her husband by Act of Parliament, had a peculiar anxiety about the child which she bore to him, it is alleged that his lordship gave him his own name, and had it duly recorded in the register of St. Andrew's, Holborn. I have," he adds, "carefully inspected that register, and I cannot find it." That Boswell should have failed in the discovery is explained by a reference to " The Earl of Macclesfield's Case," presented to the House of Lords in 1697-8, from which it appears that the child was registered by the name of Richard, the son of John Smith, and christened on Monday, January 18th, in Fox Court, and this statement is confirmed by the following entry in the register of St. Andrew's, Holborn :—

Jany., 1696-7. Richard, son of John Smith and Mary, in Fox Court, in Gray's Inn Lane, baptized the 18th.

Notwithstanding the discredit that has been thrown upon Savage's story, there can be little doubt of its truth. It was universally believed at the time, and no attempt was ever made by the countess to contradict or to invalidate any of the statements contained in it. Moreover, he was openly recognised in the house of Lord Tyrconnell, a nephew of the Countess of Macclesfield, with whom he resided as a guest for two years, and he was also on terms of acquaintance with the Countess of Rochford, the illegitimate daughter of Earl Rivers by Mrs. Colydon.*

The Earl of Macclesfield did not long survive the granting of his divorce. He was sent as Ambassador to Hanover, and died there, November 5, 1701, when the title devolved upon his younger brother, Fitton Gerard, who died unmarried in the following year, when the Earldom of Macclesfield became extinct, the estates then passing under the will of the second earl to his niece and co-heiress, the daughter of his sister, Charlotte Mainwaring, married to Charles, Lord Mohun, son of Warwick, Lord Mohun, by Philippa, daughter of Arthur, Earl of Anglesey. The preference thus shown offended the Duke of Hamilton, who had married the daughter of another niece, Elizabeth, daughter and sole heiress of

---

* In a tavern brawl, in 1727, Savage had the misfortune to kill a Mr. James Sinclair, for which he was tried and condemned to death. His relentless mother, it is said, endeavoured to intercept the royal mercy ; but he was pardoned through the influence of Queen Caroline, and set at liberty. He afterwards addressed a birthday ode to the Queen, in acknowledgment of which she sent him £60, and continued the same sum to him every year.

D'gby, Lord Gerard—by his wife, the Lady Elizabeth Gerard—the heir-general of the Macclesfield family, who felt himself injured by this disposition of the property. A lawsuit to determine the validity of Lord Macclesfield's will was commenced, much jealousy and heart-burning followed, and eventually the two disputing husbands brought their feud to a sanguinary end in the memorable duel which proved fatal to both.

The circumstances of this tragic affair are recorded in Dean Swift's " History of the Four Last Years of Queen Anne," published in 1758, and are more fully detailed in "Transactions During the Reign of Queen Anne," published in Edinburgh in 1790, by Charles Hamilton, a kinsman of one of the combatants. It appears that upon the return of Lord Bolingbroke, after the peace of Utrecht, and the suspension of hostilities between Great Britain and France, the Duke of Hamilton, long noted for his attachment to the Stuarts, and the acknowledged head of the Jacobite party, was appointed Ambassador Extraordinary and Plenipotentiary to the Court of France. Previous to his departure he wished to bring to a close the Chancery suit which had been pending between Lord Mohun and himself. With that view he, on the 13th November, 1712, attended at the chambers of Olebar, a Master in Chancery, where his adversary met him by appointment. In the course of the interview, Mr. Whitworth, formerly the steward of the Macclesfield family, gave evidence, and, as his memory was much impaired by age, the duke somewhat petulantly exclaimed, "There is no truth or justice in him," upon which Lord Mohun retorted, "I know Mr. Whitworth. He is an honest man, and has as much truth as your grace." This grating remark was allowed to pass unnoticed at the time, but Lord Mohun afterwards meeting with General Macartney and Colonel Churchill, both violent men, and declared partisans of the Duke of Marlborough, who had then been removed from the command of the army by the party to which the Duke of Hamilton was attached, it would seem that the offending person was induced by them to challenge the person offended. Preliminaries having been arranged, the combatants

met in Kensington Gardens, Hyde Park, on the morning of the
15th November—the duke attended by his relative, Colonel
Hamilton, and Lord Mohun by General Macartney. In a few
moments the affair was ended, and when the park keepers, alarmed
by the clashing of swords, rushed to the spot whence the sound
proceeded, they found the two noblemen weltering in their blood—
Lord Mohun was already dead, and the Duke of Hamilton expired
before he could be removed. Nor had the combat been limited to
the principals alone. The seconds had crossed swords and fought
with desperate rancour. Colonel Hamilton remained upon the
field, and was taken prisoner, but Macartney fled to the Continent.
Colonel Hamilton subsequently declared upon oath, before the
Privy Council, that, when they met upon the ground, the duke,
turning to Macartney, said, " Sir, you are the cause of this, let the
event be what it will." To which Macartney replied, " My lord, I
had a commission for it." Lord Mohun then said, " These gentlemen shall have nothing to do here." Whereupon Macartney
exclaimed, " We will have our share." To which the duke
answered, " There is my friend—he will take his share in my
dance." Colonel Hamilton further deposed that when the principals engaged, he and Macartney, as seconds, followed their
example ; that Macartney was immediately disarmed ; but that he
(Colonel Hamilton), seeing the duke fall upon his antagonist,
threw away the swords, and ran to lift him up ; and that, while he
was employed in raising the duke, Macartney, having taken up one
of the swords, stabbed his grace over Hamilton's shoulder, and
retired immediately.

A prodigious ferment was occasioned by this duel, which assumed
a high political character. Neither of the combatants were men
who could lay claim to any great admiration on the score of
integrity or principle. Lord Mohun had, in fact, been long known
as a brawler, and had acquired an infamous reputation for his share
in the murder of William Mountford, the player, before his own
door, in Howard Street, Strand. The Duke of Hamilton, as we
have said, was the recognised head of the Jacobite faction, whilst
his antagonist, Lord Mohun, was a zealous champion of the Whig

interest. The Tories exclaimed against this event as a party duel, brought about by their political opponents for the purpose of inflicting a vital wound on the Jacobite cause, then in the ascendant, by removing its great prop before his departure to the Court of France. They affirmed that the duke had met with foul play, and treated Macartney as a cowardly assassin. That the allegation was well founded may be doubted, for all the evidence points to the conclusion that both sets of antagonists, seconds as well as principals, were so blinded by the virulence of personal hatred as to neglect all the laws both of the gladiatorial art and the duelling code, and assailed each other with the fury of savages. A proclamation was issued by the Government offering a reward of £500 for the apprehension of Macartney, and £300 was offered in addition by the Duchess of Hamilton. After a time Macartney returned, surrendered, and took his trial, when he was acquitted of murder, and found guilty of manslaughter only. Subsequently he was restored to his rank in the army, and entrusted with the command of a regiment. After the accession of George I. he was in great favour with the Court of Hanover, and was employed in bringing over Dutch troops on the occasion of the insurrection in England, which ended in the capitulation at Preston of the Earls of Derwentwater and Nithsdale, and other English and Scottish lords and gentlemen.

The Gawsworth property, which Lord Mohun had acquired by his first wife, Charlotte Mainwaring, he bequeathed by will to his second wife, Elizabeth, daughter of Dr. Thomas Lawrence, first physician to Queen Anne; and the Lady Mohun, who thus became possessed of the estates, which she held in trust, directed that at her death they should be sold, and the proceeds, after the payment of certain specified bequests, applied to the use of her two daughters by her first husband, Elizabeth Griffith, wife of Sir Robert Rich, Bart., and Ann Griffith, wife of the distinguished soldier and statesman, William Stanhope, who, in recognition of his public services, was elevated to the peerage, Nov. 20, 1729, by the title of Baron Harrington, and subsequently raised to the dignities of Viscount Petersham and Earl of Harrington. Lord Harrington in 1727 purchased the manor from his wife's trustees, and thus passed into the family of Stanhope an estate with which they had no connection by blood or by alliance. From the first Earl of Harrington the property has descended in regular succession to the present owner, Charles Augustus Stanhope, the eighth earl.

A curious feature in connection with the Old Hall of Gawsworth, and one strongly suggestive of the warlike spirit of its former owner, is the ancient tilting ground in the rear of the mansion. Ormerod, the historian, was of opinion that this relic of a chivalrous age had been a pleasure ground ; but Mr. Mayer, the honorary curator of the Historic Society of Lancashire and Cheshire, who made a careful survey some years ago, shows, with much probab lity, that it was intended for jousts and other displays of martial skill and bravery. The "tilt-yard," the form of which may still be very clearly traced, is about two hundred yards in length and sixty-five in width, surrounded on three of its sides by a steep embankment or mound, sixteen yards in width. Within this enclosure the lists were arranged and the barriers erected, and here the knights, with pointless lances or coronels in rest, assembled to perform the *hastiludia pacifica* or peaceable jousts for the amusement of the ladies and other spectators who occupied the embankment.

At the further end of the long flat is a raised circular mound, with a base twenty-five yards square, on which was placed the tent of the Queen of Beauty, who, surrounded by her attendants, could overlook the whole field, and to her the successful competitors were heralded to receive at her hand the prize or guerdon to which their chivalrous skill had entitled them. Near to this mound is a smaller piece of ground, about fifty-seven yards in length, with three rows of seats cut out of the bank, on three of its sides, and one row on the fourth, that nearest the throne of the "Queen of Beauty." This, Mr. Mayer surmises, was intended for battles by single combat with the sword and quarter-staff, for wrestling, and other athletic displays ; where, also, at Christmastide, and at wakes and festivals, the mummers practised their rude drolleries ; where, too, the itinerant bards sang their rugged and unpolished lays in glorification of the achievements of the Cheshire warriors of ancient days, and where

> Minstrel's harp poured forth its tone
> In praise of Maud and Marguerite fair.

The level ground is divided by a small stream that flows through the middle, and the flat space beyond, which is hemmed in by a mound similar to that surrounding the "tilting ground," is supposed to have been used for such games as football, leap-frog, prison-bars, and foot-racing, in which the people generally participated. Here, too, is a raised circular earthwork, corresponding with the lady's mound already referred to, where it is probable the awards were made and the prizes distributed to the successful competitors. The stream, after passing by the eastern end of the Old Hall, empties itself into the uppermost of the series of lakes before referred to, which are divided from each other only by a narrow strip of land, and where, as has been said, in days of yore the water jousts took place.

Taken altogether, in the tilting ground, with its raised terraces for spectators—the court, which formed the arena for quarter-staff, wrestling, and similar games of strength—and the lakes or ponds, used for water jousts and other aquatic sports—we have one of the most remarkable, as well as one of the most complete, memorials to be found in the North of England illustrative of the manners and customs of our forefathers—of the military pomp and pageantry, and those displays of prowess, skill, daring, and strength, which in the reigns of the Plantagenet and Tudor Kings the English gentry so much encouraged, and the common people so greatly delighted in—the relic of an age the most chivalrous and the most picturesque in our country's history, when there was no lack of heroism and brave hearts and noble minds, when men ruled by the stern will and strong arm, and through successive ages fought the battle of England's liberties, and laid the foundations of the freedom we enjoy. The place seems to belong so entirely to a bygone age

18

that imagination wings her airy flight to those remote days, and in
fancy's eye we re-people the Old Hall, when

> Every room
> Blazed with lights, and brayed with minstrelsy;

and call up in each deserted nook and shady grove the figures of
those who have long ago returned to dust. We can picture in
imagination the time when these grass-grown terraces were thronged
with a gay company of gallant youths and fair maidens, of stern
warriors and sober matrons, assembled to witness the princely
entertainments provided by the proud owners of Gawsworth. We
see the barriers set up, and hear the braying of the trumpets, and
the proclamations of the heralds; we see the knights, with their
attendant esquires, mounted upon their well-trained steeds, with
their rich panoply of arms and plumed and crested casques, and
note the stately courtesy with which each, as he enters the arena,
salutes the high-bred queen of the tournament; we hear the
prancing of horses, the clang of arms, the shock of combat, and
the loud clarions which proclaim to the assembled throng the
names of the gallant victors. But the days of tilt and tournament
have passed away, the age of feudalism has gone by, and in the
long centuries of change and progress that have intervened, time
has mellowed and widened our social institutions, and raised the
lower stratum of society to a nearer level with the higher. Yet,
while we boast ourselves of the present, let us not be unmindful of
what we owe to the past, for those times were instinct with noble
and true ideas, and with Carlyle we may say that, "in prizing justly
the indispensable blessings of the new, let us not be unjust to the
old. The old *was* true, if it no longer is." The glories of
Gawsworth are of the past. The old mansion is still to be seen,
and the silent pools, the deserted terraces, the forlorn garden
grounds, and the stately trees still remain as representatives of the
once goodly park and pleasaunce, but those who here maintained
a princely hospitality, and bore their part in those splendid
pageantries, are sleeping their last sleep. We may not lift the
veil which hides their secret history, or reveal much of the story of

their hopes and fears, their perils by flood and field, and their deep feuds and still deeper vengeances. Their graven effigies and gaudily-painted tombs are preserved to us, but

> The knights' bones are dust,
> And their good swords rust,
> Their souls are with the just
>   We trust.

In this quiet, out-of-the-way nook, amid these old landmarks, an afternoon will be neither unpleasantly nor unprofitably spent. We may learn something of English history, and of the historic figures which played their parts in our "rough island story." Our thoughts and fancies will be stirred anew, and our sense of patriotism will be nothing lessened by the contemplation of the relics of that past on which our present is securely built.

Any notice of Gawsworth would be incomplete that did not make mention of the remarkable series of fresco paintings that were discovered during the work of restoring the church in the autumn of 1851. At that time the fabric underwent a thorough repair, and the remains of coloured ornamentation in the timber-work of the roof led to the belief that the same method of decoration had been applied to the surface of the walls. Accordingly a careful examination was made, and on the removal of the whitewash and plaster some curious and interesting examples of mediæval art were discovered ; but, unfortunately, no effort was made at the time to preserve them. Happily, however, before their destruction careful copies were made by a local artist, Mr. Lynch, which have since been published as illustrations to a work he has written. The three principal frescoes represented St. Christopher and the Infant Saviour ; St. George slaying the Dragon ; and the Doom, or Last Judgment. From the details they would appear to have been executed in the early part of the fifteenth century—probably about the time the tower was built and some important additions made to the main structure, which, as previously stated, would be between the years 1420 and 1430.

At the period referred to, St. Christopher had come to be

regarded as a kind of symbol of the Christian Church, and the stalwart figure of the saint wading the stream with the Infant Jesus upon his shoulder was a favourite subject for painting and carving in ecclesiastical buildings. The Gawsworth fresco is especially interesting, from the circumstance of its being an exact *fac-simile* (except that it is reversed) of the earliest known example of wood engraving, supposed to be of the date 1423—an original and, as is believed, unique impression of which was acquired by Lord Spencer, and is now preserved in the Spencer library. The second picture represents St. George on horseback, armed *cap-à-pie*, brandishing a sword with his right hand, whilst with the left he is thrusting a spear into the mouth of the dragon. In the distance is the representation of a castle, from the battlements of which the royal parents of the destined victim witness the fray, whilst the disconsolate damsel is depicted in a kneeling attitude. The knight's armour and the lady's costume furnish excellent data in fixing the time when the work was done. The third subject—the Last Judgment—occupied the space between the east window and the south wall. It was in three divisions, representing heaven, hell, and earth, and from the prominent position it occupied was no doubt intended to be kept continually before the eyes of the worshippers, that, to use the words of the Venerable Bede, "having the strictness of the Last Judgment before their eyes, they should be cautioned to examine themselves with a more narrow scrutiny."

Among the rectors of Gawsworth was one who added lustre to the place, but whose name is, curiously enough, omitted from the list given in Ormerod's "Cheshire"—the Rev. Henry Newcome, M.A., who held the living from 1650 to 1657, when he was appointed to the chaplaincy of the Collegiate Church at Manchester. Newcome was born in November, 1627, at Caldecote, in Huntingdonshire, of which place his father, Stephen Newcome, was rector. In January, 1641-2, both his parents died, and were buried in one coffin, when Henry removed to Congleton, where his elder brother Robert had recently been appointed by the

Corporation master of the Free School. The circumstance is thus referred to in his "Autobiography" :—

> I was taught grammar by my father, in the house with him ; and when my eldest brother, after he was Batchelor in Arts, was master of the Free School at Congleton, in Cheshire, I was in the year 1641, about May 4, brought down thither to him, and there went to school three quarters of a year, until February 13, at which time that eloquent and famous preacher, Dr. Thomas Dodd, was parson at Astbury, the parish church of Congleton, where I several times (though then but a child) heard him preach.

Newcome entered at St. John's, Cambridge, May 10, 1644, and began to reside in the following year. In 1646 he was a candidate for the mastership of a Lincolnshire grammar school, but failed in obtaining the appointment—a disappointment he bore with much stoicism. In September, 1647, he was nominated to the mastership of the Congleton School, and in the February succeeding he took his degree of B.A.

From his boyhood he seems to have had a fondness for preaching, and the inclination grew with his years. His first sermon was delivered at a friend's church (Little Dalby) in Leicestershire ; and on settling down at Congleton, as he tells us, "he fell to preaching when only 20 years old" He was appointed "reader" (curate) to Mr. Ley, at Astbury, and preached sometimes in the parish church and sometimes at Congleton. At first he "read" his sermons and "put too much history" into them, whilst "the people came with Bibles, and expected quotations of Scripture." Before he had attained the age of 21 he entered the marriage state, his wife being Elizabeth, daughter of Peter Mainwaring, of Smallwood, to whom he was married July 6, 1648. He speaks of himself as rash in taking this step at so early an age, but admits that it turned to his own good, and he dwells on the excellent qualities of his wife. It was indeed not only a happy, but in a worldly sense an advantageous match, as by his alliance with the Mainwarings he became connected with some of the most influential families in the county, and to their interest he undoubtedly owed his preferment to Gawsworth. He was ordained

at Sandbach in August, 1648, the month following that of his
marriage, and began his ministerial labours at Alvanley Chapel, in
Frodsham parish, to which place he went for many weeks on the
Saturday to preach on the following day; but before the close of
the year he had settled at Goostrey, where he officiated for a year
and a half. It was whilst residing here that he received the startling
intelligence of the trial and execution of Charles I., for, under date
January 30, 1649, he writes : "This news came to us when I lived
at Goostrey, and a general sadness it put upon us all. It dejected
me much (I remember), the horridness of the fact ; and much
indisposed me for the service of the Sabbath next after the news
came." Newcome, though a zealous Presbyterian, was a scarcely
less zealous Royalist, and boldly avowed his abhorrence of the
murder of the King.

Shortly after this event his name was mentioned in connection
with the then vacant rectory of Gawsworth, and an effort was made,
through the interest of the Mainwaring family, to secure his induction under the Broad Seal.   Under the Usurpation Independency
was in the ascendant, and " Dame ffelicia ffitton," the widow of Sir
Edward Fitton, in whom the patronage of Gawsworth had been
vested, was then included in the list of delinquents whose estates
were to be sequestered for loyalty to the sovereign.   Eventually the
instrument of institution under the Broad Seal was obtained.   It
bears date November 28, 1649, and the opening sentence sets forth
that, "Whereas, the rectory of the parish church of Gawsworth,
in the county of Chester, is become void by the death of the last
incumbent, and the Lords Commissioners of the Great Seal of
England have presented Henry Newcome, a godly and orthodox
divine, thereunto.   It is therefore ordered," &c.   Considerable
demur was made, however, to the appointment, and the people
locked the church doors against their new minister ; but eventually,
as we are told, " it pleased God to move upon the people when I
thought not of it, and they came (some of the chief of them) over
to Carincham on February 12th, and sent for me, and told me they
were desirous to have me before another ; and so were unanimously

consenting to me, and subscribed the petition, not knowing that the seal had come."

The obstacles to this induction having been removed, Newcome and his family took up their abode in the pleasant old rectory-house at Gawsworth, April, 1650, and on the 14th of the month he preached his first sermon to his new flock from Ezekiel iii., 5.

THE REV. HENRY NEWCOME.

There are several incidents recorded in his " Autobiography" which throw light on the life and habits of the youthful divine at this period. Thus he writes : —

> Whilst living here (Goostrey) my cousin, Roger Mainwaring, would needs go to Gawsworth (the park being then in the co-heirs' possession) to kill a deer, and one he killed with the keeper's knowledge ; but they had a mind to let the greyhound loose, and to kill another that the keeper should not know of, partly to hinder him of his fees and partly that it might not be known that he had killed more than one. I was ignorant of their design ; but had the hap to be one of the two that was carrying the other little deer off the ground, when the keeper came and only took it and dressed it, as he had done the other, and sent it after them to the alehouse where the horses were. But I remember the man said this word, that "*priests should not steal.*" I have oft after thought of it, that when I was

parson at Gawsworth, and that tho' Edward Morton, the keeper, was sometimes at variance with me, he never so much as remembered that passage to object against me; which, though I could have answered for myself in it, yet it might have served the turn to have been retorted upon me when the Lord stirred me up to press strictness upon them. But the Lord concealed this indiscretion of mine, that it was never brought forth in the least to lessen my authority amongst them.

It is pleasant to reflect that while Newcome was residing in his snug parsonage at Gawsworth, he was visited by his brother-in-law, Elias Ashmole, the learned antiquary and founder of the Ashmolean Museum at Oxford, who spent some time with him at the rectory and rambled thence into the Peak country. They had married sisters; Ashmole, who was Newcome's senior by ten years, having had to his first wife Eleanor, daughter of Peter Mainwaring. This lady died in 1641, and in 1649 Ashmole married Lady Mainwaring, the widow of Sir Thomas Mainwaring, of Bradfield, who died in 1668; and the same year he again entered the marriage state, his third wife being Elizabeth, daughter of Sir William Dugdale, Norroy, and afterwards Garter King of Arms. Ashmole, in his "Diary," thus refers to his visit to Gawsworth and his ramble in the Peak :—

1652.
Aug. 16.—I went towards Cheshire.
  ,, 28.—I arrived at Gawsworth, where my father-in-law, Mr. Mainwaring, then lived.
Sept. 23.—I took a Journey into the Peak in search of plants and other curiosities.
Nov. 24.—My Good Father-in-law, Mr. Peter Mainwaring, died at Gawsworth.

Oddly enough, Ashmole nowhere makes mention of Newcome's name in his "Diary," but Newcome himself refers to the visit in one of his letters to his brother-in-law, preserved among Ashmole's MSS. in the Bodleian Library, and printed by Mr. Earwaker in his "Local Gleanings," where, speaking of the Theatrum Chymicum he had lent to Hollinworth, the author of "Mancuniensis," he says, "It was with him when you were with me at Gawsworth, and I then sent for it home."

Puritan though he was, Newcome was by no means of a soured or morose disposition, nor so rigid in his notions as were some of

his southern brethren. He was fond of amusement within reasonable limits, and his experiences he relates with charming candour
and impartiality. Indeed, sometimes his hilarity was a little too
exuberant. "I remember," he says, "this year (1650), when the
gentlewomen from the hall used to come to see us, I was very
merry with them, and used to charge a pistol I had, and to shoot it
off to affright them." Notwithstanding his liveliness of disposition,
he set himself determinedly against the vices to which some of his
parishioners were addicted. Drinking and swearing seem to have
been prevalent, and he records how, one Sabbath evening, at the
house of Lady Fitton, a Mr. Constable,—

A known famous epicure. . . . told the lady there was excellent ale
at Broad [heath—what this place was does not appear], and moved he
might send for a dozen, some gentlemen of his gang being with him. I
made bold to tell him that my lady had ale good enough in her house for
any of them ; especially, I hoped, on a Sabbath day she would not let
them send for ale to the alehouse. The lady took with it, and in her
courteous way told him that her ale might serve him. But notwithstanding,
after duties, he did send ; but durst not let it come in whilst I staid. . . .
At last I took leave ; and then he said, "Now he is gone! Fetch in
the ale."

"My lady" was the beautiful and youthful Felicia Sneyd, the
second wife, and then widow of Sir Edward Fitton, who resided at
the hall, her jointure house. In all Newcome's efforts to improve
the spiritual condition of his parish Lady Fitton warmly joined ;
the Sacrament, which hitherto had been discontinued, was with her
co-operation revived. She offered herself to the minister for
instruction, and instituted family prayers twice a day in her house,
which Newcome for a while read ; and we gather from several
passages that the fascination and dignified bearing of the youthful
widow greatly attracted the divine of twenty-three. It was not
long, however, before he had occasion to describe another and
more painful scene. Lady Fitton, as has been previously stated,
re-married Sir Charles Adderley ; and on the 20th January, 1654,
Newcome writes she "was in lingering labour."

I had been at Congleton, and was just come home ; and they came
shrieking to me to pray with Lady Fitton; she did desire it, it should

19

seem. I went as fast as I could; but just as I came the fit of palsy took her. We went to prayer in the gallery for her again and again. Mr. Machin* came in, and he helped me to pray. We prayed there two or three times over. We begged life for mother and child, very earnestly at first. After we begged either, what God pleased. After the night we were brought to beg the life of the soul, for all other hopes were over. The next day I went, and prayed by her i' th' forenoon. I was much afflicted to see her die, as in a dream, pulling and setting her head clothes as if she had been dressing herself in the glass ; and so to pass out of the world. A lovely, sweet person she was ; but thus blasted before us, dyed Jany. 21 (1654), just after evening service. She was buried the next day, at night. . . . Sir C. Adderley was removed, and all manner of confusion and trouble came upon the estate, Mr. Fitton and the co-heirs striving for possession, which begat a strange alteration in the place.

Lady Fitton, "a very courteous, respectful friend to me while she lived," as Newcome observes, lies near the east end of the church of Gawsworth, close by the communion rails, and near to the stately tomb of her first husband, on which she is described as "*nulli secundam.*" In her death Newcome lost a good friend, for the living of Gawsworth was very poor, and, finding it difficult to equalise the wants of a growing family and the supplies of a small stipend, he was led to consider the expediency of removing to some other and more lucrative charge. His labours had been by no means confined to his own parish. On the contrary, he devoted a good deal of his time to ministerial work in other places. The fame of the wonderful young preacher spread to the larger towns, and those who had heard him once wished to hear him again. Among other places, he had visited Manchester, and preached in the Old Church during the sickness of Richard Hollinworth. It was only on one Sunday, but the generosity of the town brought him considerable relief at the moment that the necessities of his family were pressing inconveniently upon him. As Dr. Halley tells us, the relief produced an effect the contributors did not intend, as it induced him, when contemplating his removal, to remain in Gawsworth, where Providence had so unexpectedly

---

* John Machin was then minister of Astbury, and an intimate friend as well as neighbour of Newcome's.

relieved him of his anxieties by their liberality. He painted his rectory-house, parted off a little study from his parlour, and spent what he could of his friends' bounty in smartening his home and making it pleasant and comfortable.

Newcome was not allowed to remain long in undisturbed tranquillity in his quiet parsonage. On the 3rd November, 1656, Mr. Hollinworth died; four days later a meeting of the "Classis" was held at Manchester to nominate to the vacancy. Three persons were mentioned as suitable—Mr. Meeke, of Salford ; Mr. Bradshaw, of Macclesfield; and Mr. Newcome, of Gawsworth— but the feeling was so unanimous in favour of Newcome that nothing was said about the other two. Friday, December 5th, was fixed for the election ; but here a difficulty occurred. Newcome had spent a Sunday at Shrewsbury as well as at Manchester. He had preached at "Alkmond's, and the people of Julian's" (there were no saints in Puritanical times) "set their affections" upon him while ministering in the neighbouring church, and by a curious coincidence, on the same day that he received intelligence of the arrangement at Manchester he received letters from the people of "Julian's," from the Mayor of Shrewsbury, and from three of its ministers, entreating him to accept their invitation. On the Sunday preceding the election at Manchester he preached in the Old Church, and, as he tells us, "the women were so pleased that they would needs send tokens," which amounted to seven pounds. This gave great dissatisfaction to the proud Salopians, who were evidently afraid the young preacher might not be proof against the fascinations of the "Lancashire Witches," and so they "gave him a very unhandsome lash" for being drawn away from them by "women's favours." Angry contentions arose, Richard Baxter was asked to interfere, and a conference was suggested, but the good folks of Shrewsbury were resolved upon securing the services of Newcome, and would not agree to arbitration, or listen to any other proposition. They were doomed, however, to disappointment, and, in opposition to the advice of Baxter, Newcome, on the 24th of December, made choice of Manchester.

His removal from Gawsworth was a sorrowful time both for himself and his rustic congregation. The sight of the wagons sent to remove his furniture overwhelmed him with sorrow, and when the time came for leaving the old rectory, he says, "I was sadly affected, and broken all to pieces at leaving the house. I never was so broken in duty as I was in that which I went into just when we were ready to go out of the house;" and he adds, "I prayed the Lord the sin of the seven years might be forgiven us, and that we might take a pardon with us." On his arrival in Manchester he was welcomed with extraordinary manifestations of friendship and pleasure, and many of the townspeople went out to Stockport to meet him.

This "prince of preachers," as he has been called by his friends, continued his ministrations in the Church at Manchester until the passing of the Act of Uniformity, when, unable to conform to the discipline of the Church, he withdrew from her communion, to the great grief of his people, by whom he was greatly beloved. On the passing of the Act of Toleration, at the accession of William of Orange, the wealthy Presbyterians of Manchester gathered round their favourite divine and built him a tabernacle on the site of the present Unitarian Chapel in Cross Street—the first erected for the use of the Nonconformist body in the town. He was not long permitted, however, to continue his ministrations, his death occurring on the 17th September, 1695, little more than a year after the opening of the "great and fair meeting house."

The church in which Newcome ministered, and where rest the bones of so many of the "Fighting Fittons," well deserves a careful examination. Let us bend our footsteps towards the ancient fane. It is a fair and goodly structure—small, it is true, but presenting a dignified and pleasing exterior—

Beauty with age in every feature blending.

The bold, free hand of the old English architect is seen in every detail—in the deep mouldings, the varied tracery, and the quaintly grotesque carvings, where burlesque and satire and playful fancy have almost run riot. The restoring hand of the modern renovator—Sir Gilbert Scott—is also visible ; but what he has done has been well done, and, if we except the interesting examples of mediæval art to which reference has already been made, every-thing that was worth retaining has been carefully preserved. Though erected at different times, the general features harmonise and point to the conclusion that nearly the whole of the existing fabric was erected in the period extending from the end of the 14th to the middle of the 15th centuries.

The nave, which is three bays in length, is undoubtedly the oldest part, and the point at which it originally terminated is clearly shown by the diagonal projection of the angle buttress which still remains. The chancel appears to have superseded an older foun-dation of smaller dimensions. It is of equal width with the nave, and, in fact, a continuation of it, and both are covered in with a timber roof of obtuse pitch, with elaborately moulded and orna-mented beams and rafters. The external walls of both the nave and chancel are surmounted by an embattled parapet, relieved at intervals with crocketted pinnacles, that are carried above the edge of the parapet wall as a termination to each buttress. There being no clerestory or side aisles, the windows are unusually lofty. They are of pointed character, with traceried heads and mouldings, terminating in curiously-carved corbels, that have afforded scope for the humorous fancy of the mediæval masons. On the south side is an open porch with stone seats, that has at some time or other been added to the original structure, as evidenced by the fact that the greater portion of the buttress has been cut away where it is joined up to the main wall. It has coupled lights on each side, with hood mouldings, the one on the west terminating in a curiously-carved corbel, representing a rose with two heads enclosed in the petals, an evidence that this part of the fabric must have been built shortly after the union of the rival houses of York and Lancaster, in the persons of Henry VII. and Elizabeth the eldest daughter of Edward IV. The tower is well proportioned, and, rising gracefully as it does above the surrounding foliage, forms a conspicuous object for miles around. It is remarkable for

the armorial shields, 14 in number, carved in relief, in stone, on
each face. These insignia are especially interesting to the antiquary
and the genealogist, as showing the alliances of the earlier lords
of Gawsworth. They include the coats of Fitton, Orreby, Bechton,
Mainwaring, Wever, Egerton, Grosvenor, and Davenport, as well
as those of Fitton of Bollin, and Fitton of Pownall, and there is
one also containing the arms of Randle Blundeville, Earl of
Chester, with whom the Fittons appear to have been connected.

The interior of the church is picturesque and well cared for, and
the garrulous old lady who brought us the keys looks upon it with
an affection that is not diminished by the serving and tending of
many long years.   It is an interesting specimen of an old English
house of worship.   As you cross the threshold a host of memories
are conjured up, and you feel that you are in the sanctuary where
in times past have communed, and where now rest, the remains of
a line famous in chivalry, the members of which, in their day and
generation, did good service to the State.   The seats are low and
open, and the appearance has been greatly improved by the
removal of the heavy cumbrous pews with which until late years
it was filled.   At the east end, within the chancel rails, are the
effigies and stately tombs of the Fittons already described.   The
shadows of centuries seem to fall on the broad nave, while the
slanting rays of the westering sun, as they steal through the tall
windows, brighten the elaborate figures of the knights in armour,
and bring out the colouring of gown and kirtle, where their stately
dames are reposing by their side.   During the restorations some of
them were removed from their original positions, and shorn of their
original canopies, as the inscription upon a tablet affixed to the
north wall testifies.   Near the centre of the aisle is a plain marble
slab with a brass fillet surrounding it, on which is an inscription
commemorating the marriage and death of Thomas Fitton of
Siddington, the second son of Sir Edward of Gawsworth, by his
wife Mary, the daughter of Sir Guiscard Harbottle.

After our brief survey we passed out through the western door
into the churchyard.   The sun was circling westwards over the

woods, a warm haze suffused the landscape, and the shadows were lengthening over the hillocks and grass-grown mounds in the quiet graveyard. As our cicerone turned the key in the rusty wards of the lock and turned to depart, a robin poured out its wealth of song in the neighbouring copse, a fitting requiem to the expiring day. We stood for a moment looking through the trees at the picturesque old parsonage. What a lovely spot!—the spot of all others that a country clergyman might delight to pass his days in. Well might good Henry Newcome be "sadly affected and broken all to pieces" at leaving it.

Another celebrity connected with Gawsworth, though of a widely different character to Henry Newcome, deserves a passing notice— Samuel Johnson, popularly known by the title of "Lord Flame," and sometimes by the less euphonious *sobriquet* of "Maggotty Johnson." This eccentric character was well known in his day as a dancing master, to which he added the professions of poet, player, jester, and musician. He appears to have been among the last of the paid English jesters, those professional Merry Andrews whose presence was considered indispensable in the homes of our wealthier forefathers—their duty being to promote laughter in the household, and especially at meals, by their ready wit and drollery. Johnson was frequently hired out at parties given by the gentry in the northern counties, where he had licence to bandy his witticisms, and to utter or enact anything likely to enliven the company or provoke them to laughter. "Lord Flame" was the name of a character played by him in his own extravaganza, entitled "Hurlothrumbo, or the Supernatural," a piece which had a lengthened run at the Haymarket in 1729. It is upon this burlesque that his fame chiefly rests. After much patient labour he succeeded in getting it on the London boards. Byrom records the circumstance in his "Journal" under date April 2, 1729:—

As for Mr. Johnson, he is one of the chief topics of talk in London. Dick's Coffee-house resounds "Hurlothrumbo" from one end to the other. He had a full house and much good company on Saturday night, the first time of acting, and report says all the boxes are taken for the next Monday. . . . It is impossible to describe this play and the oddities,

out-of-the-wayness, flights, madness, comicalities, &c.   I hope Johnson will
make his fortune by it at present.   We had seven or eight garters in the pit.
I saw Lord Oxford and two or more there, but was so intent on the farce
that I did not observe many quality that were there.   We agreed to laugh
and clap beforehand, and kept our word from beginning to end.   The night
after Johnson came to Dick's, and they all got about him like so many bees.
They say the Prince of Wales has been told of " H," and will come and
see it. . . .   For my own part, who think all stage plays stuff and
nonsense, I consider this a joke upon 'em all.

On the same day, in a letter to Mrs. Byrom, he writes—

Mrs. Hyde must let her brother teach (dancing), for " Hurlothrumbo," as
the matter stands, will hardly be quitted while it brings a house, and consequently more money, into the author's pocket, than his teaching would
do of a long time.

The play was afterwards published with a dedication to Lady
Delves, and an address to Lord Walpole.   The former, while
remarkable for its extravagant panegyrism, is interesting from its
reference to many of the local female celebrities of the time.   It
is as follows :—

To the Right Honourable the Lady Delves.

Madam,—When I think of your goodness, it gives me encouragement to
put my play under your grand protection ; and if you can find anything in it
worthy of your Praise, I am sure the *super-naturals* will like it.   I do not
flatter when I say your taste is universal, great as an Empress, sweet and
refined as Lady *Malpas*, sublime as Lady *Mary Cowper*, learned and complete as *Lady Conway*, distinguished and clear as Mrs. *Madan*, gay, good,
and innocent as Lady *Bland*.   I have often thought you were a compound
of the world's favourites—that all meet and rejoice together in one : the
taste of a *Montague, Wharton*, or Meredith, Stanhope, Sneid, or Byrom ;
the integrity and hospitality of *Leigh* of *Lime*, the wit and fire of *Bunbury*,
the sense of an Egerton, fervent to serve as *Beresford* or *Mildmay*, beloved
like *Gower*.   If you was his rival, you'd weaken the strength of that most
powerful subject.   I hope your eternal unisons in heaven will always sing
to keep up the harmony in your soul, that is musical as Mrs. Leigh, and
never ceases to delight ; raises us in raptures like *Amante Shosa, Lord Essex*,
or the sun.   If every pore in every body in Cheshire was a mouth they
would all cry out aloud, *God save the Lady Delves !*   That illuminates the
minds of mortals, inspires with Musick and Poetry especially.

Your most humble servant,   LORD FLAME.

The prologue was written by Mr. Amos Meredith, of Henbury,
near Macclesfield, and, at the urgent request of its author, Byrom
was induced to write the epilogue.   Johnson's subsequent career

was marked by many whims and oddities, and even death was not permitted to terminate his eccentricity, his very grave being made to commemorate it for the amusement or pity of future generations. As we have previously stated, he is buried in a small plantation of firs near the road, and a short distance from the New Hall, in accordance with a request he had made to the owner in his life-time. His remains are covered by a plain brick tomb, now much dilapidated, on the uppermost slab of which is the following inscription :—

Under this stone
Rest the remains of Mr. SAMUEL JOHNSON,
Afterwards ennobled with the grander Title of
LORD FLAME,
Who, after being in his life distinct from other Men
By the Eccentricities of his Genius.
Chose to retain the same character after his Death,
and was, at his own Desire, buried here, May 5th,
A.D. MDCCLXXIII., Aged 82.
Stay thou whom Chance directs, or Ease persuades,
To seek the Quiet of these Sylvan shades,
Here undisturbed and hid from Vulgar Eyes,
A Wit, Musician, Poet, Player, lies
A Dancing Master too, in Grace he shone,
And all the arts of Opera were his own ;
In Comedy well skill'd, he drew Lord Flame,
Acted the Part, and gain'd himself the Name ;
Averse to Strife, how oft he'd gravely say
These peaceful Groves should shade his breathless clay ;
That when he rose again, laid here alone,
No friend and he should quarrel for a Bone ;
Thinking that were some old lame Gossip nigh,
She possibly might take his Leg or Thigh.

20

On the west side of his tomb a flat stone has been placed in later years, on which some rhyming moralist has sought to improve on his character, in a religious point of view, in a lengthy inscription which says more for the writer's sense of piety than his regard for prosody :—

> If chance hath brought thee here, or curious eyes,
> To see the spot where this poor jester lies,
> A thoughtless jester even in his death,
> Uttering his jibes beyond his latest breath ;
> O stranger, pause a moment, pause and say :
> " To-morrow should'st thou quit thy house of clay,
> Where wilt thou be, my soul ?—in paradise ?
> Or where the rich man lifted up his eyes ? "
> Immortal spirit would'st thou then be blest,
> Waiting thy perfect bliss on Abraham's breast ;
> Boast not of silly art, or wit, or fame,
> Be thou ambitious of a Christian's name ;
> Seek not thy body's rest in peaceful grove,
> Pray that thy soul may rest in Jesus' love.
> O speak not lightly of that dreadful day,
> When all must rise in joy or in dismay ;
> When spirits pure in body glorified
> With Christ in heavenly mansions shall abide,
> While wicked souls shall hear the Judge's doom —
> " Go ye accursed into endless gloom,"
> Look on that stone and this, and ponder well :
> Then choose 'twixt life and death, 'twixt
> Heaven and Hell.

Poor Johnson ! His last whim has been gratified : his "breathless clay" reposes beneath the "sylvan shade" that in life he so much delighted in. The thrush and the blackbird sing their orisons and vespers there ; the fresh and fragrant breeze sweeps by ; and the nodding trees that rustle overhead cast a verdant gloom around, that is brightened only where the warm sunlight steals through the intricacy of leaves and dapples the sward with touches of golden light. May no rude or irreverent hand disturb his resting-place, or "old lame gossip" share his sepulchre.

John Dee:.
Warden.:.

CHAPTER V.

F those who make up the mighty tide of human life that daily sweeps along the great highway of traffic between the Manchester Exchange and the Victoria Railway Station, how few there are who ever give even a passing thought to the quaint mediæval relic that stands within a few yards of them—almost the only relic of bygone days that Manchester now possesses—the College. Pass through the arched portal into the great quadrangle, the College Yard as it is called, and what a striking contrast is presented. Without, all is noise and hurry and bustle ; within, quietude and seclusion prevail. The old place is almost the only link that connects the Manchester of the present with the Manchester of yore ; and surely it is something to feel that within this eager, striving, money-getting Babylon there is a little Zoar where you may escape from the turmoil, and the whirl, and the worry of the busy city, and, forgetting your own chronology, allow the memory to wander along the dim grass-grown aisles of antiquity, recalling the scenes and episodes and half-forgotten incidents that illustrate the changes society has undergone, and show how the past may be made a guide for the present and the future.

A wealth of interest gathers round this old time-worn memorial, and its history is entwined with that of the town itself. That lively and imaginative antiquary, Whitaker, has striven to prove that upon its site the subjects of the Cæsars erected their summer camp, but the story, it must be confessed, rests on but a slender foundation. There is little doubt, however, that the Saxon thegn fixed his abode here, and dispensed justice according to the rude fashion of the times —which means that he did what seemed right in his own eyes, and hanged those who ventured to question the propriety of his proceedings. The Norman barons who succeeded him, the Gresleys and the La Warres, the men who bore themselves well and bravely at Crecy, Agincourt, and Poictiers, held their court here for generations, until good old Thomas La Warre, the last of the line, the priest-lord as he has been called—for he held the rectory as well as the barony of Manchester—gave up his ancestral home as a permanent residence for the warden and fellows of the ancient parish church which he caused to be collegiated. But the splendid provision he bequeathed was not long enjoyed by the ecclesiastics for whom it was intended. In 1547, when the minor religious houses were suppressed, the college was dissolved, and the lands, with the building of the College House, reverted to Edward VI., who granted them to Edward Earl of Derby, subject to the payment by him of some small pensions and other charges. On Queen Mary's accession the Church was re-collegiated, and the deeds of alienation in part recalled. But the College House and the lands pertaining to it were never recovered, though some of the wardens were considerately allowed by the Stanleys to occupy part of the premises that had belonged of right to their predecessors.

In the eventful times which followed, the building experienced many and various vicissitudes. At the time the fierce struggle between Charles I. and the Parliament began a part was used as a magazine for powder and arms, for we read that when the Commission of Array was issued Sir Alexander Radcliffe, of Ordsall, and his neighbour Mr. Prestwich, of Hulme, two of the commissioners nominated in the King's proclamation, attended by the under sheriff, went to Manchester " to seize ten barrels of powder and several bundles of match which were stowed in a room of the

College." During the troublous times of the Commonwealth the building was in the hands of the official sequestrators, as part of the forfe:ted possessions of the Royalist Earl of Derby; and at that time the monthly meetings of the Presbyterian Classis, the "X'sian consciensious people" as they were called, were held within the refectory. A part of the building was transformed into a prison, and another portion was occupied as private dwellings. In 1650, as appears by a complaint lodged in the Duchy Court of Lancaster, "a common brewhouse" was set up on the premises, the brewers claiming exemption from grinding their malt at the School Mills, to which by custom the toll belonged, on the plea that the brewhouse was within the College, the old baronial residence, and therefore did not owe such suit and service to the mills.

About the same time a portion of the College barn (between the prison and the College gatehouse) was converted into a workhouse, the first in Manchester, having been acquired by the churchwardens and overseers in order that it might be " made in readiness to set the poor people on work to prevent their begging." Another part was used for the purposes of an Independent church, the first of the kind in the town, and which woul l appear to have been set up without " waiting for a civil sanction." The minister was John Wigan, who at the outset of his career had been episcopally ordained to Gorton, which place he left in 1646, and fixed his abode at Birch, where, we are told, "he set up Congregationalism." This brought him in collision with the " Classis." Subsequently he left Birch, entered the army, became a captain, and afterwards a major. The church which he founded in the College barn is alluded to by Hollinworth. How it came to be established here would be inexplicable but for the explanation Adam Martindale gives of the matter. He says :—

The Colledge lands being sold, and the Colledge itself, to Mr. Wigan, who now being turned Antipædobaptist, and I know not what more, made a barne there into a chappell, where he and many of his perswasion preached doctrine diametrically opposite to the (Presbyterian) ministers' perswasion under their very nose.

Wigan had contrived to attract the notice of Cromwell, and "received some maintenance out of the sequestrations." Whether with this and from pillage and plunder while with the Republican army he obtained money enough to purchase the lease of the College is not clear, but his conduct during the later years of his life does not present him in a very favourable light. During his time a survey of the College property was made, and it then comprised :—

> Ye large building called ye College in Manchester, consisting of many rooms, with twoe barnes, one gatehouse, verie much decayd, one parcell of ground, formerly an orchard, and one garden, now in ye possession of Joseph Werden, gent., whose pay for ye same for ye use of ye Commonwealth—tenn pounds yearly. There is likewise one other room in ye said College Reserved and now made use of for publique meetings of X'sian consciensious people (*i.e.*, the Classis).

Neither the sequestrators nor Mr. Wigan were at much pains to preserve the fabric of the College while it was in their hands. The building and outhousing fell into decay, and became ruinous ; and there is little doubt this interesting relic would have disappeared altogether but for the timely interposition of one of Manchester's most worthy sons. Humphrey Chetham, a wealthy trader, who had amassed a considerable fortune, conceived the idea of founding an hospital for the maintenance and education of poor boys, and also the establishing of a public library in his native town. He entered into negotiations with the sequestrators for the purchase of the College, then, as we have seen, in a sadly dilapidated condition, for the purpose. Owing to some dispute, the project remained for a time in abeyance, but it was never entirely abandoned ; and in his will Chetham directed that his executors should make the purchase, if it could be accomplished. After his death this was done, the building was repaired, and from that time to the present, a period of more than two hundred years, it has continued to be occupied in accordance with the founder's benevolent intentions. Thus has been preserved to Manchester one of its oldest and most interesting memorials.

> Many and strange vicissitudes of fate
> Those time-worn walls have seen. The dwelling once
> Of servants of the Lord ; in stormy days,
> The home of Cromwell's stern and armèd band,
> A barracks and a prison ! Now it stands
> A lasting monument of Chetham's fame,
> Unto posterity a boon most rich—
> A refuge for the child of poverty,
> A still secluded haunt for studious men,
> The college of a merchant.

Though a mighty change has been wrought in the surroundings, the ancient pile looks pretty much the same as it must have done three centuries ago, when Warden Dee, who then occupied it, was casting horoscopes and practising alchemy, and when Drayton saw it, and in his "Polyolbion" made the Irwell sing—

> First Roche, a dainty rill, . . .
>   And Irk add to my store,
> And Medlock to their much by lending somewhat more ;
> At Manchester they meet, all kneeling to my state,
> Where brave I show myself.

The Irwell and the Irk still mingle their waters round the base of the rocky precipice on which the College stands, but alas for the daintiness or bravery of either !

As you enter the spacious courtyard a long, low, monastic-looking pile with two projecting wings meets the eye, presenting all that quaintness and picturesque irregularity of outline so characteristic of buildings of the mediæval period, with scarcely a feature to suggest the busy life that is going on without its walls. On the right is the great arched gateway giving admission from the Long Mill Gate, and which in old times constituted the main entrance. At the opposite or north-western angle is the principal entrance to the building itself. As you pass through the low portal you notice on the right the great kitchen, large and lofty and open to the roof, with its fireplace capacious enough to roast an ox ; adjoining is the pantry, and close by that most important adjunct the buttery. On the other side of the vestibule, and separated

11

from it by a ponderous oaken screen, panelled and ornamented,
and black with age, is the ancient refectory or dining hall, where
the recipients of Chetham's bounty assemble daily for their meals
and chant their "*Non nobis.*" It is a spacious apartment, with a
lofty arched roof and wide yawning fireplace, preserving not merely
the original form and appearance but the identical arrangement of
the old baronial and conventual halls. In pre-Reformation times
this was the chief entertaining room, and its appearance suggests
the idea that in those remote days the ecclesiastics of Manchester
loved good cheer, and were by no means sparing in their
hospitalities. At the further end, opposite the screen, may still be
seen the ancient daïs, raised a few inches above the general level
of the floor, on which, in accordance with custom, was placed the
" hie board," or table dormant, at which sat the warden, his
principal guests and the chief ecclesiastics ranged according to
their rank above the salt, whilst the inferior clergy and others were
accommodated at the side tables—the poor wandering mendicant
who, by chance, found himself at the door, and being admitted to
a humble share of the feast, taking his position near the screen,
and thankfully fed, like Lazarus, with the crumbs that fell from the
great man's table.

At the further end of the vestibule you come upon the cloisters
surrounding a small court, and note the crumbling grey walls and
vaulted passages of this the most perfect and most characteristic
portion of the original building.

Just before reaching the cloisters, you ascend by a stone staircase, guarded by massive oak balusters, that leads up to the library,
where, as "Alick" Wilson sings—

> Booath far and woide,
> Theer's yards o' books at every stroide,
> From top to bothum, eend and soide.

They are disposed in wall cases extending the length of the
corridors, and branching off into a series of mysterious-looking
little recesses, stored with material relics of the past, old manuscripts, and treasures of antiquity and art of various kinds, each

recess being protected from the encroachments of the profane by
its own lattice gate. Here

> The dim windows shed a solemn light,

that is quite in keeping with the character of the place, and as you
pass along you marvel at the plenteous store of ponderous folios
and goodly quartos, in their plain sober bindings, that are ranged
on either side, and you reflect upon the world of thought and the
profundity of learning gathered together, until the mind becomes
impressed with a feeling of reverence for the mighty spirits whose
noblest works are here enshrined.

Until late years this gloomy corridor was at once a library and
museum. High up on the ceiling, on the tops of the bookcases
and in the window recesses, were displayed a formidable array of
sights and monsters, as varied and grotesque as those which
appalled the heart of the Trojan prince in his descent to hell—
skeletons, snakes, alligators, to say nothing of the "hairy man,"
and such minor marvels as Queen Elizabeth's shoe, Oliver Cromwell's sword,

> An th' clog fair crackt by thunner-bowt,
> An th' woman noather lawmt nor nowt.

Formerly, at Easter and other festivals, crowds of gaping holiday
folk thronged the College, and gazed with vacant wonderment
at the incongruous collection, while the blue-coated cicerones,
to the discomfort of the readers, in sonorous tones bawled
out the names of the trophies displayed, concluding their
catalogue with an account of the wondrous wooden cock that is
said (and truly) to crow when it smells roast beef. But the
quietude is no longer broken by these inharmonious chantings—
the strange collection has been transferred to a more fitting home,
and the scholar may now store his mind with "the physic of the
soul," and hold pleasant intercourse with antiquity without being
rudely recalled to the consciousness of the present by such
startling incongruities.

At the end of the corridor a heavy oaken door admits you to the
reading-room, a large square antique chamber, with arched ceiling
and panelled walls, and a deeply-recessed oriel opposite the door,
that by the very cosiness of its appearance lures you to stay and
drink " at the pure well of English undefiled." In the window
lighting this pleasant secluded nook is a shield on which the arms
of the benevolent Chetham are depicted in coloured glass—arms
that gave him much trouble to obtain, and the cost of which led
him to facetiously remark that they were not depicted in such good
metal as that in which payment for them was made, to which
Lightbowne, his attorney, assented, sagely observing, " there is soe
much difference betwixt Paynter's Gould and Current Coyne," a
conclusion the correctness of which we will not stay to dispute.
No doubt it was the thought that he had " paid for his whistle"
that led the careful old merchant to adopt the suggestive motto,
" *Quod tuum tene.*" The furniture corresponds with the ancient
character of the room. In one corner is a carved oak buffet of
ancient date, with a raised inscription, setting forth that it was the
gift of Humphrey Chetham. There are ponderous chairs, with
leather-padded backs, studded with brass nails; and still more
ponderous tables, one of which we are gravely assured contains as
many pieces as there are days in the year. Over the fireplace,
surmounted by his coat of arms, is a portrait of the grave-visaged
but large-hearted founder, with pillars on each side, resting on
books, and crowned with antique lamps, suggestive of the founder's
desire to diffuse wisdom and happiness by the light of knowledge ;
and, flanking them, on one side is a pelican feeding its young with
its own blood, and on the other the veritable wooden cock already
mentioned; antique mirrors are affixed to the panelling; and dingy-
looking portraits of Lancashire worthies gaze at you from the walls—
Nowell and Whitaker, and Bolton and Bradford, with men who
have reflected lustre upon the county in more recent times, not the
least interesting being the two portraits lately added of the
venerable president of the Chetham Society, and that indefatigable
bibliopole, the late librarian, Mr. Jones.

On the ground floor, beneath the reading-room, is an apartment of corresponding dimensions, which at present more especially claims our attention. It is commonly known as the Feoffees' room; but in bygone days it was appropriated to the use of the wardens of the College. It is a large, square, sombre-looking chamber, with a projecting oriel at one end, and small pointed windows, with deep sills and latticed panes, that, if they do not altogether "exclude the light," are yet sufficiently dim to "make a noonday night." As you cross the threshold your footsteps echo on the hard oak floor—all else is still and silent. A staid cloistered gloom, and a quiet, half monastic air pervades the place that carries your fancies back to mediæval times. The walls for a considerable height are covered with black oak wainscotting, surrounded by a plaster frieze enriched with arabesque work. The ceiling is divided into compartments by deeply-moulded beams and rafters that cross and recross each other in a variety of ways, all curiously wrought, and ornamented at the intersections with carvings of fabulous creatures and grotesque faces. On one of the bosses is a grim-visaged head, depicted as in the act of devouring a child, which tradition affirms is none other than that of the giant Tarquin, who held threescore and four of King Arthur's knights in thraldom in his castle at Knot Mill, and was afterwards himself there slain by the valorous Sir Lancelot of the Lake, who cut off his head and set the captives free; all which forms a very pretty story, though we are more inclined to believe that the mediæval sculptor, thinking little and caring less for Tarquin or the Arthurian knights, merely copied the model of some pagan mason, and reproduced the burlesque figure of Saturn eating one of his own children.* On one side of the room is a broad fireplace, with the armorial ensigns of one of the Tudor sovereigns behind, and those of the benevolent Chetham on the frieze above. The whole of the furniture is in character with the

---

* In the church of Mont Mijour there is a bracket on which is carved a head devouring a child, closely resembling the one in the warden's room of the College, and supposed to be intended for a caricature of Saturn.

place—quaint, old-fashioned, and substantial. Shining tall-backed chairs are disposed around the room, and in the centre is a broad table of such massiveness as almost to defy the efforts of muscular power to remove it.

A special interest attaches to this sombre-looking chamber from the circumstance that tradition has associated it with the name of Dr. Dee, the "Wizard Warden" of Manchester, and that here Roby has laid the scene of one of his most entertaining Lancashire Legends. In this "vaulted room of gramarye," it is said, our English "Faust" had his

Mystic implements of magic might,

practised the occult sciences, cast his nativities, transmuted the baser metals to gold, and, as the common people believed, held familiar intercourse with the Evil One, and did other uncanny things. But of Dee and his doings we purpose to speak anon.

The wardenship of Dr. Dee forms a curious chapter in the ecclesiastical history of Manchester, and at the same time presents us with a humiliating picture of the condition of society in the golden days of the Virgin Queen. It has been said that witchcraft came in with the Stuarts and went out with them; but this is surely an injustice to the memory of Elizabeth's sapient successor, for the belief in sorcery, witchcraft, enchantment, demonology, and practices of a kindred nature were widely prevalent long ere that monarch ascended the English throne. Henry VIII., in 1531, granted a formal licence to "two learned clerks" "to practise sorcery and to build churches," a curious combination of evil and its antidote; and ten years later he, with his accustomed inconsistency, issued a decree making "witchcraft and sorcery felony, without benefit of clergy."

The belief in these abominations was not confined to any one class of the people, or to the professors of any one form of faith. On the contrary, Churchmen, Romanists, and Puritans were alike the dupes of the loathsome impostors who roamed the country, though each in turn was ready to upbraid the others with being believers in the generally prevailing error, and not unfrequently with being participators in the frauds that were practised. The great and munificent Edward, Earl of Derby, " kept a conjuror in his house secretly ;" and his daughter-in-law, Margaret Clifford, Countess of Derby, lost the favour of Queen Elizabeth for a womanish curiosity in " consulting with wizards or cunning men." The bishops gave authority and a form of licence to the clergy to cast out devils ; Romish ecclesiastics claimed to have a monopoly of the power; and the Puritan ministers, not to be behind them, tried their hands at the imposture.

Education had then made little progress, and the men of Lancashire, though the merriest of Englishmen, were as ignorant and superstitious as they were merry. Nowhere was the belief in supernatural agency more rife than in the Palatinate. The shaping power of the imagination had clothed every secluded clough and dingle with the weird drapery of superstition, and made every ruined or solitary tenement the abode of unhallowed beings, who were supposed to hold their diabolical revelries within it. The doctrines of necromancy and witchcraft were in common belief, and it is doubtful if there was a single man in the county who did not place the most implicit faith in both. Hence, Queen Elizabeth, if it was not that she wished to get rid of a troublesome suitor, may have thought there was a fitness of things in preferring a professor of the Black Art to the wardenship of Manchester ; believing, possibly, that one given to astrology, and such like practices, could not find a more congenial home than in a county specially prone, as Lancashire then was, to indulge in *diablerie* and the practice of alchemy and enchantment.

A brief reference to the earlier career of Dr. Dee may not be altogether uninteresting. According to the genealogy drawn up by himself, he belonged to the line of Roderick the Great, Prince of Wales. His father, Rowland Dee, who was descended from a family settled in Radnorshire, carried on the business of a vintner in London ; and there, or rather at Mortlake, within a few miles of the city, on the 13th July, 1527, the future warden first saw the light. After receiving a preliminary education at one or two of the city schools, and subsequently at the Grammar School of Chelmsford, he entered St. John's College, Cambridge, being then only fifteen years of age; and during the five years he remained there he maintained, with unflinching strictness, the rule "only to sleepe four houres every night; to allow to meate and drink (and some refreshing after), two houres every day; and," he adds, "of the other eighteen houres, all (except the tyme of going to and being at divine service) was spent in my studies and learning." On leaving the University he passed some time in the Low Countries, his object being "to speake and conferr with some learned men, and chiefly mathematicians." He made the acquaintance of Frisius, Mercator, Antonius Gogara, and other celebrated Flemings; and on his return to England he was chosen to be a Fellow of King Henry's newly-erected College of Trinity, and made under-reader of the Greek tongue. His reputation stood very high, and his mathematical and astronomical pursuits, in which he was assisted by some rare and curious instruments—among them, as we are told, an "astronomer's staff of brass, that was made of Gemma Frisius' divising; the two great globes of Gerardus Mercator's making; and the astronomer's ring of brass, as Gemma Frisius had newly framed it," which he had brought from Flanders—drew upon him among the common people the suspicion of being a conjuror, an opinion that was strengthened by his getting up at Cambridge a Greek play, the comedy of "Aristophanes," in which, according to his own account, he introduced "the Scarabeus his flying up to Jupiter's pallace, with a man and his basket of victualls on her back; whereat was great wondring, and many vaine reportes spread abroad of the meanes how that was affected." Though causing "great wondring," and seeming at that time too marvellous to be accomplished by human agency, it was in all probability only a clumsy performance, and much inferior to the ordinary transformation scene of a modern pantomime. The "vaine reportes," however, led to Dee's being accused of magical practices, and he found it expedient to leave the

University, having first obtained his degree of Master of Arts. In 1548 he went abroad and entered as a student at Louvain, where his philosophical and mathematical skill brought him under the notice of some of the continental *savants*. Apart from his intellectual power, he must in his earlier years have possessed considerable charms both of person and manner, for he contrived to gain friends and win admiration wherever he went. He was consulted by men of the highest rank and station from all parts of Europe, and before he left Louvain he had the degree of Doctor of Laws conferred upon him.

On quitting that University, in 1550, he proceeded to Paris, where he turned the heads of the French people, who became almost frenzied in their admiration of him. He read lectures on Euclid's Elements—"a thing," as he says, "never done publiquely in any University of Christendome," and his lectures were so fully attended that the mathematical school could not hold all his auditors, who clambered up at the windows and listened at the doors as best they could. A mathematical lectureship, with a yearly stipend of 200 crowns, and several other honourable offices were also offered him from "five Christian Emperors," among them being an invitation from the Muscovite Emperor to visit Moscow, where he was promised an income at the Imperial hands of £2000 a year, his diet free out of the Emperor's kitchen, and to be in dignity and authority among the highest of the nobility; but he preferred to reside in his native country, and, foregoing these inducements, he returned to England in 1551.

The fame of his marvellous acquirements had preceded him, and on his arrival he was presented by Secretary Cecil to the young King, Edward VI., who granted him a pension of 100 crowns a year, which was soon "bettered," as he says, by his "bestowing on me (as it were by exchange) the rec'ory of Upton-upon-Seaverne," in Worcestershire, and to this was added the rectory of Long Leadenham, in Lincolnshire. Though holding these two benefices, it is somewhat remarkable that Dee does not appear to have ever been admitted to Holy Orders. There is no very clear

22

evidence that he at any time occupied his Worcestershire parsonage,
but he must have been resident for a while at Long Leadenham, for
at that place a stone has been found inscribed with his name and
sundry cabalistic figures, indicating that he had at some time lived
in the parish. If he ever resided at Upton-upon-Severn he must
have found an uncongenial neighbour in Bishop Bonner, who then
held the living of Ripple—for the one was visionary, sensitive, and
unpractical, and the other stern, cruel, and unscrupulous, while on
religious and political questions their views were as wide apart as
the poles.

On the 6th of July, 1553, Edward VI. finished his "short but
saintly course," and the solemn sound then heard from the bell-
towers of England, while it announced the fact of his decease,
crushed the hopes of Dee, for a time at least, and in a pro-
portionate degree raised the expectations of Bonner. Mary had
not been many months upon the throne before Dee was accused
of carrying on a correspondence with Princess Elizabeth's servants
and of compassing the Queen's death by means of enchantments.
He was cast into prison and tried upon the charge of high treason,
but acquitted ; after which he was turned over to Bonner to see if
heresy might not be proved against him. Christian martyrdom,
however, was not in Mr. Dee's vocation, and so, after six months'
detention, on giving satisfaction to the Queen's Privy Council, and
entering into recognisances " for ready appearing and good abearing
for four months longer," he was set at liberty August 19, 1555, to
find that during his incarceration his rectory had been bestowed
upon the Dean of Worcester, Bonner having detained him in
captivity in order that he might have the disposal of his preferment. The following characteristic letter, written about this time,
and addressed from the Continent (endorsed "fro Callice to
Bruxells"), has been recently unearthed from among the Marian
State papers by that painstaking antiquary, Mr. J. Eglinton
Bailey, F.S.A., and printed in Mr. Earwaker's "Local Gleanings : "

My dutye premysed unto youre good L'rdshype as hyt apperteynethe.
This daye abowt iiij of the clocke at after noone my L. Chawncelare

(Gardyner) taketh his Jorneye toward England havynge rather made a meane to a peace to be hereafter condyscendyd unto, than a peace at thys tyme yn any pointe determyned. In England all ys quyete. Souch as wrote trayterouse l'res (letters) ynto Germany be apprehendyd as lykewyse oothers yt dyd calculate ye kynge and quene and my Lady Elizabeth natyvytee, wherof on Dee and Cary and butler, and on ooyr of my Lady Elezabeths . . . ar accused and yt they should have a famylyare sp (irit) wch ys ye moore susp'ted, for yt fferys on of ther a(ccu)sers-hadd ymedyatly upon thaccusatys bothe hys chyldr(en) strooken, the on wth put deathe, thother wth blyndnes. Thys trustynge shortly to doe youe yn an ooyr place bettre servyce I bed yowr good Lordshype most hartily to farewell Wryte ffro Cales ye viijth of June.

Yowr Lordshyps most asured

THO. MARTYN.

Happily for Dee, Mary's reign was not of long duration, and on the accession of Elizabeth he was at once restored to the sunshine of Royal favour and courted by the wealthy and the great. He was consulted by Lord Robert Dudley, afterwards Earl of Leicester, by the Queen's desire, respecting "a propitious day" for her coronation, and he says,—

I wrote at large and delivered it for Her Majesty's use, by the commandment of the Lord Robert, what in my judgment the ancient astrologers would determine on the election day of such a time as was appointed for Her Majesty to be crowned in.

At the same time he was presented to the Queen, who made him great promises, not always fulfilled—amongst others, that where her brother Edward "had given him a crown she would give him a noble."

Dee was a great favourite with Elizabeth, who could well appreciate his intellectual power, coupled as it was with some personal graces. She frequently visited him at his house to confer with him and to have peeps at futurity; and nothing perhaps better illustrates the faith the "Virgin Queen" had in his astrological powers than the circumstance of her consulting him, as other virgins in less exalted stations consult "wise men," upon the subject of her matrimonial projects, and also that she had her nativity cast in order to ascertain if she could marry with advantage

to the nation. The credulous Queen placed the most implicit confidence in Dee's predictions. She was full of hope that the genius
and learning which had already worked such wonders would
accomplish yet more, and that he would eventually succeed in
penetrating the two great mysteries—the Elixir Vitæ and the
Philosopher's Stone—those secrets which would endue her with
perpetual youth and fill her treasury with inexhaustible wealth.

The fame of the English seer became more and more widely
spread. Invitations poured in upon him from foreign courts, and
his visits to the Continent became frequent. In 1563 he was at
Venice; the same year, or the one following, he was at Antwerp,
superintending the printing of his "Monas Hyeroglyphica." An
original copy of this work is preserved in the Manchester Free
Library. Casauban acknowledges that, though it was a little book,
he could extract no reason or sense out of it. Possibly he was one
of those who, as Dee says, "dispraised it because they understood
it not." Let us hope Dee's patron was more fortunate, for she had
the advantage of reading it under the guidance of its author, in her
palace at Greenwich, after his return from beyond seas. The book
is dedicated to the Emperor Maximilian, to whom Dee presented it
in person, being at the time, as there is some reason to believe, on
a secret mission, for Lilly says, "he was the Queen's intelligencer,
and had a salary for his maintenance from the Secretaries of State."

After his return, he was sent for on one occasion, "to prevent the
mischief which divers of Her Majesty's Privy Council suspected to
be intended against Her Majesty, by means of a certain image of
wax, with a great pin stuck into it, about the breast of it, found in
Lincoln's Inn Fields," and this, we are told, he did "in a godly
and artificial manner." In 1571 he again went abroad, and while
returning became dangerously ill at Lorraine, where the Queen
despatched two English physicians "with great speed from Hamp-
ton Court," to attend him, "sent him divers rareties to eat, and the
Honourable Lady Sydney to attend on him, and comfort him with
divers speeches from Her Majesty, *pithy* and *gracious*." On his
return he settled in the house which had belonged to his father, at

Mortlake, in Surrey, a building on the banks of the Thames, a little westward of the church. Here for some time he led a life of privacy and study, collecting books and manuscripts, beryls and magic crystals, talismans, &c., his library, it is said, consisting of more than 4,000 volumes, the fourth part of which were MSS., the whole being valued at the time at more than £2,000.

In his "Compendious Rehearsall" there is a curious account of a visit which Elizabeth, attended by many of her Court, made to his house at Mortlake:—

> 1575 10 Martii.—The Queens Majestie, with her Most honourable Privy Councell, and other her lords and nobility, came purposely to have visited my library; but finding that my wife was within four houres before buried out of the house, her Majestie refused to come in; but willed me to fetch my glass so famous, and to shew unto her some of the properties of it, which I did; her Majestie being taken downe from her horse (by the Earle of Leicester, Master of the horse, by the Church wall of Mortlak), did see some of the properties of that glass, to her Majestie's great contentment and delight, and so in most gracious manner did thank me, &c.

The glass is supposed to have been of a convex form, and so managed as to show the reflection of different figures and faces.

On the 8th October, 1578, the Queen had a conference with Dee, at Richmond, and on the 16th of the same month she sent her physician, Dr. Bayly, to confer with him "about her Majestie's grievous pangs and paines by reason of toothake and the rheum, &c.;" and before the close of the year he was sent a journey of over 1,500 miles by sea and land, "to consult with the learned physitions and philosophers (*i.e.* astrologers) beyond the seas for her Majestie's health recovering and preserving; having by the right honourable Earle of Leicester and Mr. Secretary Walsingham but one hundred days allowed to go and come in."

After his return, Elizabeth honoured him with another visit, as appears by the following entry in his "Diary":—

> 1580. Sept. 17th.—The Quene's Majestie came from Rychemond in her coach, the higher way of Mortlak felde, and when she came right against the Church she turned down toward my howse; and when she was against my garden in the felde she stode there a good while, and then came ynto

the street at the great gate of the felde, when she espyed me at my doore
making obeysciens to her Majestie ; she beckend her hand for me ; I came
to her coach side, she very speedily pulled off her glove and gave me her
hand to kiss ; and to be short, asked me to resort to her court, and to give
her to wete when I cam ther.

In less than a month he received another visit from his patron,
when the shadow of death was over his house ; for his mother, who
shared the house at Mortlake with him, had expired a few hours
before the arrival of the Royal party. This time Elizabeth seems
to have come less to please herself than to comfort her favourite :—

Oct. 10th.—The Quene's Majestie, to my great comfort *(hora quinta)*, cam
with her trayn from the court, and at my dore graciously calling me to her,
on horsbak, exhorted me briefly to take my mother's death patiently ; and
withall told me that the Lord Threasorer had gretly commended my doings
for her title, which he had to examyn, which title in two rolls, he had
browght home two hours before ; she remembred allso how at my wive's
death it was her fortune likewise to call uppon me.

The "title" alluded to had reference to the doubts Elizabeth
affected to have as to her right to rule over the new countries that
were at the time being discovered by her gallant sea captains,
when, to ease her scruples, she had desired Dee to give her a full
account of the newly-found regions. This he did in a few days,
producing two large rolls, which he delivered to the Queen "in the
garden at Richmond ; " and in which not only the geography, but
also the history, of the English colonies throughout the world was
given at length. Dee must have made a liberal draught upon his
imagination in producing such a work ; and Elizabeth, credulous
as she was, could hardly have looked upon his account of Virginia
or Florida or Newfoundland as trustworthy history. She wished
to believe it, however, and therefore signified her gracious approval
of Dee's production, much to the disgust of Burleigh, who in the
Queen's presence openly expressed his disbelief ; and when, four
days later, Dee attended at the Lord Treasurer's house, he refused
to admit him, and when he came forth, as he says, "did not, or
would not, speak to me, I doubt not of some new grief conceyved."
On further examination of the writings, Burleigh's misgivings may

have been removed, or, as is much more likely, deeming it unwise
to provoke a quarrel with one whom the Queen delighted to
honour, he strove to make amends for his discourtesy, for he sent
Dee a haunch of venison three weeks after. Though the breach
was healed, the scholar's fear of the Lord Treasurer was not
altogether dispelled, if we may judge from a dream with which he
was troubled shortly afterwards, when, as he says—

I dreamed that I was deade; and afterwards my bowels were taken out.
I walked and talked with diverse, and among other with the Lord Threasorer,
who was come to my house to burn my bones when I was dead, and thought
he looked sourely on me.

Mr. Disraeli, in his "Amenities of Literature," rightly estimated
the character of the "Wizard Warden" of Manchester when he
remarked that "the imagination of Dee often predominated over
his science—while both were mingling in his intellectual habits,
each seemed to him to confirm the other. Prone to the mystical
lore of what was termed the occult sciences, which in reality are
no sciences at all, since whatever remains occult ceases to be
science, Dee lost his better genius." Casaubon maintains that
throughout he acted with sincerity, but this may be very well
doubted. It is true that until he dabbled in magical arts he gave
most of his time and talents to science and literature, but in the
later years of his life he laid aside every pursuit that did not aid in
his alchemical and magical studies, and rapidly degenerated into
the mere necromancer and adventurer. Conjuror or not, he
sported with conjuror's tools; and when in the ardour of his
enthusiasm he claimed to hold intercourse with angelic beings
whom he could summon to his presence at his will, and boasted
the possession of a crystal given him by the Angel Uriel, which
enabled him to reveal all secrets, he naturally subjected himself to
suspicions which, as he afterwards lamented, "tended to his utter
undoing."

Many of the incidents of his life are recorded in his "Private
Diary," edited for the Camden Society by Mr. J. Orchard Halliwell,
and the portion relating to the period of his wardenship of Man-

chester has since been edited from the autograph MSS. in the Bodleian Library, with copious notes, and the errors of the Camden edition corrected by Mr. J. Eglinton Bailey. This journal gives a curious insight into the private life and real character of the strange yet simple-minded writer, relating, as it does with much circumstantial detail, his family affairs, his labours and rewards, and his trials and tribulations. There are notes of the visits paid to him by great people; of his attendances at Court; entries of those who consulted him as to the casting of their nativities; particulars of moneys borrowed from time to time (for, though he received large fees and presents, he was almost continuously in a state of impecuniosity); and the ordinary small talk of a common-place book. On the 15th June, 1579, his mother surrendered the house at Mortlake to him, with reversion to his wife and his heirs. On the 5th February in the preceding year he had married, as his second wife, a daughter of Mr. Bartholomew Fromonds, of East Cheam, a fellow-worker in alchemical pursuits, the lady being 23 years of age and Dee 51. They do not appear to have had many sympathies in common. She was a strong-minded, shrewd, managing woman, with a somewhat vixenish temper, who exercised considerable influence over her visionary and unpractical husband, and kept him in awe of her, though not sufficiently to restrain his reckless expenditure on books, manuscripts, and scientific instruments. Occasionally he complains of her irritability, but it must be confessed that, with her domestic cares, the worry of her "mayds," the sickness of her children, and the difficulty she had in getting from her mystical husband sufficient money for the needful expenses of her household, the poor woman had anxieties enough to try the most enduring patience and sour the sweetest temper. On one occasion he writes: "Jane most desperately angry in respect of her maydes;" at another time he puts up a prayer to the angels that she may be cured of some malady that so she may "be of a quieter mind, and not so testy and fretting as she hath been." And again, "Katharin (a child under eight years) by a blow on the eare given by her mother did bled at the nose very much, which did stay for an howre and more; afterward she did walk into the town with nurse; upon her coming home she bled agayn."

Though Dee was much noticed and flattered by Elizabeth, the preferment she so often promised him was slow in coming; perhaps it was that the calculating Queen wished to ascertain the full value of his horoscope, which could be only done by the efflux of time, though, if the prosperity of her reign depended upon the day he had chosen for her coronation, she then had abundant proof of his magical skill. Dee was beginning to lose heart, his finances were getting low, he was in the usurer's hands, and his pecuniary obligations were disquieting him. At this time came the crisis of his life. In 1581 he formed the disastrous friendship with Kelly, whom he took into his service as an assistant in his alchemical and astrological labours.

This individual, whose dealings in the Black Art would fill a volume, was a crafty and unscrupulous schemer—a clever rogue, who, without a tithe of the learning or genius of Dee, contrived to work upon his credulity to such an extent that Dee believed him to have the power of seeing, hearing, and holding "conversations with spirituall creatures" that were invisible and inaudible to Dee himself. Kelly, who was nearly thirty years the junior of Dee, having been born in 1555, "left Oxford," says Mr. John Eglinton Bailey, in his admirable notes to the reprint of Dee's "Diary," "abruptly to ramble in Lancashire," and for some delinquencies, coining it is said, had his ears cut off at Lancaster. Mr. Bailey says that he had been a lawyer, and Lilly states on the authority of his sister that he had practised as an apothecary at Worcester. Of a restless, roving, and ambitious disposition, he was

> Everything by turns, and nothing long.

It was his practice to raise the dead by incantations, and to consult the corpse for the purpose of obtaining a knowledge, as he pretended, of the fate of the living. Weever, in his "Ancient Funeral Monuments" (p. 45), says that upon a certain night in

23

the park of Walton-le-Dale, near Preston, with one Paul Wareing, of Clayton Brook, he invoked one of the infernal regiment to know certain passages in the life, as also what might be known of the devil's foresight of the manner and time of the death, of a young nobleman in Wareing's wardship. The ceremony being ended, Kelly and his companion repaired to the church of Walton, where they dug up the body of a man recently interred, and whom, by their incantations, they made to deliver strange predictions concerning the same gentleman, who was probably present and anxious to read a page in the book of futurity. This feat, which was no doubt performed by a kind of ventriloquism, is also mentioned by Casaubon. It is not said when the circumstance occurred, but a local historian, anxious to supply the omission, gives the date August 12, 1560, and says that Dee was present. This, however, must be an error, for Kelly could then have been only five years of age, and Dee did not make his acquaintance until long afterwards.

Kelly was a notorious alchemist and necromancer long before Dee became associated with him, and after the unfortunate intimacy commenced he acted as his amanuensis, and performed for him the office of "seer," by looking into the doctor's magic crystal,* a faculty he himself did not possess, and hence he was obliged to have recourse to Kelly for the revelations from the spirit world. It would seem, therefore, that " mediums " are by no means a modern invention. Dee says he was brought into unison

---

* Dee's magic crystal, or show stone, was preserved at Strawberry Hill until that famous collection was dispersed. A correspondent in *Notes and Queries* (2nd S., No. 201) says that John Varley, the painter, well known to have been attached to astrology, used to relate a tradition that the Gunpowder Plot was discovered by Dr. Dee with his magic mirror; and he urged the difficulty, if not the impossibility, of interpreting Lord Mounteagle's letter without some other clue or information than hitherto gained. In a Common Prayer Book, printed by Baskett in 1737, is an engraving of the following scene : In the centre is a circular mirror on a stand, in which is the reflection of the Houses of Parliament by night, and a person entering carrying a dark lantern. Next, on the left side are two

with him by the mediation of the Angel Uriel, and their dealings and daily conferences with the spirits are fully recorded in Casaubon's work, entitled, " A True and Faithful Relation of what passed for many years between Dr. John Dee and some Spirits." They had a black spectrum or crystal—a piece of polished cannel coal, in which Kelly affirmed the Angels Gabriel and Raphael, and the whole Rosicrucian hierarchy, appeared at their invocation—and hence the author of " Hudibras" says,—

> Kelly did all his feats upon
> The devil's looking-glass—a stone ;
> Where playing with him at bo-peep
> He solved all problems ne'er so deep.

When an incantation was to take place, " The sacred crystal was placed on a sort of altar before a crucifix, with lighted candles on either side, and an open Psalter before it," and prayers and ejaculations of the most fervid description were intermingled with the account taken down at Kelly's dictation of the dress and hair, as well as the sayings and movements, of the angels. Dee was infatuated with his new acquaintance, and every experiment he suggested was tried, at whatever cost, and hence it was not long before Kelly's weak and credulous dupe found himself in straitened circumstances. It was at this time that the Earl of Leicester, the Queen's favourite, proposed dining with him at Mortlake and bringing Albert Lasque, the Palatine of Sieradz, who was then in England, with him, when Dee had to explain that he could not

---

men in the costume of James's time, looking into the mirror—one evidently the King, the other evidently, from his secular habit, not the doctor (Dee), but probably Sir Kenelm Digby. On the right side, at the top, is the eye of Providence darting a ray on the mirror ; and below are some legs and hoofs, as if evil spirits were flying out of the picture. The plate is inserted before the service for the 5th November, and would seem to represent the method by which, under Providence (as is evidenced by the eye), the discovery of the Gunpowder Plot was at that time seriously believed to have been effected. The tradition must have been generally and seriously believed, or it never could have found its way into a Prayer Book printed by the King's printer.

give them a suitable dinner without selling some of his plate or
pewter to procure it. Leicester mentioned the circumstance to the
Queen, who speedily helped her old favourite out of the difficulty
by sending him "forty angells of gold." He thus relates the
circumstance : —

> Her Majestie (A. 1583 Julii ultimo) being informed by the right honour-
> able Earle of Leicester, that whereas the same day in the morning he had
> told me, that his Honour and Lord Laskey would dyne with me within two
> daies after, I confessed sincerely unto him, that I was not able to prepaire
> them a convenient dinner, unless I should presently sell some of my plate
> or some of my pewter for it. Whereupon her Majestie sent unto me very
> royally, within one hour after, forty angells of gold, from Syon, whither her
> Majestie was new come by water from Greenewich.

At the same time he makes the following entry in his " Diary " :—

> Mr. Rawlegh his letter unto me of hir Majestie's good disposition unto me.

the writer being Sir Walter Raleigh, who was then in great favour
with Elizabeth, and himself a patron of Dee's.

The visit of Count Lasque was an important event in Dee's
career. The Polish noble was accounted of great learning, and
fond of "occult studies." He paid frequent visits to the house at
Mortlake, where he was admitted to the *séances* of the English
magician, and became much impressed with his learning and professed knowledge of the mystical world. When the time came for
Lasque to return he suggested that Dee should go out with him to
Poland, with his wife and children, accompanied by Kelly and his
wife and brother, and their servants. When in his castle at Sieradz
they could make their experiments in undisturbed seclusion.
Seeing no prospect of the fulfilment of the promises made to him
at home, and being hampered with debt, Dee, who was then in his
57th year, was nothing loth to try his fortune abroad once more.
They left in September, and it was six years before any of them
again set foot on English soil. The departure is thus recorded in
the "Diary" :—

> Sept. 21st (1583).—We went from Mortlake, and so to the Lord Albert
> Lasky, I, Mr. E. Kelly, our wives, my children and familie, we went toward
> our two ships attending for us, seven or eight myle below Gravessende.

The period of their residence abroad was a chequered one, and many and extraordinary were their adventures and experiences, alternating between honour and discredit—between luxury and distress. For many months they were hospitably entertained by Count Lasque while engaged in their researches for the Philosopher's Stone, but finding that they spent more gold than they were able to produce he got tired, and persuaded them to pay a visit to Rudolph, King of Bohemia, who, though a weak and credulous man, soon became conscious of the imposture that was being practised, and passed them on to Stephen, King of Poland, at Cracow, but he declined to have anything to do with them, and the Emperor Rudolph refused to pay their expenses, or further encourage their experiments, though he permitted them to reside at Prague, and occasionally to appear at Court, until they were banished from the country at the instigation of the Pope's Nuncio, who stigmatised them as "notorious magicians." Dee lamented the "subtill devises and plotts" laid against him, and pathetically added, "God best knoweth how I was very ungodly dealt withall, when I meant all truth, sincerity, fidelity, and piety towardes God, and my Queene, and country."

The old man had surrendered himself entirely to Kelly. Under his iniquitous influence he degenerated into a mere necromancer, and was sinking more and more into discredit. On leaving Bohemia the two adventurers found an asylum in the Castle of Trebona, whither the Count of Rosenberg had invited them, and where, for a time, they were maintained in great affluence, owing, as they affirmed, to their discovery of the secret of transmuting the baser metals into gold. Kelly would seem to have learned some secrets from the German chemists which he did not reveal to his employer, but by their possession contrived to increase his influence over him, while he himself had recourse to the worst species of the magic art for the purposes of avarice and fraud. It was while at Trebona that Kelly produced the wonderful elixir, or Philosopher's Stone, in the form of a powder, which Lilly, in his "Memoirs," says he obtained from a friar who came to Dee's door. With this "powder of projection," or "salt of metals," as it was variously

called, they were enabled to coat the baser metals with silver or
gold, and would seem to have hit upon the process which, a century
and a half later, Joseph Hancock introduced into Sheffield—that
of electro-plating. Among other transmutations they converted a
piece of an old iron warming pan, by warming it at the fire, into
(or covered it with) silver, and sent it to Queen Elizabeth.* Why,
when they were about it, they did not "transmute" the whole pan
is not stated, but it would seem they were not able to work the
discovery easily or quickly enough to make it pay, for heart-
burnings, jealousies, and disputations arose, and quarrels became of
frequent occurrence. At one time Kelly got such a hold upon his
dupe as to persuade him that it was the Divine will that they should
have their wives in common ; then a rupture occurred between the
ladies, who, however, became reconciled to each other, and we
have the entries in the Diary—

> April 10th (1588).—I writ to Mr. Edward Kelly and to Mistress Kelly ij
> charitable letters requiring at theyr hands mutual charity.

And—

> May 22nd.—Mistris Kelly received the sacrament and to me and my wife
> gave her hand in charity ; and we rushed not from her.

Peace was restored, but it must have been of short duration, for
we find a few months later—

> July 17th.—Mr. Thomas Southwell of his own courteous nature did
> labor with Mr. Edmond Cowper, and indirectly with Mistress Kelly, for to
> furder charity and friendship among us.

True to his sordid and scheming nature, Kelly, who had become
a full-blown knight, contrived to possess himself of the greater part
of Dec's treasures—"the powder, the bokes, the glass, and the
bone"—and then, having no longer any need of the old man's

---

* Ashmole, in his MS., 1790, fol. 58, says, " Mr. Lilly told me that John
Evans informed him that he was acquainted with Kelly's sister in Worcester, that she showed him some of the gold her brother had transmuted,
and that Kelly was first an apothecary at Worcester."

co-operation, took himself off to earn elsewhere a success that, however, proved only very short-lived, for it was not long before, being detected in some knavery, he fell into disgrace, and was immured by the Emperor Rudolph in one of the prisons of Prague. Queen Elizabeth hearing of him, sent a messenger—Captain Peter Gwinne—secretly for him to return; but he was doomed to end his days in a foreign land, for in an attempt to escape from one of the windows of the castle he fell to the ground, and was so bruised and shattered that he died in a few hours—his elixir, it would seem, not being sufficient to communicate immortality to its possessor.

Forsaken by his companion, Dee resolved on returning to England. Elizabeth, who had heard of the doings of the two adventurers, and being, moreover, much impressed with the silvered piece of the warming pan, sent the doctor friendly messages desiring his return, with letters of safe conduct, and Lord Rosenberg, who had welcomed the coming, was now no less hearty in speeding his parting guests, an attention that is not surprising when it is remembered that for two years or more he had had quartered upon him two families who maintained somewhat questionable relations, and lived upon anything but friendly terms with each other—two quarrelsome women, a whole bevy of turbulent and unruly children, and a staff of servants that were continually causing disquiet by their "unthankfulnesse" and discontent; to say nothing of a brace of conjurors who crowded his castle, or, at least, were believed to, with imps, hobgoblins, and ghostly visitants of various kinds, and who there practised all sorts of *diablerie.* The count made him magnificent promises, and gave him a present of money; and we can quite believe that he and those about him were not very much overcome when Dee and his household divinities left Trebona Castle and turned their faces homewards. They travelled with great pomp and state, having "three new coaches made purposely for my foresaid journey," "twelve coach horses," "two and sometymes three waines," with "twenty-four soldiers," and "four Swart-Ruiters," as a guard of

honour; the "total summe of money spent" being £796—well-
nigh sufficient for a royal progress. On November 19, 1589, the
Dees "toke ship by the Vineyard," and December 2nd "came
into the Tems to Gravesende." They landed the following day, and
on the 19th the doctor was "at Richemond with the Queen's
Majestie," when, according to Aubrey, who received the information
from Lilly, he was very favourably received.

Though Dee and his family "cam into the Tems" on the 2nd
December, it was not until Christmas Day that they again entered
upon possession of the old home at Mortlake. And a comfortless
coming home and a sorrowful Christmas Day must have been that
25th of December, 1589. Courted by "Christian Emperors," Dee
had lived long enough to realise the value of the aphorism which
says "Put not your trust in princes!" Feeble with years, broken
in health, and overwhelmed by his losses and disappointments, the
old man chafed and became fretful; while his comparatively youthful spouse—for Jane Dee was then in the prime of womanhood—
was becoming increasingly irritable under the increasing cares of a
growing family, and the difficulties she experienced in obtaining
even decent food and raiment for them.

On reaching their once pleasant abode on the banks of the
Thames, they found it dismantled and in part dilapidated. While
abroad, silvering his old warming-pan and dreaming dreams of
inexhaustible wealth, Dee had little dreamed of what was going on
at home. Scarcely had he and his quondam associate reached the
castle of Count Lasque than Nicholas Fromonds, his brother-in-
law, who had been left in charge of the old house, and was to
occupy it as tenant, "imbezeled," sold, and "unduly made away"
his furniture and "household stuff;" and a noisy rabble, believing
that the old man had dealings with the devil, broke in, ransacked
the whole place, and destroyed nearly everything that remained.
Scarcely anything was left. 4,000 volumes, including the precious
manuscripts, that had taken more than 40 years to get together,
and had cost him £2,000, an enormous sum if we consider the
value of money at that time, were scattered; though, through the

efforts of his friends, some of them were afterwards recovered, as he said, "in manner out of a dunghill, in the corner of a church, wherein very many were utterly spoyled by rotting, through the mine continually for many years before falling on them, through the decayed roof of that church, lying desolate and wast at this houre." The "rare and exquisitely-made instruments mathe-maticall," the "strong and faire quadrant of five foote semi-diameter;" the two globes, on one cf which "were set down divers comettes, their places and motions;" the sea compasses; the magnet-stone "of great vertue;" the "watch clock," which measured the "360th part of an hour," were all purloined, "piece-meal divided," or "barbarously spoyled and with hammers smit in pieces." Harland and Wilkinson, in their "Lancashire Folk-Lore," say that when the house was attacked, "it was with difficulty Dee and his family escaped the fury of the rabble;" but this is a mistake, for, as previously stated, they were at the time beyond the seas, and in blissful ignorance of what was taking place.

Dee's affairs were now in a deplorable condition. The destruction of his library was a terrible calamity. He was involved in debt, his creditors were becoming clamorous, and, as he laments, "the usury devoureth me, and the score, talley, and booke debts doe dayly put me to shame in many places and with many men." His old friend and patron, the Queen, who had not yet lost faith in his astrological powers and discoveries, sent him in the year following his return "fiftie poundes to keep Christmas with," and promised him another "fiftie poundes" out of her "prevy purse." Many other friends sent him presents, in all about £500; but he was still struggling in poverty, and craving for some lucrative office, that he might free himself from his difficulties. In his distress he memorialised the Queen, through the Countess of Warwick, earnestly requesting that commissioners might be appointed to inquire into and decide upon his claims. His indebtedness then amounted to nearly £4,000, and the story he tells of the shifts he had recourse to, to save his family from "hunger starving," is truly pathetic. He had been constrained, he says, "now and then to

24

send parcells of furniture and plate to pawne upon usury," and when these were gone, "after the same manner went my wife's jewells of gold, rings, braceletts, chaines, and other our rarities, under thraldom of the usurer's gripes, till *non plus* was written upon the boxes at home." Upon the report the Queen ".willed the Lady Howard to write some words of comfort to his wife, and send some friendly tokens beside;" she further sent through Mr. Candish (Cavendish) her "warrant by word of mowth to assure him to do what he would in philosophie and alchemie, and none shold chek, controll, or molest him," and as a mark of her regard, on two occasions, "called for him at his door" as she rode by.

About this time a domestic difficulty of a different nature occurred. Dee's nurse became "possessed," and he had to try his skill in exorcising what he believed to be the evil spirit, though, as the result showed, with indifferent success. The incident is thus referred to in his "Diary":—

Aug. 2nd, 1590.—Nurs her great affliction of mynde.

Aug. 22nd.—Ann my nurse had long byn tempted by a wycked spirit : but this day it was evident how she was possessed of him. God is, hath byn, and shall be her protector and deliverer! Amen.

Aug. 25th.—Anne Frank was sorowful, well comforted, and stayed in God's mercyes acknowledging.

Aug. 26th.—At night I anoynted (in the name of Jesus) Anne Frank, her brest with the holy oyle.

Aug. 30th.—In the morning she required to be anoynted, and I did very devowtly prepare myself, and pray for vertue and powr, and Christ his blessing of the oyle to the expulsion of the wycked ; and then twyse anoynted, the wycked one did resest a while.

Sep. 8th.—Nurse Anne Frank wold have drowned hirself in my well, but by divine Providence I cam to take her up befor she was overcome of the water.

Sep. 29th.—Nurse Anne Frank most miserably did cut her owne throte, afternone abowt four of the clok, pretending to be in prayer before her keeper, and suddenly and very quickly rising from prayer, and going toward her chamber, as the mayden her keeper thowt, but indede straight way down the stayrs into the hall of the other howse, behinde the doore did that horrible act ; and the mayden who wayted on her at the stayr fote followed her, and missed to fynd her in three or fowr places, tyll at length she hard her rattle in her owne blud.

Dee tried hard to regain the parsonages and endowments of Upton and Long Leadenham, of which Bonner had many years previously dispossessed him, but he was "utterly put owt of hope for recovering them by the Lord Archbishop and the Lord Threasorer." Elizabeth had, on one occasion, promised him the deanery of Gloucester, but objection was raised on the ground of his not being in Holy Orders; subsequently he had the promise of some small advowsons in the diocese of St. David's; but the promise which was pleasant to the bear was roken to the hope. Failing these, he applied for reversion of the mastership of the Hospital of St. Cross, at Winchester. The Queen and the Lord Treasurer were favourably disposed, and Mr. J. Eglinton Bailey, in his admirable notes, to which we have before made reference, cites a Latin document which he found among the State Papers, dated May, 1594, being a grant to Wm. Brooke, Lord Cobham, K.G., of the next advowson of the hospital of Holyrood, near Winchester, of the Queen's gift, by the vacancy of the See, to present John Dee, M.A., on the death or resignation of Dr. Robert Bennett, the then incumbent. Bennett, however, did not die, or did not resign in reasonable time, for Dee never got installed; or it may be that the Archbishop (Whitgift) had interposed, for a month after the "grant" just mentioned, we find in the "Diary" an entry in which he thus gives vent to his feeling of mortification and disappointment, after an interview with the Primate :—

June 29th, 1594.—After I had hard the Archbishop his answers and discourses, and that after he had byn the last Sonday at Tybald's (Theobald's) with the Quene and Lord Threaserer, I take myself confounded for all suing or hoping for anything that was. And so adieu to the court and courting tyll God direct me otherwise! The Archbishop gave me a payre of sufferings to drinke. God be my help as he is my refuge! Amen.

When Dee ceased to supplicate, his wife took up the parable, and with much more satisfactory results. On the 7th of December, in the same year, we read :—

Jane, my wife, delivered her supplication to the Quene's Majestie, as she passed out of the privy garden at Somerset House to go to diner to the

Savoy, to Syr Thomas Henedge. The Lord Admirall toke it of the Quene. Her Majestic toke the bill agayn, and kept (it) uppon her cushen ; and on the 8th day, by the chief motion of the Lord Admirall, and somewhat of the Lord Buckhurst, the Quene's wish was to the Lord Archbishop presently that I should have Dr. Day his place in Powles (*i.e.*, the Chancellorship of St. Paul's).

Possibly the Queen or the Archbishop, or both, were getting wearied with the constant appeals of their tedious and egotistical suitor, for a month later occurs the entry :—

1595. Jan. 8th.—The Wardenship of Manchester spoken of by the Lord Archbishop of Canterbury.

Feb. 5th.—My bill of Manchester offered to the Quene afore dynner by Sir John Wolly to signe, but she deferred it.

April 18th.—My bill for Manchester Wardenship signed by the Quene, Mr. Herbert offring it her.

And so the magician of Mortlake was commissioned to minister among the Lancashire witches, and an exceedingly unpleasant time he had of it, as we shall presently see.

Though the appointment was made, the patent was not yet sealed. Dr. Chadderton did not actually relinquish the wardenship of Manchester until the confirmation of his election to the see of Lincoln, May 24, 1595. Immediately after appears the entry in the "Diary" :—

May 25th, 26th, 27th.—The Signet, Privy Seale, and the Great Seale of the Wardenship.

The old man was evidently too poverty-stricken to pay the fees, for he significantly adds, "£3 12s. 0d. borrowed of my brother Arnold."

At last the long-hoped-for preferment was secured, and the Warden elect at once began to prepare for removal to his new sphere of duty. Though, as before stated, the building of the College had been acquired by the Earls of Derby, under the Confiscating Act of Edward VI., the Wardens continued to reside there. On the 11th June Dee "wrote to the Erle of Derby his secretary abowt Manchester College;" and on the 21st June he makes the entry :—

> The Erle of Derby his letter to Mr. Warren for the Colledge.

Mr. Warren being apparently the agent of the Earl, and the "secretary" previously mentioned. Having thus put matters in train for the occupation of his new home, he set about the letting or disposal of the old one, for we read :—

> July 1st.—The two brothers, Master Willemots, of Oxfordshere, cam to talk of my howse-hyring. Master Baynton cam with Mistress Katharyn Hazelwood, wife to Mr. Fuller.

Meantime the Manchester people, and more especially the fellows of the College, were curious to know something about the new Warden, of whom rumour had said so many strange things. On the 12th July he records that "Mr. Goodier, of Manchester, cam to me;" and on the 28th July he received "a letter from Mr. Oliver Carter, Fellow of Manchester College," of whom we shall have more to say by-and-by. Mr. Goodier, it may be presumed, was not altogether uninfluenced by worldly considerations in thus paying his respects at Mortlake. The worthy burgher was a man of some consequence in his way, and much given, it is said, to the improvement of his temporal estate. He resided at the "Ould Clough House," a building adjacent to the College, "over anendst the church," as the Court Rolls of the day describe it, had served as senior constable, and had also filled the more important office of borough-reeve. He had, moreover, farmed the tithes of the Warden and Fellows, and seems to have made a somewhat wide interpretation of his lease, for shortly before he had prosecuted one of the Fellows for withholding the surplice fees, which he claimed to have of right. It is not unlikely, therefore, he had an ulterior object in journeying to London and offering his civilities to Dee. A year or two before, he had married a rich widow, Katharine, the relict of Ralph Sorrocold, and the mother of John Sorrocold, at whose house, the Eagle and Child, opposite Smithy Door, John

Taylor, the "water poet," when on his "Pennyless Pilgrimage," lodged, and whose wife he immortalised in his homely rhymes—

> I lodged at the Eagle and the Child,
> Whereat my hostess (a good ancient woman)
> Did entertain me with respect not common.
>
> .   .   .   .
>
> So Mistress Saracole, hostess kind,
> And Manchester with thanks I left behind.

On the 31st July, the "very virtuous" Countess of Warwick, who had proved her friendship for Dee by urging his claims upon the consideration of the Queen, did this evening, as he says—

> Thank her Matie in my name and for me for her gift of the Wardenship of Manchester. She took it gratiously, and was sorry that it was so far from hers; but that some better thing neer hand shall be ffownd for me; and if opportunitie of tyme wold serve, her Matie wold speak with me l.erself.

It is significantly added that "the firstfruits were forgiving by her Matie," which was fortunate, as it saved him the necessity of borrowing money to pay them. Her Majesty, however, never found the "opportunitie of tyme" to speak with her aged *protégé*, and Dee eventually left without the satisfaction of a parting interview.

Dee's prospects were now brightening, and, though late in the evening of life, there was again a prospect of sunny weather. Misfortunes, it is proverbially said, seldom come singly—the same rule, it would seem, holds good in regard to prosperity—for scarcely had Dee obtained his preferment when Providence added to his domestic bliss. A daughter was born unto him (he was now in his 69th year), and the christening, as may be supposed, was a great affair, the sponsors, who by the way, all appeared by deputy, being the Lord Keeper—Sir Christopher Hatton, it has been said, but more probably another Cheshire man, Sir Thomas Egerton, afterwards Lord Chancellor, for Hatton had been in his grave four years or more—Lady Mary Russell, Countess of Cumberland, the mother of the stout-hearted Lady Anne Clifford, Dowager Countess of Pembroke and Montgomery, of famous memory; and the Lady

Frances Walsingham, widow of Sir Philip Sidney, and the wife of the unfortunate Robert Devereux, Earl of Essex, whom Elizabeth, in 1601, beheaded.

The time of the new Warden was now much occupied in visiting and receiving visits. On the 13th, and again on the 22nd of September, he was the guest of the Earl of Derby at Russell House, and on the 9th Oct. he "dyned with Syr Walter Rawlegh, at Durham House," in the Strand. On the 25th Oct. we find him urging " Mr. Brofelde, Atturny-General, for som land deteyned from the Coll." (ege). Then come the entries,—

Nov. 8th.—My goods sent by Percival toward Manchester.
Nov. 26th.—My wife and children all by coach toward Coventry.

Coventry was on the road towards Manchester. Finally, we have the great mathematician himself following in their wake—

1595-6. Feb. 15.—I cam to Manchester a meridie nova 5.

The severance from old scenes and old associations must have been a painful one. It could only have been dire necessity that induced the vain and pedantic philosopher to forsake the pleasant vicinity of Richmond; to leave the courtly gallants and the staid and erudite *savants* who had frequented his modest "mansion" to settle down among the hard-headed, but uncultured and unappreciative people of Manchester—to immure himself in a place that must have been even less attractive then than it was a century or more afterwhen Brummell's regiment was ordered there, and the Beau sold out rather than submit to the infliction of being quartered in it. Abroad Dee had been welcomed wherever he had gone, and received with all the state and courtly ceremonial due to one of such prodigious learning. At Mortlake he had enjoyed the sunshine of royal favour, had been honoured with the frequent visits of the Queen and her Ministers, and accustomed to the friendship and society of such polished wits as Walsingham and Raleigh, and Cavendish and Sir Philip Sidney—

Sidney, than whom no gentler, braver man
His own delightful genius ever feigned.

And whom Spenser, in his "Shepheards' Calendar," named—

The President
Of noblenesse and chivalree.

At Manchester he had to deal with a rude, boisterous, and
uncultivated people, who openly reviled him—a rough metal that
all his incantations and alchemical skill could not transform into
refined gold ; and withal he had to contend with a body of clergy
who abhorred the unlawful arts he was supposed to practice, and
who treated him in consequence with implacable hatred. Of a
truth his position was not an enviable one.

Lancashire was at that time the great scene of religious
conflict—the battle-ground of angry polemics and fiercely-
contending factions. It was accounted as more given to
Romanism than any other county in England, and in the rural
districts the Protestant cause seemed rather declining than
advancing. Dr. Chadderton, who preceded Dee in the
Wardenship, had carried on a vigorous persecution of those who
still adhered to the unreformed religion, the more obstinate of
whom he imprisoned in the New Fleet, a building adjoining his
residence in the College. He had further hit upon an ingenious
way of convincing these recusants of the error of their ways—as
they would not attend church to hear the sermons preached by
the Puritanical Fellows he gave orders to his clergy to read prayers
in the apartments where they were confined, especially at meal
times, so that they had the pleasant alternative of taking theological
nourishment with their food or going without victuals altogether.
Chadderton's Protestantism had been intensified by his exile
during the Marian persecutions, and as Dee had been deprived of
his rectories of Upton and Long Leadenham, and had suffered
imprisonment at the hands of Bonner, it was not unreasonably
believed that he would follow in the steps of his predecessor, and
be no less zealous in hunting up seminary priests, and punishing
those who resorted to their secret masses. But Dee's church
principles were not particularly pronounced. Devoted to mathe-

matical and scientific pursuits, he did not greatly concern himself
with either Popish or Puritan theology; preaching was not in his
line, and he cared little for those controversial sermons which only
provoked strife between the professors of the old and the new faith,
and excited bitterness in the minds of all. He was content to
leave the Papists to the watchful care of the powerful Earl of
Derby and their opponents to do as they pleased, provided they
gave him no trouble. His colleagues were greatly angered at his
lack of zeal, and interminable quarrels were the consequence.

Saturday, the 20th of February, 1596, was a great day in
Manchester, and one to be held in remembrance. The church
bells filled the air with their clanging melodies, and the groups of
curious onlookers at the church stile and in the grass-grown graveyard denoted that something unusual was astir. And there was,
for the great philosopher whose marvellous skill had astonished
half the Courts of Europe, and about whom rumour had told so
many curious tales, was come to preside over the ancient College,
and direct the ecclesiastical affairs of the parish, and on that raw
February morning was to be installed in his office. Manchester
had never seen such a Warden before, and has not seen such
another since. The ceremony, we are told, was gone through with
"great pomp and solemnity." Of those assisting at it were
Edmund Prestwich, of Hulme; Richard Massey, the representative
of a family of some consequence living "in the Milnegate, neere
unto a street comonly called Toad-lane;" George Birch, of Birch,
in Rusholme, the brother of Robert Birch, one of the Fellows, and
nephew of William Birch, who at one time had been the Warden
of the College; Ralph Byrom and Thomas Byrom, wealthy traders
of the Kersal stock; Ralph Houghton, another trader; Henry
Hardy, and Richard Nugent, who afterwards became a benefactor
to the town, but whose bequest, through the negligence of trustees,
has long since been lost. Dr. Hibbert mentions these names,
though he does not give his authority. Dee, however, was fond of
ostentation and display, and we may be sure would omit nothing
that would impart dignity and importance to the proceedings. We

25

are not told which of the Fellows were present. Nowell, who was then in his 90th year, would be too old and infirm to undertake the toil of a journey from London ; but the bold and outspoken Puritan divine, Oliver Carter, would of a certainty be in his place ; and probably with him would be his equally zealous coadjutor, Thomas Williamson ; though both must have been greatly exercised in spirit at the thought of God's heritage being lorded over by one of such questionable antecedents. Humphrey Chetham had not then amassed a fortune, and acquired fame as a reformer of ecclesiastical abuses. He was only in his sixteenth year ; but he may have been, and very likely was, among the spectators, and in his young mind may have wondered how and by what mysterious influences so valuable a preferment had fallen to one who, not having obtained ordination, had not even received authority to preach.

The Manchester as Dee saw it must have presented a very different aspect to the Manchester of to-day. Leland, who had visited the place sixty years previously, described it, in his "Itinerary," as "the fairest, best builded, quickest, and most populous town in Lancashire," which, by the way, was not saying very much, seeing that, as compared with other parts of the kingdom, the county was thinly-peopled and ill-cultivated, and the neighbourhood of the town little else than extensive moors, mosses, and quagmires, where the stranger rarely adventured himself, and so "very wild and dangerous" that Bishop Downham pleaded its inaccessibility as a reason for seldom or never visiting it. The extent of the town proper could have been little more than that of an inconsiderable village of the present day, for though, unfortunately, there is no plan of it as then existing, the enumeration of the streets in the old Court Rolls of the manor enables us to form a tolerably accurate estimate of its limits. Within a few hundred yards of the Church the whole of the business of the place was located, and what was then town was but a congeries of crooked lanes and devious by-ways, with quaint black and white half-timbered dwellings standing on either side in an irregular, in-and-out, haphazard sort of way, and some very much inclined to "stand-at-ease," yet rendered picturesque by their very irregularity and their innumerable architectural caprices and fantasies, their queer-looking and curiously-carved gables, their oddly-projecting oriels and cunningly-devised recesses, and the varied and broken sky-lines of their roofs, so different to those dull, dreary uniformities of brick the present generation is compelled to gaze upon. Deansgate, Market Sted Lane, and Long Millgate were the principal streets. These stretched irregularly towards the open country, and from them a few narrow intricate lanes branched off in the direction of the Church and the College. On the east and south sides of the churchyard were then, as now, several public-houses, where the bride ales and wedding feasts were held, and to restrain the extravagances of which numerous sumptuary laws had to be enacted. Round the Market Sted were the shops and "stallings" of the principal traders, who, clad in their own fustian, measured out their manufactured wares and sent out their pack-horsemen, with tingling bells, to sell them wherever and whenever they could find a buyer. Here also were located the "booths" in which the Portmotes and the Courts Leet and Baron of the manorial lords were held, and contiguous thereto were the Pillory, the Whipping Post, and the Stocks, where rogues and dishonest and drunk and disorderly townsmen were punished. On the north side of the church—Back o'th' Church, as it was called—between the churchyard and the College gates, stood the bull oak, where bulls were usually baited. The butts for archery practice, where every man between 16 and 60 had to exercise himself in the use of the good yew bow, were on the outskirts of the town, one being on the south side, where Deansgate merged into Aldport Lane, and the other, at Collyhurst, on the north. The cockpit stood on what was then called the "lord's waste," the vacant land in the rear of the Market Sted, which still retains the name of Cockpit Hill. Hanging Ditch was, as its name implied, a ditch, part of the old moat or fosse connecting the Irwell and the Irk, down which the water still flowed at a considerable depth below the footway, Toad Lane and Cateaton Street being but a continuation of it. Over this old and then disused watercourse was a stone bridge, the arch of which may still be seen—the Hanging Bridge, so named from the drawbridge which had preceded it, where officers were stationed to see that horses and cows did not pass over into the churchyard. Near the bridge was the smithy, which gave the name to Smithy Door and Smithy Bank. In Smithy Door, near the entrance to the Market Sted, was the town pump or conduit, fed from a natural spring, near the top of the present Spring Gardens, where the good wives of the town went for their water, and waited their "cale" till they got it, gossiping and quarrelling with each other the while. At the foot of Smithy Bank was Salford Bridge—the only bridge over the Irwell connecting the two towns—a structure of three arches, and so narrow that foot-passengers had occasionally to take refuge in little recesses while vehicles passed along. In the centre of it was the dungeon, which in earlier days had served the purpose of a chapel. Withy Grove was in truth a group of withies, the old "Seven Stars," and a few other dwellings, being all that existed to give the character of street. At the higher end was Withingreave Hall, the town house of the Hulmes of Reddish, progenitors of William "Hulme the Founder," with its gardens, orchard, and outbuilding, and beyond a pleasant rural lane led on to Shudehill. Market Sted Lane, a narrow and tortuous thorough-fare, extended no further than the present Brown Street, Mr. Lever's house, which occupied the site of the White Bear, standing in what was then the open country. The picturesque old black and white houses that bordered each side had their pleasant gardens in rear ; and beyond, towards Withy Grove in one direction and Deansgate in the other, were meadows and pasture fields. In one of those fields, on the south side, was the mansion of the Radcliffes, surrounded by a moat that gave the name to Pool Fold, and which was oftentimes the scene of much mob-justice and very much misery, for here was placed the ducking-stool for the punish-ment of scolds and disorderly women,—

On the long plank hangs o'er the muddy pool,
That stool, the dread of ev'ry scolding quean.

THE COLLEGE, MANCHESTER.

From its frequent use we may suppose that in those days the female portion of the community were neither very amiable nor very virtuous. Long Millgate ran parallel with the Irk, an irregular line of houses with little plots of garden behind forming the boundary on each side, and a little way up a rural lane, shaded with hedgerow trees, branched off on the right, known as the Milner's Lane—the present Miller Street. The Irk, a pure and sparkling stream, was noted for its "luscious eels." The Masters of the Grammar School had the exclusive fishery rights from Ashley Lane to Hunt's Bank, and the Warden and Fellows of the College might have envied them their monopoly had they not themselves been able to obtain their Lenten fare from the equally clear and well-stocked waters of the Irwell, which then glided pleasantly by, innocent of dyes and manufacturing refuse. Altogether the place presented more the semi-rural aspect of a country village than an important town, as Leland represented it to be. Picturesque, it is true, yet it possessed many unpleasant features withal. The streets and lanes were ill-paved and full of deep ruts and claypits, for every man who wanted daub to repair his dwelling dug a hole before his door to obtain it. The eye, too, was offended by unsightly cesspools and dunghills that were to be seen against the Church walls, on the bridges, and, in fact, at every turn.

Though some of the more remote parts of the parish were barren and uncultivated, the immediate environments of the town were characterised by much that was exceedingly beautiful, with a wilder sort of loveliness, increased by the natural irregularities of the surface, and the great masses of foliage, part of the old forest of Arden, that extended far away. On the north, Strangeways Park, with its umbraged heights, its sunny glades, and shady dingles, stretched away towards Broughton, Cheetham, and Red Bank. Near thereto was Collyhurst Park, with the common, on which the townsmen had the right to pasture their pigs, and where the town swine-herd daily attended to his porcine charge; and the deep sequestered clough through which the Irk wound its sinuous course, its surface chequered by the shadows of the overhanging hazels and brushwood ; and beyond, the extensive chase of Blackley, with its deer leaps, and its aërie of eagles, of herons, and of hawks. On the south was the stately old mansion of Aldport, standing in a park of 95 acres, occupying the site of Campfield and Castlefield, and reaching down to the banks of the Irwell, with the great parks of Ordsal and Hulme on the one side and those of Garratt and Ancoats on the other.

It can hardly be said that among the inhabitants a very high state of civilisation prevailed. If thrifty and industrious, they were certainly not very refined, nor blessed with "pregnant wits," as good Hugh Oldham affirmed, nor yet remarkable for their moral excellence. Boisterous and laughter-loving, they delighted in out-door games and uproarious sports,—the wild merriment of the day being oftentimes followed by the wilder merriment of the evening. Bull-baiting, wrestling, and cock-fighting were the leading diversions, "unlawful gaming" and "lewdness" were frequently complained of, and the ale-houses, to which the more dissolute resorted, were the scenes of riots and feuds that not only caused annoyance and scandal to the more well-disposed, but endangered the public peace to a greater degree than we can now easily conceive. Under such circumstances it is hardly surprising that they should have entertained little reverence for their spiritual pastors, many of whom, by the way, were only a degree less ignorant and disorderly than themselves, for in those days the curate of Stretford kept an ale-house, the rector of Chorlton eked out a scanty subsistence by doing a little private pawnbroking, while the parson of Blackley was "passing rich" on a stipend of £2 3s. 4d. a year.

Such was the Manchester of which Dee had become the ecclesiastical head. However apathetic he may have been as to the spiritual affairs of the parishioners committed to his care, he was by no means wanting in energy when his own temporal interests were concerned. Scarcely had he taken up his abode at the College than we find him entertaining at dinner two influential tenants—Sir John Byron, of Clayton, and his son, and bargaining with them about the price of hay before the grass was actually grown. A month later he records the "possession taking in Salford," and he quickly found himself in litigation with the College tenants of some of the lands there. The tenants were a source of trouble, and oftentimes disturbed the even tenor of his way, while the collecting of his tithes was not unfrequently a cause of anxiety also. He complains of being "occupied with low controversies, as with Holden of Salford, and the tenants of Sir John Biron, of Faylsworth," of "much disquietnes and controversy about the tythe-corn of Hulme," of the "Cromsall corne-tyth" being "dowted of and half denyed," and then "utterly denyed," and of his riding to Sir John Byron "for a quietnes," and "to talk with him abowt the controversy between the Colledg and his tenants." Notwithstanding these unhappy disputations he had some pleasant days. Thus, on the 26th June (1596), as he tells us—

The Erle of Derby. with the Lady Gerard, Sir (Richard) Molynox and his lady, dawghter to the Lady Gerard, Master Hawghton, and others, cam suddenly uppon (me), after three of the clok. I made them a skoler's collation, and it was taken in good part. I browght his honor and the ladyes to Ardwyk grene toward Lyme, as Mr. Legh his howse, 12 myles of, &c.

Dee was eager for sympathy and approval of his favourite schemes and pursuits, and, being a man of the world, he knew the value of such friendships. As he was, moreover, given to hospitality, there is little doubt the "skoler's collation" would be as sumptuous as the College larder would afford. A few days later (July 5) he was visited by Mr. Harry Savill, the antiquary, and Mr. Christopher Saxton, the eminent chorographer, who had come to make a survey of the town ; and on the following day, Dee, with Saxton and some others, rode over to Hough Hall, in Withington, the mansion of Sir Nicholas Mosley, who had in the same year become the purchaser of the manor of Manchester. The survey was completed on the 10th July, and on the 14th Saxton "rode away." It is much to be regretted that no copy of Saxton's work, so far as is known, has been preserved ; for an authentic plan of the town in Elizabeth's reign would be a valuable addition to the topographical records of Manchester, and would enable us to see exactly what

25

progress was made in the extension of the town between that time
and the Commonwealth period, when another survey—the earliest
reliable one extant—was taken.

Before the close of the first year of his Wardenship, Dee was
invited to exercise the power he was commonly believed to possess
of casting out devils; but he prudently declined. About two
years previously five members of the household of Mr. Nicholas
Starkey, of Cleworth, in Leigh parish, became demoniacally
possessed, through the influence, as was said, of a conjuror named
Hartley. Margaret Byrom, of Salford, who happened to be on a
visit at Cleworth, became infected with the malady. This occurred
on the 9th January, 1596-7; and at the end of the month she
returned to her friends at Salford, when Dee was importuned to
deliver her from the evil spirit which tormented her. The
Warden, however, refused, telling her friends he would practise no
such unlawful arts as they desired; but, instead, advised they
should "call for some godlye preachers, with whom he should
consult concerning a public or private fast," and at the same time
he sharply rebuked Hartley for following his contraband calling.
Possibly the failure of his previous attempt to exorcise the spirit in
the case of "Nurse Anne Frank" had induced a wholesome
prudence on his part, though his refusal made him unpopular with
his parishioners, who were offended at his withholding the relief
they believed it was in his power to give, and his Puritan
colleagues took advantage of his unpopularity to make his life
miserable. Oliver Carter, who had held his fellowship for more
than a quarter of a century, and had become the recognised head
of the Presbyterian faction in the district, was chief among the
malcontents, and a sore thorn in the side the doctor found him.
Carter disliked alchemical philosophers as much as he hated
Popish recusants, and denounced the Warden's intercourse with
the spirit world as a scandal upon the Church. The Presbyterian
Fellow had little respect for lawfully-constituted authority, and his
open resistance in matters of ceremony had aforetime brought him
in collision even with the cautious and temperate Bishop

Chadderton, who had found it necessary to enforce some little submission to ecclesiastical law. It is not surprising, therefore, that he should have shown little regard for the authority of the new comer, whom he looked upon as a Court spy, and detested accordingly. He was a continuous source of annoyance, and his contumacious demeanour, his " impudent and evident disobedience in the Church," and persistent obstructiveness are frequently complained of, thus—

> Jan. 22, 1579.—Olyver Carter's thret to sue me with proces from London, &c., was this Satterday in the church declared to Robert Cleg.
> Sept. 25.—Mr. Olyver Carter his impudent and evident disobedience in the church.
> Sept. 26.—He repented, and some pacification was made.
> Nov. 14.—The fellows would not grant me the £5 for my howse-rent, as the Archbishop had graunted ; and our foundation commandeth an howse.
> July 17, 1600.—I willed the fellows to com to me by nine the next day.
> July 18.—They cam. It is to be noted of the great pacification unexpected of man which happened this Friday ; for in the forenone (betwene nine and ten), when the fellows were greatly in doubt of my heavy displeasure, by reason of their manifold misusing of themselves against me, I did with all lenity enterteyn them, and shewed the most part of the things that I had browght to pass at London for the colledg good, and told Mr. Carter (going away) that I must speak with him alone. Robert Leghe (one of the four clerks) and Charles Legh (the brother of Robert, and receiver) were by. Secondly, the great sute betwene Redich (Redditch) men and me was stayed, and Mr. Richard Holland his wisdom. Thirdly, the organs uppon condition were admitted. And, fourthly, Mr. Williamson's resignation granted for a preacher to be gotten from Cambridge.

Reconciliation was thus effected, but it was not long before there was a renewal of hostilities, for, under date Sept. 11, we find—

> Mr. Holland, of Denton, Mr. Gerard, of Stopford (Stockport), Mr. Langley, &c., commissioners from the Bishop of Chester, authorised by the Bishop of Chester, did call me before them in the Church abowt thre of the clok, after none, and did deliver to me certayne petitions put up by the fellows against me to answer before the 18th of this month. I answered them all codem tempore, and yet they gave me leave to write at leiser.

Amid these harassing anxieties and unseemly disputations with the unruly Fellows, Dee's alchemical studies were not neglected.

He had secured another medium in the place of Kelly—
Bartholomew Hickman, who turned out to be nearly as great a
knave, though not nearly half so clever as his predecessor, and,
losing confidence, Dee discharged him and burnt all the records of
what he had seen and heard in the wonderful show-stone. The
next day Roger Kooke, who had previously been in the service of
the philosopher, and to whom he had revealed "the great secret of
the elixir of the salt of metals," offered "the best of his skill and
powre, in the practises chymicall." He was quickly set to work,
but young Arthur Dee finding by chance among his papers what
seemed a plot against the father, he was charged with the
conspiracy, when Dee cried, "*O Deus libera nos a malo!* All was
mistaken, and we are reconcyled godly;*" and he again dreamed
of his "working the philosopher's stone." He would appear,
however, to have subsequently parted with Kooke, for before his
death Hickman had been restored to favour.

Though devoted to scientific pursuits, it must not be supposed
that the Warden neglected his official duties, or that he was by
any means unmindful of the secular interests of the Collegiate
body. His business exactitude and active zeal in this direction,
however, did not always meet with the approval of his neighbours,
or at least of such of them as happened to be tithe-farmers or
College tenants. In May of the year following his induction we find
him with his curate, Sir Robert Barber (clerics commonly affected
the prefix of "Sir" in those days), Robert Tilsey, the parish clerk,
and "diverse of the town of diverse ages," making a careful
perambulation of the bounds of the parish with the view of deter-
mining its exact limits, a procedure that somewhat alarmed Mr.
Langley, the rector of the adjoining parish of Prestwich, who smelt
litigation in Dee's anxiety "for avoiding of undue encroaching of
any neighbourly parish, one on the other." On another occasion
he was careful to note that—

At midnight (January 22, 1599), the College gate toward Hunt's Hall
did fall, and some parte of the wall going downe the lane—

the "lane" being the narrow passage that led from the north

side of the church, by the venerable tree where bulls were baited, and past the prison to Irk Bridge, then known as Hunt's Bank, a name it retained until modern times, when it was superseded by the present Victoria Street. The gate-house, which, as before stated, was at one time used as a workhouse, stood on this, the westerly side of the great quadrangle, the gates opening into Hunt's Bank. Though they have long since disappeared, the evidences of their former existence may still be traced in the wall.

After an absence in London he paid an official visit to the Grammar School, where he " fownd great imperfection in all and every of the scholers, to his great grief," a record that must be taken as reflecting on Dr. Cogan, the head master, whose time appears to have been divided between the teaching of youth and the practice of physic. In August, 1597, the " Erle and Cowntess of Derby " having taken up their abode at Aldport Lodge, Dee entertained them at "a banket at my lodging at the Colledge hora 4½." There are many other entries of visits from distinguished personages, among them Sir Urian Legh, of Adlington, the reputed hero of the ballad of "The Spanish Lady;" Sir George Booth, sheriff of Cheshire; Mr. Wortley, of Wortley. Probably, also, Camden, the historian, for it is recorded that when that distinguished antiquary visited the town, Dee pointed out to him the inscription of some Roman remains at Castle Field, attributable to the Frisian cohort, which occupied the station there. While dispensing his hospitalities the poor old man was suffering from lack of money, his financial difficulties being as great as ever, and we find him raising loans on the security of his diminished stock of plate, &c.—

Feb. 17, 1597.—Delivered to Charles Legh the elder (the receiver of College before referred to), my silver tankard with the cover, all dubble gilt, of the Cowntess of Herford's gift to Francis her goddaughter, waying 22oz., great waight, to lay to pawne in his own name to Robert Welshman, for iiijli tyll within two dayes after May-day next. My dowghter Katherin and John Crocker and I myself were at the delivery of it and waying of it in my dyning chamber—it was wrapped in a new hand-kercher cloth.

Many similar transactions are recorded—indeed, he appears to have been continually borrowing money from his friends, and almost as frequently lending his books to them. Dee was certainly not one of those who believe that "imparted knowledge doth diminish learning's store," for he was ever ready to place his literary treasures at the service of others, and frequent entries occur of his lending rare and valuable works to those he thought capable of understanding and appreciating them.

It was some little relief to him when, on the 2nd December, 1600, his son Arthur had a grant of the chapter clerkship, though before he could pay £6 for the patent he

> Borrowed of Mr. Edmund Chetham, the schoolmaster (the uncle of Humphrey, the founder) £10 for one yere uppon plate, two bowles, two cupps with handles, all silver, waying all 32oz. Item, two potts with cover and handells, double gilt within and without, waying 16oz.

The Warden's pecuniary embarrassments kept him in discredit with his parishioners, who naturally looked with disfavour upon an ecclesiastic that did not pay his debts, especially when, as they believed, it required only a very little closer intimacy with the evil one to enable him to do so. The fellows maintained their hostility, his neighbours became more and more unfriendly, the urgency of his creditors was oppressive, and on every hand he was assailed with suspicions of sorcery. The nine years he was in Manchester was the most wretched portion of his life. Unable to bear the odium attaching to him, he petitioned King James that he might be brought to trial, "and by a judicial sentence be freed from the revolting imputations" his astrological and other inquiries had brought upon him; but Elizabeth's wary successor, who detested his mysteries, would have nothing to say to him. Weary with the struggle, he quitted Manchester in November, 1604, and once more sought shelter in the house at Mortlake. Of the closing years of his chequered life little is known, but that little is sad enough. The friends of former years had died or forgotten him, and the new generation of Court favourites left him to pass his few remaining days in poverty, sickness, and desolation. After

all his tricks and conjurations the once haughty philosopher was
reduced to such miserable straits that he oftentimes had to sell
some of his books before he could obtain the means wherewith to
purchase a meal. The prediction of the Earl of Salisbury that he
" would shortly go mad " was nearly being realised, for in the
midst of his poverty, and while on the very verge of the grave, he

MORTLAKE CHURCH.

resumed his occult practices, in which he was aided by the
formerly discarded Bartholomew Hickman. At last, in poverty
and neglect, wearied and worn out, the miserable wreck of an ill-
spent life, he, in 1608, passed away at the advanced age of 81, and
was buried in the chancel of the church at Mortlake without any
tombstone or other memorial to preserve his name.

Of the numerous family that had once gathered round his hearth few remained at the time of his dissolution, death or estrangement having removed nearly all. His son Michael had died in infancy. His busy, shrewish wife died on the 23rd March, 1605. Of the other seven children Katherine was the only one who clung to him to the last. Rowland, on completing his studies at the Manchester Grammar School, obtained an exhibition at Oxford, but of his subsequent career nothing is known, nor, with the exception of Arthur, can we trace anything of the after-history of the others. Arthur, his first-born, resided in Manchester for some time, and subsequently practised as a physician. He married Isabella, one of the daughters of Edmund Prestwich, of Hulme Hall, and afterwards was chosen physician to Michael III., the first Czar of Russia, and for many years he resided in that country, where his wife died, July 6, 1634, after having borne him 12 children. Returning to England, he was sworn physician to Charles I., and located himself at Norwich, where he continued to reside until his death, September, 1651. Anthony à Wood, in his *Athenæ*, mentions that Arthur Dee, when an old man, spoke in full confidence of his father's goodness and sincerity, and affirmed that in his youth, when he had initiated him in some of his mystical pursuits, he had seen enough to satisfy him that he had discovered many marvellous secrets, and only lacked the means to make them available. The son may not have been altogether an impartial witness, but it would be unfair to judge the father by the standard of the present day.

Dee lived in an age when everybody believed in the occult sciences, and in the power of summoning visitants from the world of shadows by incantations and other mysterious means. Half a century before his death he had been pre-eminent for his learning, his eloquence, and his scientific attainments, and he was undoubtedly one of the great lights of his era. Camden styled him *nobilis mathematicus*, and he may fairly be accounted the prophet of the arts which Bacon and Newton were afterwards to reveal. A ripe scholar, well skilled in chemistry, mathematics,

and mechanics, and the master of the whole circle of the liberal
arts as then understood—

He sought and gathered for our use the true.

He was one of the first who accepted the theory of Copernicus,
and he successfully performed the labour of correcting the
Gregorian calendar. He was, moreover, a good linguist, an
earnest antiquary, and a diligent searcher of those records which
tend to elucidate the history of the country, and to him is due the
credit of first suggesting the formation of a "National Library," for
the preservation of those ancient writings in which lie "the
treasures of all antiquity, and the everlasting seeds of continual
excellency." Paradoxical as it may seem, there was with the
splendour and universality of his genius much childlike simplicity;
and his credulous confiding nature often exposed him to the
iniquitous arts of those about him; while his reckless extravagance,
his love of ostentatious display, his debts, and his carelessness of
the method which brought relief, kept him in continuous disquiet.
He was part of the age in which he lived in that he was fond of
alchemy, a believer in the divining-rod, and a devout practitioner
of the astral science; but it is to be feared that his straitened
circumstances sometimes prompted him to have recourse to tricks
and artifices that his better judgment condemned. He was a
strange mixture of pride and gentleness, of goodness and credulity.
He discoursed learnedly with foreign philosophers, tended his little
folks in their sicknesses, and soothed them in their childish griefs
and sorrows; gazed into the glittering depths of his magic mirror and
smiled good temperedly at his shrewish wife's scoldings; dispensed
his hospitalities and gossiped freely with the aristocratic personages
who sought his society, and pawned his property to pay for their
entertainment; contended with an archbishop and sought peace
with the irrepressible Carter and his unruly associates; but we
willingly forget the weaknesses and the foibles of the man when we
remember the genius and the learning of the philosopher. With
all his failings Dee possessed much kindness of heart, and though

27

Manchester may not have been greatly advantaged by the ecclesiastical supervision of the "Wizard Warden," he was yet, in many respects, much to be preferred to the needy Scotch courtier whom King James appointed as his successor.

BEESTON CASTLE.

CHAPTER VI.

HE traveller who has ever journeyed in the "Wild Irishman" between that hive of industry, Crewe, and the ancient city upon the Dee, will have noticed upon his left, midway between the two places, a bold outlier of rock that rises abruptly from the great Cheshire plain, with the ivy-covered remains of an ancient castle perched upon its summit. A better position for a fortress it is difficult to conceive. It looks as if nature had intended it as a place of defence ; and evidently Randle Blundeville, the crusader Earl of Chester, thought so, when, in those stormy days in which the Marches were the constant scene of struggle and strife, and

> Like volcanoes flared to heaven the stormy hills of Wales !

he chose it as the site for one of his border strongholds.

Avoiding, for the nonce, the " Irishman," we will avail ourselves of the more convenient, if more common-place, " Parliamentary," as it enables us to alight at Beeston—for that is the place to which our steps are directed, and almost within bowshot of the relic of ancient days, of which we are in search. Beeston is not a town—it can hardly be called a village even, the houses are so few, and neighbourhood there is none. The little unpretentious railway station is innocent of hurry and bustle, and seems almost ashamed of disturbing the rural tranquillity ; the Tollemache Arms, a comfortable hostelrie standing below the railway, opens its doors invitingly; a peaceful farmstead or two, surrounded by verdant pastures and fields of ripening corn, with here and there a cleanly whitewashed cottage, half hidden among the trees and hedges, are almost the only habitations we can see.

A few minutes' walk along a sandy lane, that winds beneath the trees and across the sun-bright meadows, where cattle are pasturing and haymakers are tossing the fragrant grass, brings us to the foot of the castle rock. The huge mass of sandstone lifting its unwieldy form above the surrounding greenery seems to dominate the entire landscape. Few landmarks are more striking, and, as you draw near, the hoary time-worn ruin crowning the summit, and looking almost gay and cheerful in the fresh morning sunlight, reminds you, only that the water is wanting, of those picturesque strongholds that crest the rocky heights along the lonely reaches of the Rhine—

> High from its field of air looks down
> The eyrie of a vanished race ;
> Home of the mighty, whose renown
> Has passed and left no trace.

On the north-easterly side the hill rises slopingly, but towards the south and west it shoots up abruptly from the plain, presenting a mass of jagged perpendicular rock three hundred and sixty feet in height. Seen from the distance, it looks as if it had been upheaved by some convulsive effort of Nature, and then toppled over, the foundations standing up endways. Keeping to the left, we ascend by a path steep and rough, and stony withal. Brushwood and bracken, and the wild, old, wandering bramble border the way ; and now and then a timid sheep rushes out from some shady nook and gazes wonderingly at us as we go by. The turf in places is short and slippery, for the rabbits keep it closely cropped; and were it not for a fragment of jutting rock, or the branch of a tree that occasionally proffers its friendly aid, we should find the ascent at times difficult and toilsome. Little more than half way up we come to the outer line of the fortifications, where a small lodge has been erected, through which we gain admission into the dismantled interior.

The ruin is complete, and at the first glance presents only the appearance of crumbling masses of shapeless masonry, that, having outlived the necessities which called them into existence, time has clothed with saddest beauty. The ivy spreads its roots and clings with fond tenacity, the long grass waves, and the nettles grow in rank profusion ; yet the remains are so far perfect that the searching eye of the archæologist can readily discern their purpose, determine the plan, and reconstruct in every detail. The outer ballium, which is pierced by a few embrasures, extends in the form of an irregular semicircle round the sloping sides, and where the cliff is not perpendicular, about five or six acres being comprehended within the area. The entrance is so narrow that only one or two persons can pass through at a time—a feature that indicates the rude and lawless period of its erection, when strength and security were the chief objects aimed at. It has been guarded by a square tower, and the remains of seven other towers or bastions, mostly round, and similar in appearance to the Moorish towers which became so general in England after the return of the barons from the Crusades, occur at irregular intervals. The court itself is a large, rough pasture, broken and uneven. A pair of kangaroos are disporting themselves among the moss-grown fragments, and a few deer are quietly browsing upon the green turf; but there is no picturesque assemblage of ruins, or trace of any previously-existing building, though it was once a busy hive of life and work. Nothing now remains but a few weedy heaps of masonry, the shattered keep, and the small inner bailey which occupies the highest and most inaccessible part of the rock, covering an area an acre in extent.

The keep was formerly protected and is still separated from the outer court by a broad, deep moat, hewn out of the solid rock, that extends round two sides and terminates near its precipitous edge. It is now dry and partly choked with weeds and rubbish, and a path has been made across where formerly a drawbridge only gave access. The great barbican, though roofless and forlorn, is imposing even in its decay, and gives a distinct impression of its former strength and solidity. It was proof against bows and arrows, battering rams, and similar engines of primitive warfare, and, ere "villainous saltpetre had been dug out of the bowels of the harmless earth," must have been, barring treachery from within, absolutely impregnable. The round towers that flank the entrance are clothed with the greenest and darkest ivy, that mingles with and seems to form part of the ruined mass to which it clings so lovingly, making it more picturesque than it could ever have been in the days of its proud and pristine splendour. The walls are of immense thickness, and on the face of each, near the top, where the ashlar-work has not been destroyed, a kind of arcade ornament may still be discerned. An early English arch unites the two towers, and beneath it we can see the grooves wherein the portcullis used to descend to bar the ingress and egress of doubtful or suspected visitors. The entrance, like that to the outer court, is very narrow ; passing through, a few steps cut out of the sandstone rock, and which have been worn by the tread of many generations, lead to the inner court or bailey, environed on two sides by lofty walls, from which project great bastions that have for centuries braved the winter's wrath and rejoiced in the summer sunshine. The interior is now a vacant space, except for the few fragments of masonry that serve to indicate what once was there. This was the citadel, so to speak. In it was the home of the lordly owner of the castle (and scant and rude enough it must have been), the outer court being used as the quarters for the garrison. Here we are shown the well-house and the famous well from which, in bygone days, the occupants drew their supply of water, and which now forms an object of attraction to wondering visitors. It is a remarkable work, and says much for the perseverance and skill of those who made it. The depth is said to be no less than 366 feet—nearly double that of the well at Carisbrook—the water, it is believed, being level with Beeston Brook, which flows near the foot of the castle rock. A tradition was widely prevalent, and is still believed in many a rustic home in the locality, that a great amount of treasure lies buried at the bottom, having been cast in it during a time of peculiar exigence by one of the earlier lords of Beeston ; but the story may be dismissed as resting upon no better foundation than the shaping power of the imagination. There is no water in it, nor has there been for years, owing to the drainage below, and for a long time it was choked with rubbish ; but some five-and-thirty or forty years ago it was cleared out to the very bottom, when the only treasures discovered were an old spade and a fox's head. We peer into the darksome vault, but the gloom is impervious ; then the janitor produces a frame with a few lighted candles upon it, which he lets down by a rope and pulley. As it slowly descends the light gradually diminishes until it becomes a mere speck, and we are enabled to form some idea of the amazing depth to which the rock has been excavated. Having done this, he will, if it will add to your pleasure and you are ready to listen, give you his version of Beeston's history—lead you where nobles and high-born dames have held their banquets ; show you the iron rings to which, in bygone days, the troopers fastened their horses ; and then relate with circumstantial detail the legend of the lost treasure, and tell you how, long, long ago, a trusty servitor was let down to the bottom of the well in the hope of recovering it, and that when he was wound up again he was speechless, and died before he could reveal the mysteries he had seen.

For the boldness and beauty of its situation Beeston may be fairly said to be unrivalled, and from the wide extent of country it commands it must, in the days of watch and ward, have been admirably adapted either for the purposes of offence or defence. From the summit of the glorious old relic we can sweep the whole arch of the horizon, from the pale blue hills of Wales on the one hand, to the brown heathy wastes that once formed part of the great forest of Macclesfield on the other. The palatinate which boasts itself the Vale Royal of England is usually reckoned a flat county, and this is in a great measure true, for league upon league of broad, flat, fertile meadows spread before us, but the eye as it ranges into the distance passes over a rich variety of undulating country. Above the round-topped woods of Delamere we catch

28

sight of the eminence on which the Saxon city of Eddisbury once
stood, and the bold promontories of Frodsham and Halton
guarding the shores of the Mersey; eastwards are seen the
umbraged heights of Alderley, and further to the right the range of
hills that form the barrier of the county, and separate it from the
Peak district of Derbyshire; while more to the south, where a
cloud of smoke hangs lazily upon the landscape, is Crewe, the great
central point of railway enterprise and railway industry. Gleaming
in the warm sunshine upon the left we note the stately tower of
Chester Cathedral rising proudly above the humbler structures
that, like vassals, gather round, and we recall the stormy times
when from its walls, on that sad September day, the ill-fated
Charles the First, after a fitful gleam of prosperity, saw his gallant
cavaliers borne down by the stern soldiers of Cromwell's army on
Rowton Moor, a disaster that turned the fortunes of the King and
sealed the fate of Beeston. In rear one can look down the
wide estuaries of the Dee and the Mersey, and along the great
western horn of Cheshire, as it stretches away towards the Irish
Sea. More to the left the mountains of Wales loom darkly and
mysteriously, as distant mountains always do, and spread along the
line of the horizon until their further summits, softened by the
mellowing haze of distance, can hardly be distinguished from the
azure dome above; the bold form of Moel Fammau may be seen
rising conspicuously, and when the day is clear those who are
blessed with a keen eyesight may, it is said, discern even the peak
of Snowdon, seeming to touch the far-off western sky.

Glorious is the prospect that spreads around. What a wealth of
pastoral loveliness lies before us, everywhere exhibiting the signs
of fertility and cultivation. All within the limits is a green and
beautiful expanse made up of copse and lea, of level meadow
breadths and cattle-dappled pastures, that rejoice in the warm
sunshine, with little hamlets and villages and shady lanes, old
manor houses and churches—the monuments of the past mingling
with the habitations of contemporary life and activity. Natural
beauty is everywhere, and the eye is delighted with its variety of

extent. After leisurely contemplating the scene the mind is enabled
to occupy itself with the details. We can note the exquisite contrasts
of colour and the coming and going effects of the cloud-shadows
as, wafted by the softest of summer zephyrs, they slowly chase
each other over the woods and verdant glades. The slumber of a
summer day lies profoundly as a trance upon the scene. The
lowing of the kine in the neighbouring meadows, the harsh note of
the corncrake, and the soft dreamy call of the cuckoo are the only
sounds that break upon the ear. Bunbury twinkles through its
screen of leaves far below us, and we can discern the tower of the
venerable church where lie the bones of some of the lords of
Beeston, and where still may be seen the sumptuous monuments
that perpetuate their names. In front, and almost at our feet, is
the Chester and Ellesmere Canal, glistening like a line of liquid
silver, and the railway, over which the iron horse glides swiftly
every day, running parallel with it, types of the past and present
modes of travel. The white road that crosses them both leads up
to Tarporley, where there is an ancient church (or rather was, for
in the last few years it has been almost entirely rebuilt), and several
monuments that well deserve inspection. Close by is Utkinton,
for many a generation the home of the proud family of the Dones,
hereditary chief foresters of Delamere, one of whom, John Done,
the husband of that proverbial exemplar of unsurpassable per-
fection, the fair Lady Done,* in 1617 ordered so wisely the sports
of James the First, when that monarch took his pleasure and repast
in the forest, that, as the author of *The Vale Royal* tells us, he
"freely honoured him with knighthood and graced his house at
Utkinton with his presence ;" but the house which he graced by
his presence was made the scene of revelry and pillage by the
soldiers of his son, the hall being plundered, and the plate, jewels,

---

* " As fair as Lady Done " is a well-known Cheshire proverb. Pennant
(" Tour from Chester to London, 4 ed., p. 8 "), referring to this lady, who
was the daughter of Sir Thomas Wilbraham, of Woodhey, says that " when
a Cheshire man would express super-eminent excellency in one of the fair
sex he will say, ' There is a Lady Done for you.' "

and writings taken away by the Royalist forces shortly after the breaking out of the civil war.

On the western side the view is singularly impressive. The rock is perpendicular, its ruggedness being softened only by the ferns and mosses that have attached themselves to the clefts and crevices, and the shrubs and trees that grow out from the gaping stones. You look down from the giddy height on to the road immediately beneath, where the little homesteads and cottages seem reduced to lilliputian dimensions, and the laden waggon going by looks no bigger than a toy. Carrying the eye round towards the south, the Broxton hills come in view; nearer is the lofty height of Stanner Nab; and then, separated only by a narrow valley, the most prominent feature in the whole landscape, the richly-wooded eminence of Peckforton, surmounted by the castle, with its great round keep and broken and picturesque line of towers and turrets, that Lord Tollemache built some five-and-thirty years ago as a reproduction of the fortified stronghold of the early Edwardian period.

The historical associations of Beeston impart a deeper interest to the beauty of its natural surroundings. Its annals run back to the time of Randle Blundeville—Randle the Good, as he is sometimes called—the most famous of the Cestrian Earls. This Randle succeeded to the earldom on the death of his father, Hugh Cyveliock, in 1187, and shortly afterwards married the Lady Constance, widow of Geoffry Plantagenet, a younger son of Henry II., the mother of the young Prince Arthur whom King John cruelly put to death—a lady from whom he was afterwards divorced. They were turbulent times in which he lived, and he bore his full share in the stirring events that were then occurring; but, though one of the most powerful nobles of the land, his power was generally exercised in the interests of his legitimate sovereign. When Richard the Lion-hearted, returning from his encounters with the infidel in Palestine, was detained a captive in Austria, and the treacherous John, to whom he had committed the care of the kingdom, basely sought to appropriate the crown, Earl Randle and his knights and retainers, with Earl Ferrars and others, besieged his castle of Nottingham, and valorously maintained the cause of the absent King. After Richard's death, when John had succeeded to the throne, he remained loyal to him as he had done to his predecessor, though he had the courage to rebuke him for violating the wives and daughters of the nobility. Afterwards we find him taking part in that ever memorable council which assembled on the greensward of Runnymede, "encircled by the coronet of Cooper's Hill," which secured the rights of the people of England, and the Great Charter that still remains the foundation of their liberties, when—

> England's ancient Barons, clad in arms,
> And stern with conquest, from their tyrant King
> (Then render'd tame), did challenge and secure
> The charter of our freedom.

When that memorable June day had waned—when the Great Charter had been won, and the thoughtful night which followed had passed—when men began to think that the pledges so readily given would be as readily violated, and that concessions extorted could only be maintained by force of arms, Randle Blundeville remained faithful to his faithless King, and defended his cause against the Barons and the Dauphin of France, to whom they had traitorously offered the English crown.

The great Earl was then in the plenitude of his power, and when the tyrant John had paid the penalty of over-indulgence in peaches and new cider, he proved himself a firm and faithful champion of his son, the young King Henry, and, with Earl Pembroke, was mainly instrumental in securing him upon his father's throne, and by that means releasing England from the dominion of a stranger. When the kingdom had settled into peace, having assumed the cross in fulfilment of a vow he had previously made, the Earl betook himself to the Holy Land :—

> To chace the Pagans in those holy fields
> Over whose acres walk'd those blessèd feet
> Which, many hundred years before, were nail'd
> For our advantage on the bitter cross.

He remained absent for about two years, during which time he assisted in the taking of Damietta ; and immediately on the return from his crusading expedition he set about the erection of the Castle of Beeston, for the greater security of his palatinate against the incursions of the brave but troublesome Welsh, with whom he had previously had many encounters, bringing to his aid that Saracenic style of architecture he had found so well adapted for defence, and which is so admirably represented in the ivy-coloured walls and bastions of Beeston.

Randle Blundeville was a famous warrior, and withal a mighty castle builder, for, in addition to re-edifying the castle of Deganwy, on the Conway, which had been partially destroyed during the numerous conflicts with Prince Llewelyn, he built the castles of Beeston in Cheshire, and Chartley in Staffordshire. He also founded and endowed the Abbey of Grey Friars, in Coventry, and a religious house on the banks of the Churnet, near Leek, to which latter, at his wife's desire, he gave the name of Dieu-la-cresse— "May God increase it"—and transferred to it the Cistercian brotherhood of the Abbey of Poulton, near Chester, who had found their home there too circumscribed, and probably uncomfortably near the Welsh Marches—an act of piety he had been directed to perform, as the old monkish legends declare, by his grandfather in a vision. He believed in dreams, and he appears to have had equal faith in the piety of the monks, for it is recorded of him that, being overtaken in a storm at sea when returning from his crusading expedition, and the ship being in danger of sinking, he refused to lend a helping hand in righting it until midnight, when, as he affirmed, the monks of Dieu-la-cresse would be supplicating Heaven on his behalf; and that, consequently, God would then give him strength. The ship was saved, and, as their prayers had evidently availed so much, it may be assumed that the brethren of Dieu-la cresse were a more than usually righteous fraternity.

The castles of Beeston and Chartley were both commenced in the same year (1220), and to defray the cost of their erection the Earl "took toll throughout all his lordships of all such persons as pa sed by the same, with any cattel, chaffre, or merchandize."

The reason for the erection of Beeston is not far to seek. The Welsh were troublesome neighbours, for though the Red King and the English-born Henry—the "Lion of Justice," as he was called—had tried to unite their country with England, they had been neither exterminated nor enslaved, and for long years—

> All along the border here
> The word was snaffle, spur, and spear.

In these border struggles Earl Randle found himself on one occasion shut up in the castle of Rhuddlan—then called Rothe-lent—to which he had retreated, and hard pressed by his foes. At this time his constable of Cheshire, that doughty warrior Roger Lacy, baron of Halton, whose fierceness had earned for him the sobriquet of "Hell," happening to be at Chester, hastily mustered all the beggars, minstrels, debauched men, harlots, and other disorderly characters who were then assembled at the fair, and with this tumultuous company marched to his master's rescue. The Welsh, who were as much alarmed at the sight of such a multitude as the French were at the sight of Talbot, raised the siege and fled : and the Earl, returning in safety, in reward and in memory of such welcome service, conferred upon his trusty follower the government and licensing of all beggars, vagrants, strollers, and minstrels within the limits of his earldom, a privilege which Lacy in turn bestowed upon his steward, Hugh Dutton ; and the Duttons of Dutton, his successors, continued to exercise the right until the passing of the Vagrant Act, a few years ago—the custom being for them or their deputies to ride through the streets of Chester to St. John's Church every year, with the minstrels of Cheshire playing before them ; after which their licenses were renewed. After this adventure, peace was concluded (1222) between the Earl and Llewelyn, Prince of North Wales, which was happily cemented by the marriage in the same year of Randle's nephew and heir, John Scot, Earl of Huntingdon, with Llewelyn's daughter Helen.

Randle Blundeville, after having held the earldom for the long period of fifty-two years, died at Wallingford on the 26th Oct , 1232,

and was buried at St. Werburg's, Chester, his heart being deposited
in the Abbey of Dieu-la-cresse.   Having no issue, his sister's son,
John the Scot, succeeded ; but he bore rule only five years, dying
in 1237, having, as was commonly believed, been poisoned by his
wife, the Welsh princess.

That amiable lady not having borne him any children, his vast
possessions should by right have devolved upon his sisters ; but
King Henry, being unwilling, as he said, "that so great an
inheritance should be divided among distaffs," considerately took
the earldom into his own hands, and gave them other lands
instead.   In this transaction there is little doubt but that the King
got the best end of the bargain, though it might have been better
for his grandson if the "distaffs" had been left in undisturbed
possession of their property ; for in that case it is more than
probable England would not have had to deplore the defeat at
Bannockburn which made Scotland a nation.

> Maidens of England, sore may ye mourn,
> For your lemans ye have lost at Bannockburn.

Of the sisters of John Scot, Margaret, the eldest, was the grandmother of John Baliol, who became a competitor for the crown of
Scotland.   Isabella, the second sister, by her marriage with
Robert le Brus, the Lord of Annandale, had a grandson—the
brave and heroic Robert Bruce—the "Bruce of Bannockburn,"
and the idol of the Scottish people.

After Henry the Third had assumed the Earldom of Chester
the castle of Beeston was left to the charge of castellans, and the
people of Cheshire had a sorry time of it ; for David, the son of
Prince Llewelyn, endeavoured to cast off the English yoke, and
long and bloody were the struggles for freedom on the one hand,
and for dominion on the other—the county being overrun and
ravaged alternately by friends and enemies until nearly every rood
of land was soaked with the blood of the combatants.   In the
attack made by the King in 1245 the whole borderland was laid
waste, and the wyches or salt-pits were destroyed.   Eleven years

later the county was plundered and desolated by the Welsh; and in the year 1256 the young Prince Edward, to whom Henry had two years previously assigned the Principality, made his first progress into Cheshire, when his castle of Beeston was placed in the charge of Fulco de Orreby. This year was an eventful one, for before its close the Welsh again arose in insurrection, when Prince Edward was compelled to retire; but the King marched an army to his support, wasting the harvest as he advanced, and well-nigh depopulating the county, when, as the ancient chronicler, Matthew Paris, records, "the whole border was reduced into a desert, the inhabitants were cut off by the sword, the castles and houses burnt, the woods felled, and the cattle destroyed by famine."

The day was not far distant when Beeston was to be wrested from its royal possessor, and find itself garrisoned by the soldiers of a rebellious subject. The struggle between the Crown and the Barons had commenced, and was continued under varying circumstances; but the Sovereign was eventually borne down by the union of ambitious nobles. The rival armies met at Lewes, and in that hollow which the railway now traverses, on the 14th of May, 1264, the King saw his army defeated by the valorous Simon De Montfort, Earl of Leicester, aided by the forces of the Welsh Prince Llewelyn, and he himself, with his son Prince Edward and the King of the Romans, made prisoners. The next day a treaty, known as the *mise* of Lewes, was entered into; but the King and his son were detained as hostages until all matters in dispute should be settled. In this forced peace Edward was compelled, by a deed executed at Woodstock, December 24, 1264, to surrender his Earldom of Chester, and with it his castle of Beeston, to the victorious De Montfort, in whom the administration of the realm was then virtually vested.

The victory was short-lived; but it had a result that will be ever memorable, for immediately after, De Montfort summoned a great council of the nation—the first in which we distinctly recognise the Parliament of England; for he not o:ly called together the

29

barons, prelates, and abbots, but also summoned two knights from
each county, two citizens from each city, and two burgesses from
each borough. Thus was the democratic element—the foundation
of the House of Commons—first introduced; and, as the Poet
Laureate sings, England became

> A land of settled government,
> A land of just and old renown,
> Where freedom slowly broadens down,
> From precedent to precedent.

De Montfort was now in the fulness of his power; but his
elevation was dangerous for himself. His natural and acquired
superiority provoked the jealousy of those around him, and brought
about his own destruction. As when the light is brightest, so the
shadow is ever darkest, and his success was the ultimate cause of
his downfall. The Parliament which sprang out of the turbulence
of civil war assembled on the 26th January, 1265; and in the
month of May following Prince Edward, thanks to the fleetness of
his horse, having effected his escape from Hereford, where he had
been in "free custody," placed himself at the head of a numerous
army, the loyal barons being speedily in arms. Gloucester, Monmouth, and Worcester, were successively taken; De Montfort's son
was defeated at Kenilworth; and then the victorious Royalists
advanced to Evesham, to give battle to the father, who was posted
there. The contest, which lasted until night, was marked with
unusual ferocity; no quarter was asked or given; the Avon was
crimsoned with the blood of the slain; and, to add to the horrors,
while the dreadful carnage was going on, the air was darkened, and
a storm such as England has rarely witnessed burst over the
combatants. Drayton, in his "Polyolbion," describes the horrors
of that dreadful day—

> Shrill shouts, and deadly cries, each way the air do fill,
> And not a word was heard from either side but "kill!"
> The father 'gainst the son, the brother 'gainst the brother,
> With gleaves, swords, bills, and pikes were murdering one another.
> The full luxurious earth seems surfeited with blood,

Whilst in his uncle's gore th' unnatural nephew stood ;
Whilst with their charged staves the desperate horsemen meet—
They hear their kinsmen groan under their horses' feet,
Dead men and weapons broke do on the earth abound ;
The drums bedash'd with brains do give a dismal sound !

On the fatal 4th of August, 1265, the narrow bridge at Evesham afforded little chance of escape from the slaughter of Edward's horsemen, and when the storm was over, and the sun had gone down, the pale moon on that warm summer night glittered on the corslet of the gallant Simon de Montfort, whose mangled body was stiffening upon the gory sward, to be sent off on the morrow to the wretched widow as a testimony of the Royalist success ; his eldest son, Henry de Montfort, lay stretched by his side, and but for the determined bravery of a few devoted fellows, who bore his wounded form away upon their shields, Guy, the youngest, would have shared their fate. Such was the ghastly end of one of the lords of Beeston—the champion of English liberties and the originator of our representative Parliament.

When it became known that Prince Edward was in the field, his Cheshire adherents at once took up arms ; and on the Sunday following his escape from Hereford James de Audley and Urian de St. Pierre possessed themselves of Beeston, and held it in the name of the King ; and as soon as the fight at Evesham was ended, the youthful conqueror, with his victorious army, marched proudly through the undulating country and along the great northern road to his Cheshire stronghold with the wounded Guy de Montfort, Humphrey de Bohun, and Henry de Hastings, as captives ; and where, on his arrival, Lucas de Tanai, whom the elder De Montfort had made Justiciary of Chester, and Simon, the Abbot of St. Werburg's, came to surrender the city of Chester, which had then withstood a ten weeks' siege, and to bespeak the royal clemency for themselves. The whole of De Montfort's possessions, including the earldom of Chester, and with it the castle of Beeston, were forfeited by his rebellion, and reverted back to the crown ; and on the 27th August, twenty-three days after the great battle, the Prince granted a charter, confirming to the barons of Cheshire all the privileges which Randle Blundeville had previously bestowed upon them.

Once more the royal ensign with the golden lions waved above the battlements of Beeston ; a garrison was left in charge, but, the country having become tranquillised, the gallant Edward went to win fresh laurels beneath the sunnier skies of Palestine. In 1269 he took the cross at Northampton, and, accompanied by some of the more powerful nobles, set out for the Holy Land, stormed the city of Nazareth, gained several victories over the Moslems, and displayed a personal prowess equal to that of the lion-hearted Richard, and a military skill that was infinitely greater. At Acre he escaped the poisoned dagger of the treacherous Saracen by the devotion of his queen, who sucked the poison from the wound at the risk of her own life—so, at least, the old chroniclers affirm, and we are not inclined to reject so touching a story, even though it may have come to us from a Spanish source. While on his journey homewards he received the tidings of his father's death, but, instead of returning immediately, he made a triumphal progress through Italy, crossed the Alps, and proceeded to the Court of France, where he narrowly escaped death through the treachery of the Count of Chalons.

On arriving in England he was crowned at Westminster with Eleanor his wife, August 19th, 1274. The hospitalities of his coronation were scarcely over ere he set about the accomplishment of the great scheme he had resolved upon—the union of the whole island of Britain in one compact monarchy—Wales, his old battle-ground, then presenting a tempting opportunity for commencing the work of conquest. Llewelyn, the Welsh prince, though he promised fealty to the English crown, refused to appear at the coronation, whereupon Edward repaired to Chester, summoned his friends, and prepared to march against the Principality.

Beeston becomes once more the scene of bustle and excitement ; mail-clad warriors are hurrying to and fro ; the pennons of the knights, gay with their distinctive blazonings, flutter in the breeze ; lance and spear, and helm and burgonette, gleam brightly in the sunlight—and the echoes of the stern old fortress are again aroused by the sounds of martial preparation; for an army has been levied and all are eager to advance. Llewelyn was summoned to meet the King at Chester, but refused; he was again summoned to attend the Parliament at Westminster, and again he declined to appear; his lands were then declared forfeit, and Edward led his invading host into his territory. Conscious of their inability to withstand their more powerful neighbours in the field, the Welsh retired to the mountain fastnesses, which had many a time and oft enabled their ancestors to hold their own against their Saxon and Norman oppressors; but, Edward having successfully penetrated to the very heart of the country, Llewelyn was compelled to submit to the hard terms the victor thought fitting to impose, which, by the way, left only to the vanquished prince the sovereignty of Anglesey and the district of Snowdon.

Unhappily for Llewelyn, he put faith in the prophecy of Merlin, the native bard and necromancer, which, it is alleged, foretold that he should be the restorer of Brutus's Empire in Britain. His compatriots chafed under the usurped dominion, and maintained a dogged resistance to the invaders. In hope of the fulfilment of the wizard's prognostications, Llewelyn availed himself of the fancied security of England to break out into open insurrection. The castle of Hawarden was surprised, and the governor, Roger de Clifford, carried off a prisoner; the border castles of Rhuddlan and Flint were besieged; and then, leading his forces down into the lowlands, the English intruders were driven back across the Marches. Elated by his successes, he then marched into Radnorshire, where, after passing the Wye, his army was defeated by Edward Mortimer, and Llewelyn himself, while bravely endeavouring to retrieve the misfortune, met the death he had so ardently sought for; David, his brother, lord of Denbigh, was at the same time made prisoner, and executed as a traitor. Such was the end of Llewelyn, the great hero of Wales, and her last prince; and with his end expired the government and distinction of the Welsh

nation, after long centuries of warfare maintained by its sons for
the defence and independence of their homes—

> Such were the sons of Cambria's ancient race—
> A race that checked victorious Cæsar, aw'd
> Imperial Rome, and forced mankind to own
> Superior virtue, Britons only knew,
> Or only practised ; for they nobly dared
> To face oppression ; and, where Freedom finds
> Her aid invok'd, there will the Briton die !

At this time (1283) Edward held his court at Rhuddlan, and
to appease the conquered people hit upon the politic, though
dangerous, expedient of promising them for their prince a native
of the Principality, who never spoke a word of English, and whose
life and conversation no man could impugn.   By this bold
manœuvre he succeeded in obtaining their submission, and he
fulfilled his promise to the very letter ; for he removed his Queen
Eleanor to Carnarvon, which was then so far completed as to
allow of her reception, and there, on the 24th of April, 1284, she
gave birth ·to a son — Edward of Carnarvon, the victim of
Berkeley Castle, and the subject of Marlowe's tragedy—who was
created Prince of Wales—a title the heirs to the crown have ever
since retained.

The sanguinary extirpation of Cambrian independence, while
ultimately a b'essing to the native race, was also a good thing for
those who dwelt within the borderland of Cheshire, inasmuch as
it spared their country from a continuance of the bloodshed and
devastation it had been subjected to during the centuries of
struggle between the Saxon and the Celt.   The land had rest, and
for a hundred years or more from that time Beeston is found to
occupy but a comparatively small space in the chronicles of the
kingdom.

The power wielded by the first Edward fell from the feeble grasp
of his son and successor.   In the fifth year of that unfortunate
monarch's reign we find the custody of the castle being transferred
from John de Serleby to John de Modburly, who appears to have

been acting as the deputy of Sir Robert de Holland, the head of the great feudal house of that name in Lancashire, who, in the same year, by the king's favour, had been appointed his Chief Justice of Chester and custodian of his castles of Chester, Rhuddlan, and Flint, and three years later Holland was re-appointed to the same office. This Sir Robert, who had married a great-granddaughter of that paragon of beauty, if not of chastity, Rosamond Clifford—the "Fair Rosamond" of mediæval romance—founded the Benedictine Priory at Up-Holland, in his own county; he was held in great esteem by Thomas of Wood-stock, Earl of Lancaster, the king's cousin, who made him his secretary, and he was in that earl's retinue on the occasion of the rising of the barons to remove the De Spencers from the royal councils, for which act his estates were forfeited after the defeat at Boroughbridge in 1222, when the Earl, himself, was made prisoner and conveyed to Pontefract, where, to satisfy the vindictive favourites of the king, he was beheaded.

During the protracted reign of Edward III. and the long French wars, in which the Cheshire men, under the immediate eyes of the king and his son, the Black Prince, won so much renown, several castellans were appointed in succession, though it does not appear that the castle was at any time the scene of active military opera-tions. On the death of Edward, his grandson, Richard, the eldest son of the Black Prince, who was then only eleven years of age, succeeded to the throne, to find, as many others have done, what it is to be—

> Left by his sire, too young such loss to know,
> Lord of himself, that heritage of woe.

A "heritage of woe" truly, for his reign, from the beginning to its close, was one of continuous anarchy and disturbance. On the 23rd November, 1385, we find him appointing John Cartileche janitor of his castle of Beeston for life, in the room of Sir Alan Cheanie, who had then only lately died. The appointment was made under the king's seal, and about the same time Richard himself paid a visit to the chief city of his palatinate—the object, no doubt, being to ingratiate himself with his Cheshire friends, and, that being so, it is probable Beeston was on the same occasion graced with his presence. Loyalty to the crown was a strong characteristic of the Cheshire men, a feeling that was no doubt strengthened by the many marks of royal favour their county had received from its earls, in whom they recognised their titular sovereigns ; hence the intimate relations which existed between the king and the palatinate. When the Duke of Gloucester assembled a body of men in order that he might retain control of the youthful sovereign, Richard hastened to Chester and called out his loyal Cheshire guard; and when, in 1397, by what in modern times would be called a *coup d'état*, he determined on overthrowing the regency and recovering the power which Gloucester and his cabal of nobles had deprived him of, and in furtherance of that object had summoned a Parliament to meet him at Westminster in September, he, to guard against any possible resistance on the part of the disaffected nobles, surrounded the house with a guard of two thousand of his Cheshire archers, each wearing as a badge the white hart lodged, the cognisance of his mother, the "Fair Maid of Kent," which Richard had then adopted.

The power thus regained was wielded neither wisely nor well. On the death of John o' Gaunt, in 1399, Richard, to replenish his exhausted exchequer, seized his possessions into his own hands, leaving to the banished son of "time-honoured Lancaster," the youthful Bolingbroke, nothing but the empty title. This arbitrary abuse of power naturally inflamed the resentment of Bolingbroke, who resolved upon accomplishing the king's dethronement, and it was not long before the opportunity offered for putting his scheme · into execution. While the unsuspecting Richard was leading the Cheshire bowmen among the bogs and thickets of Ireland, in order to quell the insurrection and punish the murderers of Mortimer, Bolingbroke, taking advantage of his absence, embarked with a small retinue and landed "upon the naked shore of Ravenspurg," a place on the Humber, where, at a later date, Edward IV. landed on a similar errand, with an excuse plausible as that of the duke whose exploit he imitated. He quickly mustered a force of 60,000 men; towns and castles surrendered to him; and before Richard could return the invader had virtually made himself master of the kingdom. When he did arrive, there being no army to receive him, seven loyal Cheshire men, John Legh of Booths, Thomas Cholmondely, Ralph Davenport, Adam Bostock, John Done of Utkinton, Thomas Holford, and Thomas Beeston, each with seventy retainers, became his body guard, wearing his cognisance of the white hart upon their shoulders, and keeping watch over him day and night with their battle-axes.

This would appear to have been the occasion when, according to Stow, Beeston was chosen by the king, on account of its strength and the usually loyal feelings of the county, for the custody of his treasures, when jewels and other valuables said to be worth 200,000 marks ($£133,333$) were deposited in it for safety. The castle was then garrisoned by a force of a hundred men; but it says little for their valour that, without striking a blow, they surrendered it to the victorious heir of Lancaster, who, anticipating Richard's advance towards his trusty friends in Cheshire, where his power was strongest, and wishing to intercept his communications, had marched through Gloucester, Hereford, and Ludlow to Shrewsbury, crying havoc and destruction to Cheshire and Cheshire men as he went; and who was then at Chester, where he had caused to be beheaded that loyal and loving subject, Sir Piers Legh, the founder of the house of Legh of Lyme—a Cheshire worthy who had been the companion in arms of the Black Prince, and whose name is still perpetuated in the inscription which one of his descendants placed in the Lyme Chapel, in Macclesfield Church—

> Here lyethe the bodie of Perkyn a Legh,
> That for King Richard the death did die,
> Betrayed for righteovsnes;
> And the bones of Sir Piers, his Sonne,
> That with King Henrie the Fift did wonne
> In Paris.

30

The hapless king, finding his power gone and his castles of
Carnarvon, Beaumaris, and Conway destitute of provisions, gave
himself up to Percy, Duke of Northumberland, who conveyed
him to Flint, whither Bolingbroke repaired from Chester to receive
him. Thence the fallen monarch was removed to Chester; but
he could only have remained a day or two, for on the 21st August
he was at Nantwich, a prisoner on his way to the Tower, having
on the morning of that early autumn day passed with his captors
beneath the frowning walls of Beeston, so lately lost to him. The
close of that sad journey of triumph and humiliation has been
thus described by our greatest dramatist :—

> Then, as I said, the duke, great Bolingbroke—
> Mounted upon a hot and fiery steed,
> Which his aspiring rider seemed to know,
> With slow but stately pace kept on his course,
> While all tongues cried—" God save thee, Bolingbroke ! "
> You would have thought the very windows spake,
> So many greedy looks of young and old
> Through casements darted their desiring eyes
> Upon his visage ; and that all the walls,
> With painted imag'ry, had said at once—
> " Jesu preserve thee ! Welcome, Bolingbroke ! "
> Whilst he, from one side to the other turning,
> Bare-headed, lower than his proud steed's neck,
> Bespake them thus—" I thank you, countrymen ! "
> And thus still doing, thus he pass'd along.

Alas, poor Richard ! Where rides he the while?

> As in a theatre, the eyes of men,
> After a well-grac'd actor leaves the stage,
> Are idly bent on him that enters next,
> Thinking his prattle to be tedious ;
> Even so, or with much more contempt, men's eyes
> Did scowl on Richard. No man cried, " God save him ; "
> No joyful tongue gave him his welcome home ;
> But dust was thrown upon his sacred head ;
> Which with such gentle sorrow he shook off—
> His face still combating with tears and smiles,
> The badges of his grief and patience—
> That had not God, for some strong purpose, steel'd
> The hearts of men, they must perforce have melted,
> And barbarism itself have pitied him.

But Heaven hath a hand in these events,
To whose high will we bound our calm contents ;
To Bolingbroke are we sworn subjects now,
Whose state and honour I for aye allow.

Ere many moons had waxed and waned the humbled and
wretched king, who had resigned his crown to the usurper, fell
beneath the murderous battle-axe of Piers Exton, " within the
guilty closure of the walls " of Pontefract, that —

Bloody prison,
Fatal and ominous to noble peers ;

and very near the spot where, less than sixty years before, Sir
Robert Holland's patron, the "good Earl of Lancaster," had
yielded up his life.

In the fierce struggle between the Red and White Roses—that
"convulsive and bleeding agony of the feudal power" which
destroyed the flower of the English nobility, and well-nigh
exhausted the nation—we hear little of Beeston, though the
victorious Bolingbroke's son, the "nimble-footed madcap Harry,
Prince of Wales," lived much of his time within the palatinate,
and the Cheshire men figured prominently in the stirring events of
those stirring times.

In 1460, when the compromise was made by which the "meek
usurper" was to retain the crown for the remainder of his life, and
Richard of York become heir at his death, we find an entry on
the Patent Rolls granting to him the Principality of Wales and the
Earldom of Chester, in which Beeston is included in the recital
of the manors and castles considered as appendages to the
earldom. The honours and possessions thus acquired were not,
however, to be long enjoyed, for before the close of the year
Henry's Queen—Margaret of Anjou—refusing to acquiesce in an
arrangement that set aside the claims of her son, took up arms on
his behalf, and, aided by some of the most devoted supporters of
the Lancastrian cause, marched northwards. The opposing
forces met on Wakefield Green on the 31st December, 1460. The

army of the White Rose was completely routed, and Beeston's lately designated lord, the Duke of York, and his son, the Earl of Rutland, fell together—butchered, it is said, in cold blood upon the field by the black-faced Clifford.

The grant of 1460 is the last occasion on which mention is made of Beeston as an ordinary fortified stronghold. When Henry of Richmond came out of the field of Bosworth, a victor, he planted the heel of the sovereign upon the necks of the nobles, and destroyed their power by putting down their retainers. He freed their lands from the burden of supporting an army of the State; but, while doing so, he succeeded in breaking up the feudal system. From that time the decay of Beeston may be said to date, and the old fortress must have soon begun to show signs of dilapidation, for Leland, in his *Genethliacon Eadverdi Principis* written in 1548, describes it as being then in a shattered and ruinous condition. In the reign of Elizabeth the site was alienated from the Earldom of Chester, and given by the Queen to her dancing Chancellor, "the grave Lord Keeper," Sir Christopher Hatton, who subsequently conveyed it to the manorial lords of Beeston; and so it again became attached to the manor from which it had originally been severed. In this way it became part of the possessions of that famous Cheshire hero, Sir George Beeston—a veteran soldier who had borne himself bravely and well in the siege of Boulogne and the fight at Musselburg, and whose warlike spirit was not even subdued by age, for it is recorded that in the glorious victory over the Spaniards at the time of the Armada, when he was nearly ninety years old, he displayed such gallantry that Elizabeth knighted him for his achievements. The brave old knight closed a life of honour in 1601, being then 102 years of age, and was buried at Bunbury, where his recumbent effigy upon an altar-tomb beneath a pointed arch may be seen, with a long Latin inscription above it in which his services to his country are recorded. The grand-daughter of Sir George Beeston conveyed the manor and castle in marriage to William Whitmore, of Leighton, Esquire, from whom it descended through the Savages to Sir Thomas Mostyn, who died in 1831, when the property passed by sale to the present Lord Tollemache.

For more than a generation Beeston remained uncared for, and ceased to have any significance as a military station. Under the vigorous rule of the Tudor sovereigns there had been no incursion or civil commotion that rendered a display of strength and resistance necessary, and it was not until the great outbreak of the seventeenth century, when almost every considerable mansion in Cheshire was garrisoned for king or Parliament, that it was again put into a state of defence and made to undergo the ordeal of a protracted siege. At the beginning of 1643 Sir William Brereton, the Parliamentary commander, who had occupied Nantwich with a force of 2,000 or 3,000 men, found himself menaced by Sir Thomas Aston, who at the time was holding the fortified city of Chester on behalf of the King, and had attacked and pillaged Middlewich and other places. Under such circumstances, Beeston, offering as it did so many natural advantages, was too important a station to be neglected, and accordingly on the night of the 21st February (1642-3), 300 of the Parliamentary soldiers climbed the hill, and established themselves in possession, not, however, without some opposition, for it is recorded that on the same night they were met by the horse of the array on Te'erton (Tiverton, the adjoining township) townfield, where one of Colonel Mainwaring's officers was slain on the Parliamentary side, and a few others of the King's, who were buried at Tarporley. The first work of the Puritan garrison was to repair and strengthen the fortifications, and put the castle in such a condition as would secure its holders against attack. The contest between sovereign and subject continued throughout the year, with varying results. In November, General Brereton, at the head of the Cheshire and Lancashire forces, marched into Wales, but hearing of the arrival (at Parkgate, probably) of Royalist reinforcements from Ireland, hastily fell back upon Nantwich. His retreat would seem to have disheartened the garrison at

Beeston, for within three weeks Captain Steel, the commandant, surrendered the castle, without the semblance of a struggle, to Captain Sandford, an Irish officer, who, with eight men, had a little before daybreak on the morning of the 13th December (1643) crept up the hill, and got possession of the upper ward. The story of the capture is told with much circumstantiality in the "Diary" of Edward Burghall, the Puritan schoolmaster of Bunbury, and subsequent vicar of Acton :—

December 13th.—A little before day, Captain Sandford (a zealous Royalist), who first came out of Ireland with eight of his firelocks, crept up the steep hill of Beeston Castle, and got into the upper ward, and took possession there. It must be done by treachery, for the place was most impregnable. Captain Steel, who kept it for the Parliament, was accused, and suffered for it ; but it was verily thought he had not betrayed it wilfully ; but some of his men proving false he had not courage enough to withstand Sandford to try it out with him. What made much against Steel was he took Sandford down into his chamber, where they dined together, and much beer was sent up to Sandford's men, and the castle after a short parley was delivered up, Steel and his men having leave to march with their arms and colours to Nantwich, but as soon as he was come into the town the soldiers were so enraged against him that they would have pulled him to pieces had he not been immediately clapped in prison. There was much wealth and goods in the castle, belonging to gentlemen and neighbours, who had brought it thither for safety, besides ammunition and provisions for half a year at least, all which the enemy got.

Six weeks after, as we learn from the diarist, Steel was "shot to death, in Tinker's Croft, by two soldiers, according to judgment against him. He was put into a coffin, and buried in the churchyard. He confessed all his sins," it is added, "and prayed a great while, and, to the judgment of charity, died penitently." The stern Puritans could scarcely have given a milder judgment, for the dining together and regaling of Sandford's men with "much beer" must have told greatly against the recreant Steel.

The surrender of Beeston was a great blow to the revolutionary cause. The neighbouring country now lay at the mercy of Lord Byron and the Royalist troops, who ravaged the entire district. Crewe Hall capitulated ; the halls of Dorfold and Doddington surrendered without offering any resistance; Middlewich was captured, and on the 17th January, 1644, an assault was made on Nantwich, when, after some busy days of hard fighting, Captain Sandford met a soldier's death, within a day or two of that on which poor Steel was led out to execution. The siege continued for more than a week, when Fairfax, fresh from his victories in Yorkshire, with Colonel Monk, who afterwards played so prominent a part in bringing about the Restoration, came to the relief of the beleaguered town, and the Royalists gave way to superior numbers. They were, however, left in undisturbed possession of Beeston until the 20th October following, when "the council of war at Nantwich hearing that the enemy at Beeston were in want of fuel and other necessaries layed strong siege to it." For nearly five months the siege was continued, when Prince Rupert and Prince Maurice arrived with a considerable force, relieved the invested garrison on the 17th March, and two days later plundered Bunbury and burnt Beeston Hall. Scarcely had they departed than, as we learn from the "Diary," the Puritan soldiers again appeared :—

1645, April.—The Parliament again placed forces round Beeston Castle, where they began to raise a brave mount with a strong ditch about it, and placed great buildings thereon, which were scarce finished but news came that the king and both the princes (Maurice and Rupert) with a strong army were coming towards Chester. The Parliament army marched towards Nantwich, leaving the country to the spoils of the forces in Chester and Beeston Castle.

The garrison thus relieved sallied out on the 4th June, and made an unsuccessful attack on Ridley Hall. Ten days after came the disastrous defeat at Naseby, which put the Parliamentarians in possession of nearly all the chief cities of the kingdom. Three anxious months passed, and then (September 24th, 1645), the unhappy monarch, standing upon the leads of the Phœnix Tower on Chester walls, witnessed the fluctuating progress of the last effort on Rowton Moor for the maintenance of the Royal power, saw his gallant kinsman, the Earl of Lichfield, with many gentlemen besides, fall dead at his feet, and all that had hitherto survived of his broken remnant of a host either taken prisoners or driven in headlong rout and ruin from the fatal field. "Thenceforth the king's sword was a useless bauble, less significant than the 'George' upon his breast."

With the loss at Chester vanished the last hope of Charles. Three weeks after, the castle of Beeston was delivered up to Sir William Brereton, the garrison, though at times subjected to the

THE PHŒNIX TOWER, CHESTER.

severest privations, having bravely held it for the space of nearly a year. Burghall thus tells the tale of the surrender:—

November 16th.—Beeston Castle, that had been besieged almost a year, was delivered up by the Captain Valet, the governor, to Sir William Brereton; there were in it 56 soldiers, who by agreement had liberty to depart with their arms, colours flying, and drums beating, with two cart loads of goods, and to be conveyed to Denbigh; but 20 of the soldiers laid down their arms, and craved liberty to go to their homes, which was granted. There was neither meat nor drink found in the castle, but only a piece of a turkey pie, and a live peacock and a peahen.

The heroic defence of the castle by the Royalist garrison, and their long endurance, even after their cause had become hopeless and all chance of succour had disappeared, presents a remarkable contrast to the meek surrender of Captain Steel and his three hundred Puritan soldiers to Sandford's gallant little band of cavaliers. In the spring of the following year the old fortress, which had withstood the batterings of time and been so often exposed to the storms of war in the troubled reigns of the Plantagenets, but which had never yielded to assault, was dismantled, and since then it has gradually sunk into its present state of extreme but picturesque decay.

Since the days of the Stuarts little historical interest has attached to it. Its glories are of the past. Its palmy days are over—for it has outlived the needs that called it into being, and survives only to show us how men lived and acted in those stern times when they knew no other law than that which Wordsworth speaks of—

> The old good rule, the simple plan,
> That they should get who have the power,
> And they should keep who can,

and when even power could only feel secure when defended by iron force. We love our country with love far brought from out the historic past—the past on which the present is securely built—and we cherish the relics of its ancient chivalry and romance, but the spirit of the age is opposed to the revivication of feudal customs and feudal prejudices. The time when it was only possible for men to hold their own by length and strength of arm has gone by never again to return.

CHAPTER VII.

HALLEY—the Field of Wells, as our Saxon forefathers called it—is one of the most picturesque, as also one of the most interesting villages in Lancashire. It is the centre, too, of a district which almost claims to rank as classic ground. Few places possess greater charms from a scenic point of view, or a higher interest from the historical associations attaching to them. The parish to which it gives name covers a wide extent of territory. Originally, before the great parishes of Blackburn, Chipping, Mitton, Rochdale, Ribchester, and Slaidburn had been carved out of it, it embraced an area of four hundred square miles; and even now it is accounted the largest parish within the diocese, being equal to about one-ninth of the whole county. Well might the chief ecclesiastics of this, the oldest Christian edifice in Lancashire, dignify themselves in old times with the imposing title of "Deans" of Whalley, though the magnitude of their domain was surely not a sufficient justification for their setting at naught the decrees of Holy Church, and the vows of celibacy it imposed, by perpetuating a race of priests who married and transmitted their offices from father to son for successive generations: a state of things that continued until the Council of Lateran not only forbade but disannulled such marriages, and so destroyed the constitution by which the church of Whalley had been governed for nearly five hundred years.

A more charmingly diversified country than that of which this quiet little pastoral village is the centre it is difficult to conceive. Within the wide range of vision it commands we may note the type of almost every stage of civilisation the country has passed through. Though a railway viaduct, lofty as the Pont du Gard, bridges the Calder, and a tall chimney or two may here and there be seen, the virgin features of the country have as yet been happily but ·little scarred by the intrusion of manufacturing industry. The wild breezy moors and the wooded cloughs and dingles retain much of their primitive character, while the fair and fertile valley still bears evidence of the patient labour of the monks in redeeming the soil from its primeval barrenness. Every object that can beautify or adorn the landscape is there in picturesque variety, charming by the very order of Nature's disorder. The Ribble, winding its way towards the sea, as it flows by Ribchester, reminds us of the days when the Roman held dominion—when the subjects of the Cæsars built their fortresses and reared their stately temples, and their chief, Agricola, taught the naked and woad-stained Britons the science of agriculture and the arts of civilisation. The quaint Runic crosses standing in the churchyard, weathered and worn with the blasts of twelve hundred years, serve as memorials of the time when Edwin, the Saxon king of Northumbria, embraced the doctrines of the Cross, and the great missionary Paulinus brought the glad tidings to our pagan forefathers dwelling in this remote corner of Lancashire ; for tradition affirms that on this spot the Gospel of Peace and Love was proclaimed in those ancient days.

> There stands the messenger of truth ; there stands
> The legate of the skies, his theme divine,
> His office sacred, his credentials clear ;
> By him the violated law speaks out
> Its thunders, and by him, in strains as sweet
> As angels use, the Gospel whispers peace.

And the venerable church—"the white church under the Leigh," as it was anciently designated—that peeps above the enshrouding foliage, is doubtless the successor of a pagan temple, for it was then the fashion to convert the edifices of the old religion to the purposes of the new. The ruined keep of Clitheroe Castle, crowning the limestone rock that rises abruptly from the plain, carries the mind back to the times of the stout Norman earls, when men ruled by the stern will and the strong arm, and vigilant sentinels upon the watch-towers looked afar for the blaze of the baleful fires that should warn them of the approaching foe. Within a short two miles of the stately stronghold of the Lacies are the dilapidated remains of Waddington Hall—a house which, though it escaped the fiercer tide of politics and strife, is yet associated with the period when England was drained of its best blood by the Wars of the Roses; for it was at Waddington, which had for a time afforded him an asylum, that the "meek usurper," Henry VI., after the disastrous fight at Hexham, in 1464, was betrayed into the hands of his enemies, and, though he escaped for a moment, he was caught ere he could cross the Ribble at Brungerley hipping-stones, and given up to the vengeance of his successful rivals, for which act of perfidy his captor, Thomas Talbot, was rewarded by the Yorkist Edward with grants of land. He did not, however, long enjoy them, for when the White Rose of York drooped before Henry of Richmond on the Field of Bosworth, the same Talbot experienced one of the common reverses of war, and had to surrender his ill-gotten gains. Westward, lying among the tall trees, where the sharp corner of Yorkshire runs in between the Hodder and the Ribble, is Little Mitton Hall, another relic of the past that serves to tell the story of the changing life of our great nation, and to show how the frowning fortress gradually softened into the stately mansion when order spread as law succeeded might, and time had widened and mellowed our social institutions. The giant form of Pendle Hill, sloping upwards from the green valley, with its wild gorges, where the old forest of Bowland formerly stretched its length, its broad turfy swamps, its sombre masses of blackened rock, and its bleak ridges of "cloud-capped" desolation overshadowing the verdant landscape, conjures up humiliating memories of the credulity, the ignorant superstition,

and the revolting practices which obtained for merry-hearted
Lancashire so unenviable a reputation in the golden days of the
virgin queen and her successor, the vain and weak-minded
James—

> Pendle stands
> Round cop, surveying all the wild moor-lands,
> And Malkin's Tower, a little cottage, where
> Report makes caitiff witches meet, to swear
> Their homage to the devil, and contrive
> The deaths of men and beasts.

The genius of superstition that fills the mind with

> Shaping fantasies that apprehend
> More than cool reason ever comprehends,

still lingers, and the voices of tradition may occasionally be heard
in the embowered gloom of its solitary cloughs and dingles; but
under the disenchanting influences of steam Pendle has lost much
of that weird character of wonder and fear with which the shaping
power of the imagination had enshrouded it, though it still retains
much of its wild and uncultivated character, and there are spots
that remain almost as savage and unfrequented, if not as much
feared, as in the days of the "British Solomon," when its secluded
hollows and heathery wastes were commonly believed to be the
scenes of midnight feasting and diabolical revelries, and everything
and everybody were supposed to be under the evil influence of
decrepit hags who had sworn to do the devil service, and were
endowed by the Prince of Darkness with the power to work
destruction on man and beast. Happily, in these days, a gentler
species of witchcraft prevails. Though the spells of the Lancashire witches are as potent as ever, they are exercised without
fear of judge or jury. Few escape the fascinations, and, it
may be added, still fewer desire to do so. But Pendle has
other associations than those with which the pedantic Master
Potts and Harrison Ainsworth have made us familiar. It was
upon its broad peak that George Fox, the founder of the Society
of Friends, received his "first illumination." There, as he
tells us in his *Journal*, "the Lord let me see in what places He

had a great people to be gathered together;" and then he adds, "As I went down I found a spring of water in the side of the hill, with which I refreshed myself, having eaten or drunken but little for several days before." The spring is still there, and to this day is known in the neighbourhood as George Fox's well.

Wiswall, uprising in peaceful serenity upon the skirts of Pendle, calls to remembrance the conflict between monarchy and monasticism—the "Pilgrimage of Grace," and the penalty that Paslew, the last abbot of Whalley, paid for his share in that uprising—the destruction of himself and the house over which he had so long presided, for it was upon a gallows erected in front of Wiswall Hall, the place of his birth, and in sight of the abbey, which had then passed into profane hands, that Paslew was ignominiously hanged. A flat gravestone, in the north aisle of Whalley Church, marks the last resting-place of the ill-fated ecclesiastic. A floriated cross and a chalice, the emblems of his office, are carved upon it, with the simple and touching inscription—

Jhu fili dei miserere mei
J P

Well might he ask pity from above, for, poor man, in the days of his adversity he found none below. Let us hope, however, that the malediction which tradition says the dying man pronounced upon those who should despoil his house has lost its force, if it ever had any, and that a Braddyll and an Assheton may now step across his grave without risk of destruction.

But the glory of Whalley is the famous abbey, with which Whitaker's history has made us so familiar. Though it is now only a picturesque ruin—

> A pile decayed,
> . . . in cunning fashion laid,
> Ruined buttress, moss-clad stone,
> Arch with ivy overgrown,
> Stairs round which the lichens creep,
> The whole a desolated heap—

there yet remains much to delight the eye. The groined gateway shrouded in the gloom of a stately avenue of limes, the spacious hospitium, the cloister court, with its beautifully-decorated arches, the chapter-house, the abbot's lodgings, the refectory, and the huge kitchens, with their capacious fire-places, may still be seen, but the crowning feature of all, the glorious conventual church, with its choir and its transepts, has disappeared, a small fragment of the walls and the foundations of its mighty pillars alone remaining. Corbel and capital, mullion and transom, broken columns and fragments of masonry lie strewn about, some half buried in the rank grass and nettles, telling the story of its former magnificence. Until recent years, when it was blown down in a storm, an ancient cherry tree that must have been in its prime when Whalley was in the fulness of its glory, grew in one of the courts, contributing its fair white blossoms to the summer beauty. There you can see where the monks sat in the sanctuary; that grass-grown court was their cemetery; yonder is the nameless tomb of a forgotten abbot; and that arch, with a span of nearly eighteen feet, marks the resting-place of another. Verily, the monks of Whalley were as splendid in their obsequies as in their hospitalities. The floor is carpeted with turf, and the walls are canopied by the heavens; ivy, the flower of ruin, lends its melancholy charm, and

the clustering masses that uphold the crumbling buttresses spread
their garniture of green to hide the signs of decay, and mock the
greyness of time with a decoration that lasts but for a season. As
you wander about seeking for the best points of view, or musing
upon the fallen fortunes of the house, you will gaze again and
again upon the broken arches and the empty windows, and think

> How many hearts have here grown cold,
>   That sleep these mouldering stones among ;
> How many beads have here been told ;
> How many matins have been sung.

A spot more suited to the contemplative mind you will rarely
see. Sequestered, solemn, still, the calm tranquillity is in perfect
keeping with the sepulchre of human greatness, and the mind
brooding upon the past overleaps the boundaries of centuries. In
this spot orisons and vespers have been sung ; the low sweet music
of the Litany of the Cross has rolled ; through the " long drawn
aisle and fretted vault " the pealing organ has swelled the anthem's
note ; and where now the sod is shaded by the overhanging
verdure the funeral procession has often passed, the white-robed
monks chanting awhile the soul-stirring "*Supplicante parce Deus.*"
The following lines seem so applicable to the place that we make
no apology for transcribing them :—

> Around the very place doth brood
> A strange and holy quietude,
> Where lingers long the evening gleam
> And stilly sounds the neighbouring stream.

> I know not if it is the scene,
> Bosom'd in hills by the ravine,
> Or if it is the conscious mind
> Hallows the spot and stills the wind,
> And makes the very place to know
> The peace of them that sleep below,
> Investing Nature with the spell
> Of that strange calm unspeakable.

Methinks that both together blend
To hallow their calm peaceful end—
The thoughts of them that slumber there
Seem still to haunt the holy ground ;
And e'en the spot and solemn air
Themselves partake that calm profound.
Methinks that He who oft at even
Brings stillness o'er the earth and heaven,
Till mountains, skies, and neighbouring sea
Blend in one solemn harmony,
Hath caused e'en Nature's self to grace
This sweet and holy resting-place.

Amid the venerable and peaceful shade we seem again to hear

Litanies at noon,
Or hymn at complin by the rising moon,
When, after chimes, each chapel echoed round,
Like one aerial instrument of sound,
Some vast harmonious fabric of the Lord's,
Whose vaults are shells, and pillars tuneful chords ;

and we are almost tempted to forget the errors of the monks, and to think only of them as the precursors of a simpler and purer religion. In the seclusion of their solitary lives they laboured earnestly and with prayerful zeal, for with them *laborare est orare* was no idle expression. They threw the fervour of their souls into their work, and dispensed their hospitalities with a lavish hand ; but they taught no liberty, and preached no freedom, to a Christian world. The knowledge they cherished most was as a lamp beneath a bushel—it kept all in darkness but themselves. Better that their system should pass away, and that their houses should be dismantled and left only to beautify and adorn the landscape, than that we should have a return to their sensual pageantry and pent-up learning.

Many stories are related of the doings and misdoings of the brotherhood at Whalley in those far-off days ; but the legend that they disturbed the peace of the fair anchorites who had their habitation in the hermitage close by the great gate of the abbey must surely be a fable, though tradition affirms that the lady hermits were not always spotless in their lives, and a more trust-

32

worthy authority records that one of them, Isold de Heton, a fair widow, who, in the first transports of her grief, had vowed herself to Heaven, led a disorderly life there, to the scandal of the abbey and the prejudice of the morals of the fraternity. Here is the story of the profane doings of this dissolute votaress, as set forth in the representation made to that paragon of virtue, King Henry the Eighth, of blessed memory : —

Be it remembered that the please and habitacion of the said recluse is within place halowcd and nere to the gate of the seyd monastre, and that the weemen that have been attendynge to the seyd recluse have recorse dailly into the seyd monastre for the levere of brede, ale, kychin and other things; the whych is not accordyng to be had withyn such religyous plases : and how that dyvers that been anchores in the seyd plase have broken owte and departed : and in especyal how that now Isold of Heton is broken owte, and so levying at her owne liberte by this two ycre and mor, like as she had never been professyd ; and that dyvers of the wymen that have been servants there, have been misgovernyd and gotten with chyld within the seyd plase halowyd, to the great displeasuance of hurt and disclander of the abbey aforeseyd, &c.

On this report the pious Henry, as in duty bound, suppressed the little hermitage, and cast its inmates upon the world.

The Calder still flows on bright and clear as it did of yore ; but the glories of the abbey of Whalley have for ever passed away, and the roofless ruined walls serve only to remind us of the days of the old Catholicism ; whilst across the valley, crowning a thickly-wooded eminence that rises from the slopes of Longridge Fell, we can see the tall towers of Stonyhurst, which may be said to typify the new—for the monasticism which Henry so ruthlessly rooted out has been revived in a new form in the stately mansion which once formed the home of the Sherburns. To that seminary of learning, the college of the fathers of the Society of Jesus, and the *alma mater* of so many of the Catholic gentry of England, let us now bend our steps, taking in the way the little hamlet of Mitton, and its ancient church, in which so many of the former lords of Stonyhurst repose.

Leaving the village of Whalley at the upper end, we pass beneath the viaduct, and continue along a pleasant rural high road that winds away to the right in sweetest solitude. The tall hedgerows are fresh with their summer foliage, and fragrant with the odours of the honeysuckle, the sweetbriar, and the wealth of floral beauty that spreads around. Now and then we get a glimpse of the Calder, flowing "with liquid lapse serene," here coming out of the verdant shade, and there going into it again, and murmuring its admiration of the scene in a perpetual song of joyousness. Presently the trees thicken, and through the openings we look over a country serenely pastoral in its character, with its wooded bluffs, its level holms, and wide-spreading pastures, through which the

> Cold springs run
> To warm their chilliest bubbles in the grass.

Behind us rises Whalley Nab, with the old abbey nestling at its foot; the wooded heights above Wiswall, Billinge Hill, and the bleak, cloud-mottled heights of the majestic Pendle. In mid-distance the broken keep of Clitheroe Castle gleams in the mellow light, and just below the tower of Clitheroe Church may be discerned. Sweeping round towards the north, Waddington Fell, Bleasdale Moor, and the wooded heights of Bowland Forest come in view; and, far beyond, the shadowy peaks of Pennygent and Ingleborough, reminding us of the old saw—

> Pendle Hill and Pennygent and Little Ingleborough,
> Are three such hills as you'll not find by searching England thorough.

Nearer we see the woods about Whitewell, a spot dear to every lover of the gentle craft, and to the artist a very storehouse of scenic beauty; the opening shows where the Hodder flows down to add its tributary to the Ribble; further westward we have the huge form of Longridge Fell stretching across the landscape, with Kemple End, and the wooded eminence rising from its lowest spur, on which stands the stately hall of Stonyhurst.

A little more than half an hour's walking brings us to Mitton, a pleasant little rural hamlet occupying a narrow tapering strip of land that runs in between the two rivers, the Hodder and the .

Ribble, and very near the point where the latter is joined by the
Calder. As the old distich reminds us—

The Hodder, the Calder, the Ribble and rain
All meet in a point on Milton's domain.

The rivers keep us in pleasant companionship, but, happily, the
rain is absent. Before we cross the Ribble we get sight of the
ancient hall of Little Mitton, lying among the trees; on the left a
gabled mansion built by the Catteralls in the days of the seventh
Henry, which, though it has been modernised and part rebuilt in
recent years, still retains its spacious entrance hall, with the
original arched timber roof, the exquisitely carved oaken screen,
and the gallery above. With the exception of the great hall at
Samlesbury it is the finest room in any house in the country, and
its erection must well-nigh have laid a forest prostrate. Well
might Whitaker express the hope that "it might never fall into
the hands who have less respect for it than its (then) owner; and
that no painter's brush or carpenter's hammer might ever come
near it, excepting to arrest the progress of otherwise inevitable
decay." Thomas Catterall, the last of the name who held Little
Mitton, granted the manor in 1579 to his daughter Dorothy, and
her husband, Robert Sherburn, a younger son of the house of
Stonyhurst, and their grandson, Richard Sherburn, in the reign of
Charles the Second, sold it to Alexander Holt, of the ancient
family of Holt of Grislehurst. Subsequently it passed by purchase
to John Aspinall, Esq., and his grandson, Ralph John Aspinall,
Esq., of Standen Hall, the late High Sheriff of Lancashire, is
the present possessor; Mr. John Hick, formerly M.P. for Bolton,
being the occupant.

The village of Mitton is finely embosomed among tufted trees
upon a slope that rises gently from the valley, watered by the
Ribble and its tributary streams, and is as thoroughly picturesque
and "old English" as you would wish to see. As you
approach, the grey embattled tower of its venerable church
peeping above the umbrage forms a pleasing object, but its

appearance does not improve on a closer acquaintance, for the hand of the spoiler has been busy, and a coating of coarse stucco effectually conceals the ancient masonry. It should be said, however, that a good deal has been done in recent years to atone for the tasteless barbarism of bygone churchwardens, and Nature has lovingly aided in the work by spreading a mantle of living green so as to hide many of the tasteless deformities. The church is a small and unpretending structure, though of considerable antiquity, some parts dating as far back as the reign of the third Edward, and probably it occupies the site of a still earlier building. The tower is of much later date, and like many other old churches the exterior, by its architectural diversities, gives ample proof of alterations and "improvements" at distant periods. The churchyard delights you by its placid beauty, and the little hamlet sleeping peacefully at the foot is in perfect harmony with the scene. When we entered the enclosure the doors of the church were fastened, but the sexton, who was pursuing his vocation in the corner of the graveyard, offered to bring the keys and show us whatever was worth seeing.

The interior has been lately restored, and the old timber roof of the nave, which was previously hidden by a flat plaster ceiling, has been again exposed to view. There are also some remains of ancient carving, carefully preserved, and an oaken screen separating the nave from the chancel that well deserve inspection. The lower portion belonged originally to Cockersand Abbey, the monks of that house being patrons of Mitton ; and it was removed to its present position when the fraternity was dissolved. The fragment of an inscription still remaining shows that it was made in the time of William Stainford, and this helps us to fix the date, as Stainford was abbot of Cockersand from 1505 to 1509. One peculiarity noticeable is that, unlike other churches, you have to descend into the chancel from the nave by a few steps, an arrangement necessitated by the natural formation of the ground, which declines considerably towards the east. Within the chancel is an old oak chest, bound with iron, and triple-locked, with the date

1627 carved upon it. On the top is a copy of Burkett's "Expository Notes on the New Testament," a paraphrase on the Book of Common Prayer, and one or two other theological works fastened with chains—the village library of former days, as the inscription in one of them testifies: "*Ex Libris Ecclesiæ Parochialis de Mitton* 1722."

But the great feature of Mitton, and that which most attracts the attention of visitors, is the Sherburn Chapel, the mausoleum of the former lords of Stonyhurst. It is situated on the north side of the chancel, from which it is separated by a parclose screen, and is remarkable as containing an assemblage of recumbent figures and other family memorials such as very few old country churches can boast.

It was erected on the site of the ancient chantry of St. Nicholas by Sir Richard Sherburn, of Stonyhurst, who died in 1594, as appears by his will, which expressly directs that his body shall "be buried at my parish church of Mitton, in the midest of my new quere." His tomb is the oldest in the chapel, and upon it are the recumbent figures in alabaster, life size, of the knight and "Dame Maude, his wife," a daughter of Sir Richard Bold, of Bold, who predeceased him. The body of the tomb is enriched with heraldic shields representing the family alliances, and there are some panels of figures. The inscription, which is in old English characters, describes Sir Richard as "master forrester of the forest of Bowland, steward of the manor of Sladeburn, Lieutenant of the Isle of Man, and one of Her Majesty's Deputy Lieutenants." He commenced the building of the present mansion of Stonyhurst, or rather the rebuilding, for it stands on the site of an older house, a portion of which still exists, employing in the decoration some of the stone carvings from the neighbouring Abbey of Whalley, among them being noticeable two shields of arms, one bearing the cognisance of the Lacies, the founders of that house. Sir Richard lived during the eventful reigns of the Tudor sovereigns, and he seems to have accommodated himself very happily to the varying circumstances of those stirring times, conforming without scruple to the religious changes which occurred in the days of Henry, Edward, Mary, and Elizabeth, and to have succeeded in making considerable additions to his patrimonial estates the while. His friend and contemporary, Edward, Earl of Derby, told George Marsh, the Bolton martyr, that the true religion was that which had most good luck, and this article of faith Sir Richard Sherburn very rigidly maintained. He succeeded to the family estates on the death of his father, Thomas Sherburn, in 1536, and two years later, being then only 15 years of age, he married his first wife, the daughter of Sir Richard Bold. He was nominated one of the commissioners for the suppression of the religious houses in the reign of Henry VIII., and for the sale of the chantry lands in that of Edward VI., and in 1544 he had the honour of knighthood conferred upon him for his bravery at the burning of Leith. In the first year of Edward VI., when a writ of Parliamentary summons was re-issued to Lancaster, Liverpool, Wigan, and Preston, he was returned as member for the last-named borough, and in the first Parliament of Mary's reign he was returned as knight of the shire for the county of Lancaster, and shortly afterwards was nominated high steward and master forester of the Forest of Bowland, where he gave evidence of his faith in the excellency of the game laws by "vigorously prosecuting various individuals for unlawfully hunting deer and other game within the forest." In the reign of Elizabeth he was associated with the Earl of Derby, the Bishop of Chester, Sir John Radcliffe, and Sir Edward Fitton in executing the penal laws against those who adhered to the Romish faith, and in 1581 he was appointed by Cecil, Lord Burleigh, along with other commissioners, to compound with the tenants who had obtained fraudulent leases of the tithes and other properties of the College of Manchester. Four years later he was one of the Lancashire magistrates who promulgated an order against the profanation of the Sabbath by "wakes, fayres, markettes, bayre-baytes, bull-baits, ales, May-games, resortinge to alehouses in tyme of devyne service, pypinge, and dauncinge, huntinge, and all maner of vnlawfvll gamynge." In 1588, on the occasion of the threatened invasion by Spain, he was one of the eighty loyal gentlemen of Lancashire who formed themselves into an association for the defence of Queen Elizabeth against "Popish conspiracies," and from the "intolerance and insolence" of the Papacy. Baines says that he was allowed by Elizabeth, as an especial favour, to have his chapel and his priest at Stonyhurst, but the accuracy of this statement may very well be doubted, for it is more than probable, as the late Canon Raines observed in the "Stanley Papers," that "at this time, and long afterwards, the family held the Reformed faith, nor does it appear when they became absorbed by the Church of Rome." Under his munificent hand the splendid mansion of Stonyhurst arose, but death overtook him before he had completed his work. He died July 26th, 1594, leaving to his son and heir, Richard, among other things, "all my armor at Stonyhurste, and all my iron to build withall, so that he fynishe the buildinge therewith now already begonne—the leade, buildinge, stone, and wrought tymber."

The monument perpetuating the names of this Richard, the "fynisher" of Stonyhurst, and his first wife, Katharine, daughter of Charles, Lord Stourton, is affixed to the north wall of the chapel. The pair are represented as kneeling before a faldstool or litany desk, with their hands uplifted, as if in prayer, the figures strongly thrown out and gorgeously coloured. The man wears a full skirted jerkin and the Elizabethan ruffs, and his wife is habited in a long gown with a hood falling over the top of her head. The inscription records that he was Captain of the Isle of Man for fifteen years, and that his wife died there in childbed of twins, "and their lieth intomb'd." In the panel beneath is a carving in *alto relievo*, representing the twins in bed with their nurses watching over them.

Richard Sherburn again entered the marriage state, his second wife being Ann, daughter of Henry Kighley, and widow of Thomas Hoghton, of Hoghton Tower; but this lady, who died at Lea, October 30th, 1609, bore him no issue. He died in 1629, at the advanced age of eighty-three, and was in turn succeeded by a son, also named Richard, whose altar-shaped tomb, on which are the recumbent figures of himself and his wife, bears a lengthy inscription recording the family history for four generations. " He was," it states, "an eminent sufferer for his loyal fidelity to King Charles I. of ever blessed memory." He lived to see the restoration of the Stuarts, and died February 11th, 1667, aged eighty-one years.

Another altar-tomb, on which lie the recumbent effigies of a knight and his lady, is to the "pious memory" of Richard Sherburn, son of the last-named, and his wife Isabel, daughter of John Ingleby, of Lawkeland, in Yorkshire. The inscription, among other things, records that "he built the almshouse and school at Hurst Green, and left divers charitable gifts yearly to the several townships of Carleton, Chorley, Hamilton, and Lagrim, in Lancashire; Wigglesworth and Guisely in this (York) county; departing this life (in prison for loyalty to his sovereign), at Manchester, August 16th, A.D., 1689, in the 63rd year of his age. He, like many other of the Catholic gentry of Lancashire, being devoted to the family of the expatriated James by hereditary attachment and personal affection, looked upon the exiled monarch as a martyr to his religious convictions, and could not therefore be persuaded that he was absolved from his allegiance or at liberty to transfer it to the Prince of Orange." The inscription on his tomb adds—"The said Isabel (his wife), by whom, at her own proper charge, these four statues were erected, died April 11th, 1663, whose mortal remains are together near hereunto deposited."

As the "four statues," *i.e.*, of Richard Sherburn and his wife, and his father and mother, were not erected until 1699, thirty-six years after the lady's death, it may be assumed that she bequeathed the funds "necessary to defray" the cost of their erection. Whitaker, in his "History of Whalley," remarks that the two male figures on these tombs are probably the latest instances (that is, of former days) of cumbent cross-legged statues in the kingdom, and this is

33

probably so, as it has been commonly supposed that the latest recumbent monumental figure is that enshrined in Westminster Abbey, and erected in 1676, to the memory of William Cavendish, Duke of Newcastle. The effigies at Mitton were executed by Stanton, the well-known lapidary, at a cost, it is said, of £253.

There is another monument to the memory of Richard Sherburn, eldest son of the Richard just named, who succeeded on his father's decease, but enjoyed the estates only for a few months, his death occurring April 6th, 1690, when, having no issue, the Stonyhurst possessions devolved upon his brother Nicholas, who had had the dignity of a baronetcy conferred upon him by Charles II. during the lifetime of his father. He was the last of the name who resided at Stonyhurst, and died without surviving male issue December 16th, 1717. His monument was placed beside those of his ancestors by his only surviving daughter and heir, Maria Winifred Francesca, Dowager Duchess of Norfolk. The inscription, which is said to have been written by the duchess herself, is perhaps unsurpassed in prolixity and extravagant adulation, and deserves to be noted as a specimen of the way in which great families were wont, a couple of centuries ago, to glorify themselves in their own charnel houses, forgetting that of the long laudatory inscriptions which family pride had made fashionable,

> One half would never be believed,
> The other never read.

Here it is :—

This monument is to the sacred and eternal memory of Sir Nicholas Shireburn and his lady. Sir Nicholas Shireburn, of Stonyhurst, Bart., was son of Richard Shireburn, Esq., by Isabel his wife, daughter of John Inglesby, of Lawkeland, Esq. Nicholas Shireburn had by his lady, whose name was Katharine, third daughter and co-heir to Sir Edward Charleton, of Hesleyside, in Northumberland, Bart., by Mary, eldest daughter and co-heir of Sir Edward Widderington, of Cartington, in Northumberland, Bart., three children ; the eldest, Isabella, died the 18th of October, 1688, and is buried at Rothburgh, in Northumberland, in the quire belonging to Cartington, where Sir Nicholas then lived ; a son named Richard, who died June 8th, 1702, at Stonyhurst ; another daughter named Mary, married May 26, 1709, to Thomas, Duke of Norfolk.—Sir Nicholas Shireburn was a man of great humanity, sympathy, and concern for the good of mankind, and did many good charitable things whiles he lived ; he particularly set his neighbourhood a spinning of Jersey wool, and provided a man to comb the wool, and a woman who taught them to spin, whom he kept in his house, and alloted several rooms he had in one of the courts of Stonyhurst, for them to work in, and the neighbours came to spin accordingly ; the spinners came every day, and span as long a time as they could spare, morning and afternoon, from their families. This continued from April, 1699, to August, 1701. When they had all learn'd, he gave the nearest neighbour each a pound or half a pound of wool ready for spinning, and wheel to set up for themselves, which did a vast deal of good to that north side of Ribble, in Lancashire. Sir Nicholas Sherburn died December 16, 1717. This monument was set up by the Dowager Duchess of Northfolk, in memory of the best of fathers and mothers, and in this vault designs to be interr'd herself, whenever it pleases God to take her out of this world.

Lady Sherburn was a Lady of an excellent temper and fine sentiments, singular piety, virtue, and charity, constantly imployed in doing good, especially to the distressed, sick, poor, and lame, for whom she kept an apothecary's shop in the house ; she continued as long as she lived doing great good and charity ; she died Jan. 27th, 1727. Besides all other great charities which Sir Nicholas and Lady Sherburn did, they gave on All Souls' Day a considerable deal of money to the poor ; Lady Sherburn serving them with her own hands that day.

Of a truth man is a noble animal—splendid in ashes and pompous in the grave !

There is yet another inscription from the pen of the dowager duchess, to the memory of her second husband :—

In this vault lies the body of the Hon. Peregrin Widderington. The Hon. Peregrin Widderington was youngest son of William, Lord Widderington, who died April 17th, 1743. This Peregrin was a man of the strictest friendship and honour, with all the good qualities that accomplished a fine gentleman. He was of so amiable a disposition and so ingaging that he was beloved and esteemed by all who had the honour and happiness of his acquaintance, being ever ready to oblige and to act the friendly part on all occasions, firm and steadfast in all his principles, which were delicately fine and good as could be wished in any man. He was both sincere and agreeable in life and conversation. He was born May 20th, 1692, and died Feb. 4th, 1748-9. He was with his brother in the Preston affair, 1716, where he lost his fortune, with his health, by a long confinement in prison. This monument was set up by the Dowager Duchess of Norfolk, in memory of the Hon. Peregrin Widderington.

Though careful to record the descent as well as the "good qualities" and "delicately fine principles" of the amiable Peregrin,

her grace, whose grammar, by the way, is somewhat obscure, has
curiously enough, while perpetuating the fact of her previous
marriage, omitted all mention of her relationship to the dear
departed, and has thus inadvertently done an injustice to his
memory as well as to her own, for ill-natured people have
wickedly suggested that their union never had the sanction of a
priest, and that, as the old sexton assured William Howitt when he
visited Mitton nearly half a century ago, the "accomplished fine,
gentleman" was only a "tally husband," a belief that still prevails
in many a cottage home in the district. The "Preston affair," so
delicately alluded to, was the occasion when the old Pretender,
the Chevalier de St. George, made the rash and abortive attempt
to recover the Crown of England by an appeal to civil war, and a
portion of the rebel army, headed by the ill-fated Lord Derwentwater and General Foster, penetrated as far south as Preston,
where it was met by the King's forces, under Generals Wills and
Carpenter, and compelled to surrender ; when no fewer than seven
lords and 1,500 men, including officers, were made prisoners, among
them being the Hon. Peregrin Widderington and his father,
William, Lord Widderington, the latter of whom was impeached
before the House of Lords for high treason, but afterwards
reprieved and pardoned. The Widderingtons, like the Sherburns,
had for successive generations been devotedly attached to the
Stuart cause, the Lord Widderington of a former day having lost
his life at Wigan Lane on the 25th August, 1651, while bravely
fighting by the side of Lord Derby and the gallant Sir Thomas
Tyldesley.

As previously stated, Sir Nicholas Sherburn was the last of the
name who resided at Stonyhurst. In his time considerable
additions were made to the mansion. He rebuilt the principal
front, placed the two eagle-crowned cupolas on the summits of the
old battlemented towers, dug out the ponds in front of the hall,
and laid out the gardens in the stiff fantastic Dutch style then
fashionable ; but before he had completed the work he had the
misfortune to lose his only son, Richard Francis, a youth of nine

years, who, as tradition affirms, was poisoned with eating yew
berries gathered in the dark avenue at Stonyhurst—the fruit of

> Some dark, lonely, evil-natured yew,
> Whose poisonous fruit—so fabling poets speak—
> Beneath the moon's pale gleam the midnight hag doth seek.

The untimely death of his heir so affected Sir Nicholas that he
abandoned his design, quitted Stonyhurst, and never returned. A
monument to the memory of the ill-starred boy adorns the chapel
at Mitton, and among the floral decorations upon it is a bunch of
yew berries ; beyond this there is no evidence of the cause of death
save the tradition which has been handed down through successive
generations, and is still implicitly believed by the village gossips.

On the death of Sir Nicholas Sherburn, in 1717, the baronetage
became extinct, and the extensive possessions of his house, in
default of a male heir, passed, in accordance with the provisions of
his will, dated August 9th of that year, after the decease of his
widow, to his only daughter, Maria Winnifred Francesca, wife
(first) of Thomas, eighth Duke of Norfolk, and (secondly), as
already stated, of the Hon. Peregrin Widderington. The
duchess died without issue September 25th, 1704, and was buried,
in accordance with her expressed desire, at Mitton, when the
estates reverted to the issue of her aunt Elizabeth, sister of Sir
Nicholas Sherburn, who had married William, son and heir of
Sir John Weld, of Lullworth Castle, in Dorsetshire. Edward
Weld, the grandson by this marriage, was the first to inherit the
property, and from him the estates passed in 1761 to his eldest
son, Edward Weld, Esquire, who had to his second wife Mary
Anne, youngest daughter of William Smyth, Esquire, of Bram-
bridge, in Hampshire, who survived him, and in her second
widowhood, as the relict of Thomas Fitzherbert, of Swinnerton,
was privately married to "the first gentleman of Europe"—
George, Prince of Wales, afterwards George the Fourth. On the
death of Edward Weld, the first husband of Mrs. Fitzherbert, in
1775, without issue, the property passed to his only surviving

brother, Thomas Weld, of Lullworth, who in 1794, when through the fury of the French Revolution the Jesuits were driven from their college at Liege, granted that body a lease of the Stonyhurst estate, and subsequently the property became theirs by purchase.

Looking upon these magnificent memorials—this blazonry of human greatness—and contrasting the achievements of the sculptor's art as here displayed with the bare simplicity and, until recent years, we might have said meanness, of the sanctuary itself, from which they are only separated by an open screen, it is difficult to avoid the conclusion that the proud Sherburns were more concerned for the perpetuation of their own greatness than for the honour and glory of God. Infinitely more appropriate is the humble and prayerful ejaculation we found graven upon the stone of poor Abbot Paslew, at Whalley, than this ostentatious chronicling of the virtues of poor frail humanity.

Having spent some time in the examination of the Sherburn Chapel we stepped out into the quiet graveyard, among the grass-grown hillocks where the "rude forefathers" tranquilly repose, and—

> Their name, their years, spelt by th' unletter'd muse,
> The place of fame and elegy supply.

Underneath one of the windows on the north side, half hidden in docks and nettles, we noticed the cumbent figure of a knight in armour sculptured in stone, the counterpart of one of those we had seen inside. There is a curious tradition connected with it. It is said that when the effigies of the Sherburns came down from London they were a good deal talked of in the neighbourhood. A village stonemason hearing of the sum they had cost, and piqued at the want of appreciation of his own skill, declared that he could have done the work equally well. This was repeated at the hall, when the man was sent for, questioned, and ordered to make good his boast. This he did by producing the imperfect copy now in the churchyard, and the story adds that the Sherburns gave him £20 in acknowledgment of his skill. On the south side of the church yard is the circular carved head of an ancient cross that was dug up by a former clerk; there are also several curious gravestones, including one to the memory of an ecclesiastic, Thomas Clyderhow, the same, probably, whose curious will, made in 1506, or rather the copy of it, is preserved in the Townley MSS. Many members of the great family of Talbot, as well as that of Winckley, have here found a resting-place, and altogether Mitton is full of interest, as well from its associations as from the secluded beauty of its situation.

But we have loitered long by the way—who would not loiter in such a pleasant old-world nook?—and must now betake ourselves to Stonyhurst.

From the silent resting-place of the Sherburns to their old ancestral home the walk is little more than a couple of miles, and a pleasanter bit of country is rarely traversed. Half a mile brings you to the banks of the Hodder, where a noticeable feature meets the eye that brings to remembrance the "twa brigs of Ayr." At this point two bridges bestride the river, which, by the contrast in their appearance, not inaptly symbolise the difference between the old times and the new. One, that by which we cross, is a comparatively modern erection, with parapet walls and bold projecting piers; the other, which is placed a hundred yards or so lower down, is a primitive-looking structure of ancient date, extremely narrow, as most old bridges are, and now only serving as a footpath to the cottages close by, though rendered picturesque by the profuse growth of ivy and weeds upon it. The old bridge, however, possesses more than a passing interest, and may fairly claim to rank as one of the historic sites of Lancashire ; for it was here that Cromwell held a council of war with General Ashton, on the 16th August, 1648, when the Scots had penetrated into Lancashire, and there was a general fear that they might reach London, in which case the hopes of the Parliamentarians would be crushed. The Duke of Hamilton had at the time entered the county with a large force ; and Sir Marmaduke Langdale, with another army, acting in concert, was moving in a parallel direction. The Roundhead troopers, under General Lambert, being insufficient in number to arrest their progress, withdrew into Yorkshire ; when Cromwell, who had just succeeded in reducing Pembroke, marched northwards, and, forming a junction with Lambert at Knaresborough, hastened into Lancashire to attack the invaders. On the 16th August he arrived at the little bridge over the Hodder, where he met Major-General Ashton, with a Lancashire force ; and, after consultation with him, determined upon the plan of operations—the result, as is well known, bringing victory to the arms of the invincible Ironsides and overwhelming disaster to the Royalist cause. That night the future Lord Protector was an unbidden guest at Stonyhurst, and was, doubtless, more free than welcome. Tradition still points to the old oak table near the entrance, on which it affirms that Cromwell slept, while his men bivouacked in the grounds,* though the accuracy of the story may well be doubted, for the stern warrior was hardly likely to put up with so indifferent a couch when the " Papist's

---

* In his despatch to the Speaker of the House of Commons, Cromwell says : " That night quartered the whole army in the field by Stonyhurst Hall, being Mr. Sherburn's house, a place nine miles distant from Preston ; " and Captain Hodgson, an officer who accompanied him, writes : " We pitched our camp at Stanyhares Hall, a Papist's house, one Sherburn's.

house" afforded so much better accommodation. The next morning he marched with his followers towards Preston, forced the bridge, and in a conflict which lasted several hours completely routed Hamilton's army, the waters of the Ribble and the Darwen being crimsoned with the lifeblood of the combatants. It was Charles's last appeal to arms, and when intelligence of the disaster reached him in the Isle of Wight he told Colonel Hammond, the governor, that "it was the worst news that ever came to England." For the king it was; for there is little doubt that Cromwell's victory hastened the action of the Republicans, and precipitated that event which the world has ever since condemned.

But we are wandering from our story, and more peaceful scenes await us. As we approached the Hodder the sun shone full and strong, and flashed and glittered upon its rippling surface, broken at the time into innumerable wavelets where the full-uddered kine were plunging and wading in the shallows to cool themselves after the heat of the bright summer day. Half a mile or so up the river, half hidden among the trees on the hillside, we catch sight of the Hodder Place, or Hodder House, as it is sometimes called—a kind of novitiate or preparatory school in connection with the seminary at Stonyhurst. After crossing the river, our road lay along a wild old wandering lane that winds away to the left, rising and falling in a succession of gentle eminences,

34

filled with quiet nooks, whose vernal shade tempts you to relax
your speed and while away the passing hours in listless contemplation of the wealth of beauty that Nature, with lavish hand, has
spread around.   Then a steep ascent occurs, and as we mount the
stony and intricate path we look through the tangled vegetation to
the green links of undulating woodland and the distant hills that
swell gently into the blue of infinite space, and now and then get a
glimpse of the tall towers and dome-crowned cupolas of Stonyhurst
shooting above the rich umbrage that environs them.   Then
another climb, and we are in front of the old mansion of the
Sherburns, though, in truth, it now presents a different aspect to
that it must have done when Sir Nicholas "set his neighbourhood
a spinning of Jersey wool," and my Lady Sherburn—playing the
part of Lady Bountiful—"kept an apothecary's shop in the
house," and distributed her alms to her poorer neighbours "with
her own hands."

Before venturing upon a description of the building, let us refer
for a moment to the account which Dr. Whitaker, in his "History
of Whalley," gives of the circumstances that led the disciples of
Ignatius Loyola to establish a seminary in this picturesque corner
of busy, practical Lancashire : —

On the north-west border of the county is the ancient seat of the Shireburn family. After the death of Sir Nicholas Shireburn, Bart., in 1720, it
was possessed by his daughter Mary, Duchess of Norfolk, till 1754.
It then became the property of Edward Weld, Esq., of Lullworth Castle,
Dorset, whose son, the late Thomas Weld, Esq., converted it, in 1794, into
a college, or house of education, for young pupils of the Roman Catholic
religion. This gentleman's benevolent view was to facilitate the means of
religious and literary instruction for persons of his own persuasion, who had
now lost all the resources which the British transmarine colleges and
seminaries had afforded during two hundred years. He had received his
education among the English Jesuits abroad, and he had witnessed the
violent seizure and ejection of his old masters from their College of St.
Omer, which was perpetrated by the French Parliament of Paris in 1762.
This college was one of the principal houses of education which the
British Catholics had formed on the continent, while the severity of the
penal laws prohibited such institutions in their own country. The
English fathers of the society, not disheartened by persecution, proceeded
to form new establishments, for the same purpose of education, in the

Austrian Netherlands, and again in the city of Liege ; and they were dislodged, pillaged, and ejected, with similar injustice and violence, by the governments which admitted the suppression of their order, by Pope Clement XIV. in 1773, and finally, by the revolutionary armies of France in 1794. In their uttermost distress they took advantage of the humane lenity of our Government, which allowed them to settle and to open schools for pupils of their own religion, under security of the oath of civil allegiance which was prescribed by the Act of 1791. Under the immediate protection of Thomas Weld, Esq., the gentlemen expelled from Liege by the French conducted the small remnant of their flourishing seminary to Stonyhurst ; and, in the course of twenty-one years, by unremitting industry, they have improved it into a distinguished seminary and house of education, of which they justly acknowledge Thomas Weld, Esq., as the founder and principal benefactor. It is filled at present (1816) by more than two hundred and fifty students of the Roman Catholic religion, sent thither from most parts of the world ; and their established reputation for good order and regularity has justly procured for them the countenance and favour of their neighbours.

An amusing story is related of the eagerness of the students of Liege to get possession of their new quarters in Lancashire. Tradition says that the last person to quit the college at Liege was George Lambert Clifford, and that he was the first to enter the new institution at Stonyhurst. Another student, Charles Brooke, was equally anxious for the honour ; and when they came in sight of the building both ran at their utmost speed down the avenue. Brooke reached the entrance first ; but Clifford, arriving almost at the same moment, and seeing a window open, scrambled through it, and so entered the building while his competitor was waiting for admission by the ordinary way.

In addition to that from Mitton, there is another road by which Stonyhurst may be reached, leading up from Hurst Green—a little village near the bottom of the hill, half a mile away, and past the cemetery. The approach is by a broad avenue of spreading trees, a quarter of a mile in length, the vista being terminated by the principal front of the mansion, half revealed through the leafy screen, and which gains in importance and architectural effect by its natural surroundings. At the end of the avenue the road is flanked on each side by an ornamental sheet of water, part of the old pleasure grounds as laid out in the stiff and formal fashion prevalent in the time of the last Sherburn; and, beyond, a dwarf wall is carried across, forming the boundary of the court. In the centre is an ample gateway, with ornamental gateposts on each side; and from this point the entire front of the mansion, in all its stately proportions, appears in view.

As previously stated, Sir Nicholas Sherburn made considerable additions to the old home; but was prevented from carrying out to their fullest extent the plans he had prepared, through the untimely death of his only son. The work, however, which he left undone has been completed on an even more extensive scale by the present owners. A college church and other buildings have also been erected to meet the requirements of the institution; and altogether the place presents a much more imposing appearance than it could at any time have done during its occupancy by the Sherburns. The chief feature in the main façade is the entrance tower, which forms the central compartment, and is advanced slightly from the line of the main structure. It is a handsome erection, essentially Italian in character, though exhibiting some details of the late Tudor type, and is ascribed, though erroneously as we believe, to Inigo Jones. The basement is occupied by an arched portal, forming the chief entrance, and is surmounted by an ornamental cornice supported on each side by double-fluted columns, above which is a carved escutcheon, with the arms of the Sherburns quartered with those of the Bayleys— the family through whom they acquired the Stonyhurst property. The "red hand" of Ulster is also displayed—an evidence that the shield must have been placed there in the time of Sir Nicholas Sherburn, he being the only member of the house who had the baronetcy. The three upper stories are each pierced with a square window, mullioned and transomed and flanked with coupled columns, similar to those on the basement. An embattled parapet surmounts the structure, and in the rear rise two octagonal towers, covered with dome-like cupolas crowned with eagles. These latter were erected in 1712 for the modest sum of £50, as

ST. PAUL'S.

appears by the "artickles of agreement" made in that year and still preserved among the Stonyhurst muniments. From the entrance tower two wings extend, one on each side, both being similar in style and dimensions, though they are of different dates; that on the south being coeval with the tower itself, whilst the one on the north was erected so recently as 1842. From the south-west angle a corridor extends at right angles, connecting the main building with the chapel, a handsome Gothic edifice in the florid or perpendicular style of architecture, erected in 1835, from the designs of Mr. Scoles, of London, and resembling very much in external aspect that splendid monument of mediæval art—the chapel of King's College, Cambridge.

The recollection of the doings of the order which at one time exercised such a powerful influence over the cabinets and councils of Europe, if it did not create a feeling of awe, at least induced one of curiosity to see the system pursued in what has been the *alma mater* of so many members of that notable fraternity. Though we had omitted to provide ourselves with that customary "open sesame," a letter of introduction, our request to see over the establishment was at once courteously complied with.

Passing beneath the great arched portal and along a corridor on the left we were ushered into a waiting-room the walls of which are hung with a series of views, engravings, and photographs representing the hall of Stonyhurst at different periods of its history. The attendant then led the way into a paved court directly opposite the principal entrance. It is quadrangular in form, and from it you can note the general disposition of the buildings, their architectural characteristics, and the difference between the old and the new work. The additions harmonise and exhibit a striking unity with the general features of the pile, while possessing the conveniences required by the present occupants. Altogether it conveys the idea of the ancient baronial hall erected when the manor house had disengaged itself from the castle, and law having succeeded to the reign of the strong hand, beauty and ornament were considered more than strength and resistance. The south side is the more ancient, the greater part having been erected during the lifetime of Sir Nicholas Sherburn, though there are some remains of a still earlier date. There are unmistakable evidences, however, of substantial repairs having been made at the time the house was transferred to the Jesuit Fathers, and the leaden waterspouts bear the date 1694, the year they acquired possession. A handsome oriel projects from the main wall, and beneath is a doorway giving admission to the range of apartments on this side of the building; there are also indications of several other doors that formerly existed, but in the rearrangement of the interior they have been built up. The north wing, which has been added in recent times, is of corresponding form and dimensions, though much plainer in detail, its severity of character almost approaching to baldness.

Entering by the door beneath the oriel on the south side we pass into a corridor that runs the entire length of the wing. At the western end is an antiquated apartment lighted by a five-light pointed window with traceried head, the old chapel or domestic oratory of the Sherburns, but now used for school purposes. Quitting this room we are next conducted through a series of corridors, galleries, and apartments, a detailed description of which is not only beyond our purpose but would be wearying to the reader. Among them is a room deserving of especial notice—the refectory—the banquetting hall of the former lords of Stonyhurst, which, though it has been extended at one end and subjected to other alterations, still retains many of its ancient features unimpaired. It is a spacious apartment, ninety feet by twenty-seven feet, with two recessed oriels and a fireplace capacious enough to roast an ox. It is fitted up in a style harmonising with its ancient characteristics, and is very suggestive of the abundance and lavish hospitality that were here displayed in bygone days, when the "two-hooped pot" was indeed a "four-hooped pot," and fell felony it was to drink small beer. The floor is of marble, arranged in lozenge-like patterns, and a raised daïs or platform of the same material extending across the southern end terminates in the oriel

recesses before referred to. The walls have the addition of a dado
of oak and an elaborately ornamented frieze in relief. Across the
northern end is a gallery protected by an open balustrade, adorned
in front with the head and antlers of the moose deer and other
trophies of the chase, and having the following inscription carved
beneath :—

QUANT JE PUIS. HUGO SHERBURN ARMIG. ME FIERI FECIT. ANNO
DOMINI 1523. ET SICUT FUIT SIC FIAT.

Over the fireplace is the Sherburn coat of arms, with the motto,
" *Quant je Puis*," and the date, MDCLXXXIX. A large number
of portraits are placed against the walls, many of them those of
distinguished alumni of Stonyhurst, while others are again
commemorated by their heraldic shields in painted glass placed
in the two oriel windows. At one end of the room is a large
painting, the "Immaculate Conception," which is said to be an
original of Murillo.

Contiguous to the great dining-room is the library and museum,
which may be reckoned among the chief attractions of the place.
The library certainly contains a remarkably fine collection of
works, including many of extreme rarity and value. There are
about thirty thousand volumes in all, and the collection of ancient
MSS., missals, black-letter books, and examples of early typography
are especially interesting. Upon shelves reaching from floor to
ceiling, in galleries and recesses, upon tables and in glass cases,
and, in short, in every nook and corner, are these literary treasures
displayed. A world of thought, a mighty mass of intellectual
matter, is spread about, before which the haughty Aristarch himself,
without any consciousness of humiliation, might have doffed "the
hat which never veiled to human pride." Every school of thought,
every department of literature is represented ; here are sombre-looking
folios of ancient date that scholars of the old English school might
well delight in, and there, dapper duodecimos of the present age
to gratify the taste of the modern dilettante reader whose platonic
love of literature is influenced more by the external vanities— the

35

gold and glitter without than the solid thought within. Among these curiosities of book-craft, and especially deserving of note, is a copy of Caxton's "Boke of Eneydos" (1490), a translation of a French novel partly based upon the Æneid of Virgil, which provoked the anger of Gavin Douglas, who savagely attacked Caxton for translating a book from the French, professing to be a translation of Virgil when it had nothing to do with it—

> Clepaud et Virgil in Eneados
> Quihilk that he sayes of French he did translait.
> It has nothing ado therewith, God wate,
> Nor na mare like than the Devil and Sanct Austin.

There is also an imperfect copy of that remarkable work, the "Golden Legend"—the first attempt to render hagiology amenable to the laws of reason and decency, and which from its containing a translation into English of the whole of the Pentateuch, and a great part of the Gospels, became one of the principal instruments in preparing the way for the Reformation. The first edition of the work was printed by Caxton in folio 1483-4, the Stonyhurst copy is of the date 1493, and must, therefore, be the third, the one generally accepted as having issued from the press of Wynkyn de Worde, and of which only nine copies are known to exist. A singularly interesting relic, screened in a glass case, is a small prayer-book which tradition affirms to be the identical one that Mary Queen of Scots carried with her to the scaffold when she was beheaded. It is said to have been given by her confessor to the library at Douay; subsequently it was tranferred to the college at Liege, from which place it found its way to Stonyhurst when its owners removed there. It is remarkable for the sharpness and beauty of the type, which bears a close resemblance to the court-hand of the Tudor period, as well as for the richness of the binding. The cover is of crimson silk velvet, embossed, with the words "Maria" and "Regina" in silver gilt capitals, with the arms of France and England quartered, and a crown, rose, and pomegranate. If this book ever belonged to the Queen of Scots there is good reason to believe that it must previously have been owned by her kinswoman and namesake, Mary of England, for the reason that the pomegranate was the emblem of Spain, and one of the badges of Catherine of Arragon, and Mary herself used as a device the pomegranate and rose combined.

Another feature of the library is the collection of ancient illuminated missals, the largest and probably the most beautiful in the kingdom. There is also a copy of the Gospel of St. John, believed to have been transcribed in the seventh century, and said to have been found in the tomb of St. Cuthbert in Durham Cathedral, and a MS. copy of the Homilies of Pope Gregory, attributed to Simon, Abbot of St. Albans, in the twelfth century. In another room is the valuable collection of books presented to the college in 1834 by the Lady Mary Ann, widow of James Everard, tenth Lord Arundell of Wardour, and numbering about five thousand volumes.

The contents of the museum at Stonyhurst are many and varied; some are ancient, some modern, some of great historic interest, and some, it may be said, of little or no interest at all. To learn what they are we must yield ourselves and listen *auribus patulis* to the descriptions of our courteous cicerone, who is familiar with the history and uses of each and all. Here we find displayed the cap, rosary, seal, and reliquary of that impersonation of goodness and incorruptibility, Sir Thomas More, and near it a fragment of chain mail taken from one of the dusky warriors of King Theodore; porphyry from the ruins of ancient Carthage, and pistols that played a part in the fight at Navarino; chips from the cedars of Mount Lebanon, and prize cups of silver awarded to shorthorns of the Stonyhurst breed, for be it known that Papal bulls are not the only ones with which the Jesuit Fathers at Stonyhurst have concerned themselves. Now our attention is drawn to the seals of James the Second and Fenelon, and to a quaint old jewel case of lapis lazuli once possessed by Queen Christina of Sweden; and anon to the tobacco pouch of a Sioux Indian; next we are shown a huge rusty key that belonged to the far-famed abbey of Bolton, and an antique gold ring turned up by the plough near Hoghton

Tower some years ago with the arms of Langton on the seal, and the motto "*De bon cuer*" on the inner side, and that, for aught we know, may have been dropped at the time of that lawless foray in 1589 which cost Thomas Hoghton, the builder of Hoghton Tower, his life, and lost the manor of Lea to the proud family of the Langtons. Here is a bit of masonry brought from one of the Holy Places, and there a bullet taken from the body of a British soldier at Sebastopol. Indian bows and arrows, swords, spears, and other implements of warfare are exposed to view, with grim relics from Waterloo, the Crimea, and Lucknow, that call up mingled memories of bloodshed and bravery. Many of the curiosities are deposited in glass cases to protect them from the touch of the vulgar or profane; there are ivory carvings of wonderful workmanship; crucifixes, triptychs, and devotional tablets; ancient bronzes, Papal medals, seals, and coins of every nation under the sun, sufficient in number and variety to turn the head of a numismatist and set the student of history a-thinking of the changes the whirligig of time has brought about, and the dynasties that have risen and passed away since they received the impresses they still display.

From the library we return through the dining-hall to an apartment named, from its proportions, the Long Room, occupied chiefly as a museum of natural history. Tables run the entire length, filled with geological and mineralogical specimens illustrative of every epoch in the world's history; precious stones of every hue; fossil remains and skeletons of creatures of various kinds; delicately-tinted shells, and eggs of every shape and size; butterflies, beetles, and birds the splendour of whose plumage would defy the painter's art to imitate, many of them the gift of a former student of the college, the distinguished naturalist and genial, hospitable, and cultivated gentleman, Charles Waterton. Another room is fitted up with mechanical appliances, models of steam engines, &c., and adjoining it is one devoted to the purposes of a laboratory.

One of the great attractions of the place is the Sodality Chapel, as it is called, devoted to the use of the students whilst "saying their office," small, but a very marvel of architectural skill and decorative art. As we pass through the ante-chapel our attention is arrested by a large plaster model of Auchterman's celebrated sculpture, the Dead Christ supported by the Virgin, placed there to commemorate the services of Father Clough, who for a period of twelve years was rector or principal of the college. The Sodality Chapel was erected in 1856 from the designs of Mr. C. A. Buckler, of Oxford. It is Gothic in character of the 15th century period, and is remarkable for the elaborate carving and sculpture, and the profuse decoration in polychrome displayed. There is an apsidal termination lighted by three two-light windows with oak traceried panelling carried round; the altar has wreathed columns of alabaster, and the reredos is of stone and alabaster, with a statue of the Virgin in the centre, surmounted by a richly-decorated canopy. The windows are filled with stained glass, the work of Hardman, of Birmingham. Close to this beautiful example of Gothic art is the Community Chapel, in which the students attend mass every morning.

As previously stated, there is another church connected with the institution, St. Peter's, erected nearly half a century ago, and of much larger dimensions, being intended for the use of the neighbourhood as well as that of the inmates of the college. It will accommodate about 1,500 worshippers, and, considering the date of its erection, will bear favourable comparison with many of the Gothic structures of more recent years. Painting, carving, and sculpture have been freely employed, with everything that could add to that architectural effect the love of which forms so distinguishing a feature of the Roman Church. The interior, with its spacious nave, its "long drawn" aisles, its lofty arches, and its elegant oak-panelled roof, has a very imposing appearance. The high altar has a reredos behind, rich in carving, and above is a magnificent window divided into five lights with a traceried head, and sub-divided by double transoms into fifteen compartments, each filled with the image of one of the apostles or saints in stained glass, while the storied windows of the clerestory " shoot down a stained and shadowy stream of light." Within the sanctuary are two niches occupied with statues of SS. Peter and Paul, and we also noticed two coloured frescoes, the work of Wurm and Fischer, of Munich, the one representing Ignatius Loyola, the founder of the order, administering the communion to his first missionary companions, and the other, St. Francis Xavier, "the apostle of India and Japan," who threw around the society the lustre of poetry in action, and "the mists of the wonderful, if not the dignity of historic heroism," preaching to the Indians, some of whom are represented as breaking their idols in his presence.

The college chapel, as we have said, is situated near the south-west angle of the main structure. Occupying very nearly a corresponding position at the north-west side is the hospital, connected with the main building by a broad corridor, the walls of which are hung with portraits and engravings.

Any notice of Stonyhurst would be incomplete that did not make mention of the gardens and pleasure grounds. Though somewhat diminished in size by the additions made from time to time to the college buildings, they remain pretty much in the same stiff and formal style in which they were laid out a couple of centuries ago. They are pleasant in themselves and pleasantly situated, commanding as they do a widespread view of the surrounding country, a country rich in everything that can beautify or adorn the landscape. A curious feature noticeable is the lofty, solid, well-trimmed walls of yew which extend in various directions. Though more remarkable for their quaintness than their natural beauty, they furnish a pleasant shade for the students, and have a certain air of antiquity that well accords with the surroundings. In one part of the grounds is a large circular bowling green, on the edge of which is placed the Roman altar found among some rubbish in the neighbourhood in 1834, and evidently the one found at Ribchester which Camden saw in 1603. It originally bore an inscription setting forth that it was dedicated by a Captain of the Asturians to the mother-goddesses, but this can now only in part be deciphered, the greater portion of the lettering having become obliterated by exposure to the weather. The following is Camden's rendering :—

DEIS MATRIBVS
M. INGENVI
VS. ASIATICVS
DEC. AL. AST.
SS. LL. M.

Within the garden is a capacious circular basin, in the centre of which, on a square pedestal, is the figure of a man in chains, said to be that of Atilius Regulus ; and near thereto is the observatory, a building consisting of a central octagon and four projecting transepts, fitted up with every necessary scientific appliance. The kitchen gardens are on the south-east side, and eastward of them is the famous "Dark Walk," a long avenue of firs, cedars, and yews, very patriarchs of their kind, that meet overhead, and impart a green tinge to everything around, creating a solemn and mysterious gloom, fitted for reflection and the meditations of the religious devotee—a solemn, cool, and shady retreat— a very grove of Academe, and the place of all others to dream away a summer afternoon. These trees must have budded and flourished through long centuries of time ; successive generations of Sherburns have paced beneath their vernal shade ; here the tender tale, the word that sums all bliss, the—

> Sweet chord that harmonises all
> The harps of Paradise,

has doubtless oft been breathed to the fair daughters of the house ; and here, if tradition is to be believed, the last scion of the Sherburns plucked the poisonous fruit that terminated a long and illustrious race.

The college at Stonyhurst has accommodation for 300 students, and we were informed at the time of our visit that, including the pupils at the Hodder House, about 250 were receiving instruction. It does not come within our province to enter into the scholastic arrangements of the place or the educational course pursued, and the domestic life of the establishment is a subject too lengthy for our notice. It may be said, however, that everything which efficient teaching can accomplish is done ; everything that skill and ingenuity and means can provide in the shape of scientific and mechanical appliances to aid the efforts of the teacher is there. As you pass along the corridors, and through the halls and classrooms, you are struck with the quietude, the order, and the perfect discipline which prevail. Morality among the students is maintained by the strictest supervision, and equal care is bestowed in the development of their mental powers, with the natural result that the institution has earned the fullest confidence of its Catholic patrons, while its pupils have given proof of the excellence of their training by their scholarly attainments, and the distinctions so many of them have earned in the competition for honours at the examinations of the London University. The life at Stonyhurst is one in which teacher and taught are in kindly sympathy with each other, and where associations are formed productive of quiet happiness to the one and joy and gladness to the other.

After our perambulation of the college we lingered for some time in the gardens enjoying the prospect from the high ground, looking across the broad fertile valleys of the Ribble and the Calder to the bleak ridges of Pendle and the wooded heights of Bowland Forest. Daylight was melting away into the soft warm haze of a summer eve, deepening in splendour the woods and meads and darkening hills beyond. A peaceful calm pervaded the scene, the stillness being only broken as now and then some feathered warbler trilled out its evening lay, or the wind rustled with plaintive cadence through the trees that waved sleepily overhead, making a dreamy lullaby. Then, as the sun circling towards the glowing west, and the chapel bell summoning the collegiates to vespers, warned us of the approach of night, we bade adieu to Stonyhurst, and, descending by a steep path that winds round the edge of a thick wood, were soon wending our way along the quiet old country lanes to our quarters at Whalley.

36

ADLINGTON HALL.

CHAPTER VIII.

HESHIRE, says Speed, in his "Theatre of the Empire of Great Britain" (1606), "may well be said to be a seed-plot of gentilitie and the producer of many most ancient and worthy families." Smith says that "it is the mother and nurse of gentility of England;" and, if we may believe the author of "The Noble and Gentle Men of England," it contains at the present day a larger number of old county families than any other English shire of equal size. "Cheshire, Chief of Men," or, as it is versified,

> Cheshire, famed for chief of men,
> High in glory soars again,

is a popular proverb in the palatinate, though Grose maliciously insinuates that the Cheshire men fabricated the proverb themselves. If, however, Menestrier's definition of a gentleman, that he must be one "*de nom d'armes et de cir*," holds good, then the men of Cheshire may pride themselves upon a lineage unsurpassed by the gentry of any other county. Among those who have brought renown, the Leghs have ever held a foremost place, and have proved themselves the worthy compeers of the Grosvenors, the Egertons, the Davenports, and other of the valiant men of Cheshire whose names are

> Writ in the annals of their country's fame.

Adlington, the ancestral home of one of the older branches of this widespread family, is a pleasant old mansion, possessing, besides its own particular attractions as a good specimen of the half-timbered manor house of bygone days, much that is interesting in its memories and associations. It lies, too, in the midst of a spacious park, prettily feathered with woodlands, and environed with much rural beauty, so that it is altogether a pleasant place to spend a summer day in—a spot where you may find enough to occupy your thoughts without satiety or weariness.

The railway carries you within a hundred yards or so of the park-gates. A roadside inn—the Unicorn's Head—(the crest of the Leghs), and a few picturesque cottages, with cunningly devised porches of open rustic work, and little plots of garden in front, gay with flowers of every hue—tall lilies and roses that sway their heads in the passing breeze, and sweet-scented creepers that trail around and half hide the little old-fashioned windows—constitute what there is of village. Close by the station, and abutting upon the high-road, is the old smithy. As we go by, the smith is hard at work, the sparks fly merrily, and under the ponderous strokes of his hammer the anvil rings as melodiously as it did a hundred years ago, when, on a bright morning, Handel, while taking a constitutional with his host, Charles Legh, of Adlington, listened to it and first conceived the idea of the "Harmonious Blacksmith," the score of which he wrote down immediately on his return to the hall, where it was long preserved. The park, which is well stocked with deer, is of considerable extent, varied and picturesque, and marked by much unrestrained beauty; for Art and Nature seem both to have stopped short of "improvement," and to have given Time the opportunity of softening the harsh outline of man's labours. It is not too tamely kept, however, nor yet too rigidly subjected to rule, the open lawns and broad sunny glades being chequered with clumps of wood and sturdy trees—

Whose boughs are moss'd with age,
And high top bald with dry antiquity,

whilst through the grassy meads and beneath the woodland shade,

pranked with a thousand silvery shapes of beauty, the freakish
Deane—

> A gentle stream,
> Adown the vale its serpent courses winds,
> Seen here and there through breaks of trees to gleam,
> Gilding their dancing boughs with noon's reflected beam,

as it hastens on to mingle its waters with the Bollin, and unite with
it in helping the Mersey to do honour to the British Tyre. It is
a lovely summer day, with just sufficient breeze to cool the over-
heated atmosphere, and give a pleasant and invigorating freshness
to it ; the sunbeams are dappling the rich sward with their playful and
ever-changing patches of light, and the air is balmy with the odours
of the new-mown hay. The lark carols joyously in the bright blue
sky, the insects are busy in the tall grass, and the lowing of the
kine in the distant meadows, the merry song of the haymakers
spreading out the fresh-cut swaths, and the creaking of the waggon
as it bears its fragrant load to the stackyard, blending together,
make a rustic music delighting to the heart of him who loves the
sounds of country life.

As we leisurely wend our way along the broad gravelled path we
have time to note the more prominent features of the surrounding
country ; and assuredly there are few localities in the county
where the scenery is more agreeably diversified, the prospect
embracing—

> Hill and dale, and wood and lawn,
> And verdant fields, and darkening heath between,
> And villages embosomed soft in trees.

A long line of stately chestnut trees bounds one side of the walk.
Eastward the view is limited by a range of undulating eminences
that stretch along the line of the horizon, dark, shadowy, and
lonely-looking, in places, a kind of mountain wall—the outwork, so
to speak, of the Peak hills beyond—with upland pastures and
sweet verdant slopes, green where the grass has been newly mown,
and tinged with yellow where the grain is ripening in the bright

August sunshine, showing where man has encroached upon Nature's wild domain, and what good husbandry has won from the bleak wastes that once formed part of the great forest of Macclesfield. Hidden from view in a green, cup-like hollow in the hills is the "lordly house of Lyme," that calls up memories of the deeds at Crescy, in which the flower of the Cheshire chivalry were engaged; for it was in acknowledgment of the seasonable aid Sir Thomas Danyers rendered to the "Boy Prince," when on that bloody field his Royal father bade him "win his spurs and the honour of the day for himself," that Richard the Second bestowed the fair domain of Lyme upon Sir Piers Legh, a younger son of the house of Adlington, who had wed Sir Thomas's daughter. Just above the hall the "Knight's Low" lifts its tree-crowned summit; tradition hovers around it, and tells us that far back in the mist of ages a knightly owner of Lyme there found his resting-place.

Peeping out from the thick umbrage on the adjacent height we get a glimpse of the modern mansion of Shrigley—the successor of an ancient house that for full five centuries and a half was the abode of the once famous, though now extinct, family of Downes; the chiefs of which held the hereditary forestership of Downes and Taxal, in the Royal forest of Macclesfield, with the right of hanging and drawing within their jurisdiction, and further claimed the privilege of holding the King's stirrup when he came a-hunting in the forest, as well as of rousing the stag for his amusement; in allusion to which office they bore a white hart upon their shield of arms, with a stag's head for crest. But Shrigley has other associations. In more recent times the name was identified with an outrageous case of abduction—the carrying off and pretended marriage of the youthful heiress of that pleasant domain by the notorious adventurer, Edward Gibbon Wakefield, in 1826. Below, where the great break occurs in the mountainous ridge, and the hills look as if riven asunder by the stroke of a giant's hand, lies the little town of Bollington, where the cotton trade has established itself, and the tall chimneys—the "steam towers," as Crabbe calls them—do their best, though in a small way, it is true, to detract from the natural beauties of the landscape. The hill which terminates the ridge nearest to us bears the name of the Nab, and the one that bounds the opposite side of the defile, the summit of which is crowned with a whitewashed summer-house that gleams brightly in the sunshine, is popularly known as White Nancy. With White Nancy the Kerridge hills, famed for their freestone quarries, come in view. The name (Cær Ridge) suggests the idea that the Romans had a camp or minor station in the vicinity, and the opinion is strengthened by the fact that one of their highways led eastwards over the rocky ridge.

Southwards, near the foot of the Kerridge range, lies the old and somewhat dingy-looking town of Macclesfield, the view of which is, however, happily shut out by intervening plantations and the eminence on which stands Bonishall, for a time the residence of Lord Erskine, the grandson of the distinguished Lord Chancellor, and occupying the site of an older house, where, in the days of the Virgin Queen, a branch of the Pigots of Butley, had their abode. Round towards the right, through the openings in the dark belt of trees, the long crescent-like sweep of Alderley Edge is seen rising sheer from the plain to a considerable elevation, and extending a couple of miles or so, with its rough projecting rocks full of changeful picturesqueness of indentation, and rich in their exquisite variety of form and colour. The steep slopes are clothed with vegetation and crested with a miniature forest of pines and fir trees that mingle their dark-hued verdure with the brighter foliage of the oak and the birch, making a little fairyland of woodland beauty, the natural charm of which is heightened by the cloud-shadows gliding slowly across. With a keen eye Stormy Point can be discerned standing out a mass of sombre crag, in striking contrast to the scenery around. The Beacon close by reminds us of the troublous times when our grandfathers were in daily dread of invasion, and erected this signal that they might pass the warning on should their Gallic neighbours put foot on British soil. The Edge is not without its tale of wonder, nor will it lose the recollection of it while the sign of "The Wizard" adorns the neighbouring hostelry, or "The Iron Gates" that of its rival. But we are not now concerned with the legend of the countless milk-white steeds or the nine hundred and ninety-nine slumbering knights—"the wondrous cavern'd band "—

> Doom'd to remain till that fell day,
> When foemen marshall'd in array,
> And feuds intestine shall combine
> To seal the ruin of our line.

Our walk has brought us to the lawn in front of the mansion, but before we enter let us take a glance at the past history of the house and its possessors.

Before the days of Duke William, the Norman conqueror, Adlington formed part of the demesne of the Saxon Earl of Mercia. The name is supposed by some authorities to be derived from the Saxon words *adeling* (noble), and *ton* (a town), but in the Doomsday Book it is written Edulvintone, signifying Edwin's town, the inference being that Edwin, then Earl of Mercia, a grandson of Earl Leofric and that fair Lady Godiva whose memory the good people of Coventry delight to honour, had a residence here, and this is the more probable origin. The account in the great Norman survey is summed up in the word "Wasta," from which it is clear that the district had at that time been devastated or laid waste by the invaders, and the reason of this is not far to seek, though the story is not without a spice of romance. Edwin and his brother Morcar, Earl of Northumberland, were two of Harold's chief generals at the battle of Hastings. Knowing the power and influence they possessed throughout the country north of the Trent, William set himself diligently to discover the means of effecting their overthrow. The Saxons generally were more impassioned than politic, and Edwin, having conceived an affection for the conqueror's daughter, Adela, consented to abdicate his position as a condition of obtaining that princess's hand. As far as a Norman word could bind she was given to him, whereupon he laid down his arms and undertook to pacify and to bring over to the invader nearly a third of the kingdom. Immediately he had done so the treacherous William, feeling himself secure, broke the promise he had given and refused to accept him for his son-in-law. Stung with the insult thus offered to himself and his house, Edwin and his brother flew to arms, and roused their countrymen into open revolt. The brave Saxons entered into a solemn league and covenant to expel the foreigners from their soil, or perish in the attempt. Famine, pestilence, and war did their worst. The Normans devoted themselves on the one hand to havoc, ruin, and desolation ; while on the other, the outraged Saxons dealt death around them wherever they had the power. The foreigner was bent upon extermination, and between him and the native Saxon no intercourse existed save that of revenge and a rivalry as to which should inflict the greatest amount of injury upon the other. As a consequence, the country was drenched with slaughter and made the scene of violation, rapine, and murder. In the bloody conflict no place suffered more than this part of Cheshire, the frequent occurrence of the phrase " Wasta" in the survey evidencing the destruction accomplished by fire and sword. After fruitless struggles, Edwin, with a small band of followers, fled towards Scotland, but being overtaken near the coast he turned upon his pursuers. A fierce resistance was made, in which he was slain, when his head was cut off and sent as a trophy to the victorious William, and so perished the first owner of Adlington of whom history has furnished us with any particulars.

On the death of Edwin the manor with other of his possessions were given by the Conqueror to that pious profligate, Hugh d'Avranches, surnamed Lupus, whom he had created Palatine Earl of Chester, and who, being more concerned for the pleasures of the chase than the cultivation of the soil, appears to have retained Adlington in his own hands as a hunting seat, for in the Norman Survey it is mentioned as then having no less than seven " hays" (deer-fences or enclosures in which deer could be driven) and four aeries of hawks. It remained in the possession of the

37

Norman earls until the time of John Scot, the seventh and last, who died without male heirs, when Henry the Third, with somewhat indistinct ideas with regard to *meum* and *tuum*, took the earldom into his own hands, deprived Earl John's sisters of their heritage, and so sowed the seeds of discontent that produced a plentiful crop of troubles for King Henry's grandson when he succeeded to the crown.

Immediately after this high-handed procedure Adlington is found in the possession of Hugh de Corona, who would appear to have held it by a grant direct from the Crown, for a Crown rental was payable for the manor for centuries. He also held the superior lordship of Little Neston-cum-Hargrave, in the Hundred of Wirral, as well as lands in Penisby, in the same hundred, formerly belonging to the hospital of St. John, at Chester. By his wife Amabella, daughter of Thomas de Banville, of Storeton, near Chester, he had, in addition to a son, Hugh, two daughters—Sarah, to whom he gave his lands in Penisby, and Lucy, who became the wife of Sir William Baggaley, or Baguley, according to the modern orthography, whose monumental effigy has lately been placed in the old hall at Baguley.* In 1316 Hugh de Corona gave the whole of his manors of Parva Neston and Hargrave, excepting a third part of the same held in dower by his wife Lucy, and the tenements held in dower by Margaret, his mother, to John de Blount, or Blound, citizen of Chester, in consideration of an annual payment of ten marks; by another charter, executed about the same time, he granted the reversion of the said third part to the said John, and in the same year the grantee was released from the payment of the ten marks, and an amended grant of the manors

---

* The mutilated effigy of Sir William Baggaley, after being discarded from the church at Bowdon and lost for several generations, was, some years ago, discovered by Mr. John Leigh, of Manchester, and the author, affixed to a wall in the garden of a house at Mill Bank, Partington, near Warrington. It was subsequently acquired by Mr. T. W. Tatton, and removed by him to its present position in the hall at Baguley. An account of it was given in the *Manchester Courier*, March 13, 1866.

"in fee simple" was made to him, with the exception of the dower estates. On the 15th March, 10 Edward II. (1316-17), Thomas de Corona appeared in the Exchequer at Chester, and prayed that these three grants might be enrolled, and they now appear on the Plea Rolls, together with a separate one granting the reversions. Finally, in the 27 Edward III., Thomas de Corona, the grandson of Hugh, quit-claimed to John, son of John de Blound, all title to the manors.

Having in this way completely alienated the Wirral estates, Adlington seems to have been made the chief abode of the Coronas. Lucy, the daughter of Hugh de Corona, who became the wife of Sir William Baggaley, had a son, John, who died without issue, and two daughters—Isabel, who married Sir John de Hyde, and Ellen, who became the wife of John, son of Sir William Venables, of Bradwell, Knight, younger brother of Sir Hugh Venables, Baron of Kinderton, but who assumed the surname of Legh, the maiden name of his mother, Agnes de Legh, as also of the place (High Legh) where he was born and resided until he became the possessor by purchase of Knutsford-Booths-cum-Norbury-Booths, from William de Tabley, 28 Edward I., 1300.

Hugh de Corona, the second of the name who resided at Adlington, had a son, John, who inherited the estates, and was in turn succeeded by his son, Thomas de Corona, who died unmarried in the reign of Edward III., when the male line of the family became extinct. By a deed executed in the early part of Edward II.'s reign, this Thomas granted to John de Venables, *alias* Legh, and Ellen de Corona, or Baggaley, his wife, all his part of the manor and village of Adlington, excepting the lands which Margaret, his mother, and Lucy, the widow of his grandfather, Hugh de Corona, the second of the name, had in dower; and by another charter, dated 9 Edward II., he gave to the said John Legh and Ellen, his wife, all the rest of his lands in Adlington previously held in dower by his mother and grandmother. Thus John de Legh became lord of Adlington, and on the paternal, as his wife Agnes de Legh was on the maternal side, founder of the house of Legh of Adlington, a house that has held possession of the manor for an uninterrupted period of more than five centuries and a half.

John de Legh, who acquired the lordship of Adlington by his marriage with Agnes de Corona, could boast a lineage as ancient and honourable as that of the Conqueror himself. When the subjugation of England was accomplished the Norman invader was enabled to reward his faithful followers out of the numerous forfeitures that had accrued through the fruitless insurrections of Earl Edwin and the other Saxon nobles. Hugh d'Avranches, or Hugh Lupus, as he was more generally designated, from the wolf's head which he bore for arms, and which may have been given as symbolical of his gluttony, a vice Oderic says he was greatly addicted to, though he does not appear to have been with the invading army at Hastings, having followed the victor in the succeeding year, was largely instrumental in establishing William upon the English throne. In acknowledgment of his services, as well as for his valour in reducing the Welsh to obedience, he had conferred upon him in 1070 the whole of the fair county of Cheshire, " to hold of the King as freely by the sword as the King himself held the realm of England by the crown "—he was, in fact, a Count-Palatine, and all but a king himself. Thoroughly appreciating the conditions of his tenure, he, in order the more effectually to secure it, divided his palatinate into eight or more baronies, which he distributed among his warlike followers upon the condition of supporting him with the sword as he was in turn to support the King. He also established his officers as well as his own courts of law, in which any offence against the dignity of "the Sword of Chester" was as cognisable as the like offence would have been at Westminster against the dignity of the Royal crown.*

---

* The "Sword of Chester" is now preserved in the British Museum. The last instance of the exercise of the Earl's privileges was in 1597 when the Baron of Kinderton's Court tried and executed Hugh Stringer for murder.

One of the eight barons created by Hugh Lupus was Gilbert, a younger son of Eudo, Earl of Blois, and a first cousin of the Conqueror. He was one of the combatants at Hastings, where he received the honour of knighthood for his valour in the field, and he afterwards rendered important services against Edgar Atheling, as well as in the subjugation of the Welsh, for which welcome aid Earl Hugh rewarded him with considerable estates in the newly-acquired county, and he chose Kinderton as the seat of his barony. Like his patron, he was devoted to the pleasure of the chase, and from that circumstance acquired the name of Venables (*Venator abilis*), which some of his descendants have retained to the present day, in the same way that another Norman chieftain, a nephew of Hugh Lupus, and a mighty hunter withal, took the name of Grosvenor—Gilbert *Le Gros venor*—which is now perpetuated by the ducal house of Westminster.

Gilbert Venables, Baron of Kinderton, who was a widower at the time of the Norman Conquest, again entered the marriage state, his second wife being Maud, the daughter of Wlofaith Fitz Ivon, another Norman soldier, who had the lordship of Halton, near Daresbury, conferred upon him by the gift of his brother Nigell, Baron of Halton. This lady bore him in addition to a son, William, who succeeded to the barony of Kinderton, and a daughter, Amabella, who became the wife of Richard de Davenport, a second son, Thomas Venables, whose exploits, if that most respectable authority, tradition, is to be believed, rivalled those of the mythical champion, St. George, and that more modern hero, More of More Hall, who—

> With nothing at all,
> Slew the Dragon of Wantley.

Here is the story as veraciously recorded by an ancient chronicler in the Harleian MSS. (No. 2,119, art. 36.) In the time of this Thomas Venables, it says, "Yt chaunced a terrible dragon to remayne and make his abode in the lordshippe of Moston, in the

sayde countye of Chester, where he devowred all such p'sons as
he lay'd hold on, which ye said Thomas Venables heringe tell of,
consyderinge the pittyfull and dayly dystruction of the people
w'thowte recov'ie who in followinge th' example of the valiante
Romaynes and other worthie men, not regarding his own life, in
comparison of the commoditie and safeguard of his countrymen,
dyd in his awne p'son valiantlie and courragiouslie set on the saide
dragon, where firste he shotte hym throwe with an arrowe, and
afterward with other weapons manfullie slew him, at which instant
tyme the sayd dragon was devowringe of a child. For which
worthy and valiant act was given him the Lordshippe of Moston by
the auncestors of the Earle of Oxford, Lord of the Fee there. And
alsoe ever since the said Thomas Venables and his heires, in
remembrance thereof, have used to bear, as well in theire armes,
as in their crest, a dragon."* The old chronicler has omitted to
give us a description of this wonderful creature, but doubtless it
bore a close resemblance to the monster of Wantley, whose
appearance is thus pourtrayed in the "Percy Reliques" :—

> This Dragon had two furious Wings,
> Each one upon each Shoulder.
> With a sting in his Tayl
> As long as a Flayl,
> Which made him bolder and bolder.
> He had long Claws,
> And in his Jaws,
> Four and Forty Teeth of Iron,
> With a Hide as Tough as any Buff,
> Which did him round Inviron.
>
> Have you not heard that the Trojan Horse
> Held seventy men in his Belly !
> This Dragon was not quite so big,
> But very near, I'll tell ye.

---

* The Venables, Barons of Kinderton, bore for their crest a wivern (*i.e.*,
dragon), with wings endorsed, gules, standing on a fish weir, or trap, devour-
a child, and pierced through the neck with an arrow, all ppr.

Devour did he,
Poor children Three,
That could not with him grapple;
And at one Sup
He eat them up,
As one should eat an Apple.

The sixth in direct descent from the first Baron of Kinderton was Sir William Venables, who, by his wife Margaret, daughter of Sir Thomas Dutton of Dutton, had two sons, Sir Hugh, who inherited the barony, and Sir William, to whom his father gave the lordship of Bradwall, near Sandbach. This William was twice married, his second wife being Agnes, daughter and heir of Richard de Legh, of the West Hall, near Knutsford, and the widow of Richard de Lymme. By her he had John Venables, who, as previously stated, assumed his mother's maiden name of Legh. He became the owner by purchase of Norbury Booths, and married some time previous to 1315 Ellen de Corona, who inherited the Adlington estates under the settlement of her grand-nephew, Thomas de Corona. Four sons were born of this marriage, three of whom became the founders of distinct houses : John, ancestor of the Leghs of Booths; Robert, to whom, at the death of his mother in 1352, the manor of Adlington reverted under the Corona settlement, and who thus became progenitor of the Leghs of Adlington, Lyme, Ridge, Stoneleigh, Stockwell, &c. ; William, founder of the line of Isall in Cumberland, and from whom descended Sir William Legh, Bart., Lord Chief Justice of England ; and Peter de Legh, who in right of his wife Ellen, daughter and heir of Philip de Bechton, acquired the Bechton estates, which were in turn conveyed by his two daughters, Margaret and Elizabeth, to their respective husbands, Thomas Fitton, of Gawsworth, and John de Davenport, of Henbury.

Robert de Legh, who succeeded to the manor of Adlington on the death of his mother in 1352, had a commission as a justice in eyre for Macclesfield, and was also appointed a steward of the manor and forest of Macclesfield. He was twice married, his first wife being Sibilla, the daughter of Henry de Honford, of Honford

(Handforth), by whom he had, in addition to two daughters, Robert, who succeeded as heir to the Adlington estates, and Hugh, who predeceased him. His second wife was Maud, the daughter and heir of Adam de Norley of Northleigh, of the manor of that name, near Wigan, Knight. This lady, who is said to have been his second cousin, and very young at the time of her marriage, bore him two sons in his old age, Peter or Piers, and John. Peter, who was born about the year 1361, married in 1388, Margaret, the daughter and heiress of that famous Cheshire hero, Sir Thomas d'Anyers, who distinguished himself at the battle of Crescy* by taking prisoner the Count de Tankerville, chamberlain to the King of France, and rescuing the standard of the Black Prince when it was in danger of being captured, in acknowledgment of which services his daughter afterwards received a Royal grant of the manor of Lyme Handley, and, with her husband, became progenitor of the Leghs of Lyme and the Leghs of Ridge. John de Legh, the younger son by the second marriage, was keeper of Macclesfield Park prior to 1395, and was sometimes designated John de Macclesfield. He was living in 1399, and had issue.

Robert de Legh died at Macclesfield, about the year 1370. Before his death his wife Maud, who survived, conveyed to him all her estates in trust for their son, Piers Legh, who, at the time of his father's death, was a child of nine years. Six years after the death of Sir Robert the name of his widow was unpleasantly associated with a charge of fraud, as appears by the Chamberlain's accounts at Chester, she being indicted with one Thomas le Par, who possibly may have been more active in the matter than herself, with fabricating, in the name of Adam de Kingsley, the trustee, a false settlement of the Broome estates within Lymm in fraud of the heir and in favour of her youngest son, John, and his

---

* It has been frequently stated that Peter Legh, the first of Lyme, also fought at Crescy ; but he was not born until fifteen years after that famous victory.

heirs male; and with having, through such false charter, unjustly retained possession of the land for six years after her husband's death. The issue of the indictment is not recorded; but it is clear that if she had succeeded her act would have given to her son John a considerable estate, to the disadvantage of his elder brother.

Robert de Legh, who inherited the manor of Adlington on the death of his father, *circa* 1370, was, in 1358, in the retinue of Edward the Black Prince in the war in Gascony; and there is an entry in the Palatinate Rolls at Chester that he, with William de Bostock and Hugh, son of Thomas le Smyth, of Mottram, entered into a recognisance indemnifying the chamberlain for any moneys that might be due to two of the Cheshire archers who were serving under him while with the prince. In 1360-61, as appears by the Recognisance Rolls, he had granted to him the custody of the lands in Cheshire lately belonging to Henry de Honford, then deceased, with the wardship and marriage of his daughter and heiress, Katherine. In 1382, Joan, Princess of Wales, the widow of the Black Prince, and the once "Fair Maid of Kent," gave to him and William del Dounes a lease for twelve years of her part of the town of Bollington, with the water-mill there, on a payment of eight marks yearly. He appears to have succeeded his father in the office of bailiff of the manor of Macclesfield, and to have held it until 1382, when his half-brothers, Peter and John, were appointed in his stead. He died on the 9th November, 1382, leaving by his wife Matilda, daughter of Sir John Arderne, of Aldford, Knight, a son, Robert, born at Roter-le-Hay, and baptised at Audlem on the 2nd March, 1361-2, and then aged 20; and two daughters—Margery, who became the wife of Thomas de Davenport, of Henbury, and Katherine, who married Reginald Downes.

Robert de Legh made proof of age on the 3rd March, 1382-3. On the 13th May following he had livery of his father's lands, and on the 18th June he had also, as heir of his mother, livery of what pertained to her as one of the heirs of Alina, daughter of

38

Robert Daa, whose lands were then in the king's hands. In 1385, or thereabouts, he married Isabel, daughter and heir of Sir Thomas de Belgrave, Knight, who brought him the manor of Belgrave, with several other estates in Cheshire and Flintshire. With these, and the lands in Hyde, Stockport, Romiley, and Etchells, the inheritance of his mother, the influence and social importance of the family were largely increased, while Robert de Legh himself, by the active part he took in the service of his country, as well as in the administration of the affairs of his own county, attained to considerable distinction, and well sustained the honour and dignity of his house. In July, 1385, shortly after his marriage, he had protection of his lands guaranteed to him on his departure to Scotland in the King's service, the occasion being the expedition headed by Richard in person, following upon the invasion of John of Gaunt, which, however, terminated without any trial of strength in battle, for while the English army proceeded northwards, took Edinburgh, and marched towards Aberdeen, wasting the country as it advanced, the Scotch, with their French allies, in turn entered Cumberland and Westmorland, burning and plundering as they went on every side. In the succeeding year Robert de Legh had the honour of knighthood conferred upon him, and shortly after (September 26, 1386), on the threatening of a French invasion, he, with Robert de Grosvenor, Knight, Reginald del Dounes, and William de Shore, had protection granted on his departure for the coast, there to stay for the safe custody of those parts and the defence of the realm. In 1389 a contention arose between Sir Robert and his kinsmen Peter, of Lyme, and John, his brother, a renewal probably of a former dispute, touching the manner in which they should discharge their several offices within the hundred of Macclesfield, when Sir Robert with his sureties entered into recognisances to the King for one thousand marks, to keep the peace towards Peter and John Legh, they at the same time entering into counter-recognisances of the same amount to keep the peace towards Sir Robert. He and Peter de Legh, of Lyme, having been entrusted with the custody of John, the son and heir of William Launcelyn, during his minority, an order was made to them in 1392, as appears by the Recognisance Rolls, to deliver possession of all his inheritance to the said John on his making proof of age; at the same time a like order was made with reference to Thomas, son and heir of William Voil, who, while under age, had been in their custody, and in the same year a commission was issued to Sir Robert, jointly with Peter Legh, to arrest all malefactors and disturbers of the peace within the hundred of Macclesfield. On the 12th October, 1393, John de Massey, of Tatton, Sheriff of Cheshire, having been attainted, a commission was issued to Sir Robert Legh and others, directing them to arrest him and Thomas Talbot, Knight, and convey them to the castle of Chester, and two days afterwards another commission was issued appointing Sir Robert de Legh sheriff of the county during pleasure, in the place of Massey. In 1394, when Richard the Second proceeded to Ireland to quell the revolt which had broken out among the native chiefs, taking with him four thousand knights, and thirty thousand archers, including many of the noted Cheshire bowmen, we find Sir Robert Legh, of Adlington, accompanying him, he being in the train of Thomas, Earl of Nottingham; before his departure license was given to William de Shore, William de Prydyn (afterwards rector of Gawsworth), and Henry Marchall, to act as his attorneys during his absence. On the 23rd September, 1396, a commission was issued appointing him one of the King's justices for the three hundreds of the eyre of Macclesfield; on the 12th February following he was a second time made Sheriff of Cheshire; six months later (August 20th, 1397) he had a grant of an annuity of £40, the King retaining him in his service for life; and as a further mark of his sovereign's favour he had conferred upon him on the 4th October following the office of Constable of the Castle of Oswaldestre (Oswestry) for life, with £10 yearly and the accustomed fees. In 1398 he was again named one of the justices for the three hundreds of the eyre at Macclesfield, and on the 20th August in the following year, when the banished Bolingbroke, taking advantage

of the King's absence in Ireland, had returned to England, raised the
standard of insurrection, and eventually compelled the humbled
and wretched Richard to renounce the crown, John de Legh, of
Booths, one of the seven gallant Cheshire men who had met the
King on his landing in Wales, submitted himself to the usurper,
when Sir Robert de Legh of Adlington and Sir John Stanley
became sureties in £200 for his good behaviour. Unlike his
relative of Lyme, Peter Legh, who remained true to his sovereign
to the last, and at Chester sealed his loyalty with his life, as his
monumental inscription in Macclesfield old church still testifies,
and whose name Daniel thus perpetuates —

> Nor thou, magnanimous Legh, must not be left
> In darkness, for thy rare fidelity—
> To save thy faith—content to lose thy head,
> That reverent head, of good men honoured—

Sir Robert of Adlington elected to join the winning side, and
repaired to Shrewsbury, where he made his submission to the
victorious Bolingbroke, and afterwards joined with Sir James Booth
and other Cheshire men in furthering his cause. In this it must
be admitted the lord of Adlington showed as little gratitude as
loyalty, for it was only a few short months before that he had been
retained and pensioned by the king, and made constable or keeper
for life of Oswestry Castle, with an adequate salary; and had,
moreover, been honoured in receiving his sovereign as his guest
during the sitting of the Parliament at Shrewsbury, the occasion
being the memorable one when Bolingbroke charged the Duke of
Norfolk with treason to his liege lord the king. After Richard's
deposition and the accession of Bolingbroke as Henry IV., Sir
Robert was made one of the conservators of the peace for the
hundred of Macclesfield, and about the same time had a confirmation of the letters of the 20th August, 1397, granting him the
annuity of £40 for life. Hugh le Despencer, Knt., having in
1401 been appointed steward of Macclesfield, and surveyor,
keeper, and master of the forests of Macclesfield and Mara, and all
other of the Prince's forests in Cheshire for life, Sir Robert de

Legh was appointed by him to act as his deputy. In the follow-year (Oct. 16, 1402) he was again named one of the justices for the three hundreds of the eyre at Macclesfield, and at the same time a commission was issued to him and the other justices, directing them to inquire into the doings of certain malefactors and disturbers of the peace in the hundred of Macclesfield of whose enormities the Prince (as Earl of Chester) had been informed. After the battle of Shrewsbury, in which the valorous Hotspur lost his life, Henry, who had found the throne of an usurper only a bed of thorns, had to direct his arms against the obnoxious Glendower, and the young Prince of Wales, then only seventeen years of age, who was appointed to head the expedition, issued his precept (11th January, 1403-4) to Sir Robert Legh and others "to hasten to his possessions on the Marches of Wales, there to make defence against the coming of Owen Glendower, according to an order in council, enacting that, on the occasion of war against the King and the kingdom of England, all those holding possessions on the Marches nearest to the enemy should reside on the same for the defence of the realm." This order, however, would seem to have been countermanded, for in an old MS. account of the family, beautifully written on vellum, and still preserved at Adlington, it is stated that on the breaking out of the revolt in the north of England, when the Earl of Northumberland, the Earl of Nottingham, Lord Bardolf, and Scrope, Archbishop of York, confederated to place the Earl of March on the throne, Sir Robert Legh received a summons from the Prince of Wales, as Earl of Chester, countermanding one previously issued, and "requiring him to attend him (the Prince) in person at Warrington on Thursday then next, or on Friday at Preston, or on Saturday at Skipton-in-Craven, with 100 defensible, honest, able bowmen, in good array for war, to go with him thence to his father the King, then on his journey to Pontefract." This was on the 26th May, 6 Henry IV. (1405), and it is the last occasion on which Sir Robert's name occurs in connection with any important move-ment, for three years later (August, 1408) he brought to a close a short but very active and eventful life, being then only forty-seven years of age.

Sir Robert Legh, of Adlington, made his will on the 9th August, 1408, and he must then have been *in extremis*, for he died before the 18th, and was buried, in accordance with his expressed desire, in the Church of St. Mary de la Pree, near Northampton. Among other things, he directed the payment of 14 marks (£9 6s. 8d.) to a priest celebrating in the church of Prestbury for two years— probably the priest serving at one of the chantry altars there. The inquisition taken after his death is interesting as showing the extent of the family possessions at that time. They included the whole of the manor of Adlington, a moiety of the manor of Hyde, the manor of Belgrave, 40 acres of land in Eccleston, 12 messuages and 20 acres of land in Stockport, three messuages and 20 acres of land in Romiley, one messuage and 20 acres of land in Cheadle, one messuage in Macclesfield, one messuage and three acres of land in Rainow within the forest of Macclesfield, two messuages and two acres of land in Bollington, one messuage and 10 acres of land in Budworth, in the Fryth (the forest of Delamere), one messuage and 10 acres of land in Tyresford, two messuages and two acres of land in Kelsall, one messuage and 20 acres of land in Legh, four salt pits, four shops and land in Northwich, three mes- suages in Chester, one messuage and 20 acres of land in Warford, two messuages and 40 acres of land in Mottram Andrew, one messuage and 20 acres of land in Fulshaw, and the third part of one messuage and two acres of land in Mottram-in-Longdendale. By his wife, Elizabeth Belgrave, he had two sons—Robert, who inherited Adlington, and Reginald, of Mottram Andrew, who built the tower and south porch of Prestbury church, as the inscription on his sepulchral slab in the chancel there, which may still be seen, testifies,* and two daughters. The name of his second wife is not

---

* It is somewhat remarkable that though the Leghs have been settled in the parish for more than five centuries, and have been patrons of the church for many generations, there is not a single monumental inscription or other memorial of them in the church, excepting that of Reginald Legh, of an earlier date than the one of Charles Legh, who died in 1781.

known with certainty, but she did not long wear the trappings of widowhood, for on the 28th February, 1409-10, as appears by an enrolment on the Recognisance Rolls in the Record Office, she had a pardon granted to her for marrying Richard de Clyderhow without the licence of the Earl of Chester.

Robert Legh, who succeeded as lord of Adlington, though he was only twenty-two years of age at the time of his father's death, did not long enjoy possession of the property. Dr. Renaud, relying apparently on the MS. at Adlington, says that he died in 1410, but this statement, as we shall hereafter see, is inaccurate. Shortly after he entered upon his inheritance, a dispute arose between him and the Grosvenors, of Eaton, touching their respective rights to certain lands at Pulford and other places in the neighbourhood of Chester, under the settlement of Robert Legh's maternal grandfather, Thomas de Belgrave, and his wife, who was heiress of Pulford. Eventually the two disputants, with their relations and friends, on the 14th April, 1412, repaired to the "Chapel" at Macclesfield—the old church of St. Michael—when a very remarkable ceremony took place, which is thus recorded in the pages of Ormerod :—

A series of deeds relating to these lands having been publicly read in the chapel, it was stated that Sir Robert de Legh, Isabel, his wife, and Robert de Legh, their son and heir, having claimed them, it had been agreed, in order to settle their differences, that Sir Thomas Grosvenor should take a solemn oath on the body of Christ, in the presence of 24 gentlemen, or as many as he wished. Accordingly Robert del Birches, the Chaplain, whom Robert de Legh had brought with him, celebrated a mass of the Holy Trinity, and consecrated the Host, and after the mass, having arrayed himself in his alb, with the amice, the stole, and the maniple, held forth the Host before the altar, whereupon Sir Thomas Grosvenor knelt down before him whilst the settlements were again read by James Holt, counsel of Robert de Legh, and then he swore upon the body of Christ that he believed in the truth of these charters. Immediately after this Sir Lawrence de Merbury, sheriff of the county, and 57 other principal knights and gentlemen of Cheshire affirmed themselves singly to be witnesses of this oath, all elevating their hands at the same time towards the Host. This first part of the ceremony concluded with Sir Thomas Grosvenor receiving the sacrament, and Robert Legh and Sir Thomas kissing each other in confirmation of the aforesaid agreement. Immediately after this,

Sir Robert publicly acknowledged the right to all the said lands was vested in Sir Thomas Grosvenor and his heirs, and an instrument to that effect was accordingly drawn up by the notary, Roger Salghall, in the presence of the clergy then present, and attested by the seals and signatures of the 58 knights and gentlemen.

The historian of Cheshire, in commenting upon the pomp and circumstance attending the settlement of this family dispute, remarks: "Seldom will the reader find a more goodly group collected together, nor will he easily devise a ceremony which will assort better with the romantic spirit of the time, and which thus turned a dry legal conveyance into an exhibition of chivalrous pageantry."

Robert Legh inherited the martial spirit of his father, and was not long, after he had succeeded to the estates, in seeking an opportunity to display his prowess. In 1415, Henry V., having revived the old claim to the crown of France, determined upon an invasion of the French King's dominions, whereupon Robert Legh engaged himself to join in the expedition, and accordingly, on the 18th July, protection of his lands whilst abroad in the retinue of the King was granted him. The force mustered at Southampton early in August, and on the 11th of the month the fleet, consisting of 1,400 vessels, with 6,000 men-at-arms and 24,000 archers, an army of picked men, strong of limb and stout of heart, caring little for the abstract justice of the cause for which they were to fight, content to know that they would receive their due share of the "*gaignes de guerres*," set sail. On the 14th, the force—

A city on the inconstant billows dancing,

arrived in the Seine, and landed near the fortified town of Harfleur, which surrendered on the 22nd September. Henry's army had, however, to contend with a more powerful foe than the French. Disease made frightful ravages in his camp, the poisonous miasma of the marshes of Harfleur carrying off in those few weeks fully five thousand of the besiegers. On the 7th October the remnant of the army advanced, and on the 25th the splendid victory of

Agincourt was achieved. Robert Legh, however, was not permitted to share in the glories of that memorable day, he having died of the pestilence five days after the surrender of Harfleur, and an inquisition by virtue of a writ of *diem clausit extremum*, dated 16th October, 1415, was taken.

He was succeeded by his only son, also named Robert, who, though then only five years of age, boasted the possession of a wife, he having, in accordance with the fashion of the time, and well nigh before he could quit his cradle, been wedded to Isabel, one of the daughters of Sir John Savage, of Clifton, Knight, who was entrusted with the custody of his lands during his minority. On the 16th October, 3 and 4 Henry V. (1416), Robert Legh's young widow petitioned for and had livery of dower, and shortly after she became the wife of William Honford, of Chorley, a younger brother of Sir John de Honford, of Handforth.

On the 4th May, 1431, Robert Legh made proof of age, when his mother's second husband, William Honford, "aged 60 and upwards," was one of the witnesses, and testified "that the said Robert was born at Adlynton, and baptized in the church at Prestbury, the Tuesday on the feast of the Annunciation of the Blessed Virgin Mary (March 25, 1410), and was aged 21 on the feast of the Invention of the Holy Cross (May 3) then last past : and that he, William, was present at Prestbury the day when Robert Hyde, his godfather, came to the church at Prestbury with the said Robert." (Earwaker.)

The name of Robert Legh appears among those who on the 3rd March, 1435-6, were summoned to attend the Council of the boy King Henry VI. at Chester, when he and the others then assembled, in the name of the whole community of the county of Chester, granted to the King a subsidy of 1,000 marks (£666 13s 4d.) ; and on the 28th May, in the same year, he with Robert de Honford, Knight, Robert Massy of Godley, and John Pygot were appointed collectors of the subsidy within the hundred of Maccles-field.   In March, 1441-2, a further subsidy of 3,000 marks (£2,000) having been granted by the county, Robert Legh was

39

again deputed, with the others named, to collect the same within the hundred.

In the MS. account of the Legh family, preserved at Adlington, and to which reference has already been made, it is said that, in 1447, Robert de Legh obtained a licence from the Bishop of Coventry "to keep a chaplain to perform mass and other divine offices in any of his manor houses within the diocese for the term of thirty years, without prejudice to the curate of the place, on which licence a domestic chapel was built at Adlington." The chapel thus erected stood in the park, within a few hundred yards of the front of the present mansion, and on the site known at the present day by the name of the Chapel Field.

The first connection of the Leghs with the manor of Prestbury dates from 1448, when the manor with the great and small tithes, which had previously been leased to the Pigots, of Butley, were demised by the Abbot of St. Werburgh's, Chester, to Robert Legh for thirty-nine years, together with the Heybirches and Ewood, and also the advowson of the church of Prestbury, and all other rights and appurtenances belonging to it and the manor, the vicar's endowment excepted—one of the conditions being that the lessee should provide a fit and proper chaplain to celebrate divine service in the chapel of Poynton, within the parish of Prestbury, during the continuance of the lease, a condition, however, that was not always observed, for in 1500 the tithes of Poynton were sequestrated in consequence of the omission or neglect to fulfil the condition named. Some dispute having subsequently arisen, a new lease was granted in 1461, which was renewed in 1493. This last expired in 1524, and in the year following another lease was granted for forty years. On the 9th March, 1462 (2 Edward IV.), the King, as Earl of Chester, granted to Robert Legh a licence to enclose and impark a certain wood called Whiteley Hay and Adlington Wood, and also a place called Whiteley Green, with liberty to hold the park so enclosed and imparked to him and his heirs for ever. The place remained enclosed until the early part of the last century, when it was disparked, and a tract of land more conveniently near the hall applied to the purpose. In 1478 his mother, Matilda, who had survived her first husband sixty-three years, and had also outlived her second husband, William de Honford, died. She must have been very old, for in the inquisition taken after her death her son Robert was said to be sixty-eight years of age. He had livery of the lands held by her in dower, but did not long enjoy possession of them, for his death occurred on the 21st January following. As already stated, he had been married in his infancy to Isabella, daughter of Sir John Savage, of Clifton. This lady predeceased him, and he afterwards married Isabella, a daughter of Sir William Stanley, of Stanley, Stourton, and Hooton, who, according to the Adlington MS., was within the prohibited degrees, being of the blood of his first wife, and, consequently, it was thought prudent, if not indeed necessary, to make the marriage valid, to obtain a dispensation from the Pope.

On the death of Robert Legh, his eldest son, who bore the same name, and who was then fifty years of age, and married to Ellen, daughter of Sir Robert Booth, of Dunham Massey, Knight, succeeded to the patrimonial lands. Two years afterwards, a quarrel having arisen between Edward IV. and James III. of Scotland, which resulted in the breaking off of the marriage treaty between the English Princess Cicely and the son of the Scottish King, and the resumption of hostilities between the two countries, a commission was issued (November 18, 1480) to Robert Legh, and other persons therein named, requiring them to array the fencible men of the hundred before the Christmas following, and to command the same to be in readiness in warlike attire to attend upon the Earl of Chester on three days' notice ; and on the 15th January following another commission was issued to the same persons, requiring them to communicate with the gentlemen of the hundred to determine the number of horsemen, with their harness, that could be raised in their households, and to make a return before the Wednesday next before the Feast of the Purification. A third commission was issued to them in May, 1481, to array the fencible men of the hundred between the ages of sixteen and sixty, and to appoint a certain day for the same to depart "*pro viagio dicti partes nostri versus partes scocie.*" Mr. Earwaker cites a deed from which it appears that on the 6th December, 1483, John Legh, a younger brother of Robert, a priest in orders, and then rector of Rostherne, and Douce or Dulcia, his sister, granted to the said Robert all their right and title to the manor and church of Prestbury.

The fierce struggle of the Red and White Roses destroyed the power and weakened the influence of the English nobility and their feudatory chiefs by sweeping away the heads of the principal families. Their sun went down when the stout Earl of Warwick, the renowned "King-maker," lay weltering in his gore upon the field at Barnet ; Tewkesbury extinguished their hopes ; and the fight at Bosworth ended a contest which, in the field and on the scaffold, had cost the lives of more than sixty princes of the royal family, above one-half of the nobles and principal gentlemen, and above a hundred thousand of the common people of England. Fortunately for themselves, the lords of Adlington passed harmless through that eventful period. It does not appear that Robert Legh took any very active part in the protracted struggle between the rival houses of York and Lancaster. The Lyme Leghs had plucked the "pale and maiden blossom" and given their verdict "on the White Rose side," but there is reason to believe that, in the closing years of his life at least, the sympathies of Robert Legh were on the side of the Red Rose of Lancaster. It may be that, like the kinsmen of his father's second wife, the Stanleys of Lancashire, he believed that to be "the true policy which had the most success," and, like them, have been a faithful adherent of the party of "good luck." Certain it is that the great and exhausting quarrel between these rival houses, which brought death and destruction to so many an English home, left his house with unimpaired estates and undiminished power ; but he did not long survive the close of that unhappy struggle, his death occurring on the 8th December, 1486, when he must have been sixty-eight years of age. By his wife, whom he predeceased, and who died in 1504, he had Thomas Legh, who succeeded as his heir, four younger sons, and one daughter.

Thomas Legh was thirty-five years of age when he entered upon his inheritance, and he had then been married about seven years, his wife being Katharine, daughter of Sir John Savage, of Clifton, and sister of Thomas Savage, Archbishop of York, the founder of the Savage chantry in Macclesfield church, and of Ellen Savage, who married Sir Piers Legh, of Lyme.

Two years after the victory at Bosworth, which gave the crown of England to Henry of Richmond, a desperate effort was made by the friends of the fallen tyrant, Richard III., to secure the throne for the impostor Lambert Simnel, and when the new King's crown was in peril at the battle of Stokefield, Thomas Legh's relative, Piers Legh, of Lyme, drew his sword and fought valiantly to defend it. In November of that year (1487) a subsidy was voted to the King by his loyal subjects in the county of Chester, and the name of Thomas Legh, of Adlington, occurs *inter alia* among those authorised to collect the portion due from the hundred of Macclesfield.

In 1498 he obtained a licence from the Bishop of Lichfield and Coventry to have mass and other divine offices performed by a fit chaplain in the chapel situated within his manor of Adlington—a renewal, it would seem, of the privilege conceded to his grandfather, Robert Legh, in 1447. When Henry's eldest son, Arthur, Prince of Wales, succeeded to the earldom, he was at great pains to guard against any encroachment affecting the "sword and dignity of Chester," and with that object made a searching inquiry as to the authority in which many of his feudatories exercised their privileges. Among them Thomas Legh, in 1499-1500, had a *quo warranto*, requiring him to show cause why he claimed to have a park at Whiteley Hay and to hold a court-leet, &c. He replied, setting forth the grant made by Edward IV. to his grandfather; he further pleaded right of free-warren in all his Cheshire possessions, and claimed the assize of bread and ale, the punishing of scolds by the cucking-stool, of bakers by amercement or the pillory, and brewers by judgment of the tumbrell, and to have amercements and fines for trespasses, offences, and effusions of blood in affrays presented within the leet to be assessed by the jury. The answer must have been deemed satisfactory, for no further action appears to have been taken against him in the Earl's court.

If we may judge from some of the enrolments on the Recognisance Rolls, Thomas Legh must have been a somewhat turbulent subject, and have been frequently at variance with his neighbours and friends. Impatient of the dilatory and uncertain processes of the law, he sometimes had recourse to the simpler and less tardy method of taking the adjustment of his differences into his own hands, a mode of procedure that occasionally brought him into trouble, and subjected him to the inconvenience of having to find sureties for his good behaviour. He oftentimes appeared in the legal arena, and not unfrequently his quarrels were with his wife's father, Sir John Savage, who was then residing at the park at Macclesfield, the custody of which had been granted him by King Henry in acknowledgment of his services at Bosworth. Thus, on the 14th November, 1488, he was required to enter into a recognisance of 1,000 marks that he and all his children and servants would keep the peace towards Sir John Savage, sen., knight, and on the same day he entered into another recognisance of the like amount that he, his children, and servants would keep the peace towards Nicholas Davenport, of Woodford, and his servants. On the 28th April, 1489, he again gave sureties in two sums of 1,000 marks each that he would keep the peace towards his father-in-law, Sir John Savage, his children, and servants, and Nicholas Davenport, of Woodford, his children, and servants, and at the same time he entered into a further recognisance of £200 to keep the peace towards Hamo Ashley, Esq. Whatever may have been the cause of the difference with his father-in-law, it was a long time before the variance was composed, for on the 20th April, 1490, he again appeared in the law courts, when he was required to find sureties in 1,000 marks to keep the peace towards him. On the

11th May, 1495, he and his brother, John Legh, of Lawton, entered into recognisances of 1,000 marks each to abide the award of Hamnet Massy and others named, touching all disputes between the two brothers and Nicholas Davenport and William Honford, of Davenport and Honford, at the same time entering into recognisances for the same amounts. The arbitration must have been very protracted, for the recognisances and counter recognisances were renewed on the 12th April, 1496, again on 9th September in the same year, and a third time on the 19th June, 1498. On the 8th June, 1501, Thomas Legh was again required to give sureties, this time in £100, to keep the peace towards John Carter and Robert Rokeley; and on the 19th September, 1502, he entered into recognisances of £100 to keep the peace towards Richard Phillips, chaplain. He either lacked prudence, or his neighbours must have been more than ordinarily litigious, for it was not long before he was again involved in a suit, this time at the instance of Robert Walls, the representative of a family located at Adlington. He appears to have been then outlawed in error, for on the 5th March, 1st and 2nd Henry VIII., proceedings were taken against Roger Downes and others for restitution of goods seized under the outlawry. In July of the same year he entered into recognisances to the Earl of Chester to keep the peace towards his neighbour, Sir John Warren, of Poynton.

In the Calendar of Warrants, removed from Chester to the Public Record Office, London, there is one dated at Ludlow Castle, 1st April, 12th Henry VII., 1497, appointing the Bishop of Lincoln, the Bishop of Lichfield and Coventry, and others named, a commission to levy money in the counties of Chester and Flint, to aid the King in repelling the unprovoked invasion of James IV. of Scotland, who, in violation of the treaty of 1493, had raised an army in support of Perkin Warbeck and crossed the borders, spoiling and plundering the country. The Parliament which assembled at Westminster in January of that year had granted him £120,000 under certain restrictions, and on the 6th April, Thomas

Legh, and other loyal men of Cheshire, assembled at Chester, and in the name of the county granted him a further sum of 1,000 marks. Four days later a commission was issued to Thomas Legh and others to array the fencible men of the hundred before the 1st May following, for the purpose of aiding in the war against the Scotch. Henry VII., in the indulgence of his inordinate passion for money, had frequent recourse to a system of benevolences or contributions, apparently voluntary, though, in fact, extorted from his wealthier subjects, and also to the granting of subsidies— "reasonable aids," as they were called. In 1501, on the occasion of the marriage of Arthur, Prince of Wales, with Katharine of Arragon, afterwards the unhappy queen of Henry VIII., a subsidy was granted by the county of Chester, and Thomas Legh was appointed with others to collect the portion due from his own hundred.

When Henry of Richmond came out of the field of Bosworth a victor it was to rule over a nation weak and impoverished, and bleeding at every vein. The sword had vied with the axe, and the nobles had shown themselves too powerful for the comfort or security of the monarch. To destroy their influence the King determined upon the suppression of their retainers—virtually the rent of the lands granted in knights' service, thus freeing their properties from the burden of supplying the armies of the State. In this way peace and good order were re-established, and an end put to those intestine wars which had well-nigh exhausted the country. Though the Leghs had not suffered to any appreciable extent from these internal broils, it is more than probable that less attention had been paid to their ancestral home than would have been the case had public affairs been in a more settled state. With the return to a more peaceful order of things they had leisure to add to the beauty and convenience of their permanent home. Architecture marks the growth and development of human society, and the progress of refinement as well as the changes society had undergone rendered alterations at Adlington necessary for the comfort and convenience of the inmates. Thomas Legh, if he did not

rebuild the house, remodelled and greatly enlarged it; and much
of the traceried panel-work forming part of the ancient screen, as
well as other carved work still remaining, was no doubt executed
during his time. In commemoration of his work, he caused his
name and that of his wife, with the date, to be affixed in carved
Lombardic letters—

Thomas Legh & Catarina Sauage uxor ejus

Ao. Doi. Mo^{cc}_{ccc}Vlo R.R.Y. bij., rr.

The inscription appears over the high-place at the west end of the
great hall, and was probably replaced in the last century during the
occupancy of Charles Legh.

Thomas Legh died August 8, 1519, leaving, with other issue, a
son, George Legh, then aged 22 years, who succeeded as his heir.

"Better marry over the mixen than over the moor" has ever
been a favourite proverb with the men of Cheshire; and the heads
of the house of Legh evidently believed in the soundness of the
advice it conveyed, for, from the time their Norman progenitor
first settled in the county, they had been content to mate within
their own shire. The first of the manorial lords of Adlington to
depart from this long-established custom was George Legh, who, in
1523, married the daughter of a Huntingdonshire squire—Joan,
daughter of Peter Larke, and a sister of that Thomas Larke on
whom Cardinal Wolsey had bestowed the rich rectory of Winwick,
in Lancashire—and it can hardly be said that the departure added
much to the reputation of his house, the supposed antecedents of
the lady having given rise to no inconsiderable amount of scandal.
It is said that, previous to her marriage with Thomas Legh, Joan
Larke had been the mistress (not the illegitimate daughter, as a
recent writer has unnecessarily sought to disprove) of Cardinal
Wolsey. The statement is evidently made on the authority of
one of the "Articles of Impeachment" against Wolsey presented
to Parliament by a committee of the House of Lords, December 1,
1529, and quoted in Lord Herbert of Cherbury's "Life of
Henry VIII." The story is a curious one, and, if true, reflects

40

little credit either upon the Cardinal or his frail companion. The accusation is embodied in the 38th article—

That the sd Cardinal did call before him Sir Jno. Stanley, kt., which had taken a farm by convent seal of the Abbot and Convent of Chester; and afterwards by his power and might, contrary to right, committed the said Sir Jno. Stanley to the prison of Fleet by the space of one year, until such time as he compelled the sd S'r Jno. to release his convent seal to one Leghe, of Adlington, which married one Lark's daughter, which woman the sd lord cardinal kept and had with her two children ; whereupon the sd Sir John Stanley, upon displeasure taken in his heart, made himself monk in Westminster, and there died.

The story, it must be confessed, has much improbability about it; and may, as has been suggested, have been prompted by feelings of malice against the fallen ecclesiastic. Certain it is, the charge was not pressed to a direct issue. Whatever may have been the relations existing between Wolsey and the wife of Thomas Legh, there is no doubt that in the short interval between the expiry of the lease of the Prestbury tithes, in 1523-4, and the granting of a new one by the Abbot of St. Werburg, in the following year, a dispute had arisen between George Legh and Sir John Stanley respecting them. It is not improbable that the latter had endeavoured to steal a march upon his neighbour by securing a lease of a portion of them to the disadvantage of the Leghs, who, as we have seen, had been farmers of the impropriate rectory for a lengthened period, and that the Cardinal, who is known to have been a patron of the Larkes, was then appealed to with a view of inducing the monks of Chester to grant George Legh a renewal of the privileges his family had so long enjoyed. If so, the appeal was unsuccessful, for in 1524-5 a new lease for forty years was granted, which was subsequently renewed.

Sir John Stanley was a natural son of James Stanley, warden of Manchester, and afterwards Bishop of Ely, a younger son of that Thomas, Lord Stanley, who placed the crown of the vanquished Richard upon the head of the victorious Richmond on the field of Bosworth. He commanded his father's retainers at the battle of Flodden Field, in 1513, when his uncle, Sir Edward Stanley, after-

wards created Lord Monteagle, led the forces of Lancashire and
Cheshire, and Sir Edmund Savage, mayor of Macclesfield, and so
many of the burgesses of that town were slain ; and on that
occasion by his valour in the field won his golden spurs.   He
married Margaret, the only daughter and heir of William Honford,
of Honford, by his wife Margaret, daughter of Sir John Savage, and
was consequently closely allied to the Leghs of Adlington.   In
1528 he and his wife prayed for a divorce in order that they might
severally devote themselves to a religious life, and be quit of the
world for ever.   The divorce was granted, and he became a monk
of Westminster, where he died ; his wife also entered a religious
house, but must have abandoned her intention of becoming a
recluse, for she afterwards married Sir Urian Brereton, by whom
she had a family, who through her inherited the Honford estates.
Though Sir John assumed the cowl and tonsure of a monk, it is
hardly credible, even supposing the story of Wolsey's arbitrary
exercise of power to have been true, that he forsook the society of
his wife, retreated from the world, and disappeared in the shadow
of the cloister " from displeasure taken in his heart " upon a matter
of such comparatively little moment, and occurring four or five
years previously.

A recent writer, in an account of Adlington, says that Sir John
Stanley " was himself an ecclesiastic and warden of Manchester ;"
that his claim " was espoused by the Bishop of Ely, his father ;"
and that " the battle seems in reality to have been fought between
the powerful Bishop of Ely on the one hand, and the yet more
powerful Cardinal on the other."   These statements are entirely
erroneous.   Sir John, in early life, had embraced the profession of
arms ; as a soldier he had earned his knighthood by bravery on the
field ; and, being married, he would by the canons of the Church be
disqualified from holding an ecclesiastical preferment, while, as a
fact, his father, the Bishop of Ely, had been in his grave eight or
nine years when the dispute respecting the Prestbury tithes arose.

George Legh died on the 12th June, 1529, at the early age of
thirty-two.   His will was only made on the day preceding his

decease, and the broad lands of Adlington were transmitted to his only son, Thomas Legh, then an infant two years of age. His wife survived him, and was remarried to George Paulet, brother of the Marquis of Winchester, and she with her second husband appear to have resided at Adlington during the minority of the heir, for in a return of the clergy serving at the various chapels of ease within the parish of Prestbury there occurs the name of Sir James Hurst, a stipendiary priest, paid by George Pollet (Paulet), and apparently serving in the chapel at Adlington. By an unaccountable error Thomas Legh, of Adlington, has been confounded with another personage of the same name, who, as one of the commissioners under Sir Thomas Cromwell, took an active part in the suppression of the religious houses. The mistake will be apparent when it is remembered that at the time (1536) that worthy was denouncing monachism and despoiling the monks of their lands and houses Thomas Legh, of Adlington, was only in his ninth year, and before he had attained to manhood the great and lesser monasteries had been swept away.

Whilst he was in his minority he had been united in marriage with one of the younger daughters of the great house of Grosvenor—Mary, the daughter of Robert Grosvenor, of Eaton, the direct ancestor of the present Duke of Westminster. It is not known with certainty how the match was brought about, but in those days the lord of the fee was entitled to the wardship of the heir, with the right to put up his or her hand to sale in marriage ; and if Richard Grosvenor, as is not unlikely, had the wardship of the Adlington estates, he may have thought the alliance a desirable one for a younger member of his numerous family. It was to avoid the evil arising from this feudal practice that so many early marriages were in former times resorted to, parents being oftentimes prompted to seek an eligible match for their heirs while under age to free them from the exactions and other consequences of wardship—a circumstance that could have been little understood by the President Montesquieu, when he cast the sneer upon our country in saying there was a law in England which permitted girls of

seven years of age to choose their own husbands, and which, he
added, was shocking in two ways, since it had no regard to the time
when nature gives maturity to the understanding, nor to the time
when she gives maturity to the body. Mary Grosvenor survived
her husband and remarried Sir Richard Egerton, of Ridley, Knight,
with whom she appears to have resided at Adlington during the
minority of the son by her first husband. She had the manor and
tithes of Prestbury settled upon her as dower ; and in 1558 her
second husband is found attending a meeting in the church at
Prestbury, and acting there in the capacity of warden—an office
then held in much higher esteem than at the present day. The
lady deserves to be held in special remembrance by the men of
Cheshire, from the circumstance that she is generally believed to
have superintended the education and taken a kindly interest in
the well-being of a notable Cheshire worthy, who attained the
highest honours of the peerage, Richard Egerton's base-born son
by Alice Starke, of Bickerton—Thomas Egerton, Viscount
Brackley, Lord Keeper and Chancellor of England, ancestor of
the great Duke of Bridgewater, as well as of the present Earl of
Ellesmere—a worthy who, if precluded by the circumstances of his
birth from deriving honour from an illustrious ancestry, reflected
on them, his descendants, and his county the lustre of a name
brighter than any other its annals can boast. It is pleasant to
think that some of the earlier years of the great Chancellor were
spent within the old house at Adlington, and that the generous-
hearted lady to whom he owed so much was not forgotten when he
had attained to distinction, and she in her old age had become the
victim of religious persecution.* She died in 1599, having survived her first husband for the long period of fifty-one years. In
her will, dated 18th October, 1597, she appoints the Lord Keeper
Egerton, whom she designates her " wellbeloved sonne," one of

---

* Lady Egerton, who remained a firm adherent of the ancient faith, is
frequently named in the prosecutions for recusancy under the severe statutes
of Elizabeth, but appeals for mitigation were often and successfully made
through, as would seem, the influence of the Lord Keeper Egerton.

her executors, and bequeaths to him "one ringe of Goulde having thereon a Dyamond." She is buried at Astbury, where her altartomb, with a recumbent effigy upon the top, may still be seen.

Thomas Legh, the first husband of Mary Grosvenor, did not long enjoy possession of the ancestral domains, his death occurring at Eaton, May 17, 1548, the year in which he attained his majority. The only issue by his marriage was a son, Thomas, aged one year at the time of his death, so that the broad lands of Adlington were once more held in ward through the infancy of the heir.

On the 21st April, 1548, three weeks before his death, Thomas Legh granted to his wife's eldest brother, Thomas Grosvenor, of Eaton, all the lands which his family had held in Belgrave from the time of the marriage of Sir Robert Legh with the heiress of Sir Thomas Belgrave, *circa* 1385; and four days later he settled the remainder of his estates, including "the Hall of Adlington," in trust for the benefit of himself and his wife and his heirs in tail male.

Sir Urian Brereton, who married the widow of Sir John Stanley, the quondam recluse, seems to have acquired, with the lady, Sir John's craving for the Prestbury tithes, for in 1538, during the minority of Thomas Legh the elder, he obtained from the Abbot of St. Werburg's, in the names of himself and John Broughton, the reversion of the lease of the manor and advowson, to commence on the expiry of the one, for 40 years renewed to George Legh in 1524; and this reversion was afterwards purchased by Richard and John Grosvenor, the brothers of Mary, the wife of Thomas Legh, in trust, and to prevent their alienation from the other Adlington properties. But a great revolution in religious thought and action was then gradually gaining strength and power, and the day was near at hand when the monks and their system were to be overthrown. On the dissolution of St. Werburg's Abbey the manor and advowson of the church of Prestbury were granted to the Dean and Chapter of the newly-founded Cathedral of Chester. They did not, however, long enjoy possession ; William Clyve, the third dean, and two of the prebendaries, were confined in the Fleet by procurement of Sir Richard Cotton, of Werblington, comptroller of the King's household, a Hampshire knight, who appears to have shared the acquisitive properties of his elder brother, Sir George Cotton, another courtier and favourite of the King, who had had conferred upon himself the dissolved abbey and the greater part of the demesne of Combermere, in Cheshire, and who, in other ways, had increased his worldly possessions out of the spoils of the religious houses. While in the Fleet, under intimidation, as was alleged, the dean and canons granted to Sir Richard (20th March, 1553), for ever, most of their lands on the payment of a yearly rental; he in turn, on the 28th July, 1555, re-conveyed the manor and advowson of Prestbury to Richard and John Grosvenor, who, in 1559, are found presenting to the vicarage. The validity of the grant to Cotton was subsequently disputed, and on the Cheshire Recognisance Rolls, under date January 13th, 5 and 6 Elizabeth (1563-4), there is the enrolment of a complaint exhibited by Richard and John Grosvenor. Eventually the feoffees surrendered to the Crown; on the 19th December, 1579, the whole of the lands formerly held by the abbey were granted by Elizabeth to Sir George Calveley, Knight, George Cotton, Hugh Cholmondeley, Thomas Legh, Henry Mainwaring, John Nuthall, and Richard Hurleston, Esquires, and their heirs for ever; and, by another indenture, dated 6th August, 1580, the counterpart of which is preserved among the Adlington charters, these fee farmers, after reciting the grant of Elizabeth, for divers good causes and considerations them specially moving, demised and quit-claimed to Thomas Legh and his heirs the rectory, church, and manor of Prestbury, with the appurtenances, excepting the certain messuages, tenements, and hereditaments, with the appurtenances and the tithes, oblations, and obventions, of Chelford and Asthull (Astle). They have since continued in the possession of the Leghs, and have descended with their other estates.

Thomas Legh had a long minority, and it was a fortunate thing for him that in those early years of his life he had a good mother,

who, with the aid of her powerful kinsmen, was able to guard his
estates and protect him from undue taxation. On the 16th March,
1567-8, he obtained livery of his father's lands, he being then of
full age.   He had, five years previously (29th June, 1563), being
then in his sixteenth year, married, at Cheadle, Sybil, the youngest
daughter of Sir Urian Brereton, of Honford, by his first wife,
Margaret, daughter and heir of William Honford, and widow of
Sir John Stanley, a marriage that it may be fairly assumed happily
terminated the long-standing disputes between the two houses
respecting the tithes of Prestbury.

Following the example of his father-in-law, who rebuilt the hall
of Handforth, Thomas Legh, in 1581, rebuilt, or at all events,
greatly enlarged, the house at Adlington, as the following inscription, in black-letter characters, over the entrance porch leading
from the court-yard testifies : —

Thomas Legghe esquyer who maryed Sibbell doughter to Sir Urian Trerrton
of honbforbe knight, and by her had Issue four sonnes & foure doughters, made
this buylbinge in the geare of or lorbe god 1581 And in the raigne of our
sobragnine laby Quene Elizabeth the rriijth.

In 1587 Thomas Legh had the shrievalty of Cheshire conferred
upon him.   The time was one of considerable excitement and no
little anxiety, for scarcely had he entered upon the duties of his
office than news came that the "Invincible Armada," so long
threatened and so long deferred, had unfurled its sails, and was
then actually advancing towards the English coast.   The spirit of
patriotism was aroused ; Roman Catholic and Protestant united
as one man to repel the haughty Spaniard, and the Queen issued a
proclamation to her sheriffs and others, urging them by every
consideration of social and domestic security to call forth the
united energies of their respective counties, in common with the
country in general, to resist the meditated attack.   Thomas Legh,
who was then in the prime of manhood, was not likely to be idle
on such an occasion, and doubtless he acted with much the same
spirit that Macaulay's sheriff did when the signal fires announcing

the approach of the enemy flashed along the southern coasts,—

> With his white hair unbonneted, the stout old sheriff comes,
> Behind him come the halberdiers, before him sound the drums ;
> His yeomen round the market cross make clear an ample space,
> For there behoves him to set up the standard of Her Grace.
> And haughtily the trumpets peal, and gaily dance the bells,
> As slow upon the labouring wind the royal blazon swells.

In the later years of his life Thomas Legh added considerably to the patrimonial lands. Towards the close of the century, when the Butley estates, which had been held for so many generations by the Pigots, were partitioned among three co-heiresses, he acquired by purchase the manor and a moiety of the lands, which descended with the Adlington property until the present century. On the 20th April, 1596, an enrolment was made, as appears by the Cheshire Records, at the instance of Dame Mary Egerton, his mother, then a widow, of a covenant by which he undertook to convey the mansion house of Adlington, with other properties, to her use for life, and afterwards to himself with successive remainders in fee tail to his sons Urian, Thomas, and Edward, and his daughter, Maria Legh, and his right heirs for ever. In the same year his eldest son, Urian Legh, brought distinction to the family by his gallant bearing at Cadiz, where he earned for himself the honour of knighthood, an event respecting which we shall have more to say anon. Proud as the father must have felt at his son's conspicuous bravery, the pleasure must have had its alloy when, in the following year, he had the misfortune to lose his younger son, Ralph, who was slain by the insurgents in an attack upon Newry, in Ireland; and, to add to his sorrow, in the next year, 1598, he lost another son, Thomas Legh, who, with his commander, Sir Henry Bagnall, was killed in the disastrous attempt to relieve the fortress of Blackwater,—the most signal defeat ever experienced by an English force in Ireland,—when Hugh O'Neill, Earl of Tyrone, who had been for some time in insurrection against the English rule, was besieging it, and who had, at the same time, burned down the castle of Kilcoleman, where

> Amongst the coolly shade
> Of the green aldars, by the Mulla's shore,

41

the "Faery Queen" had been written, and its gifted author, Edmund Spenser, was then residing.

Thomas Legh died at Adlington on the 25th January, 1601-2, in the fifty-fifth year of his age, and was buried at Prestbury, on the following day, as the parish registers show. The same year his widow caused a memorial window, a portion of which still remains, though in a very mutilated condition, to be placed in the church, on which is a shield of arms, with several quarterings, representing the alliances of the two families. Beneath is this inscription :—

ORATE PRO BONO STATV THOMÆ LEYGHE DE ADLINGTON ARMIGERI ET SIDILLA VXORIS SVÆ VNI' FILIORVM VRIANI BRERETON DE HANDFORD MILITIS DEFVNCTI QVI HANC FENESTRAM FIERI FECERVNT IN ANNO DOMINI 1601.

She survived her husband eight years, and was buried at Prestbury, February 19th, 1609-10.

Sir Urian Legh, who succeeded as heir on the death of his father, in 1602, was born at Handforth in 1566, and was, consequently, in his thirty-sixth year when he entered upon his inheritance. As we have seen, he had early embraced the profession of arms, and in the service of his country had already won renown. It was the time when Elizabeth's sea captains, Howard and Essex, and Raleigh and Drake, were adding to the national laurels by their achievements on the main, justifying the witty and well-timed impromptu which one of the courtiers gave when lament was made that England was then under the rule of a queen, instead of that of a king,—

> O fortune! to old England still
> Continue such mistakes,
> And give us for our Kings such Queens,
> And for our dux such Drakes.

In 1596, when Philip of Spain was preparing for a second invasion of England, Howard, the Lord Admiral, with his characteristic daring and love of adventure, urged that, instead of waiting for the enemy's attack, a blow should be struck at Spain herself, by destroying the fleet before it could leave her harbours.

The more cautious Burleigh counselled the less hazardous policy, but was overruled by the dashing and impetuous Devereux, Earl of Essex, who, with Howard and Raleigh, was eventually entrusted with the command of the expedition. Young Urian Legh could not remain a laggard when such opportunities for distinction offered; leaving the bower and the tilt yard for the Spanish main, and the saddle of the war horse for the deck of the war ship, he joined the expedition, and on the 1st of June, the fleet, then lying at Plymouth, loosed its sails and bore away towards the shores of Spain, arriving before Cadiz on the 12th. Essex, whose impetuosity could brook no restraint, and who had, moreover, a bitter aversion to the tyrant Philip, was so eager for action that he threw his hat into the sea in the exuberance of his delight. The attack was commenced on the following day, and with such fury that the Spanish Admiral's ship and several others were blown up with all their crews on board, whilst the few vessels which were not either sunk or burned were run on shore, the English admiral refusing to accept a price for their release, declaring that "he came to burn and not to ransom." This daring and successful enterprise was followed up by an attack on the strongly-fortified town of Cadiz. The impetuous Essex threw his standard over the wall, "giving withal a most hot assault unto the gate, where, to save the honour of their ensign, happy was he that could first leap down from the wall, and with shot and sword make way through the thickest press of the enemy." The daring of the leader called forth the courage of his followers. The town was captured on the 26th June, and six hundred and twenty thousand ducats were paid as a ransom for the lives of the inhabitants. The heir of Adlington took the leading part in the attack, and displayed such conspicuous bravery that the Earl knighted him upon the spot. The display of British valour on the occasion has been justly described by Macaulay ("Essays," art. "Lord Bacon,") as "the most brilliant military exploit that was achieved on the continent by English arms during the long interval which elapsed between the battle of Agincourt and that of Blenheim."

Sir Urian Legh stands out with marked individuality in any record of the house of Adlington. The Leghs have ever looked with pardonable pride upon the doughty deeds of their warlike ancestor, and the feeling has been nothing lessened by the romantic incident which tradition has linked with his name. He is commonly believed to have been the hero of the old legendary ballad,—"The Spanish Lady's Love," written by Thomas Deloney immediately after the return from Spain, and reprinted by the Percy Society from "The Garland of Goodwill"—

> Will you hear a Spanish lady,
> How she wooed an English man?

The story is that, while with Essex in Spain, a captive maid, "by birth and parentage of high degree," was so overcome by Sir Urian's kindness that she conceived an ardent attachment towards him, and when he was about to return, the amorous and high-born beauty, flinging aside the trammels of country and kin, begged that she might be allowed to accompany him and share his lot in life— a request the gallant Cheshire man, after urging many other objections, was compelled to refuse, for the best of all reasons—he had already a wife.

> Courteous ladye, leave this fancy,
> Here comes all that breeds the strife;
> I in England have already
> A sweet woman to my wife;
> I will not falsify my vow for gold nor gain,
> Nor yet for all the fairest dames that live in Spain.

To which the disappointed lady magnanimously replies—

> Ah! how happy is that woman
> That enjoys so true a friend!
> Many happy days God send her!
> Of my suit I make an end.
> On my knees I pardon crave for this offence,
> Which did from love and true affection first commence.
>
> Commend me to thy loving lady,
> Bear to her this chain of gold,
> And these bracelets for a token;
> Grieving that I was so bold.
> All my jewels in like sort bear thou with thee,
> For they are fitting for thy wife, but not for me

It has been stated by some writers that the ballad has reference not to Sir Urian Legh, but to Sir John Bolle, of Thorpe Hall, in Lincolnshire, the representative of a family remotely connected in a later generation with the Leghs of Adlington; while Dr. Percy, in his introductory remarks, inclines to the opinion that the original was either a member of the Popham family or Sir Richard Leveson, of Trentham, in Staffordshire, an ancestor of the Duke of Sutherland. The legend has doubtless some foundation in fact, though the *actores fabulæ* may be phantoms; it should, however, be said that, until recent years, when they were removed to Shaw Hill, in Lancashire, the Leghs, in proof of the identity of their kinsman with the hero of Deloney's ballad, were able to show the veritable "chain of gold" and the casket in which through long generations it had been carefully preserved as a heirloom of the family. A half-length portrait of Sir Urian hangs upon the staircase at Adlington. It has been taken when he was in the fulness of manhood, and represents him as fresh complexioned, with a regular and rather handsome cast of features, suggesting the idea that comeliness of face and figure blended with courage and courtesy,—the characteristics of an old English gentleman. He wears a black felt hat with jewelled front, a black gown with vandyked and richly embroidered points, and round his neck a gold chain of many links that hangs down almost to the waist—whether the one given him by the "Spanish Lady" or not we will not undertake to say. In one corner of the picture is a shield of six quarters, and in the opposite corner this inscription :—

SIR URIAN LEGH OF ADLINGTON IN THE COUNTY OF CHESTER KNIGHT WHO WENT WITH ROBERT DEVEREUX EARL OF ESSEX TO THE SIEGE OF CADIZ AND WAS BY HIM KNIGHTED IN THE FIELD FOR HIS GREAT SERVICES IN TAKING THAT TOWN IN 1575 (SHOULD BE 1596). HE MARRIED MARGARET DAUGHTER OF SIR EDMUND TRAFFORD IN THE COUNTY OF LANCASTER KNIGHT BY WHOM HE HAD FOUR SONS AND THREE DAUGHTERS.

On succeeding to his inheritance Sir Urian appears to have settled down to the discharge of his duties as a country gentleman, and to have applied himself to the further improvement of his

patrimony, which he managed with so much thrift and care that
before the close of the century he was able to make an addition to
the family estates by the purchase of the lands and hall of Foxwist,
in Butley township, from William Duncalf, whose ancestors had
been resident there for more than three centuries, and in 1603 he
built the Milne House, which long afterwards continued to be used
as the dower house of the family. In 1613, the year following that
in which Cecil died and the notorious Carr, a raw Scotch lad, was
made Prime Minister, he was entrusted with the shrievalty of the
county, and in local affairs he appears to have taken an active
part, his bold and clearly defined autograph being of frequent
occurrence in the parochial records. He was a man of some

culture, had had the advantage of a university education, having
matriculated at Oxford, and in his private life he would seem to
have had a sweet fancy, turning to literature in the absence of
action, for in the inventory of his effects, taken after his death, it
is mentioned that there were in his closet at Prestbury "his bookes
valued at xvjli." He affected the society of men of letters: Dee,
the "Wizard Warden" of Manchester, in his "Diary," under date
April 22nd, 1597, records that he was visited at his residence in
the College by Sir Urian Legh and his brother (Edward Legh,
probably, for the other brothers, Thomas and Ralph, were at the
time in Ireland engaged in the suppression of O'Neill's rebellion),
a Mr. Brown, and Mr. George Booth, of Dunham, then Sheriff of
Cheshire.

On the 6th of September, 1586, ten years before the affair
at Cadiz, Sir Urian Legh was united in marriage to Mary, one of

the daughters of Sir Edmund Trafford, of Trafford, Knight, that "hunter out and unkeneler of those slie and subtil foxes Iesuites and semenarei Priests." The guests who graced the ceremony by their presence must have formed a goodly company, for William Massie, the rector of Wilmslow, who preached a sermon on the occasion, speaks of it as being delivered "before the right honourable the most noble Earle of Derby, and the right reuerend father in God the B(ishop) of Chester with diuerse Knightes and Esquires of great worship at the solemne marriage of your (Sir Edmund Trafford's) daughter, a modest and vertuous Gentlewoman, married to a young gentleman of great worship and good education."

Sir Urian Legh died at Adlington on the 2nd June, 1627, and two days afterwards, as the registers show, he was buried at Prestbury.

It is somewhat singular that Thomas Newton,* the famous Cheshire poet, who sang the glories of Essex and Drake in Latin verse, should have remained silent upon the daring deeds of his quondam friend and neighbour, Sir Urian Legh, leaving the "Water Poet," John Taylor, to record in rhyme the virtues of the hero of Cadiz. Taylor was a guest at Adlington some time before the close of the century, and in his "Pennilesse Pilgrimage" describes the reception he met in a manner that recalls Ben Jonson's lines in praise of the daily hospitalities at Penshurst :—

> This weary day, when I had almost past,
> I came vnto Sir Urian Legh's at last,
> At *Adlington*, neer *Macksfield*, he doth dwell,
> Belou'd, respected, and reputed well.

---

*Thomas Newton, before his removal into Essex, resided at Park House, in Butley, little more than a mile distant from Adlington. His mother, Alice Newton, in her will, dated December 22, 1597, leaves "one spurill ryall or XVs. in money to each of the right worshipful Thomas Legh, of Adlington, and Sybell, his wife," the testatrix's "worshipful good frendes;" and she also appoints "the right worshipful Thomas Legh, of Adlington aforesaid, Esquire," overseer, earnestly entreating him to assist and direct her executors.

Through his great loue, my stay with him was fixt,
From Thursday night till noone on Monday next,
At his own table I did daily eate,
Whereat may be suppos'd did want no meate.
He would have giu'n me gold or siluer either,
But I with many thankes receiued neither.
And thus much without flattery I dare sweare,
He is a knight beloued farre and neere.
First, he's beloued of his God aboue,
(Which loue he loues to keep beyond all loue),
Next with a wife and children he is blest,
Each hauing God's feare planted in their brest.
With faire Demaines, Reuennue of good Lands,
He's fairely blest by the Almightie's hands.
And as he's happy in these outward things,
So from his inward mind continuall springs
Fruits of deuotion, deedes of Piety,
Good hospitable workes of Charity;
Iust in his Actions, constant in his word,
And one that wonne his honour with the sword.
He's no Carranto, Cap'ring, Carpet Knight,
But he knowes when and how to speake and fight.
I cannot flatter him, say what I can,
He's euery way a compleat Gentleman.
I write not this for what he did to me,
But what mine eares and eyes did heare and see,
Nor doe I pen this to enlarge his fame,
But to make others imitate the same.
For like a Trumpet were I pleased to blow,
I would his worthy worth more amply show,
But I already feare haue beene too bold,
And craue his pardon, me excusd to hold.
Thanks to his Sonnes and seruants euery one,
Both males and females all, excepting none.

Sir Urian Legh, as we have said, died in 1627; and his eldest son, Thomas, was approaching the meridian of life when he succeeded as heir to the family estates. It was a memorable epoch in English history, for in that year Buckingham, the King's favourite, by his inglorious expedition to France, had brought dishonour on his country's arms, and was impeached in Parliament; and in the following year the Commons, before they would grant the supplies necessary to retrieve the disaster, extorted from

Charles the Petition of Rights, confirming the liberties that were already the birthright of Englishmen—a measure which, had it been accepted by its authors as final, would have spared the country the calamities of civil war. Thomas Legh had married in his father's lifetime (1610) a rich heiress, one of the daughters of Sir John Gobert, of Boresworth, in Leicestershire; with whom he acquired considerable property, including the estate of Clumber,* forming part of the royal manor and forest of Sherwood, which subsequently passed into the possession of the Pelham-Clintons, Dukes of Newcastle; so that by the time he came into his patrimony he had added considerably to the territorial possessions as well as to the social status of his house. On the death of Sir John Gobert, dame Lucy, his widow, appears to have resided with her daughter and son-in-law at Adlington, and to have remained with them up to the time of her death in 1634. In 1628-9 Thomas Legh was chosen to fill the office of high sheriff of the county, a distinction that was again conferred on him in the year 1642-3. The year of the second appointment was a portentous one, for the seeds of civil strife which had been sown in previous years had ripened, and King and Commoner—sovereign and subject—were then placing themselves in open array against each other. The Royalists of Cheshire, though in a minority, were prompt in obeying the King's summons. Thomas Legh, in whom the blaze of youth was then sinking into the deep burning fire of middle age, for fifty summers had passed over his head, at once placed himself at the disposal of his sovereign, and had a colonel's commission in the Royalist army; Thomas, his eldest son, had a lieutenant-colonel's commission; whilst his four

---

* A recent writer says (*Contributions towards a History of Prestbury*, p. 102): "Clumber appears to have been sequestrated from the Leghs during the Civil War, and never restored." This is not quite accurate, for Thomas Legh, who died in 1687, by his will, dated 20th August, 1686, bequeathed to his younger son, Richard Legh, and his heirs for ever, "all that mannour or capitall messuage called Clumber, in the county of Nottingham, and all buildings, tenements, and hereditaments in Clumber aforesaid."

42

younger sons—John, Charles, Peter, and Henry—and his brother Urian, who had previously been in the wars in the Low Countries, had also commissions.

The attempt to maintain the neutrality of the county by the Treaty of Pacification, as it was called, having failed, the commission of array was issued, requiring the receivers to see that the tenantry and others in their respective districts were mustered and properly armed and accoutred, and each of the hostile parties set to work to procure military stores in anticipation of approaching conflict. The King's troops were at Chester under the command of Sir Thomas Aston, and the Parliamentarians, led by Thomas Legh's relative, Sir William Brereton, of Honford, established themselves at Nantwich, which subsequently became the scene of important military operations. In March, 1643, the rival forces met at Middlewich, when an engagement took place in which the Royalists were defeated, Sir Edward Mosley, of Manchester, and several Cheshire men of mark being made prisoners; but Sir Thomas Aston and Colonel Legh, who was present with him and at the time sheriff, being more fortunate, succeeded in making good their escape. Before the close of the year the Royalists suffered a series of reverses. At Nantwich they sustained a defeat at the hands of General Fairfax; on the 4th of February, 1643-4, Crewe Hall.was attacked and taken; three days later Doddington Hall shared the same fate; in the same month Adlington was besieged by a force under Colonel Duckinfield, and a few days after its surrender Mr. Tatton's house at Wythenshawe, was also stormed and taken.

The probability of an attack on their home must have been foreseen by the Leghs, and, consequently, the house was put in a state of defence on the outbreak of hostilities, and stores of provisions and ammunition for the use of the garrison collected in anticipation of any attack that might be made upon it. Colonel Legh appears to have been absent at the time of Duckinfield's assault, being probably with the King's forces in some other part of the country, and the defence, therefore, fell to the lot of his eldest son—a brave scion of a brave ancestry, who must have conducted it with considerable energy and judgment, for the garrison held out a whole fortnight, notwithstanding that the siege was carried on with a good deal of vigour. The attacking party appear to have encamped on the south side of the hall, and the assault must have been made from that direction, for the door on the south front is pierced in several places where the bullets and cannon shot passed through. The garrison, by their obstinate bravery, must have won the respect of their assailants, for, unlike the case of Biddulph, which surrendered a week afterwards, when quarter for life only was granted, the defenders of Adlington when they did capitulate (Feb. 14) had full leave to depart. Burghall, the Puritan vicar of Acton, thus records the circumstance in his " Diary " : —

> Friday, February 14th.—Adlington House was delivered up, which was besieged about a fortnight, where was a younger son of Mr. Legh's and 140 souldiers, which had all fair quarter and leave to depart, leaving behind them, as the report was, 700 arms and 15 barrels of powder.

By an order of the Parliament, dated March 18, 1643, Sir William Brereton, of Honford, Thomas Legh's second cousin, and then major-general of the Cheshire forces, entered upon possession and seized the family estates into his own hands, so that the owner of Adlington could hardly say of Sir William what, according to the old ballad, his kinsman Lord Brereton said when he espied him on the hill overlooking Biddulph—

> Yonder my uncle stands, and he will not come near,
> Because he's a Roundhead and I am a Cavalier.

The house was pillaged, though the fabric itself does not appear to have sustained any very serious injury considering the quantity of powder that was burned and the efforts that were expended upon it. Shortly afterwards it was retaken and held for the King, but it must have been stormed and taken a second time by the Parliamentarian soldiers, for when Colonel Legh's widow appealed to Sir William Brereton to be allowed to occupy the hall, and to have a portion of her late husband's estates assigned to her for the maintenance of herself and children, the request was denied, so far as the occupancy of the house was concerned, on the plea that as Adlington Hall had been garrisoned twice against the Parliament it was not judged fitting it should be ventured a third time.

Colonel Legh's active zeal in the Royalist cause made him so obnoxious to the Parliament party that in the preliminary proposi009 for the abortive Treaty of Uxbridge he was specially named as one of those to be excluded from the councils of his sovereign, and from holding any office or command from the crown under pain of forfeiture of his estates and the penalties attaching to high treason. The stipulation was unnecessary, for before the commissioners had assembled he had entered into his rest. It is not known with certainty when or where his death occurred; the Prestbury registers for this period are imperfect, and no entry of burial can be discovered; it is not unlikely, however, that he found an unknown grave at some place distant from his home where he may have lost his life in the service of the King.

His widow took up her abode at the Miln House—the picturesque old black and white gabled structure, now occupied as a farmhouse, standing near the railway midway between Adlington and Prestbury, built in the time of Sir Urian Legh—which she held in jointure. She could hardly have been as uncompromising a Royalist as her husband, for in a petition to the committee for compounding with "delinquents," praying that she might be allowed to compound for her deceased husband's estates, she sets forth that "she had long before the death of her husband misliked the course of the enemy (*i.e.*, the Royalists) in the parts where she resided, and had departed thence into the Parliament's quarters, where she had ever since remained and conformed herself to all the orders of Parliament." The statement was no doubt made in good faith, for some little time after Thomas Legh's death she married an ardent Republican, who had been as active in furthering the Parliament's interest in Lancashire as her first husband had been in defending that of the King in Cheshire—Sir Alexander Rigby, of Middleton-in-Goosnargh, a lawyer, statesman, magistrate, and colonel, and eventually one of the barons of the

Exchequer. Rigby, who represented Wigan in the Long Parliament, was head and heart and hand and almost everything else of importance in Lancashire; his activity was unwearied : his energy irrepressible, and his influence unbounded. He was engaged in every important action ; he commanded at the siege of Lathom, the fight in Furness, the capture of Thurland Castle, and the defence of Bolton-le-Moors ; and he was nominated one of the King's judges, but declined to act, the only occasion in his life, it is said, in which he hesitated to do his worst against royalty. Dr. Halley, in his "Lancashire Puritanism," describes him as " rash,

SIR ALEXANDER RIGBY.

impetuous, rude, haughty, severe, implacable ; admired by many, esteemed by few, and loved by none," and the same writer adds, " he is said to have contrived a scheme and bargain by which the Royalist masters of three Cambridge colleges—St. John's, Queen's, and Jesus'—were to be sold for slaves to the Algerines.

The "insolent rebell, Rigby," as Charlotte Tremouille, the heroic Countess of Derby, designated him when he was besieging Lathom House, though possessed of only a small estate, was connected by birth and marriage with many of the best families in Lancashire; he was also closely allied with the Leghs, of Adlington, having married for his first wife Lucy, the daughter of Sir Urian, and sister of Thomas Legh, so that he stood in the relationship of brother-in-law to his second wife.

The marriage of their mother with the "insolent rebell" could hardly have been viewed with much satisfaction by the sons, who were all fighting on the side of the ill-fated Charles, and, therefore, accounted "delinquents," one of them being specially mentioned as "very active against the Parliament" and continuing "extreamelie malitious," though, in other respects, it was fortunate, as Rigby's influence as a member of the House of Commons in the Parliament interest was no doubt used in protecting the estates from the more ruinous exactions to which they would otherwise have been subjected, as well as the illegal challenges which might have wrested them absolutely from their rightful owners.

Sir Alexander Rigby died in 1650, having caught the gaol fever of the prisoners while on circuit at Croydon, and some time after his widow, who appears to have had a penchant for matrimony, again entered the marriage state, her third husband being John Booth, of Woodford, in Over, the uncle of Sir George Booth, of Dunham Massey, the head of the Presbyterian interest in Cheshire. John Booth was also a staunch Puritan; like the knight in "Hudibras," he had ridden out "a-colonelling" in the interest of the Parliament, and may have been the identical Puritan whom "Drunken Barnaby," when on his "Four Journeys to the North of England," saw and thus immortalised:—

> I came to Over—O, profane one—
> And there I saw a Puritane one,
> A-hanging of his cat on Monday
> For killing of a mouse on Sunday.

The marriage with John Booth could not have been a very felicitous one, for, according to Sir Peter Leycester, husband and wife lived apart from each other. She resided at the Miln House, and died there in February, 1675-6, and was buried at Prestbury. By her first husband, Thomas Legh, she had five sons, all of whom served in the Royalist army, one of them, John, losing his life in the war; and seven daughters, one of whom, Margaret, became the second wife of the eldest surviving son of her mother's second husband, Alexander Rigby the younger, who, like his father, was an active soldier on the Parliament side, and the representative for Lancaster in the House of Commons in 1658.

At the time of Colonel Legh's death, in 1644, his eldest son and heir, Thomas Legh, was a prisoner of war at Coventry, having been captured in the engagement at Stafford in May in the preceding year, where he was detained until June, 1645, when he was exchanged for his brother-in-law, Alexander Rigby,* who had been taken prisoner during the siege of Lathom House. He had then been married some few years, his wife being Mary, the daughter of Thomas Bolles, of Osberton, in Nottinghamshire.

Civil war has ever a devouring and insatiable maw, and in those days of political trouble and disturbance, when hostile armies were marching and counter-marching through the country, neither persons nor property were safe. It was the time—

> When nobles and knights so proud of late,
> Must pine for freedom and estate,

especially if they were suspected of having any political partialities, whether on the "malignants" or the "roundheads" side. The Leghs were all active partisans, and no family in Cheshire sustained heavier losses or endured greater hardships in defending what they believed to be the rights of their sovereign. While Thomas Legh was a prisoner at Coventry his young wife petitioned the sequestrators that some provision might be made for her, and eventually she had allotted to her a small portion of her husband's lands. In June of the following year she again memorialised the sequestrators that her husband might be allowed to compound for his estates, pleading that since his release he

---

* According to Colonel Fishwick it was Urian Legh, the uncle of Thomas, who was exchanged for Alexander Rigby the younger.—*History of Goosnargh*, p. 148.

had foreborne to repair to the enemy's quarters, and setting forth the miseries which she and her children were enduring, being destitute of the means of livelihood until relieved. Mr. Legh also presented a petition praying that he might be allowed to compound, when a statement of his "delinquencies" and a report upon his estates was submitted, which is preserved among the State papers in the Record Office. The charges exhibited against him were—

(1.) That he led a company of musquetiers into Adlington Hall when it was first garrisoned against the Parliament, and brought some who were well affected to the Parliament prisoners into the garrison, and kept them there till they compounded with him.

(2.) That he bore arms in that garrison; was governor of it; and gave directions to the inferior commanders therein.

(3.) That he refused to deliver up the said house to Colonel Duckinfield for the use of Parliament.

(4.) That he went from that garrison to Shrewsbury, thence to Chester, and thence to other garrisons of the enemy, and that he associated himself and held intercourse of intelligence against the Parliament with them.

On the 10th March, 1645-6, the Committee of Sequestrators agreed that Thomas Legh should be permitted to compound on payment to them of the sum of £2,000. This amount having been secured he, in July, obtained his discharge, and in the succeeding year sued out a pardon under the great seal for himself and his three surviving brothers, Charles, Peter, and Henry (John having been killed in action), who had also been admitted to compound. But his troubles were not yet ended. In November, 1648, he was required by the commissioners to settle the tithes of Bosley in Prestbury parish, valued at £56 a year, in trust for the minister of Bosley, the following being the minute of the Commissioners of Augmentation :—

Thomas Leigh, of Adlington, in ye said countie (Cheshire), by deeds dated ye 16th of November, A.D. 1648, hath settled ye tithes of Prestbury, of ye value of £56 per ann. upon George Booth, Esq., in trust for ye minister of Boseley, and his successors for ever. Consideration £560.

Before the close of the year, in pursuance of an order of Parliament, he was ordered to pay £220, being an assessment of one-twentieth part of the estate. Subsequently he was required to furnish a particular account of his real and personal estate, which being done, it was submitted to Major-general Worsley and the Commissioners then assembled at Middlewich, in February, 1655.

In November, 1656, he had the misfortune to lose his wife, who had borne him a family of six sons and four daughters. She was buried at Prestbury, November 22, and at the very time she lay dead his estate was again decimated and himself secured. Whereupon he presented a petition to the Lord Protector, alleging that he had behaved peaceably under the then government, and praying that he might no longer be looked upon as an enemy, but might partake of the Protector's grace and favour. The petition was referred to Worsley and the Commissioners for securing the peace of the county, who in January, 1656-7, reported that since his composition he had behaved peaceably and respectably to the Parliament party, soldiers and friends, and had not been concerned in any plots against the Protector or Parliament to their knowledge; that he had constantly paid all taxes for the use of the Commonwealth; had sent forth such forces, both horse and foot, for the service of the late Parliament as required; and had, moreover, offered his personal assistance for them at the battle of Worcester; and, finally, that they considered him a person capable of favour. From this time he appears to have been left in undisturbed possession of his property. He survived these troublous times, and lived to see the overthrow of the Commonwealth and the restoration of monarchy in the person of Charles the Second. In 1662 he was nominated sheriff of his native county—the only recognition he ever received of the losses sustained and the great services which he and his family had rendered to the cause of the Stuarts. Fortunately for his house, those losses were in some measure made up from another source. In the year in which he served the office of sheriff his late wife's mother, Dame Mary Bolles, who, in 1635, had been created a baroness in her own right, the only instance of such a creation, died, leaving property, to the value, it is said, of £20,000 to be divided between her two sons-in-law, Sir William Dalston and Thomas Legh—in the case of the latter a welcome addition to an estate which during the usurpation had been so greatly impoverished. The fortune thus acquired he seems to have employed in improving and extending his territorial possessions, for about the year 1669 he is found purchasing from Sir Thomas Brereton the old manor-house of Handforth, which one of his progenitors, Urian Brereton, erected in 1557, and subsequently (1681) he became the owner, also by purchase, of lands in Newton, adjoining Butley, that have since descended with the other Adlington properties. Thomas Legh survived all his brothers,

and died in December, 1687, being then in his seventy-third year. In accordance with his expressed desire, his remains were "decently buried amongst his Ancestors in the Chancell of the parish church of Prestbury."

Thomas Legh, the third of that name, was in his forty-fourth year when he succeeded to the Adlington estates—those in Leicestershire and Nottinghamshire passing under his father's will to his two surviving brothers, Edward and Richard. Shortly after the Restoration (1666) he chose himself a wife from the historic house of Maynard—Johanna, the daughter, and eventually heir, of the distinguished statesman and lawyer, Sir John Maynard—a match that must have brought him considerable wealth, and have added to his social influence. Sir John had been an active member of the Long Parliament, in which he distinguished himself as one of the prosecutors of Strafford and Laud, but afterwards, for his opposition to the violent acts of the army and the unconstitutional proceedings of Cromwell, he was twice committed to the Tower. At the conference between the Lords and Commons at the time of the Revolution he displayed considerable ability, and warmly advocated the abdication of James II. He was appointed one of the Commissioners of the Great Seal in 1689, being then eighty-seven years of age. He had frequently to submit to the coarseness of Jeffries' ribald tongue. On one occasion, when addressing the court, that unjust dispenser of justice interrupted him with the rude remark, "Mr. Serjeant, you've lost your knowledge of law; your memory is failing you through age." "It may be so," responded Maynard, "but I am sure I have forgotten more law than your lordship ever knew." And it is said of him that when William III., alluding to his great age, remarked that he must have outlived all the lawyers of his time, he happily replied, " Yes, and if your highness had not come over to our assistance I should have outlived the law itself."

Political prudence was not always a distinguishing characteristic of the lords of Adlington, and Thomas Legh does not seem to have profited greatly by his father's and grandfather's experiences of political partisanship, for he contrived to get himself involved in the troubles which fell upon Cheshire in 1683, the year of the notorious Rye House Plot, when he was suspected of conspiring with others to place the Duke of Monmouth upon the throne.

Monmouth, who had been expatriated, had returned a year or two previously to find himself hailed as the " Protestant Duke," and exalted into a popular hero. He made a partisan progress through Cheshire, with the view of ingratiating himself with the men of the county; while at Chester, courting popularity, a violent "No Popery" mob broke into the Cathedral, and, amongst other outrages committed upon the contents of the sacred building, wholly destroyed the painted glass of the east window of the Lady Chapel, broke up the organ, and knocked the ancient font to

pieces. Enquiries were instituted as to those who were believed
to sympathise with the action of Monmouth, when Thomas Legh's
name was included in the list of persons, who, being suspected, it
was deemed expedient should give security for their good behaviour.
He must, however, have regained the Royal favour, for he
retained his commission as colonel of militia, and the year
following that in which he entered upon possession of his
patrimonial lands he was honoured with the shrievalty of the
county. He did not live long to enjoy the estates, having met his
death by an accident on the 6th April, 1691, as thus recorded in a
MS. diary, preserved at Tabley :—

1691, April 6th.—Col. Legh, of Adlington, layning on a raile in Adlington,
whch breaking he fell and broak his neck and dyed.

His wife, who survived him several years, resided at the Miln
House, in Adlington, and died about November, 1700. The
bulk of her personal property was, in accordance with her
directions, invested in the purchase of lands for the benefit of her
second surviving son, Robert, who married Mary, daughter of Sir
Richard Standish, of Duxbury, and settled at Chorley, in Lancashire, on the lands purchased under his mother's will. Thomas
Legh, by his wife had, *inter alia*, Anne, his co-heiress, who became
the wife of Thomas Crosse, of Crosse Hall and Shaw Hill, in
Lancashire, by whom she had a son, Richard Crosse, of Shaw
Hill, who, through failure of direct male heirs, eventually succeeded
to the Adlington estates, and took the name and arms of Legh
by Royal license.

Thomas Legh, who died in 1691, was succeeded in the estates
by his eldest son, John, who was then thirty-two years of age,
having been born in 1668. Two years after he entered upon his
inheritance (July, 1693) he married Isabella, the daughter of
Robert Robartes, Viscount Bodmin, and granddaughter of the first
Earl of Radnor. During his time some important additions were
made to the family estates. In the year of his marriage he
purchased from William Sherd, of Sherd and Disley, the descendant

of an old companion in arms of his grandfather, the estate of Sherd-fold, on the confines of Adlington; three years later he purchased Hope-green from Edward Downes, and in 1696 he acquired the property known as "Day's Tenement," in Prestbury. In 1705 he was nominated sheriff of the county, and he appears to have succeeded his father as colonel of the militia, in which capacity he was called upon to aid in suppressing the political disturbances that arose in Lancashire on the occasion of the Hanoverian succession.

At the time of Queen Anne's death, in 1714, the country was divided into two powerful factions, a large number of the people, with that old English feeling of which we see traces even yet, preferring as their monarch the son of an English king to the son of a petty foreign prince. The flames of rebellion were kindled, and a determined effort was made to restore the direct succession to the throne, in the person of the Chevalier de St. George, the eldest son of James II., and a half-brother of the deceased queen. On the 10th June, 1715, the birthday of the Chevalier, a Jacobite mob, headed by "Tom" Syddall, a peruke maker, attacked the Nonconformist Chapel in Cross Street, Manchester—the only dissenting place of worship at that time in the town—smashed in the doors and windows, pulled down the pulpit and pews, and carried away everything portable, leaving only the ruinous walls; and, a few days later, sacked and destroyed the meeting-houses at Blackley, Monton, and Greenacres. In October of the same year the Earl of Derwentwater and General Foster, with the Earls of Wintoun, Nithsdale, and Carnwath, and Lords Widdrington and Nairne, raised the standard of the Pretender, and, with a small army, crossed the border, passed through Kendal and Lancaster, and as far as Preston—that "Capua" of Scotchmen, as it has been called—on their way south. In the last-named town, if we are to believe the Jacobite journalist, Peter Clarke, they were so fascinated by the good looks and the gay attire of the Lancashire witches that "the gentleman soldiers from Wednesday to Saturday minded nothing but courting and feasting." While they were thus "courting and feasting" the news of their advance reached General Willes, who was then in command of the garrison at Chester, and he at once set out to attack them, passing through Manchester on his way. Finding a strong Jacobite feeling existing there, he caused several of the more influential leaders of the faction to be secured, and disarmed the others, leaving a troop behind him to overawe the disaffected. Before leaving he wrote to the Earl of Cholmondeley, the lord lieutenant of Cheshire, urging him to send on the militia while he with his regular forces marched against the insurgents, and in the "Memoires of the family of Finney, of Fulshaw," written by Samuel Finney in 1787, it is recorded that in October a warrant from three of the deputy lieutenants was directed to John Legh, of Adlington, or, in his absence, to John Finney, his captain-lieutenant, requiring them to give notice to the constables of Macclesfield Hundred to order all persons charged with any foot soldiers to send on the same by the 17th of the month, "every Soldier to appear compleatly armed with musket, bayonet to fix in the muzel thereof, a Cartooch Box, and Sword, to bring pay for two days, and the Salary for the Muster Master. Every Muskateer to bring half a pound of powder, and as much (sic) Bullets, and the said Constables to appear and make returns." On the 27th October another warrant was issued requiring them to assemble the forces at Knutsford on the 7th November, when, as we are told in the "Memoires," "having exercised their appointed time, and the Rebells advancing, the Regiment was ordered to advance northwards and secure the town of Manchester, whilst Generals Willes and Carpenter advanced with the horse to attack the Rebells at Preston. When," it is added, "the Cheshire Regiment was advanced to the Top of Deansgate, the Entrance of the Town, they made a Halt to wait for Billets from the Constables, which were so long in coming and the Weather extremely wet and cold, and the road Miry, that both Officers and Men grew so impatient that a messenger was despatched to the Constables to tell them that if they did not immediately send them Billets they would fire the Town ; this had an immediate good Effect ; they

soon got into warm quarters. The King's Head in Salford fell to
the share of Sir Samuel Daniel, Coll. Legh, and Captain Finney,
intimate Friends, and jolly brave Fellows, who, instead of saying
their prayers and going to bed like good Folks, expecting to be
killed next day, sat drinking, laughing, and taking Spanish Snuff
till the morning, when they expected to come soon into action ;
but Willes and Carpenter soon eased them of that trouble, by
forcing the Town of Preston."

Mr. Legh's military experiences were not of a very sanguinary
character, and this appears to have been the last occasion in which
he was employed in any soldierly capacity. He died in 1739, and
on the 12th December was buried in the family vault at Prestbury,
having had in addition to a son Charles, who succeeded, two
daughters, who pre-deceased him ; Elizabeth, who died unmarried,
and was buried at Westminster, August 20th, 1734, and Lucy
Frances, second wife of Peter Davenport (afterwards Sir Peter),
of Macclesfield, who died in November, 1728, leaving an only
daughter her sole heiress, Elizabeth Davenport, who became the
wife of John Rowlls, of Kingston, in Surrey, Receiver-General, who
afterwards assumed the surname of Legh.

Charles Legh, who succeeded as heir on the death of his father,
John Legh, in 1739, was born at Adlington, September 17, and
baptised at Prestbury, October, 1697, so that he must have been
in his forty-fourth year when he entered upon his inheritance. He
had then been married some years, his wife being Hester, daughter
of Robert Lee, of Wincham, in Bucklow Hundred, who by the
death of her brothers, Robert and Clegg Lee, and her sister,
Elizabeth, without issue, became heir to the manor of Wincham.

In earlier years the Leghs had evinced their piety by important
additions made to their parish church, as well as by the erection of
a chapel on their estate for the convenience of their more immediate
dependents ; and Charles Legh, on first coming into his patrimony,
applied himself to the work of enlarging the old church of Prestbury by the rebuilding of the north aisle and the Legh chapel, to
the cost of which he was the chief contributor. He could not,

however, have felt much appreciation of the beauties of the
original design, or he would not have replaced a Gothic structure
with the unsightly, barn-like erection which has happily within the
present year been superseded by one of more ecclesiastical character.
The following year was one of considerable excitement, for it
was that in which Prince Charles' Edward, the Young Pretender,
renewed the attempt to recover the throne of his ancestors—the
fatal '45. On the 28th November the rebel army reached
Manchester, which, as the story goes, was taken by "a sergeant, a
drum, and a woman;" three days later the march towards London
was resumed, Macclesfield being chosen as the terminus of the
first day's journey. The Prince marshalled his forces in two
divisions, and, leading one of them, forded the Mersey at Stockport, and then marched through the level country, by way of
Woodford, Adlington, and Prestbury, to Macclesfield. The story
is told that as they were passing through Adlington they came up
with a carter, named Broster, returning from Stockport, who was
forthwith "pressed" into the service and ordered by the soldiers
to convey their baggage to Macclesfield. Among the chattels put
into Broster's cart was a heavy chest evidently containing treasure,
the money possibly in which the Manchestrians had been mulct,
and which poor James Waller, of Ridgefield, the borough-reeve,
had been compelled to gather in. The darkness of a December
night had fallen upon the scene by the time they approached Prestbury, and, the baggage guards not being over vigilant, Richard
Broster watched his opportunity and made the most of it when it
came. Suddenly turning up a bye-lane, he whipped his horses
briskly, and succeeded in reaching his home at Old Hollin Hall
Farm, near Bollington, before he was missed; arrived there, the
box was quickly tipped into the yard pit as a hiding-place from the
troopers who might be sent in search of the lost treasure, and
there it lay until the rebels had started upon their march to Derby,
when it was fished up.*

---

* It is said that in the cellar at Old Hollin Hall there is a stone bench
with this inscription graven upon it :—"This must stand here for ever—
Richard Broster, 1757."

Though the Leghs of Lyme, who were suspected of favouring the cause of the Pretender, might not be able to wipe out altogether from their hearts the old Stuart affection, their kinsman of Adlington could not have had much sympathy either for the young Chevalier or the cause he represented, or, if he had, his Jacobitism must have been under the control of a very cautious possessor, and not so demonstrative as to imperil his personal and family interests, for when Joseph Ward, the Vicar of Prestbury, preached a sermon on the occasion of the "General Thanksgiving" for the suppression of the "unnatural rebellion" it was published, as by the title-page appears, "at the request of Charles Legh, of Adlington, Esquire."

In 1746 Mr. Legh added to his territorial possessions by the purchase, from Thomas Pigot, of the estate of Bonishall, which for several generations had been the residence of a younger branch of the Pigots of Butley, the representative of which had then migrated to Fairsnape, near Preston, and from that time Bonishall has descended to the successive owners of Adlington with the other estates of the family. In the following year Mr. Legh had the shrievalty of Cheshire conferred upon him, a dignity that, as we have seen, had been enjoyed by his ancestors in six consecutive generations previously. He does not, however, appear to have devoted much attention to public matters, preferring to reside upon his own estate and there discharge the duties devolving upon him as a country gentleman. In the later years of his life he occupied his time in remodelling, and in part rebuilding, the home of his fathers; in doing so, however, it is to be regretted that, influenced by the then prevailing fancy for works of classic type, he was led to adopt a style so much at variance with the character of the original structure, and which, outwardly at least, robbed it of its most picturesque and interesting features. In commemoration of his work he inscribed his own name and that of his wife with the year of its completion, 1757, upon the frieze of the portico, and on the pediment above affixed a shield of arms—Legh quartering Corona, with Lee of Wincham, on an escutcheon of pretence.

While engaged in the re-edification of his house the barony of

44

Kinderton became extinct, when Mr. Legh set up a claim to be considered heir male of the family, in right of his descent from Gilbert Venables, the first baron, and, as such, entitled to bear the Venables coat without any mark of decadence. The claim was never admitted, but Mr. Legh assumed the arms notwithstanding, and, in assertion of his supposed right, caused them to be placed conspicuously in the hall at Adlington, and also on the chancel screen in the church at Prestbury, where they may still be seen.

Unlike his mother, who, if we may judge from the directions she gave respecting her funeral, had as little respect for the blazonments of chivalry and that ancient and respectable guild, the College of Arms, as Macaulay's old Puritan who wished to have his name recorded in the Book of Life rather than in the Register of Heralds, Mr. Legh had a great fondness for heraldry, and was much given to the study of the "noble science."

> The boast of heraldry, the pomp of power,

was with him no meaningless phrase, and before he began the rebuilding of the south front of his mansion he had been at considerable pains to adorn the interior of the great hall of Adlington with the armorial ensigns of his progenitors and the families with which they had severally become allied, like the lord of Gray's "ancient pile" at Stoke-Pogeis, upon

> The ceiling's fretted height
> Each panel in achievements clothing.

The fine series of armorial shields which still appear were painted under his directions, and are in place of a series, one hundred and eighty-one in number, which were affixed shortly after the rebuilding of the mansion by Thomas Legh, in 1581,* about which time that

---

* In the Chetham Library there is a curious MS. folio volume purchased at the sale of the Adlington Library in 1846, and now known as the "Adlington MS." On the fifth page from the end is written, "*Finis, Quod sum non curo quod ero spero Thomas Leyghe.* Thomas Legh, it would seem

assiduous worthy, William Flower, Chester Herald, and subsequently Norroy King of Arms, was corresponding with and enjoying the friendship and hospitality of the owner of Adlington, and his kinsman, Sir Peter Legh, of Lyme.

In 1758, the year following the rebuilding of the south front of Adlington, Charles Legh's only son, Thomas Legh, was united in marriage with Mary, daughter of Francis Reynolds, of Strangeways, Manchester, who represented Lancaster in Parliament for the long period of forty-five years, and the sister of Thomas and Francis Reynolds, who inherited successively the barony of Ducie of Tortworth. The young couple took up their abode at Wincham, which had come to Thomas Legh's mother by inheritance, and there he died, in his forty-first year, on the 15th June, 1775, without surviving issue—thus terminating a line which had maintained an unbroken succession for more than four centuries. His widow survived him for the long period of forty-three years, her death occurring March 26, 1818.

Charles Legh is said to have been somewhat autocratic and austere in his bearing, and to have ruled his little kingdom with a strong hand, dispensing justice in a summary fashion, and not scrupling at times to administer correction to the refractory with his own hand. Many curious stories concerning him are related and still find credence in the cottage homes around Adlington. There is a tradition that it was his daily practice to perambulate the boundaries of his domain with the object of discovering and expelling any marauder or sturdy rogue who might be prowling about his lands. Notwithstanding these little peculiarities, he kept up a style of true old English hospitality, and was greatly esteemed and respected by his neighbours. With his fondness for heraldry, he united a love of music; and he had, moreover, some claim to rank as a poet, though his muse, it must be confessed,

---

being the compiler. Among other interesting matters relating to Cheshire which it contains are "The Armes of Gentlemen as they be placed over the Chimney in Adlington Hall, 1611."

was at times a little halting. When Handel* was in the zenith of his popularity he was for some time a guest at Adlington, and there is a common belief that while there he composed his charming piece, "'The Harmonious Blacksmith," in response to a request made by his host for an original composition, the melody being suggested by the natural music of the smiths plying their vocation at Hollinworth smithy, close by the park gates.†

The original score is said to have been preserved at Adlington until the sale of the library in 1846, but the music is undoubtedly

---

* A story is told respecting the great composer which, as it associates his name with Cheshire, we may be excused for repeating. As is well known, his masterpiece, the *Messiah*, was first performed in Dublin, in 1741. While on his way there he was detained for a time at Chester, the wind being unfavourable for his embarkation at Parkgate. Wishing to employ the time in trying some pieces in his new oratorio, he inquired for some one who could read music at sight, and a printer, named Janson, who had a good bass voice, was recommended to him as one of the best musicians attached to the cathedral. A time was fixed for a private rehearsal at the Golden Falcon, where Handel was staying; but, alas! on trial of the chorus in the *Messiah*, "And with His stripes we are healed," poor Janson after repeated attempts, failed so egregiously that Handel let loose his great bear upon him; and, after swearing in four or five different languages, cried out, in broken English, "You schauntrel! Tit not you dell me dat you could sing at soite?" "Yes, sir," replies the printer, "and so I can; but not at *first sight!*" Handel on this burst out laughing, and the rehearsal, it is said, proceeded no further.

† According to another version, it was at Edgeware, and not at Adlington, that Handel heard the anvil sounds which suggested the "Harmonious Blacksmith." The great composer dwelt at Canons, the guest of the Duke of Chandos, within three quarters of a mile of Edgeware, and was for three years the organist of Little Stanmore Church. The authority for the Edgeware or Little Stanmore version rests mainly on local tradition and the following inscriptions:—On the organ of Little Stanmore Church: "Handel was organist of this church from the year 1718 to 1721, and composed his oratorio of 'Esther' on this organ." On a tombstone in the churchyard: "In memory of William Powell, the 'Harmonious Blacksmith,' who was buried 27th February, 1780, aged 78 years. He was parish clerk during the time the Immortal Handel was organist of this church." Powell was a blacksmith at Edgeware smithy. [Information obligingly communicated by J. Oldfield Chadwick, Esq.]

a variation of an old French air. There is also preserved in the
[drawing-room at Adlington a hunting song written by Charles
Legh, and set to music by Handel, which may find a fitting place
in the anthology of the county :—

HUNTING SONG,

The words by Charles Legh, Esq.   *Set by Mr. Handel.*

The morning is charming, all Nature is gay !
Away, my brave boys, to your horses, away ;
For the prime of our pleasure and questing the hare,
We have not so much as a moment to spare.

Chorus of the Hunters.

Hark! the merry loud horn, how melodious it sounds
To the musical song of the merry-mouth'd hounds !

In yon stubble field we shall find her below,
So ho ! cries the huntsman ; hark to him, So ho!
See, see, where she goes, and the hounds have a view !
Such harmony Handel himself never knew.
 Gates, hedges, and ditches to us are no bounds,
 But the world is our own while we follow the hounds !

Hold, hold ! 'tis a double ; hark ! hey, *Tanner*, hey !
If a thousand gainsay it, a thousand shall lie ;
His beauty surpassing, his truth has been try'd —
At the head of a pack an infallible guide.
 To his cry the wild welkin with thunder resounds
 The darling of hunters, the glory of hounds !

O'er high lands and low lands and woodlands we fly,
Our horses full speed and the hounds in full cry ;
So match are their mouths and so even they run,
As the tune of the spheres and their race with the sun.
 Health, joy, and felicity dance in the rounds,
 And bless the gay circle of hunters and hounds !

The old hounds push forward, a very sure sign
That the hare, though a stout one, begins to decline.
A chase of two hours or more she has led ;
She's down, look about ye ; they have her ; 'ware dead.
 How glorious a death, to be honoured with sounds
 Of the horn, with a shout to the chorus of hounds !

Here's a health to all hunters, and long be their lives!
May they never be cross't by their sweethearts or wives
May they rule their own passions, and ever at rest,
As the most happy men be they always the best!
And free from the care the many surrounds,
Have peace at the last when they see no more hounds!

Hunting was a favourite pursuit of Mr. Legh's. In Prestbury churchyard, near the lych gate, is a flat stone, with an inscription recording the death of one of his huntsmen, and a couplet, which he no doubt wrote.—

Here lye the Remains of Thomas Bennison,
Head Huntsman many years to Charles Legh,
of Adlington, Esq. He died the 17th of February,
in the year of our Lord 1768. Aged 75.

The Joys of his Heart were good Hounds and good Nappy,
Oh! wish him for ever still more and more Happy.

On the 26th July, 1781, Mr. Legh, who had attained the ripe age of 84, was removed by death, and on the 3rd August his remains were committed to the family vault which he had himself erected at the east end of the north aisle of Prestbury Church. His wife survived him some years. By her will, which bears date September, 1787, the manor of Wincham passed to her second cousin, Colonel Edward Townshend, of Chester, whose great grandson, Edward Townshend, Esq., is the present possessor.

By the death of Charles Legh without surviving issue the direct succession ceased, and the manor and dependencies of Adlington reverted to his niece Elizabeth, the only child of Lucy Frances Legh, by her husband, Sir Peter Davenport, who was then married to John Rowlls, of Kingston. She assumed, by royal licence, the surname of Legh, as did also her eldest son John, who had married Harriet, daughter and co-heir of Sir Peter Warburton, of Arley. He pre-deceased his mother, and, his two sons dying in infancy, the estates, with the exception of Butley Hall and some lands adjacent, which were alienated to his daughter Elizabeth Hester, who married, in 1800, Thomas Delves, third son of Sir Thomas Delves Broughton, Bart., and died in 1821, reverted in 1806, on the death of Mrs. Elizabeth Rowlls Legh, to Richard Crosse, of Shaw Hill, Lancashire, great grandson of Robert, the third son of Thomas Legh, of Adlington, who took the name and arms of Legh by royal licence. He served the office of sheriff of Lancashire in the succeeding year, and died on the 11th August, 1822, at the age of sixty-eight, leaving by his wife Anne, only surviving daughter of Robert Parker, of Cuerden, who pre-deceased him, two sons and three daughters. Thomas (Crosse) Legh, the eldest son, succeeded to the broad lands of Adlington; the Lancashire estates of Shaw Hill, Chorley, and Liverpool devolving upon his younger brother, Richard Townley Crosse, who died, unmarried, February 27, 1825, when they reverted to his sister Anne Mary, married to Thomas Bright Iken, of Leventhorpe House, Yorkshire, who assumed the name of Crosse, the father of the present possessor.

Thomas Crosse Legh, of Adlington, was accidentally drowned in crossing the river at Antwerp, April 25, 1829, being then only thirty-six years of age. By his wife, Louisa, daughter of George Lewis Newnham, of New Timber, Sussex, who survived him, and married, May 12, 1830, the Hon. Thomas Americus, third Lord Erskine, the grandson of the distinguished Lord Chancellor of that name, he had, with other issue, Charles Richard Banastre Legh, the present representative of this ancient stock. *Esto perpetua.*

As previously stated, the hall of Adlington stands in the midst of an undulating and well-timbered park, from the higher parts of which the views are extensive and pleasingly diversified. It is a remarkably fine example of the ancient manorial residence of the time when the power of the feudal chief had waned and the great landowners were no longer under the necessity of cooping themselves up in their fortified strongholds—a type of building that is rapidly passing out of existence, and, with the exception of the part rebuilt in the middle of the last century, furnishes an excellent illustration of a style of architecture which, if not altogether peculiar to, was certainly nowhere else practised so commonly or on so extensive a scale as in Cheshire and Lancashire. The timber-work is remarkable for its strength and solidity, an evidence that our forefathers were by no means economists in the use of their building materials; and, though the lighter ornaments of architecture which give grace and beauty to the more stately fabrics of brick and stone raised in other parts of the country, may not be apparent, there is yet a rude magnificence and ingenuity of construction, as well as excellence of decoration, that make it well deserving of examination.

The principal front has a southward aspect; it is the latest built and most pretentious part of the mansion, but, withal, the least interesting. It is of brick, with a portico of four columns in the centre, surmounted by a frieze, bearing the inscription, "Charles and Hester Legh, 1757," with a pediment above, in which is a shield with the Legh arms quartered with those of Corona, and an escutcheon of pretence over all on which is the coat of Lee of Wincham.

On entering, the first thing that meets the eye is the ponderous oaken door, thickly studded with iron nails and black with age, which stirs the fancy with images of the strife with Roundhead and Cavalier, for it bears abundant evidence of the rude assaults of Colonel Duckinfield's troopers in the shot-holes with which it is pierced in several places. Over the door within the vestibule is written, *Sic vos nunc vobis mellificatis apes*, one of the four lines by which Virgil exposed the imposture of Bathyllus. At the further end of the corridor we enter the courtyard, on the opposite side of which is the great hall, one of the finest in the county, if, indeed, it has its equal, with its projecting porch, its long lofty windows, its high-pitched roof, and quaint chequer work of black and white. Over the doorway as we enter we notice the old black letter inscription which Thomas Legh placed when, as he tells us, he " made this buyldinge in the year of or lorde god 1581."

The "hall" itself is an admirable and almost perfect specimen of the period when that apartment constituted the chief feature of every mansion, serving not only as an audience chamber on occasions of state and ceremony, but as the place where the owner and his family, with his guests and dependents, assembled daily at the dinner hour, and where, in fact, the public life of the household was carried on. Though perhaps not so large as in some of the baronial mansions of the country, it is yet a noble apartment, and sufficiently spacious for the hospitalities which in bygone days the lords of Adlington maintained. It occupies the entire height of the building, the form being that of a parallelogram, and, being the master feature of the house, is superior in architectural adornment, as well as in the amplitude of its dimensions, to any of the other rooms. The floors are laid with polished oak, and the walls, which are elaborately carved and ornamented, support a roof of dark oak acutely pointed and open to the ridge piece. The framework of this roof is divided by massive principals into bays, the collar braces being so arranged as to form a series of fine Gothic arches, springing from bold projecting hammer-beams that terminate in carved figures of angels holding heraldic shields, each being in turn connected by a hammer-brace with the main timbers of the walls. The daïs, or high place, which undoubtedly had its position at the further end, and where the master and mistress with their chief guests sat above the salt, as Chaucer relates in his " Marriage of January and May "—

> And at the feste sitteth he and she
> With other worthy folk upon the deis

has disappeared, and the screen which separated the lower end from the passage communicating with the buttery and the kitchener's department has been subjected to considerable alterations, though the original form may be distinctly traced, and much of the exquisitely ornamental panel work remains, though now well-nigh hidden from view. These panels, though mutilated in places, are deserving of careful examination; the design of the tracery is very beautiful, and the carving, where not broken, remains almost as sharp and as fresh as the day it left the workman's hands, save that time has given that sombre tint which so

45

well harmonises with the ancient character of the house. Above
the screen a gallery, the front of which is ornamented in arabesque
work, extends the entire width of the apartment; in it is an organ
elaborately painted and decorated, which, from the two shields of
Corona and Robartes on the top, would appear to have been
erected during the occupancy of John Legh, who married Isabella
Robartes, and died in 1739, and no doubt it was at this time the
original screen was subjected to so much injury. In addition to
the organ gallery there are two small side galleries near the
opposite end, each lighted by a dormer window, to which, in time
past, the ladies of the household and the more honoured guests
could retire to witness the revelries of the assembled retainers
below.

Though it can no longer be said that—

> With heraldry's rich hues imprest
> On the dim window glows the pictured crest

for every trace of the "storied pane" has disappeared, the want of
this species of decoration is in some measure compensated for by
the remarkable series of armorial shields with which the upper end
of the hall is adorned. At this end the roof is coved and divided
into square panels, each panel containing the arms of one of the
Norman Earls of Chester, the barons of their court, or of some
Cheshire family with whom the Leghs could claim kindred.
There are eight rows of panels in all. The upper ones
contain the heraldic insignia of the seven Norman Earls
of Chester in their successive order; immediately beneath
are the arms of the eight Norman baronies—Halton, Montalt,
Nantwich, Malpas, Shipbrooke, Dunham, Kinderton, and
Stockport; and below these again, and separated by an
elaborately carved oak cornice, the coats of the chief Cheshire
families, including those with which the Leghs are allied—fifty-
four in all. In the centre is placed an achievement of arms—
quarterly (1) Corona impaling Venables (for Legh, of Adlington),
(2) Honford, (3) Arderne, and (4) Belgrave; over all an

escutcheon of pretence bearing the coat of Legh of Wincham, with a crescent for difference. Beneath is the motto *Da gloriam Deo*, and, to give effect to his work, the artist, with scant regard for the laws of heraldry, has added a couple of unicorns as supporters; honourable accessories which it was not in the power of Garter King or even the Earl Marshal himself to bestow. On the knots of the framework of the panels is an inscription in single letters carved in relief—

THOMAS LEGH & CATARINA SAVAGE UXOR EIUS

AO DOI MO $\frac{CC}{CCC}$ VTO R.R.H. VIJ., XX.

The walls on the west and north sides are adorned with paintings of scenes from the "Æneid"—the one on the west end, which occupies the entire width, representing Hector taking leave of Andromache, and those on the north Venus presenting Æneas with armour, and Andromache offering presents to Ascanius. The wall spaces on each side of the organ at the west end are similarly decorated, one representing St. Cecilia and the other a figure playing upon the harp.

Nash, in his "Ancient Mansions," has given a characteristic view of this glorious old banquetting room, and it requires little stretch of the imagination to picture it as it must have appeared in its pristine state in the days of bluff King Hal and the maiden Queen—of Thomas Legh who built it, and his son, the valorous Sir Urian, when banners gay with many a proud device floated overhead; when the huge fire blazed cheerfully upon the halpas, and the long windows shed a profusion of light and dyed the pavement with the reflected hues of the heraldic cognisances with which they were dight; when the walls were draped with richest arras, and the screen, wrought with all the nicety of art, was hung with arms and armour—halberds, bills, and partisans, and the spreading antlers of deer captured in many a memorable chase; to re-people it with the departed forms of sturdy warriors and sober matrons, of gallant youths and lovely maidens; to see again the figures and faces of those who have long ago returned to dust, and listen

in imagination to the lusty laugh and the jocund song of the nameless men who, at the trumpet call of "boot and saddle," were
ready to mount and ride away wherever their lord might lead,

> Alike for feast or fight prepared.
> Battle and banquet both they shared,

Giving the rein to fancy, we may see the stately owner with his
dependents seated at the well-spread table, and hear the thrice-
told tale, while

> flagons pass along the board,
> Filled to the brim with foaming ale;
> And goblets flash with ruby wine,
> And merrily speeds the glad wassail.

The hall was proverbially the place of festivity, and many a scene
of jocund mirth and roystering revelry, unrestrained by the laws
which modern civilisation imposes, has, doubtless, here been
witnessed, as the nut-brown ale, the mead and the sack, the
Malmsey, and the Rhenish, the mazer-bowl, and the highly-
spiced claret cup passed from hand to hand, and the "top beam
of the hall" was enthusiastically toasted as symbolising the health
of the lordly owner, whose armorial ensigns occupied that elevated
position, for

> Merry swith it is in halle
> When the berdes waveth alle.

On the north side of the hall, near what was the "high-place," a
doorway communicates with the dining-room and some of the
principal apartments, and also with the staircase leading to the
drawing-room and the corridor which extends the entire length of
the south front; but these parts of the mansion have been greatly
modernised, and, with the exception of the dining and drawing
rooms, remodelled by Charles Legh about the middle of last
century, and in each of which are some exquisite carvings, said to

be by Grinling Gibbons,* but more probably the work of Sephton, which well deserve examination, do not call for any special description.

In 1846 a large portion of the contents of Adlington, including many family portraits by Vandyke, Lely, and Kneller; books, manuscripts, and curiosities, were sold by auction. Some of the books and manuscripts are now in the Chetham Library, and others were purchased for the Portico in Manchester. Fortunately many of the family portraits have since been recovered and restored to their original positions, among them being the one of Sir Urian Legh already referred to, and a large-sized picture in the dining-room by Cornelius Janssens; a full length of Thomas Legh, the Royalist soldier, and his wife Mary, daughter of Thomas Bolles.

Apart from its memories, its traditions, and its associations as the home of an ancient Cheshire stock, Adlington possesses a deep interest as an example of old English domestic architecture. Whilst retaining many of the more striking and important of its ancient features comparatively unimpaired, it marks the growth and development of human society, and expresses the needs and ideas of changeful centuries, the varied and somewhat rude magnificence of the Tudor and Stuart periods and the classic forms of the earlier Georgian era mingling in curious contrast, and carrying the mind rapidly through a long series of years. Happily, within the present century the house has been subjected to but little change or innovation, and has escaped, in a great degree, the evil influ-

---

* Gibbons, of whom Horace Walpole said "there was no instance of a man before who gave to wood the loose and airy lightness of flowers, and chained together the various productions of the elements with a freer disorder natural to each species," died in 1721, and, while there is good reason for supposing that the reconstruction of the dining and drawing rooms was effected at a later date, Sephton was certainly employed by Charles Legh, and it is more than probable that the carvings at Adlington were his work. Possibly, the close resemblance which these productions of the chisel bear to the well-known works of the great artist led to their being attributed to Gibbons.

ences of "renovators" and "improvers." It is one of the comparatively few old places that have remained to the descendants of the ancient worthies by whom they were erected, and we may venture to indulge the hope that as it has endured for centuries past, so for centuries to come it may be preserved a genuine relic of mediæval England—a monument and a memorial of what men call "the good old times."

KERSALL CELL.

CHAPTER IX.

N the township of Lowton, within the limits of the ancient and far-reaching parish of Winwick, and a short distance from the little town of Leigh, is an old-fashioned building of no great architectural pretensions, erected apparently in the reign of one of the Stuart kings, and now in the occupancy of a farmer. Byrom Hall, for that is the name, stands upon the site of an earlier structure, described in ancient writings as a manor house, though there is no evidence that the reputed manor ever enjoyed manorial privileges, and gave name in times past to a family ranking with the smaller gentry, who could boast a line of succession reaching as far back as the time of the second Edward. The Byroms of Byrom, notwithstanding their ancient lineage, do not appear to have ever attained to any very great distinction, or to have held any very important offices in the county; they married and were given in marriage among the best families of the shire, and they maintained the outward evidences of gentility by the use of armorial ensigns, but how or when those were acquired is not clear, and it is somewhat singular that they did not attend at any of the Herald's visitations to justify their right to the use of them, or to register their descent, at least not until September, 1664, when, in answer to the summons of Sir William Dugdale, Norroy King of Arms, Edward Byrom attended at Ormskirk, and on behalf of his elder brother, Samuel Byrom cf Byrom—the grandfather of a certain "Beau"

46

Byrom who wasted his substance in riotous living, and less than half a century afterwards parted with his patrimonial lands— registered a pedigree of five generations.

In the reign of Henry VII., when the Wars of the Roses were ended, and the people had settled down to more peaceful pursuits, a cadet of the family, Ralph Byrom, repaired to Manchester, established himself in trade, and throve apace by transactions which in those days were accounted considerable.

From the earliest period Manchester had exhibited an aptitude for manufacture. Kuerden tells us that as far back as the reign of Edward II. there was a mill for the manufacture of woollen cloths, and in the succeeding reign the industry and wealth of the town were greatly promoted by the encouragement given to a number of Flemish artisans who were induced to leave their homes in Flanders and settle in Lancashire, where they revealed the secrets of their craft to the peasantry of the neighbourhood, and thus planted the sapling of that industry which, taking root, flourished and gradually spread through the Lancashire valleys, the fulling mills and dyeworks then established in Salfordshire being the auspicious beginnings of that vast manufacturing industry which has enriched the kingdom and made Manchester the commercial capital of the Empire.

The old chronicler, Hollinworth, quoting an ancient writer, says that in 1520 "there were three famous clothiers living in the north countrey, viz., Cuthbert of Kendal, Hodgkins of Halifax, and Martin Brian, some say Byrom, of Manchester. Every one of these kept a greate number of servants at worke, spinners, carders, weavers, fullers, dyers, shearemen, &c., to the greate admiration of all that came into their houses to bechould them." Whether Hollinworth's authority is historically correct, or the persons he names only fictitious, certain it is that at that time Manchester was "a greate cloathing towne;" the Byroms had become noted as one of the great trading families, and took their places with the Galleys, the Beckes, the Pendletons, and other of the merchant princes of the day.

Adam Byrom, of "Saulforde, merchaunt," as he is styled, the son of Ralph, who first settled in the neighbourhood and diverged into trade, was, with one exception, the largest merchant in the Salford Hundred, and in 1540 was assessed by the commissioners of. Henry VIII. at a larger amount even than Sir Alexander Radcliffe, of Ordsall, who was accounted the great magnate of the district. Manchester was even then a thriving and prosperous mercantile town. Mills had been placed on the waters of the Irwell and its affluent streams, and " Manchester Cottons," as they were called, and which, be it known, were then and for a hundred years to come Lancashire woollens, were carried on pack-horses to London and Hull, and were frequently sent to the great fairs at Amsterdam, Frankfort, and to other foreign marts. So important had the trade become that it was found necessary, after a year's experience, to repeal the statute bestowing upon the town the privilege of sanctuary, and to send the sanctuary men, who by their idleness and other enormities were " prejudicial to the wealth, credit, great occupyings, and good order " of the place, to Chester, which, being poor, was less likely to suffer by the presence of such thriftless and disorderly characters—

> Cantabit vacuus coram latrone viator.

The wealth which Adam Byrom acquired in his business was at different times invested in the purchase of lands, &c , in Salford, Darcy Lever, Ardwick, Bolton-le-Moors, and other places, including the chief messuage or manor-house called Salford Hall, in which he resided. He appears to have been a free-trader in principle, and opposed to the feudal monopolies that were then in vogue, for it is recorded in the Kalendar of Pleadings that he prosecuted William Arram, the mayor of Preston, claiming exemption from the payment of tolls and other imposts in the fairs and markets of Salford and Preston. This worthy died on the 25th of July, 1558. His wife, a daughter of one Hunt, of Hunt's Hall—the Hunt's Bank, probably, of later days—bore him six children, three sons and three daughters; and it is a noteworthy fact that the two elder sons, George and Henry, died within a month of their father's demise. George, the first-born, was succeeded by his eldest son, Ralph, then a child of three years of age. One of his daughters was Margaret Byrom, the ill-fated victim of the memorable case of supposed witchcraft in 1597, of which mention has been made in our notice of Dr. Dee, the Wizard Warden of Manchester, who was solicited by her friends to cast out the devil with which it was believed John Hartley, a conjuror, had possessed her, while staying on a visit at the house of Nicholas Starkey, of Cleworth.

It is, however, with the descendants of Henry, the second son of Adam Byrom, the "merchaunt," that we are at present more immediately concerned. This Henry had in his father's lifetime been united in marriage with Mary, one of the daughters of Thomas Becke, a wealthy trader in the town, an alliance that introduces us to quite a group of Manchester worthies. The Beckes had been for years engaged in trade, and numbered among them some of the earliest benefactors of Manchester, and some of her most generous churchmen. Isabel, the widow of Robert Becke, and the mother, probably, of Henry Byrom's father-in-law, at her own cost erected the conduit in the market-place, the first "water works" in Manchester, conveying the water in pipes from a natural spring at the upper end of the town, which gave name to the present Spring Gardens and Fountain Street. Her father was Richard Bexwyke, another opulent merchant, who founded the Jesus Chantry on the south side of his parish church—the one which his descendant Henry Pendleton, in 1653, gave to the parishioners of Manchester for the purpose of a "free" public library, the first of the kind in the town, if not, indeed, in the kingdom; he also restored the choir and nave of the church, erected the beautifully carved stalls on the north side of the choir, and founded a grammar school, which one of his chantry priests was to teach. It is probable that he was the husband of Joan Bexwyke, the sister of Bishop Oldham, who, with Hugh Bexwyke and Ralph Hulme (ancestor of William Hulme, the "Founder,") was named in the first charter of feoffment of the Manchester Free

Grammar School, the three being, in fact, not only trustees, but special benefactors and co-founders in the endowment, if not in the first erection, of the Manchester school, which absorbed the original foundation of Richard Bexwyke. Another of these Bexwykes, Roger, a son or nephew of the Richard just named, married Margaret, the sister of John Bradford, the "martyr," a "worthy" whose name Lancashire men will always revere; and it is recorded that this Roger attended Bradford at the stake at Smithfield, but he was prevented by the brutal violence of one of the officials from helping to soothe the martyr's last agonies.

Henry Byrom left two sons—Robert, who succeeded as heir, but died unmarried in May, 1586, when the property passed to his younger brother, Lawrence. Of this representative of the family but little is known. He was in infancy at the time of his father's decease, and he was yet only young when he became heir to his brother, and succeeded to an inheritance that seems to have involved him in no small amount of litigation—generally with his own kinsmen, and for the purpose of adjusting differences respecting properties bequeathed by his father and grandfather. Ultimately, an agreement was come to, as appears by the following deed, dated 13th December, 1586:—

Be yt knowne to all men by these p'sents that wee Raphe Byrom a cousin of Lawrence), of Salford, in the countye of Lancaster, gent., Richard Hunte of the same Town, gent.; Adam Byrom (another cousin, of the same Town, gent.; and Raphe Houghton, of Manchester, in the countie afforesaid, gent.; for dyvers good causes and consideracons vs movinge Have Remysed, &c., and quyteclaymed vnto Lawrence Byrom, of Sallforde afforesaid, gent.; &c. All and all maner of accons, sutes, querells, trespasses, &c. by reason of any Lease made unto us of confidence and truste by Roberte Byrom (the elder brother of Lawrence and then deceased) to us, &c. ffrom the beginning of the worlde till this p'sent daye except onlie for the Release or discharge of one Obligacon of a thousande poundes made &c. by Lawce. to Ralfe & Adam j Maye 28 Eliz. that the sayde Lawrence B. shall not alter the state tayle made by Henry Byrom, father of the said Robte B. & Lawrence B. Witnessed by "William Radclyffe" and "Roberte Leighe." Dated 13 Dec., 29 Eliz. (1586).*

---

* Local Gleanings (Lancashire and Cheshire), V. ii. p. iii.

The late Canon Parkinson, in his notes on the "Private Journal of John Byrom," says that "after an unsettled life, and a too keen sense of his own infelicity, at least towards the close of his earthly struggles, he found at last a haven of rest in the Collegiate Church, being buried there June 26, 1598. There was," he adds, "more than ordinary sorrow in his family on that day, and probably some ground for his son not appearing at the Herald's Visitation in 1613, as well as for his own Christian name not being borne by any of his descendants." The appearance at the Visitation (Richard St. George's) was scarcely necessary, for on the same occasion Adam, the son of Ralph (Lawrence Byrom's cousin), entered a pedigree of six generations, claiming descent from Ralph, "second sonne to Byrom of Byrom," the first occasion on which any pedigree of the family had been entered, and at the same time he asserted his claim to and was allowed the arms borne by the Byroms of Byrom—Argent, a chevron between three porcupines, sable, a crescent for difference, with a porcupine, sable, charged with a crescent for crest.

Edward Byrom, the son who succeeded him, married, about the year 1615, Ellen, the daughter of Thomas Worsley, of Carr in Bowdon, an alliance that brought him in relationship with the Worsleys, of Platt in Rusholme, of which family was the distinguished Parliamentarian soldier, Major-general Charles Worsley, returned as the first representative for Manchester in Cromwell's Parliament of 1654. Like his progenitors, he was engaged in trade, and carried on an extensive business as a "linen draper," a phrase that meant a good deal more in those days than it does now. In local affairs he took an active part, and in 1638-9 his name occurs on the Court Leet Rolls as one of two constables of the town. His lot was cast in troublous times. Unlike his contemporary, Humphrey Chetham, he seems to have escaped the attentions of the money-seeking functionaries of Charles the First. Greatness was not thrust upon him, and he had not, as Chetham had, to pay smart for refusing to take upon himself the "honour" of knighthood—a distinction in those days of doubtful value.

Manchester had oftentimes been the scene of conflict. Roman and Saxon, Dane and Norman, had each in turn striven for supremacy; but well nigh six hundred years had elapsed since the tranquillity of the inhabitants had been disturbed by the presence of contending armies. The day, however, was near at hand when the sounds of war were once more to be heard, and that of war the most unnatural; when members of the same family, and often the same blood, were to contend with each other in deadly strife. When the storm burst, and the struggle between Charles and the Parliament began, the Byroms of Salford and the Byroms of Manchester, with whom the recollection of the vexatious lawsuits of Lawrence Byrom had not yet died out, ranged themselves on opposite sides. The Byroms of Salford, like those of the parent house, took up arms on behalf of the King, John Byrom receiving a commission as sergeant-major in the regiment of Lancashire militia commanded by Colonel Roger Nowell, of Read, for which, and other acts of delinquency, his estates were seized by the Commissioners of Sequestration, when he was obliged to compound for them by the payment of £201 16s. 6d. ; his brother, Edward Byrom, being at the same time required to pay £2 6s. 8d.

Edward Byrom, the representative of the Manchester stock, though in earlier life a contributor to the building of Trinity Church, in Salford, and accounted a moderate Churchman, was strongly inclined to Presbyterianism, and, with two of his sons, William and John, took an active part in promoting the cause of the Parliament. Manchester was at the time the great stronghold and rallying point of the Puritan party, and it is worthy of note that it was here the first blood was shed in that unhappy conflict. When the town was in peril of assault from Lord Strange's (afterwards Earl of Derby) forces, Heyricke, the Puritan warden, engaged the services of a German engineer, John Rosworm, who had served in the Low Countries, and happened at the time to be in the town ready to be employed by either party, and bargained with him to superintend the defences for six months for the modest sum of thirty pounds. Edward Byrom, "Sergeant Mr.

Byrom the elder," as he is called, served under Rosworm, and it is recorded that he was the means of discovering a villainous plot of certain individuals to seize and plunder the town, through which the chief conspirators were apprehended and their designs frustrated.*   At a later date, when Cromwell had been appointed "Lord Protector of the Commonwealth," and had summoned a Parliament to meet on his "fortunate day," September 3, 1654, the anniversary of the battles of Dunbar and Worcester, we find "Sergeant" Byrom among those of the witnesses to the return of "Charles Worsley, of Platt," his wife's kinsman, as the first member for Manchester. This appears to have been his last official act, and his death occurred shortly after. His wife, Ellen Worsley, bore him three sons and eight daughters. John, the second son, was a zealous Puritan, and held a lieutenant's commission in the Parliamentarian army; his military experiences were, however, cut short by an accident which cost him his life, almost immediately after the outbreak of the war, and which is thus recorded in a chronicle of the time :—

1642, October.—The two and twentieth day store of powder came in (to Manchester) and the foure and twentieth day some (more powder) coming was stayed. The joy of this last supply was sadly tempered with the accidentall, but mortall, wound of a skilful and active souldier. †

The "skilful and active soldier"—John Byrom—who was in his twenty-second year, was buried in the Collegiate Church, October 31, 1642.

William Byrom, the eldest son, who succeeded as heir to his father, was an active Presbyterian, and an elder in the Manchester Classis.   In 1656 he was one of the chief inhabitants who elected Richard Radcliffe, of Pool Fold, as the representative of Manchester in the Commonwealth Parliament in the place of Worsley, who was then dead.   Edward Byrom, the youngest of

---

* Ormerod's Civil War Tracts, p. 238.

† Lancashire's Valley of Achor, p. 123.

the three sons, was twenty-eight years of age at the time of his father's death, and had been then married only a few months, his wife being Ellen, the daughter of John Crompton, of Halliwell. He inherited the Puritan principles of his father and grandfather, and was one of those who, on the death of Richard Hollinworth, signed the invitation to Henry Newcome to supply the vacancy, and, with his brother William, accompanied the deputation to Newcome's quiet little parsonage at Gawsworth to entreat the famous preacher to comply with the wishes of the Church at Manchester.

This Edward was the first of the family who resided at Kersall Cell, a house occupying the site of a religious settlement that originally formed part of the possessions of the Cluniac monks of Lenton, and which had been confiscated to the Crown in the reign of Henry VIII. After its suppression the place, with the manor, had been granted to Baldwin Willoughby, who, in 1540, sold it to Ralph Kenyon, of Gorton, and he in turn conveyed it, eight years afterwards, to Richard Siddall, of Slade Hall, an old black and white house still standing in Burnage-lane, Rusholme. The estate remained in the possession of the Siddals until 1613, when it was alienated by Richard Siddal's great grandson, George Siddal, who seems to have been the spendthrift of his family.

Edward Byrom made his will on the 14th June, 1668, being then, as he states, " sick and weak of body," and he must have died within a day or two, for on the 18th June in the same year he was laid to rest with his fathers in the Collegiate Church. By his wife he had a family of six children, four of whom died in infancy, two sons only surviving, Edward and Joseph Byrom.

Joseph Byrom, the younger son, was largely engaged in trade, and, in 1703, served the office of borough reeve. He acquired considerable wealth in his business, and with the profits thus made he, on the 10th July, 1710, purchased from Samuel Byrom, of Byrom, the "Beau Byrom" before referred to, "the manor, demesne and hall of Byrom," the ancient house of his progenitors, and it has continued in the family ever since.

47

Edward Byrom, the eldest son, took up his abode at Kersall, and he had also a house at Hyde's Cross, which, with Withy Grove—Within Greave, as it was called—was then a pleasant outskirt, and the fashionable quarter of Manchester. In 1680 he married Dorothy, daughter of Captain John Allen, of Redvales, near Bury, and granddaughter of the Rev. Isaac Allen, rector of Prestwich, by whom he had, in addition to seven daughters, two sons, Edward, who, on his death in 1611, succeeded as heir, and John Byrom, the famous poet and stenographer.

The men of seclusion were by no means insensible to the beauties of Nature, but, on the contrary, in the selection of the sites for their religious houses usually displayed considerable judgment—

> The cunning rooks,
> Pitched, as by instinct, on the fattest fallows—

and Hugo de Buron was no exception, for he must have been imbued with the feeling so characteristic of the monkish fraternity when, in the days of Ranulph Gernons, he withdrew himself from the world and settled as a solitary recluse in the quiet secluded hermitage on the banks of the Irwell, which afterwards became an appendage of the Cluniac monastery of Lenton, in Nottinghamshire, and, in turn, the home of the opulent Manchester merchant, Edward Byrom, and his descendants. Fairer spot than that which Hugh de Buron chose it would be difficult to conceive, or one better suited for a life of monastic seclusion. It was then remote from the haunts of men, the atmosphere was not dimmed by the smoke of innumerable chimneys, nor the broad stream polluted with the abominations of countless manufactories. With its breezy moor and low wooded hills, its ferny hollows and forest avenues, and its wide shimmering river gliding swiftly yet silently along, and heightened in beauty by the noble oaks and stately elms that feathered down almost to the water's edge, it was just the place where the soul might commune with itself, and feed on thoughts and fancies ever new and ever beautiful. A place where the purest and noblest impulses might be awakened and the mind stirred to many a holy thought and deed—where in leaf and blossom, in wood and water, might be discovered the parallelism between the Great Artificer's work and His precepts, or, as Charles Kingsley puts it, "The work of God's hand, the likeness of God's countenance, the shadow of God's glory."

> It stood embosomed in a happy valley,
> Crowned by high woodlands, where the Druid oak
> Stood like Caractacus, in act to rally
> His host, with broad arms 'gainst the thunderstroke.

After the Reformation, when this little sanctuary passed into lay hands, a house was built upon the site—a picturesque black and white structure with projecting oriels, quaint mullioned windows, and gabled roofs, and here Edward Byrom took up his abode when he attained to manhood, for he was a youth of but twelve summers when his father died; to this house he took his youthful bride, Dorothy Allen, in 1680, and here many of his children were born. He had another house, as already stated, at Hyde's Cross, and, besides this, his burgage shop or place of business in the market stead opposite the Cross, to which he afterwards added a stall, as appears by the following entry on the court rolls of the manor of Manchester :—

1692, May 16th.—Stallinged and installed Edward Byrom, of Manchester, milliner, in one stall, stallinge, or standing roome at or neare the Crosse, in the Market Place, in Manchester aforesaid, formerly in the possession of Francis Rydings, deceased, being next to Robert Pelton's, towards the Crosse, conteyning in breadth two yards, and length three yards.

The spot thus indicated was in close proximity, if not, indeed, actually in front of the shop—the quaint black and white structure in the Market Place, which has been for many years a licensed house, and is now known as the "Wellington." The building has ever since continued in the possession of the family, the present owner being Mr. Edward Byrom, who assumed that name in lieu of Fox on his succeeding at her death to the property of his godmother, Miss Eleanora Atherton, the great granddaughter of Edward Byrom's distinguished son, John Byrom. The "milliner's" business was in reality that of a mercer or haberdasher. It must have prospered, for subsequently the two adjoining stalls were absorbed; and it would seem to have been carried on after Edward Byrom's death by his youngest daughter, Phœbe, for in Mrs. Raffald's "Directory" for 1773 the name occurs, "Miss Phœbe Byrom, milliner, 1, Shambles," and in that for 1781, "Miss Phœbe Byrom, milliner, Market Place." The lady, who was five years younger than her brother John, died on the 20th February, 1785, at the ripe old age of 88.

It seems strange in these days to read of a·merchant or trader having a stall in the Market Place, but the mode in which business was conducted in the earlier years of the last century was very different to that with which the present generation is familiar. Dr. Aikin, in his "Description of the Country Round Manchester," says that "When the trade began to extend, the chapmen used to keep gangs of pack-horses, and accompany them to the principal towns with goods in packs, which they opened and sold to shop-keepers, lodging what was unsold in small stores at the inn. The pack-horses brought back sheep's wool, which was bought on the journey and sold to the makers of worsted yarns at Manchester or to the clothiers of Rochdale, Saddleworth, and the West Riding of Yorkshire." When at home the trader was invariably in his warehouse or place of business at six o'clock in the morning; at seven he and his children and apprentices had a "plain breakfast" together, the "plain breakfast" being "one large dish of water pottage, made of oatmeal, water, and a little salt, boiled thick and poured into a dish." "A pan or basin of milk" was placed by the side, and each, using a wooden spoon, dipped first into one and then into the other. The shops in the Market Place which were occupied by clothiers, mercers, and the better class of tradesmen were for the most part open to the street, and a loose stall or standing in front, where their wares could be more advantageously displayed, was not thought at all derogatory.

In the "Private Journal and Literary Remains of John Byrom," edited for the Chetham Society by the late Canon Parkinson, we have pleasant glimpses of the daily doings of the worthy linen-draper or milliner, as he was indifferently styled, Edward Byrom, and an admirable picture of the habits and modes of life in the household of a well-to-do trader as well as of the literary and social characteristics of the better class of people in Manchester a century and a half ago. Edward Byrom had a numerous family—seven daughters, six of whom died unmarried, and, in addition, two sons. Edward, the eldest son, who was brought up to the business which had been carried on with so much success for so many generations, was born March 4, 1686-7. John was baptised at the Collegiate Church, 29th February, 1691-2, and was his junior therefore by about five years. Having, as good old Bishop Oldham expressed it, much "pregnant witte," he was trained for one of the learned professions, and in due course was sent to Chester and placed under the tuition of his relative, the eminent schoolmaster, Mr. Francis Harper, preparatory to his being entered at Merchant Taylors'—then famous as a seminary of learning—in which it was expected that his father's influence with the city traders would secure him admission. He proceeded from Chester to London in January, 1707-8, and in the following month he writes to his father :—

London, Feb. 170?.

Hond. Sir [such was the form in which a young gentleman addressed his "governor" in the days of Queen Anne] I received yours in answer to mine of the 10th and 27th inst. Our feast was on Tuesday last ; the boys went to school, had wine and biscuit, then walked to Bow Church, where one Mr. Dunstan preached on Prov. xix. 8; from thence they walked to Leathersellers' Hall, where the gentlemen had a feast. The boys who were my schoolfellows at Chester came up soon to London, which turned to their advantage. I think it not prudence to go to University too soon, both for Mr. Ashton's opinion, and because I believe that when they come there they are expected to know enough of school learning so as to read authors, compose exercises, &c., with their own help and the instruction of a tutor. I cannot have the opportunity of seeing the Register Book till doctor's day, which will be about Easter, when I shall take particular notice how I stand as to election ; in the meantime strive to improve myself in virtue, knowledge, and learning. We went to Bow Church on Sunday to hear the Archbishop of York.—I am your dutiful son,   J.B.

In another letter he writes :—

My master is very kind to me, and never yet spoke a cross word to me, and I think I never gave him occasion, which is an encouragement and satisfaction to me, and I will strive to preserve it."

Young Byrom's progress in the classics was so satisfactory that in 1709 he was admitted a pensioner of Trinity College, Cambridge, and in a letter, dated 14th May in that year, he gives his father a detailed account of the examination and the circumstances attendant upon his election. His career at the university was anxiously watched by his father, whose letters, many of which have been preserved, contain many admonitions and much excellent advice. Thus, apparently in response to a request for a copy of Locke's great work, he writes,

I have not Mr. Locke's book of "Human Understanding," it is above my capacity ; nor was I ever fond of that author, he being (though a very learned man) a Socinian or an atheist, as to which controversy, I desire you not to trouble yourself with it in your younger studies. I look upon it as a snare of the devil, thrown among sharp wits and ingenious youths to oppose their reason to revelation, and because they cannot apprehend reason, to make them sceptics, and so entice them to read other books than the Bible and the comments upon it.

In another letter he says :—

I lately brought home Mr. Melling and Mr. Worsley from evening prayers to drink a dish of tea in your remembrance. . . . good son, look now before you to consider how precious your time is, and how to improve yourself, to consider the design and end proposed in your education, to fit you for sacred orders, which ought most considerately to be undertaken . . . whatever books you read, be sure to read Dr. Hammond upon the Psalms and Lessons, with Dr. Whitby every day ; it is not every young scholar hath them, but you have, and shall want no necessary thing I can buy you. I was reading, the other evening, the 2nd lesson ; Hebrews vi., 7, 8, made a deeper impression on my mind now, after receiving the holy sacrament on Good Friday and Easter day, than I ever noted in them before, which may be applicable to you. In your case, when the good education bestowed upon youths designed for the ministry bringeth forth herbs meet for them to whom it is dressed, it receiveth God's blessing ; but if thorns and briars, &c. Reading this, I applied it so on you, who I then thought of, but on myself as in my own case.

No wonder that with such counsel from such a father, the young undergraduate should have become imbued with a spirit of piety that influenced every action of his future life. But that father was soon to be taken from him. In August, 1711, Edward Byrom, whose health had been failing for some time, passed away at the comparatively early age of fifty-five, and on the twenty-first of the same month was laid to rest by the side of his fathers in the Jesus chantry, then called the Byrom chapel, in the old church of Manchester—the church in which in life he had so often delighted to worship.

In December, 1711, young Byrom took his B.A., and in his exuberant joy he thus writes from Cambridge to his confidential friend, John Stansfield, the assistant manager of his late father's place of business in London, whom he frequently commissioned to purchase books for him :—

I would fain have nothing hinder the pleasure I take in thinking how soon I shall change this tattered blue gown (the undergraduate's gown, which was then, as now, blue) for a black one and a lambskin, and have the honourable title of Bachelor of Arts. BACHELOR OF ARTS! John, how great it sounds! the Great Mogul is nothing to it. Ay, ay, sir, don't pride yourself upon your fine titles before you have them. Are you sure of your degree? Can you stand the test of a strict examination in all these arts you are to be bachelor of? Has not one of your blue gowns been stopped this week for insufficiency in that point already, and do you hope to escape better? Why, sir, you say true, but I will hope on, notwithstanding, till I see reason to the contrary.—Yours, J. B.

The "black gown," the "lambskin," and the "honourable title" were gained notwithstanding, and the vacation which followed was spent by the young Bachelor of Arts with his widowed mother and sisters in his Lancashire home at Kersall. His sister, Sarah (Mrs. Brearcliffe), in a letter to John Stansfield, writes—

Brother John is most at Kersall : he goes every night and morning down to the water side and bawls out one of Tully's orations in Latin, so loud they can hear him a mile off ; so that all the neighbourhood think he is mad, and you would think so too if you saw him. Sometimes he thrashes corn with John Rigby's men, and helps them to get potatoes, and works as hard as any of them. He is very good company and we shall miss him when he is gone, which will not be long to now; Christmas is very near.

From orating on the banks of the Irwell, and "threshing corn with John Rigby's men," Byrom returned to his studies at Cambridge. His lively and cheerful disposition made him popular with his brother collegians, and secured for him many friendships. He was, too, a welcome visitor in the house of the master of Trinity, Dr. Richard Bentley—the great Bentley; one of his most intimate associates was the doctor's nephew, "Tom," and he was also on friendly terms with the doctor's young and fascinating daughter, Joanna—"Jug," as she was familiarly called— if, indeed, they did not entertain something more than friendly feelings towards each other. In July, 1714, we find him writing to his old friend Stansfield as to his prospects of a fellowship, and in the following month he writes to his brother Edward, who was then in London:—

I have wrote to Mr. Banks to desire his interest at fellowships, but must leave it to you to direct it and send it to him.

It was about this time that his passion for poetry first manifested itself. He had before (August 17, 1714), under the signature of "John Shadow," contributed a paper to the *Spectator* on the subject of dreams, which elicited a complimentary editorial note from Addison. This was followed on the 6th October in the same year by his pretty pastoral, "Colin and Phœbe," prefaced by another complimentary note, which at once brought him into general notice:—

> My time, O ye muses, was happily spent,
> When Phœbe went with me wherever I went,
> Ten thousand sweet pleasures I felt in my breast ;
> Sure never fond shepherd like Colin was blest !
> But now she has gone, and has left me behind,
> What a marvellous change on a sudden I find !
> When things were as fine as could possibly be,
> I thought 'twas the spring, but alas! it was she.

The poem, which comprises ten stanzas, at once became generally popular; it was his first production in verse, and gained the admiration of Chalmers and the praise of Bishop Monk, the latter pronouncing it "one of the most exquisite specimens in existence." It is commonly supposed that the Phœbe of the pastoral was Bentley's witty and accomplished daughter, "Jug," who, Bishop Monk says, "from her earliest youth captivated the hearts of the young collegians," and for whom Byrom is said, though without any evidence, to have conceived a passion. It is more than likely that he wished to attract the attention of Bentley, who was an ardent admirer of the *Spectator*, and who, finding in its columns a poem of such merit from one of his own college might be induced to use his influence in obtaining for the author the fellowship which Byrom so much desired. Certain it is that he got the fellowship he had previously despaired of, and did not gain the hand of Bentley's daughter, that young lady a few years afterwards becoming the wife of Dr. Dennison Cumberland, afterwards Bishop of Clonfert and Killaloe, the issue of the marriage being Richard Cumberland, the well-known dramatic writer.

The year following his election to a fellowship of his college (1714) Byrom proceeded to his master's degree. The ardent aspirations of his father that he should enter the Church were not, however, to be realised, for in 1716 he was obliged by the statutes of his college to vacate his fellowship in consequence of his declining to be admitted to holy orders. The reason of this is not very clear, but it is evident from his correspondence that he had then become strongly imbued with Jacobitism, and, in the unsettled state of society consequent upon the Hanoverian succession and the determined efforts that were made to restore the crown to the exiled Stuarts, he may have felt a desire to be free from the obligations his ordination vows would impose. Be that as it may, he visited the continent in 1717, and remained for some time in seclusion. There was some mystery about his movements at the time, and it has been surmised that his retirement was not altogether unconnected with politics, if, indeed, it

48

was not for the actual purpose of fomenting another Jacobite
insurrection. During his stay he met with Malebranche's
"Search after Truth," and some pieces of Mademoiselle
Bourignon, the consequence of which was that he became strongly
impressed with the visionary philosophy of the former, and the
enthusiastic extravagance of the latter. He resided for a while at
Montpelier, where he applied himself to the study of medicine.
His brother Edward, writing to him on the 17th August, 1717,
says :—

> I hope you have improved yourself in physic since your being there
> (Montpelier). I would gladly have you employ yourself that way, and you
> need not doubt of encouragement here. Not one person but ourselves
> knows where you are, but we think now to let our friends know that you
> are studying physic at Montpelier. . . . You may save yourself any
> trouble of inquiring after Mr. Roberts, for he is in these parts, but thinks
> himself excepted out of the act of grace, as are all persons who have gone
> beyond seas, or all who have been with the Pretender.

While away there was a probability of the librarianship of the
Chetham Library falling vacant, a post which Byrom was rather
anxious to obtain, though the emoluments were very small. In a
letter to his brother, written from Montpelier, January 3, 1718,
he writes :—

> My wife (his youngest sister Phœbe, whom he playfully spoke of by that
> name) writes me word that Mr. Lesley, your library keeper, is going to
> die ; that the feoffees ask if I will have the place. I could like it very well,
> but I suppose it tied to certain engagements which I do not like so well ;
> I suppose the feoffees (are) at liberty to give it to one *in* or *out* of orders,
> but whether he must take the oaths or no depends not upon them. If I
> may be as I am, I shall be glad to visit the skeleton. You all invite me
> home very kindly, and in spring I think to come to you by way of Paris, if
> you know of no other by any of the ports. I have nothing should tempt
> me from your company at present but the occasion of a little insight into
> physic in this place.

The "insight" having apparently been obtained, he returned to
England, and on the 3rd May he writes a hurried note to his
brother from Cambridge.

The post is this moment going out, so I run to the coffee-house to return you an answer in haste to yours, and let you know that I should be very willing to have the library, and am very much obliged to you for your pains in engaging the feoffees; if you can be sure of it, let me know further; it will be better worth while than staying for a doubtful chance of a fellowship whose profit will be slow in coming; besides, 'tis in Manchester, which place I love entirely.

Whether admission to orders was a condition, or the taking the oaths an obstacle, is not clear, but, though Byrom returned to Manchester, he did not succeed to the office.

The prospect of the librarianship of Chetham's Library was not the only inducement for Byrom to settle in his native town. His uncle, Joseph Byrom, had a pretty daughter, then blooming into womanhood, who had made an impression on his susceptible heart, and, in short, the ardent young Jacobite, who awhile before had penned verses in praise of Bentley's fascinating daughter—

> Moving all nature with his artless plaints,

fell in love with his cousin; but the course of true love was ruffled by the proverbial obstructions. The young lady's favour was quickly gained, but her father's approval was not so easily secured, and that is scarcely to be wondered at. Byrom at the time had not settled down to any profession; his prospects were doubtful; he had been obliged to seclude himself on account of his political proclivities; and had, moreover, come to be accounted an eccentric and somewhat dreamy philosopher, infected with the mysticism of the French school. The practical, hard-headed Manchester merchant could, therefore, hardly look upon him as an eligible suitor or a promising husband for a young lady destined to inherit the ancestral home of the Byroms. Everything, however, comes to him who can wait. Byrom did wait; and eventually the obdurate parent yielded, and gave his consent to, if he did not actually express approval of, the match; and on Valentine's Day, 1720-1, at the old church, the young couple were united, the bride having just completed her twenty-first year, and Byrom being then in his twenty-ninth.

Chalmers, in his biography of Byrom, represents the marriage as a clandestine one. He says the lady's father " was extremely averse to the match, and when it took place without his consent, refused the young couple any means of support ; and, as a means of supporting himself and his wife, Byrom had recourse to the teaching of shorthand writing." But this is an error, as evidenced by a passage in a letter addressed by the bride's elder sister, Anne Byrom, to Mr. Stansfield, under date February 18, 1720-1, four days after the wedding :—

> I received yours last week, and designed answering it by first post, but could not have an opportunity, we having been pretty much engaged this week; for on Tuesday last sister Elizabeth was married to Dr. Byrom, with consent of father and mother, and the wedding kept here, and we having had a deal of company.

His sister here designates him "Dr." Byrom, and the prefix to his name was through life commonly accorded by his friends and acquaintance. He does not appear ever to have taken a degree entitling him to it, though in one of his letters written from Montpelier he styles himself " Dr. of Physic." There is a common belief that he practised medicine in Manchester ; but this was only upon rare occasions, chiefly among the poor and the members of his own family ; and he threw physic to the dogs when he applied himself to the perfecting of his system of shorthand. Shortly after his marriage he became the occupant of a house belonging to Mr. Hunter, standing at the corner of Hanging Ditch, and what is now the lower end of Cannon Street, but then called Hunter's-lane, and here his family resided for many years. His journal affords pleasant glimpses of his home life and surroundings at this time :—

> October 5, 1722.—This day we came to Mr. Hunter's house. Saturday, 6th.—Laurenson's wife died. Sister Ellen ill. Sorted my papers all morning. Mr. Hooper came about one to ask me to go to Holme (Hulme Hall). I followed 'em thither ; Mr. M. and R. and Mrs. H. Malyn. Dr. Mainwaring there. We bowled, read Haddon's verses on the eclipses, &c. Mr. Leycester came, and Mr. Kate.

The Mr. Hooper here referred to was the recently-appointed librarian to Chetham's Library, and the chaplain to Lady Anne

Bland, of Hulme Hall, lady of the manor of Manchester. Massey Malyn was a son of Dr. Malyn, who had acquired by his marriage the Sale Hall Estate, in Cheshire, and was himself the rector of Ashton-upon-Mersey; Robert Malyn, his younger brother, was an undergraduate of Cambridge; Peter Mainwaring was a well-known medical practitioner in the town, who subsequently married one of the sisters and co-heiresses of Massey Malyn; and John Haddon

was the rector of Warrington. Hulme Hall was at that time the centre in which gathered the wit and learning and intellectuality of the neighbourhood. Lady Anne Bland, the widowed owner, and the foundress of St. Ann's, was accounted the leader of fashion among the Hanoverian and Whig party, and the rival of Madam Drake, who carried the palm among the Jacobite and Tory fashionables; the former deeming it not inconsistent with her dignity to resent the exuberant display of Stuart tartan at the newly-built Assembly-rooms, in King Street, by arraying her party in orange-coloured ribbons, and dancing a minuet with them by moonlight in the open street. Byrom was always a welcome guest at Hulme, where his sprightliness and epigrammatic humour was highly appreciated, and with the pious, if somewhat imperious, owner he was, in spite of his Jacobite proclivities, an especial favourite. He was a frequent worshipper at St. Ann's, the "new church" as it was called, in contradistinction to the "old" or parish church, oftentimes occupying Lady Bland's seat, and occasionally going back to tea with her in her own coach :—

1725.—Wednesday, Twelfth-day (January 6th), went to the new church in the morning with Beppy (his eldest daughter Elizabeth, then a child of three years), and sat in Lady Bland's seat ; dined at Father Byrom's; called to see the Wild Irishman in Smithy-door.

Tuesday, 12th,—Young Tarboc called on me, and we went to Hulme to take the inscription off the stone (a Roman altar found in Castle Field). I came home with Lady Bland in the coach, and went with Mr. Cattel and Mr. Brettargh to dinner. I went to Hulme again with young Tarboc.

Wednesday.—Lady Bland sent to invite me to the dancing to-night. I walked to Hulme in the evening, when I found them dancing. We came home between twelve and one in Lady Bland's coach and father Byrom's chariot, which sister Ann had ordered.

Sunday.—New church ; sat with Mr. Mynshull (of Chorlton Hall); took leave with Dr. Malyn, Mr. Chetham, and Lady Bland.

It is pleasant to think that at this time, when in Manchester political and religious feeling was at fever heat, and the place had become little else than a hot-bed of contending factions, there was a disposition to observe the amenities of life, and people of the most conflicting political opinions were able to meet in social intercourse with every appearance of complaisant good humour.

When Byrom married he obtained the consent of his bride's father, but he obtained little else ; his own means were scanty, and with the increasing demands of an increasing family he was compelled to follow some occupation as a means of earning a livelihood. While pursuing his studies at Cambridge he had invented a system of shorthand, the leading principle of which was to denote the different sounds of language by strokes of the shortest and simplest form. Reporting, as a profession, was all but unknown, but in private life stenography was much more generally practised than at the present time, especially among students and the better educated members of society, who, before the age of cheap literature, had recourse to it to reduce the labour of frequent transcription. Cypher-writing had long been in vogue, the "Diary" of Pepys being a notable illustration, but the system which Byrom introduced was the first that was based upon any clearly defined principle, and, though now out of date, may be said to be the parent of all subsequent and "improved" systems. Unfortunately for him the men of Manchester a century and a half ago thought more of looms than of literature, and were more intent on manufactures than on metaphysics; hence the place afforded little scope for the practice of the art which he had invented. London was a more promising field, and during several years he made lengthened visits to the metropolis, where he met with very encouraging support, his patrons and pupils including some of the most eminent statesmen and divines of the day—the Duke of Devonshire, the Archbishop of York, Lord Chesterfield, Lord Hartington, Hoadley, Bishop of Salisbury, Horace Walpole, Pope, and others of equal celebrity. In his Journal he records :— "Proposals printed May 27, 1723, for printing and publishing a new method of shorthand;" and on the 30th January, 1724, he writes to his wife :—

> I told you I was to see the Archbishop of York. I did so on Tuesday morning, and talked with him and his son about our art. They entered into the notion of it very readily, and his grace promised to recommend it wherever he had an opportunity. New proposals are now printing off, dated February 1st, 1724, that is, Saturday, on which day I intend to advertise in the *Daily Post, Evening Post*, and *London Journal.* They are the same as the old proposals, only Mr. Leycester's (of Toft) approbation is added to Mr. Smith's. Now the thing receives a formal publication I shall see what I am likely to expect from my friend Mr. Public, and whether he will have a true relish for clever things or no.

"Mr. Public" had the desired "relish," and the "clever things" obtained for their inventor the honour of admission into the Royal Society.

Thursday, March 19th (1724).—This day I was admitted Fellow of the Royal Society by Sir Hans Sloane, and Mr. Robert Ord at the same time. He and I went there together, gave Mr. Hawkshee two guineas, and signed bond to pay fifty-two shillings a year."

Byrom found a competitor in the person of a Mr. James Weston, who claimed to be the inventor of a superior method of stenography, and the journalist thus writes of his "furious antagonist" :—

> Mr. Hooper and Jo. Clowes have been to pay Mr. Weston a visit, and we have had good diversion with the account of it. . . . He describes me seven foot high,* tolerably dressed in a tie-wig, spent my fortune, and a little light-headed, and showed 'em all his challenge, and how he had frightened me from dispersing my proposals publicly, but seemed at the bottom to be plaguily afraid. He says I come to Dick's coffee house almost every night when he intends to come and challenge me before the company ; when he does, I shall let you know in what manner he (de)molishes me.

During his visits to London Byrom became associated with the leading literary and political characters of the day—with Sir Hans Sloane, Bentley, the great Newton, the Wesleys, and others—over whom his great intellectual ability and ceaseless industry, blended as it was with a high tone of religious and moral feeling, enabled him to exercise considerable influence. His "Journal," in which from day to day he records the trifling occurrences of his life, contains many references to his literary friends, and embraces a variety of information interesting as illustrative of the manners and habits of the age. In his long absences, however, he never forgot the ties of home and family. His letters addressed " To Mrs. Eliz. Byrom, near the Old Church, in Manchester," relating his daily doings, are full of entertaining gossip, and couched in terms of the fondest endearment. Here is a passage taken at random :—

---

* Byrom was of unusual stature ; on one occasion he records having met with a Mr. Jefferson, who was " taller than I by measuring," the only instance, it would seem, of his having met with such a person.

Kent's Coffee House, May 20, 1729.—I am sorry to hear of Nelly's being so ill and weakly; but I am not able to add anything to the care which you take of her by any physic of mine. The diet of children is the only thing to look after. . . . My dearest love, as thou takest all possible care of thy infants, make not thyself uneasy about them: but secure thine own health for the sake of them, and thy most affectionate husband and friend.

A week later he writes:—

I promise myself that you are all pretty well at Kersall and Nelly better, not having any letter last post. . . . Prithee let the children have some sort of things that will keep the sun off 'em. Why should one let their faces be spoiled when a little custom might prevent it? Oh, dear! that I was with ye all. I long to jump into Kersall river.

If he could revisit his dearly-loved haunt at Kersall he would find the river now not quite so inviting.

In one of his letters to Mrs. Byrom he speaks of meeting with Whitefield, the great preacher and founder of the Calvinistic Methodists, who had then just returned from a visit to the American settlement of Georgia, when it was proposed to sing a hymn; and he remarks, "If I was to sing with 'em, it must (be) nearer homeward than Georgia. The tune that I should sing would be something like this, I believe :—

> Partner of all my joys and cares,
> Whether in poverty or wealth,
> For thee I put up all my pray'rs;
> Well heard if answer'd by thy health.
>
> Long absence, cruel as it is,
> Content still longer to endure,
> If ought conducive to thy bliss
> The tedious torment could procure.
>
> Joyous or grievous my employ,
> Absence itself would give relief,
> Could I but give thee all the joy,
> And bear myself alone the grief.
>
> Lost in this place of grand resort,
> Though crowds succeeding crowds I see,
> Quite from the city to the court—
> 'Tis all a wilderness to me!

Amidst a world of gaudy scenes
    Around me, glittering, I move;
I wander, heedless what it means,
    Bent on the thoughts of her I love.

Still I usurp that sacred sound
    Too often and too long profan'd;
When shall I tread the happy ground
    Where love and truth may be obtained?

Let me and my beloved spouse,
    With mutual ardour, strive to quit
False, earthly, interested vows,
    And Heaven into our hearts admit.

There let th' endearing hope take place,
    Though parted here to meet above
In a perpetual chaste embrace,
    United, Jesu! in thy love!"

It was during the time of these visits to London that the wordy war arose between the admirers of Handel and his great Italian rival Bononcini, which Byrom ridiculed in a witty epigram that will remain famous for all time :—

Some say compared to Bononcini
    That Mynheer Handel's but a ninny.
Others aver that he to Handel
    Is scarcely fit to hold a candle;
Strange all this difference should be
'Twixt Tweedle-dum and Tweedle-dee.

Its publication created quite a sensation in the literary world; the wits of the day attributed it to Swift, and he has been often credited with it in later times. Handel's biographer, M. Victor Schoelcher, thus refers to it—" Swift, who admired nothing, and who had no ear, wrote an epigram upon the subject," and adds, " the angry injustice of the nobles" who were in league against the great composer was " far preferable to the empty eclecticism of the Dean of St. Patrick's." The question of authorship is, however, easily disposed of by a reference to Byrom's journal, in which, writing under date, Saturday, June 5, 1725, he says :—

We went to see Mr. Hooper, who was at dinner at Mr. Whitworth's; he came over to us to Mill's Coffee House, told us of my epigram upon Handel and Bononcini being in the papers. . . . Bob came to supper; said that Glover had showed him the verses in the *Journal*, not knowing that they were mine."

And so the years went round. The summer months he usually spent with his family and kindred in Lancashire ; looking in now and then at the " College ;" discussing learnedly with Dr. Deacon, Clayton, Thyer, and other of the local *literati* ; paying court to Lady Bland ; spending the day with " Mother Byrom " at Kersall ; dining with " brother Byrom at the Cross " (Edward Byrom's, in the Market Place) ; " drinking a dish of tea with sister Brearcliffe " at her stately house in Spring Gardens ; or taking an evening walk " after sermon by the river side by Strangeways with Mr. Leycester and Dr. Mainwaring ;" for Strangeways Walk, as it was called, was then a pleasant tree-shaded lane, with the pleasaunce belonging to Hunt's Bank Hall, the residence of Mr. Clowes, and the stately woods of Strangeways Park on the one hand, and verdant meadows and pastures reaching down to the banks of the pure and sparkling Irwell on the other. In London his time was pretty well occupied with his pupils, the brief intervals of leisure being spent in social intercourse with his Lancashire and Cambridge friends, writing epigrams, disputing on religious doctrines, attending meetings at the (Royal) " Society," " making merry at the Mitre," and lamenting the shortcomings of his laundress.

The practice of reporting was not then universally popular, and Byrom occasionally met with a humorous adventure. " Orator" Henley, whom Pope has immortalised—

> The great restorer of the good old stage,
> Preacher at once and zany of his age,

objected to his sermons being reported on the ground that " he might have his discourses printed against him." He threatened to turn out the " chiel amang them takin notes," and when Byrom would not desist, even when the " manager" offered to return the shilling he had paid for admission, " went on so much faster than usual that he took the only way to stop me," thus effectually getting rid of the unwelcome attentions of the inexorable shorthand writer. On another occasion when Byrom exercised his talents in assisting the High Church party to oppose the application to Parliament for an Act to establish a workhouse in Manchester for the employment of the poor, a scene occurred which is best related in his own words. A subscription had been raised in the town to defray the cost of erection, and it was proposed that the house should be managed by twenty-four guardians, eight to be nominated by the Whigs, eight by the Tories, and the remainder by the Presbyterians. Dr. Peploe, the Whig Bishop of Chester, who was also warden of Manchester, undertook to present the Bill for forming the guardians into a corporation ; but the Tory and High Church party offered a strong opposition to the scheme. Through some delay the measure was defeated in the first session of Parliament, and on being reintroduced in the succeeding year it was opposed by Sir Oswald Mosley, of Ancoats, who, fearing that his interests as lord of the manor might be prejudiced, had, in the meantime, caused a large building to be erected for the purpose near Miller's Lane—the present Miller Street. Byrom, whom the Whigs denounced as an incendiary and threatened to pull to pieces, was very active in supporting the Tory opposition, and gave evidence before the Commissioners. He appears on the same occasion to have occupied himself in taking shorthand notes, when the scene occurred which he thus describes in a letter dated February 20, 1731 :—

I must tell you to get another petition ready to offer to the House that a body may write shorthand in the cause of one's country. I have ventured to stand the threats of a complaint and the danger of a committee in defence of that natural right of exercising the noble art which I have acquired. At the last committee but one I was threatened by a Scotch knight (Sir James Campbell) whom I provoked to execution of his said valiant threatening yesterday, for in the midst of Serjt. Darnel's reply out he comes at the instigation of one Brereton, and suddenly and loud pronounces these terrible words—*To oadur, oardur, I speak to oadur; I desair to knaw if any mon shil wrait here that is nut a clairk or solicitur ?* and an universal silence ensuing I was going to speak for myself but a member of my acquaintance

winking that I had better not, I repressed my rising indignation. Nobody
said anything to the knight's query, only Sir Ed. Stanley (M.P. for the
county of Lancaster, and afterwards eleventh Earl of Derby) hinted that
there was no great harm done; and my friend the serjeant himself said
that the gentleman was famous for writing shorthand, and for his part he
was under no apprehension by his taking down anything he should say,
and so returned to his matter; and the apparition of danger vanished:
but if these attacks upon the liberty of shorthand men go on I must have
a petition from all countries where our disciples dwell, and Manchester
must lead 'em on.

On the 12th May, 1740, Byrom's elder brother, Edward, the
"Brother Byrom at the Cross," died unmarried, when John, the
poet and stenographer, became the head of the family and owner
of the estates at Kersall.

Mr. Espinasse, in the first of his admirable series of "Lancashire
Worthies," says that Byrom's biographers "do not give the precise
date of the death of his elder brother, Edward." The information
is supplied in the stenographer's "Shorthand Journal," in which
occurs this entry:—

May 12th (1740).—Edward Byrom, of Kersall, elder son of Edward
Byrom, of Manchester, and Dorothy, daughter of John Allen, of Redivales,
near Bury. He was born March 4th, 1686, and died May 12th, 1740.

By his acquisition of the family estates at Kersall, Byrom was
placed in a position of comfortable independence, and able to relax
from the drudgery of teaching shorthand, though it was some time
before he could be induced to withdraw from London and its
pleasant society to settle down in quiet retirement in Manchester.
Two years after this addition to his fortune he received the welcome
intelligence from Lord Morton that the crowning act of all his
anxieties—the Act securing to him for a period of twenty-one
years the exclusive right of publishing his "Art and Method of
Shorthand"—the nation's testimony to the merits of the system —
had passed the House of Lords and received the royal assent ; an
Act which, singular to say, appears to have been obtained without
any cost.

From this time his journeyings to London became less and less frequent, and his life seems to have been passed for the most part in his native town in a calm round of social and domestic enjoyment, his playful fancy finding vent in squib and pasquinade, and in sparkling epigrams, an easy and unshackled style of versification for which he had a special aptitude. Not the least popular of his effusions was the one directed against the farmers or tenants of the Grammar School Mills, Messrs. Yates and Dawson, who had involved the town in the costs of a lawsuit because the inhabitants had refused to observe the old feudal monopoly and grind all their corn, grain, and malt at the mills : —

> Here's Bone and Skin,
> Two millers thin,
> Would starve the town, or near it,
> But be it known
> To Skin and Bone
> That Flesh and Blood can't bear it.

The point of the epigram was in the allusion to the professions of Yates and Dawson, *Skin* being Joseph Yates, a barrister, the father of Sir Joseph Yates, one of the Judges of the Common Pleas ; and *Bone*, Dr. Dawson (Byrom's relative), a well-known medical practitioner in the town, and the father of the ill-fated "Jemmy Dawson," the hero of Shenstone's pathetic ballad. He also, on the occasion of the Pretender's visit to Manchester, wrote the lines which have since become almost as famous as his epigram on Handel and Bononcini :—

> God bless the King! I mean the faith's defender ;
> God bless (no harm in blessing) the Pretender ;
> But who Pretender is, or who is King,
> God bless us all—that's quite another thing.

The period was one of great political excitement. The men of Manchester, who a century previously had barricaded their town and defied the soldiers of Charles the First, became jubilant on the restoration of monarchy in the person of his son, and, to prove their loyalty, caused the conduit in the market place to flow with claret and the gutters to swell with strong beer ; their sons were noted for their Jacobite proclivities, and nowhere did the young Pretender receive a heartier welcome than in the old Puritan town where, as has been said by a popular writer (Dr. Halley), "the orange plumes seemed to have grown pale and faded into white feathers before the bright colours of the Stuart tartan." The barbarous severities with which the rebellion of 1715 was crushed had only served to perpetuate and increase the feeling of bitterness against the Whig Government, and this feeling was intensified by the religious feuds that sprang up in the town. The Tories and High Churchmen, though they had taken the oath to King George and desired to maintain the Protestant succession, were for the most part Jacobites, while the Low Churchmen and Nonconformists were staunch partisans of the house of Brunswick—the one proclaimed the divine right of kings, and the other was equally zealous in upholding the "Glorious Revolution."

Byrom's intimate friend, Dr. Deacon, a nonjuring minister, who had incurred the suspicions of the Government through his supposed connection with the former rebellion, and on that account had removed to Manchester, where he combined the profession of theology with the practice of physic, assembled a congregation of nonjurors at his house in Fennel Street, adjoining the present "Dog and Partridge"—the "Schism Shop," as it was irreverently called—while Joseph Owen, a fierce Presbyterian polemic, declaimed with angry invective against the clergy of the "Old Church" for their alleged sympathy with the nonjuring divine. The quarrel became fiercer than ever, and the coarse sermons of Owen were answered by the satire and clever epigrams of Byrom : —

> Leave to the low-bred Owens of the age
> Sense to belye and loyalty to rage,
> Wit to make treason of each cry and chat,
> And eyes to see false worship in a hat.

Meetings of the rival factions were regularly held at the different taverns in the town, the "Angel" in Market Street Lane being the head-quarters of the Whigs, and the "Bull's Head," opposite

Phœbe Byrom's in the Market Place, the resort of those disaffected
to the reigning family; "John Shaw's," too, a "public" in the Old
Shambles, kept by a veteran trooper, who in his campaigns abroad
had acquired the art of brewing punch of unrivalled quality, and
who was as famed for the discipline and the autocratic rule he
maintained as for the excellence of the beverage he brewed,
received under its hospitable roof the more thorough-going Church
and King men and supporters of the Stuart cause.* Byrom was a
frequent attender at the convivial gatherings at "John Shaw's," and
the only portrait of him in the later years of his life that has been
preserved, was one taken by stealth by his friend Dorning
Rasbotham, "after spending an evening at Shawe's Coffee House,"
prefixed to the Leeds edition of his poems, and reproduced in
Gregson's "Fragments."

Byrom's pen was ever at the service of his political friends, and
the "Laureate of the Jacobites," the "Master Tool of the Faction,"
as he was indifferently styled, was more than a match for his Whig
antagonists. Imbued, however, with strong religious feelings, there
was little of bitterness in his compositions; the shaft of ridicule
was never envenomed, his playful wit and genial good-humoured

---

* "John Shaw's" eventually assumed the character of an organised
club, and after an uninterrupted career of a century and a half it still
remains in a flourishing state, and is as convivial in its "green old age" as
in the days when John Shaw cracked his whip, and with loud voice and
imperative tone exclaimed, "Eight o'clock, gentlemen, eight o'clock," and
his serving maid, Molly, followed with her mop and bucket ready to
expedite the movements of the loiterer, should the cracking of the whip
have failed to "speed the parting guest." The club has an official staff
elected annually and with much mock formality, and what Dr. Johnson
calls "obstreperous merriment," and the members, who are true "Church
and Queen" men, assemble once a month under the shadow of the "Mitre"
to discuss punch and politics, and drink old wine, and the traditional old
toasts, omitting, however, the very suggestive one of the King "over the
water." Among the most treasured relics in the possession of the club,
and which now adorn the room where the members assemble, are the
original portraits in oil of the autocratic and inflexible John and Molly
Owen, his prime minister, and factotum—the Hebe of the house, and the
veritable china bowl in which John brewed his seductive compound.

satire telling with far greater effect than the coarse and angry invectives with which he was at times assailed. If he was ready to lampoon a foe, he never lacked the courage to rebuke a friend. This is evidenced by his well-timed admonition against swearing, "addressed to an officer in the army," Colonel Townley, the commander of the regiment raised in Manchester in the service of the Pretender :—

> O that the muse might call, without offence,
> The gallant soldier back to his good sense,
> His temp'ral field so cautious not to lose;
> So careless quite of his eternal foes.
> Soldier! so tender of thy prince's fame,
> Why so profuse of a superior name?
> For the King's sake the brunt of battles bear;
> But, for the King of King's sake do not swear.

In his early youth Byrom had manifested strong Jacobite tendencies, but in the interval between the two rebellions—the Sacheverel riots of '15 and the rising of '45—his political opinions, if in no degree modified, had become much less demonstrative, and his Jacobitism was under the control of a possessor sufficiently cautious to prevent its imperilling his family interests or endangering his personal safety. His daughter "Beppy" was then a young lady of three-and-twenty; following her father's example she had set up a diary, and some of the entries in her journal, with a letter written by Byrom to his kinsman and friend, Mr. Vigor, furnishes the most circumstantial and entertaining accounts of the Pretender's visit to Manchester extant. The doctor's gossiping daughter was an ardent Jacobite, though a very prudent one, her sentimental devotion to the Stuart cause being most pronounced when personal danger was remote, the fair young diarist having little scruple in designating the wearers of the white cockade "rebels" when peril was at hand. For all that, her "Diary" is very entertaining. Apart from the vivid portraiture of the excitement and consternation into which the Manchestrians were thrown by the presence of the rebel army, it is impossible to read it without feeling that you are listening to the sprightly chat of the lively and unsophisticated writer.

50

On Tuesday, the 25th of November, news came that Prince Charles Edward had marched his forces into Lancashire. The town was in a state of great excitement. The Presbyterians and Whigs deemed it prudent to get out of the way ; the militia, which had been very valiant before the approach of the rebels, followed the example ; the wealthier householders removed their families into the country ; and even furniture and provisions were conveyed to places of more assured safety. On the afternoon of Friday, the 28th, Sergeant Dickson, a dashing young Scotchman, with his sweetheart and a drummer, entered the town and proclaimed the Chevalier King ; and on the following morning the Prince with the main body of his army joined them, and encamped in St. Ann's Square. " Manchester," says Ray, in his " History of the Rebellion," " was taken by a sergeant, a drum, and a woman, who rode to the market cross on horses with hempen halters on, where they proclaimed their King." Here is " Beppy" Byrom's version :

Tuesday (November) 28.—About three o'clock to-day came into town two men in Highland dress, and a woman behind one of them with a drum on her knee, and for all the loyal work that our Presbyterians have made they took possession of the town, as one may say, for immediately after they were 'light they beat up for volunteers for P(rince) C(harles). . . . . They were directly joined by Mr. J. Bradshaw, Mr. Tom Sydall, Mr. Tom Deacon, Mr. Fletcher, Tom Chaddock ; and several others have listed, about 80 men by eight o'clock, when my papa came down to tell us there was a party of horse come in. He took care of me to the Cross, when I saw them all. It is a very fine moonlight night. . . . My papa and uncle are gone to consult with Mr. Croxton, Mr. Fielden, and others how to keep themselves out of any scrape, and yet behave civilly (a very prudent pro- cedure in such a crisis). All the justices fled, and lawyers too, but coz. Clowes.

Friday, 29th.—They are beating up for the P.; eleven o'clock we went up to the Cross to see the rest come in ; then came small parties of them till about three o'clock, when the P. and the main body of them came ; I cannot guess how many. . . . Then came an officer up to us at the Cross, and gave us the manifesto and declarations. The bells they rung, and P. Cotterel made a bonfire, and all the town was illuminated, every house except Mr. Dickinson's (the house in Market-street-lane, where the Prince took up his quarters, and thenceforward known as the Palace). My papa, mama, and sister, and my uncle and I walked up and down to see it,

About four o'clock the King was proclaimed, the mob shouted very cleverly, and then we went up to see my aunt Brearcliffe, and stayed eleven o'clock making St. Andrew's crosses for them ; we sat up making till two o'clock.

Colonel Townley, a member of the great Catholic family of that name, who had arranged for the Prince's reception in Manchester, and had engaged several of the principal residents for officers, speedily mustered and enrolled a regiment in the service of the Prince. Each recruit received a white St. Andrew's cross, which cost little, and a *promise* of five guineas, which, as they were never paid, cost less. In the next entry the enthusiastic young Jacobite describes her impressions of the "yellow-hair'd laddie," and the way in which her father made homage to him :—

Saturday, 30th (St. Andrew's Day).—More crosses making till twelve o'clock; then I dressed up in my white gown and went up to my aunt Brearcliffe's, and an officer called on us to go see the prince. We went to Mr. Fletcher's and saw him get a horseback, and a noble sight it is [no wonder that amid such excitement the young lady got a little " mixed " in her moods and tenses]. I would not have missed it for a great deal of money. His horse had stood an hour in the court without stirring, and as soon as he got on he [*i.e.* the horse, not the prince] began a dancing and capering as if he was proud of the burden, and when he rid out of the court he was received with as much joy and shouting almost as if he had been King, indeed I think scarce anybody that saw him could dispute it. As soon as he was gone the officer and us went to prayers at the old church at two o'clock by their orders, or else there has been none since they came. Mr. Shrigley read prayers; he prayed for the King and Prince of Wales, and named no names. Then we called at our house and eat a queen cake, and a glass of wine, for we got no dinner ; then the officer went with us all to the Camp Field to see the artillery; called at my uncle's and then went up to Mr. Fletcher's, stayed there till the prince was at supper, then the officer introduced us into the room, stayed awhile and then went into the great parlour where the officers were dining, sat by Mrs. Stark(ey); they were all exceeding civil and almost made us fuddled with drinking the P. health, for we had had no dinner ; we sat there till Secretary Murray came to let us know that the P. was at leisure and had done supper, so we were all introduced and had the honour to kiss his hand; my papa was fetched prisoner to do the same [another testimony to the doctor's discretion]. as was Dr Deacon; Mr. Cattell and Mr. Clayton [two of the Old Church clergy who were less cautious] did it without ; the latter said grace for him . then we went out and drank his health in the other room, and so to Mr. Fletcher's, where my mamma waited for us (my uncle was gone to pay his land tax) and then went home.

December 1st.—About six o'clock the P. and the foot set out, went up Market-street Lane and over Cheadle ford; the horse was gathering together all forenoon; we went up to the Cross to see them, and then to Mr. Starkey's, they were all drawn up in the Square and went off in companies, Lord Elcho's horse went past Baguley.

What follows is matter of history.

> The Stuart, leaning on the Scot,
> Pierced to the very centre of the realm,
> In hopes to seize his abdicated helm.

The Pretender's cause was soon lost, the progress of his army being as brief as it was disastrous. Hearing, on their arrival at Derby, that the Duke of Cumberland with an army of veterans was in the neighbourhood, and distrusting the skill of their own officers, they returned northwards, their vanguard reaching Manchester on the 9th of December, where the regiment which Colonel Townley had raised only a few days before was disbanded, though some of the more resolute supporters of the Prince pushed on to Carlisle, where, after a feeble effort to hold the city, they were compelled to surrender. Chaplain Coppock was executed in the border city, wearing his canonicals; ten of the others, including a son of Dr. Deacon, and the adjutant, Syddal, whose father had given up his life in the same cause thirty years previously, and Beppy Byrom's cousin, Jemmy Dawson, were executed on Kennington Common. The heads of Deacon and Syddal were sent to Manchester and fixed upon spikes on the top of the Exchange,* to be reverenced by friends and execrated by foes, an exhibition that called forth the following lines :—

> The Deel has set their heads to view,
> And stickt them upon poles;
> Poor Deel! 'twas all that he could do
> Since God has ta'en their souls.

---

* In the accounts of the Constables of Manchester occurs this entry—
1745. Sept. 18: Expenses tending the sheriff this morn, Syddal's and Deacon's heads put up, £00, 01, 06.

In Manchester the suppression of the rebellion of '45 was hailed with delight by the partisans of the house of Brunswick ; the church bells rang throughout the day, bonfires blazed at night, and orange-coloured ribbons were flaunted in the streets as gaily as the Stuart tartan had been only a few months before. That day must have been a sorrowful one for Byrom and his enthusiastic daughter, for they could hardly have escaped the insults of the Hanoverian mob when Dr. Deacon's house was attacked and that of poor widow Syddal demolished.

The ill-feeling engendered by these events was of long duration, and the toast of "The King" was not unfrequently a cause of angry disputation. The adherents of the exiled dynasty continued their meetings, though they usually assembled in secret, and their movements were carefully watched by the local authorities, sus-pected persons being required to take the oath of allegiance to the reigning monarch and abjure Popery and the Pretender. Some of the more prominent sympathisers took alarm and fled, among them being Clayton, the chaplain of the Collegiate Church, who was said to have offered public prayers for Prince Charles in one of the streets of Salford. Byrom, in describing this period, says—

We ourselves were many of us fugitives ; and had we not met with some kind asylum towns, might have wandered among the inhospitable hills, like the present mountaineer rebels.

His Journal shows that at this time he was frequently away from Manchester, and not unfrequently endeavouring through the influence of his former patrons to obtain a mitigation of the punish-ment of such of the Manchester rebels as had survived the thirst of Whiggish vengeance, but were yet undergoing imprisonment. Thus he wrote to his wife (June 18, 1748) : —

On Friday the 10th of June I had been asked to meet Mr. Folkes at Mr. Ch. Stanhope's, where I found likewise Lord Linsdale, Duke of Moun-tague, and Mr. Stanhope's brother, Lord Harrington, with whom we passed the dinner and an hour or two after very agreeably. They asked me a great many questions about the Pretender, and circumstances when he was at Manchester, &c., and I told them what I knew and thought without any reserve, and took the opportunity of setting some matters in a truer light than I suppose they had heard them placed in, and put in now and then a word in favour of the prisoners, especially Charles D, (Charles, youngest son of Dr. Deacon, who had acted as secretary, and superintended the recruiting of the Manchester regiment). They were all very free and good natured, and did not seem offended with anything that I took the liberty to enlarge upon. When Mr. Folkes came away, about seven o'clock, I came with him, and he said that what had passed might possibly occasion young D.'s liberty, that they were not violent in their tempers, and that he took notice that they listened very much to what I had been telling them of Manchester affairs. I was much pleased with the openness of conversation which we had upon several subjects; and as Mr. St(anhope) had made me promise him some verses that I had lately writ, I added a Latin copy to his brother the Viceroy of Ireland, which I brought him yesterday, for he had sent a servant for me to dine with again, and then we had Lord Harrington, Lord Baltimore, D. of Richmond and a lady—Lady Townshend—and somebody else—oh, Sir John Cope. The Duchess of R. should have been there, but the Duke made an excuse for her. As we had a lady, however, and one (as Mr. St. had hinted to me) of great wit and politeness, who stayed the afternoon, complaisance to her turned the conversation upon suitable subjects, so that I could not well introduce the fate of Ch. D. &c. before the D. of R. who is one of our present kings,* as I wanted to do. Mr. St. had read the Latin verses and given them before dinner, and the Duke might have seen them if he would, but the lady and the Latin did not suit politely enough, and there was no urging anything untimely, or else I could have been glad to have heard what he would have said about the lot of the imprisoned. . . . One can only try as occasion offers, what mercy can be got from trying.

He did try, and on the 23rd July he again writes :—

I have heard nothing new about Ch. Deacon. I sent him (Mr. Stanhope) a copy of the petition representing his case, and some further urging of my own. By a report not being made, I understand that the judges have made no report, which I am surprised at if that be the real meaning.

In a subsequent letter (August 4, 1748) to his "Dear Dolly" (his younger daughter, Dorothy, then a maiden of 18) he sends a translation of the verses, that young lady, as he says, not being " so book-learned as to understand them in the original." They are as creditable to the heart as to the head of the writer for the

---

* The Duke of Richmond was at the time one of the Lords Justices for the administration of the Government during the absence of George II.

evidence they afford of his unswerving fidelity to a friend in adversity. The following lines are a fair specimen :—

> Three brothers—I shall only speak the truth—
> Three brothers, hurried by mere dint of youth,
> Precautious youth, were found in arms of late,
> And rushing on to their approaching fate.
>
> One, in a fever, sent up to be tried,
> From jail to jail, delivered over, died ;
> Sick and distressed, he did not long sustain
> The mortal shocks of motion and of pain.
>
> .   .   .   .   .
>
> The third was then a little boy at school,
> That played the truant from the rod and rule ;
> The child, to join his brothers, left his book,
> And arms, alas! instead of apples took.
>
> Now lies confined the poor unhappy lad—
> For death mere pity and mere shame forebad—
> Long time confined, and waiting mercy's bail,
> Two years amidst the horrors of a jail.
>
> I spare to mention what, from fact appears,
> The boy has suffered in these fatal years.
> Pity, at least, becomes his iron lot ;
> What ruin is there that a jail has not ?
>
> He is my countryman, my noble lords,
> And room for hope your genius affords ;
> Be truly noble ; hear my well-meant prayer,
> And deign my fellow citizen to spare.

In the letter accompanying the English verses, he says :—

I have not such good hopes as I had of the young boy being set at liberty upon whose account they were made ; he has some enemies or other that have represented him in so ill a light that I much question at present if he will meet with the favour which has been so long expected except affairs shall take a turn with relation to him (other) than I was told they had done. But I am not sorry I have spoken my thoughts about him as opportunity offered.

On " Prince Charles's Birthday " (November 30th), he writes to his daughter Beppy :—

Mr. Nanny, a Welsh gentleman, told me he had heard that Ch. Deacon was set at liberty ; but such a world of false reports have gone about him that I can only wish this may prove true.

And on the 3rd of January following, writing to his wife, he remarks :—

> I was taken ill so that I could not go into Southwark to enquire after Charles Deacon as I thought of, nor have I had any opportunity since, nor can I learn anything of the truth or falsehood of the report of his going abroad.

The report was unfortunately but too true, for the *Gentleman's Magazine* (v. xix., p. 41) records that on the 11th January Charles Deacon, with William Brettargh, also of the Manchester regiment, were conveyed from the new gaol, Southwark, to Gravesend, for transportation during life.

With the expatriation of this hapless youth may be said to have closed the darkest and most sorrowful page in Manchester's annals. In that sanguinary chronicle of ruthless savagery there was perhaps no more melancholy episode than the misfortunes of the nonjuring divine of Fennel Street, who lost three of his sons in the Pretender's cause. Thomas Theodorus, the eldest, as already stated, was executed, and his head fixed on the Manchester Exchange; Robert Renatus died in prison while awaiting trial, and Charles Clement, as we have seen, was sent beyond seas. The father passed into his rest on the 16th February, 1753. He lies in the north-east corner of St. Ann's Churchyard, where his raised altar-tomb may still be seen with an inscription setting forth that he was " the greatest of sinners and most unworthy of primitive bishops "

There is a tradition current that the heads of Thomas Deacon and Tom Syddal, after being exposed for some time on the Exchange, were one night surreptitiously removed by Mr. Hall, a son of Dr. Richard Edward Hall, who resided in a large house at the top of King Street, and that they were secretly buried in the garden behind his residence. This garden with the rookery in it, which reached down to the present Chancery Lane, existed within the recollection of the present generation, and it is said that on the death of Mr. Hall's last surviving sister, Miss Frances Hall, in 1828, the grim relics of mortality were by her expressed desire exhumed and buried in St. Ann's Churchyard. It was to Dr. Hall, the father, whilst paying his addresses to the lady whom he afterwards married, that Byrom sent the following epigram :—

> A lady's love is like a candle snuff,
> That's quite extinguished by a gentle puff ;
> But, with a hearty blast or two, the dame,
> Just like a candle, bursts into a flame.

It was very shortly after the event just related that Byrom received the first intimation of his son's having formed an attachment for the lady who became his wife, Eleanor, daughter of William and sister of Domville Halsted, of Lymm, the representatives of an ancient and honourable family in Cheshire, who had been owners of the Domville moiety of Lymm from the time of Edward III., when it was inherited from Agnes de Legh, the common ancestress of the Domvilles, Halsteds, and the Leghs of Adlington and Lyme. The letter written on the occasion to Mrs. Byrom is so thoroughly characteristic of the man that we make no apology for reproducing it :—

Tuesday night, Feb. 28, 1748-9.

My dearest love : I received this afternoon the potted hare from Mr. Wilkinson, which Tedy mentioned in his last letter, together with thy letter concerning Miss Halsted, &c., which has thrown me into a great but really very loving concern, for the consequence of an affair in which the family happiness so much depends. As I am quite a stranger to the young lady, and have no remembrance of having ever seen her, I cannot judge how I should like her person and behaviour ; but for my beloved son's sake, I should wish her possessed of every qualification that might justly be agreeable to thee, his sisters, uncle, aunts, and friends, as well as to himself. I guess by the contents of thy letter that he has made his addresses to her, and his Aunt A. (Mrs. Byrom's sister Anne) has given her a good character, which does not seem to amount to any absolute approbation ; his uncle, too, seems neither for it nor against it ; what his aunts say of it, thou dost not hint at, by which I presume that they suppose that he is determined himself, and they would not disoblige him by making any objection to his choice. For my part, if my son be inclined to marry, I can only wish that he may make a proper choice ; but whether he has or not, it is not in my power to determine, nor in my will to oppose his inclination, without cause, for I love him too well not to consent with great readiness to anything that others of his friends who heartily interest themselves in his happiness should approve of; but at present their approbation seems only to be negative, and his uncle's "What will his father say to it?" does not seem to impart any great encouragement. His father would gladly hope that his son, in a thing of this consequence, might so behave as to please all his relations, and thereby acquire a title to his father's approbation, who, considering him as the only youth of the name at present, would wish them all to assist, encourage or prevent him as their love and judgment shall find occasion to show itself in his favour. As to fortune, report but seldom lessens it, though it has hardly much increased it, I suppose, in Miss H.'s case; but as to that, though it is undoubtedly a very prudential consideration, yet the qualities which the lady herself may or may not have, may make her a good wife with less than she has, or a bad one with a great deal more. I am full of wishes, hopes, and fears, and can think of nothing else at present than to refer myself to thy sentiments, which I wish thee to give me, and my son to be so much master of himself as to act on this occasion with all necessary discretion. I wish that whenever he marries he may meet with one that he may have as just reason to love, honour, and cherish as his father has his Valentine, whom he begs to take all possible (care) of a life and health so dear to him, who is, with hearty prayers to God for her and hers—hers and theirs.   J. BYROM.

     To Mrs. Eliz. Byrom, near the Old Church in Manchester, Lancashire.

With the exception of an occasional journey to London, and a visit now and then to his *alma mater*, Cambridge, the remaining portion of Byrom's life was passed in comparative quietude, sometimes at the pleasant rural retreat at Kersall, "that quiet place of yours," as his loving sister Phœbe, in one of her letters, styles it, and where, as she says, she "was very glad to be a bit from the hurry of the market place;" but oftener enjoying the society and pleasant gossip of his friends in the snug parlour of his comfortable dwelling at the corner of Hunter's Lane—that quaint black and white house with a curious raised walk in front, the outlines of which the pencil of that industrious antiquary, Thomas Barrit, has happily preserved to us. The struggles of his earlier years gave a zest to the comforts of domestic life, and in his *otium cum dignitate* he whiled away the hours, poetising on subjects grave and gay; now and then ridiculing with good humoured banter some Presbyterian zealot or recalcitrant Whig, though always in a spirit calculated to soften asperity; and occasionally retaliating upon his Hanoverian opponents in some *jeu d'esprit* or sparkling epigram,

to the great delight of the *beaux-esprits* who met in social intercourse at the Bull's Head—a house that still remains, and the
gruff countenance of whose ancient sign may yet be seen over the
archway leading to the inn-yard and the old-fashioned and much-
frequented parlour. The great truths of Christianity had from his
earliest years made a deep impression on his mind, and many of
his writings are characterised by strong religious feeling; indeed,
it was the spirit of piety breathed into his poems that led to his
being accounted a mystic by the mere lukewarm professors, a
reproach that was, however, undeserved. His religion was without gloom, and by no means inconsistent with the maintenance of
habitual cheerfulness. His utterances are marked by a manly,
nervous style; his imagination was fertile, and his imagery happily
conceived, though there is sometimes a lack of smoothness that
suggests the idea that his effusions were hastily penned—the
impromptu utterances of the man of genius with the happy facility
of versification. Some of his pieces—the once popular "Three
Black Crows*" for example—were written for the annual speech
days at the Free Grammar School; he was, too, the first writer
who employed as a literary vehicle the broad, racy vernacular of
Lancashire, which in later times has been used with such signal
success by Bamford, and Waugh, and Brierley. One of the
happiest specimens of the playfulness of his muse was the poetical
epistle "On the Patron Saint of England," addressed to Lord
Willoughby, the President of the Society of Antiquaries, and which
Samuel Pegge, the antiquary, was at such pains to refute; but
perhaps the one by which he will be best remembered is the ever
popular Christmas hymn, "Christians, Awake," which John
Wainwright, the organist of the "Old Church," at Manchester, set
to music, the tune being called after his native town, "Stockport."

---

* It has been frequently stated that the story of the "Three Black
Crows" was inspired by the London edition, but in a recent communi-
cation to the Manchester Literary Club, Mr. John Evans has proved
conclusively, from a letter in Byrom's own handwriting, that it was
founded on a story related to him by Dr. John Taylor.

Byrom outlived most of the friends of his youth, and maintained
the natural cheerfulness of his disposition throughout his last
lingering illness until, in the words of his obituary notice, "the
scholar, the critic, the gentleman, became absorbed in the resigned
Christian." He died at the old house at Hanging Ditch, on the
26th September, 1763, having attained the ripe old age of 72, and
three days later his remains were interred in the Byrom Chapel, on
the south side of the "Old Church." Strangely enough, there is
no monument or other sepulchral memorial to mark his resting
place or perpetuate his name ; the register of burials is the only
record, and that is brief indeed :—

1763.—September 29.   Mr. John Byrom.

A tribute to his memory in Latin verse from the pen of his
friend and correspondent, William Cowper, of Chester, M.P.,
appeared in the newspapers of the time, of which the following is
a translation :—

> No, much-loved friend! this breast can never lose
> The dear remembrance of thy pleasing form,
> Thy gentle manners, and thy placid mien ;
> The smile of innocence, th' unstudied grace
> Of honest countenance, th' high-season'd wit,
> The copious stores of conversation sweet,
> Which to my ravish'd ears so oft supplied
> Luxurious banquet, whilst th' indulgent flow
> Of thy rich genius filled my thirsty mind.
> But who can tell the gifts of innate worth,
> The bosom beating to the cries of woe,
> The heart of soft benignity, wherein
> True honour, piety, and faith have fix'd
> Their everlasting mansion ? Who can trace,
> Alas ! the portrait of such excellence
> In any other mortal mind but thine ?

In violation of the "Woollen Act," a statute made famous by
the allusions of Pope and Dryden, he was buried "in a shirt, shift,
sheet, or shroud not made of sheep's wool," and, consequently, a
direction was issued by "John Gore Booth, Esquire, one of his
Majesty's Justices of the Peace," to the constables of Manchester

to levy the sum of £6 by distress and sale of his goods and chattels.

Mrs. Byrom survived him several years, and died on the 21st December, 1778, at the age of 78; of his children three died in infancy, and three survived him—two daughters and a son. Elizabeth—Beppy, as she was familiarly called—the first-born, and the gossiping chronicler of the fatal '45, died in 1801, her sister Dorothy having died three years previously, both unmarried. Edward Byrom, the eldest and only surviving son, succeeded as heir. Of this worthy son of a worthy sire we need say little; his biography has been undertaken by an able writer, and with such a congenial theme as the projected " Memorials of St. John's" we may rest assured that the accomplished editor of the " Old Church Clock" will do ample justice to his memory. He was born on the 13th June, 1724, and baptised at the old church on the 24th of the same month. On the death of his uncle, Edward Byrom, in 1740, he became devisee in fee of his estates, and in the spring of 1750 he added to his worldly wealth the fortune he acquired by his marriage with Miss Halsted, already referred to, a marriage that, in accordance with the fashion of the times, is thus chronicled in the *Chester Courant* of the 6th March in that year :

A few days ago, Mr. Edward Byron. son of Dr. Byrom, was married to Miss Halsted of Limm, co. Cest., a lady of great merit and a handsome fortune.

He took up his abode in the large detached house in Quay Street, now occupied by Dr. Blackmore, and which continued to be the residence of his grand-daughter, Miss Atherton, up to the time of her death, in 1870. Mr. Grindon, in his pleasant volume, " Manchester Banks and Bankers," says : " There is a legend that he removed thither on account of the delicate health of his little Nelly, the atmosphere of Quay Street being purer than that of the town," and he adds, " the house was obviously intended to be the first of a row. Mr. Byrom preferred that it should stand alone, arranging also for the preservation in perpetuity of the meadow in front, which served as a playground for the children." The house was

Mr. Byrom's own, and in all probability its erection was begun by his uncle, Edward Byrom, shortly before his death, for in the "Shorthand Journal" there occurs the entry :—

1741.—Thursday. August 11th or 12th. Dined at new house in Quay Street; . . . We came from Macclesfield yesterday—Mrs. Byrom, Beppy, Dolly, David and I.

The neighbourhood was then unbuilt, and formed a pleasant suburb of Manchester, but with the increase of trade the tide of population spread in that direction ; new streets were laid out, houses were built, and the locality became what might be called the "Court-end." The house has survived the mighty changes that time has wrought ; it stands alone, as it did in Byrom's days ; the remnant of the old garden and orchard are there, and the "meadow" in front still struggles to look green, but its sylvan beauties are only a memory of the past.

With the increase of the population came the necessity for a new church, and on the 28th April, 1768, Edward Byrom laid the foundation stone of St. John's—so named in compliment to his father—which was consecrated on the 7th June in the following year. Little more than two years later he joined Messrs. Sedgwick, Allen, and Place, in establishing the first bank in Manchester, the doors of which were opened on the 2nd December, 1771, under the style of Byrom, Sedgwick, Allen, and Place. It occupied the site of Messrs. Hunt and Roskell's shop in St. Ann's Square, and the name is perpetuated in Bank Street, leading from it. Less than seventeen months after, Edward Byrom was laid to rest, his death occurring on the 24th April, 1773, at the early age of forty-nine. Under his will the Quay Street property passed to his daughter Ann, who became the wife of Henry Atherton, of the Middle Temple, the issue of the marriage being an only daughter, the estimable and much-honoured Miss Eleanor Atherton, the foundress of Holy Trinity Church, in Hulme, and the last representative in a direct line of the Byrom family, who died at the old home in Quay Street, on the 12th September, 1870, at the age of eighty-eight. In accordance with the provisions of her will, the greater portion of her property, including the Kersall estates, passed to her godson, Mr. Edward Fox, who, in accordance with her expressed desire, assumed the name and arms of Byrom—the arms John Byrom was so proud of, and of which he made such frequent mention in his Journal :—

> Some sire of ours, beloved kinsfolk, chose,
> The hedge-hog for his arms; I would suppose
> With aim to hint instruction wise, and good.
> To us descendants of his Byrom blood,
> I would infer, if you be of this mind,
> The very lesson that our sire design'd.
>
> At last the hedge-hog came into his thought,
> And gave the perfect emblem that he sought.
> This little creature, all offence aside,
> Rolls up itself in its own prickly hide,
> When danger comes ; and they that will abuse,
> Do it themselves, when their own hurt ensues.

CHAPTER X.

HERE is much truth in the remark that it is more in the
lives of England's worthies than in the lives of
England's warriors that we may discover the true secret
of England's greatness. Yet, of those master-spirits
who by their inventive genius, their patient industry,
and indomitable perseverance have been the greatest
benefactors to their country, and who, on that account, deserve
ever to be held in honoured remembrance, how many have had to
battle with untoward fate, to

> Wage with fortune an eternal war,
> Checked by the scoff of Pride, by Envy's frown,
> And Poverty's unconquered bar.

Of such men was Samuel Crompton, the inventor of the spinning
mule, whose mechanical achievement may be said to have laid
open the prospect of unbounded wealth to the industrious of his
native shire, and to have wrought in Lancashire changes well-nigh
as wondrous as any recorded in the fictions of Eastern romance.

Hall-in-the-Wood, or Hall-i'-th'-Wood, according to the vernacular, the ancient dwelling-place in which Crompton spent his
toilsome days and thoughtful nights—the shrine to which our
present pilgrimage is directed, and which deserves to be hallowed
as one of our sacred temples—is situated in the midst of scenery
strangely at variance with the associations the name calls forth ; for

HALL-i'-TH-Wood.

though, with Firwood, the Lower Wood, the Oaks, and other places of similar designation immediately adjacent, it recalls the sylvan beauty of former days, so complete has been the disafforesting that, with the exception of the blighted and blackened relics of a sturdy oak or stately elm here and there dotting the landscape, scarce a remnant remains of the old forest that once formed its pleasant environment. Yet withal, if the surroundings have lost much of their picturesqueness and are not altogether lovely, they are under their present aspect far more suggestive of the manufacturing enterprise, the permanent utility, and the universal good which is the natural outcome of Crompton's invention, than they would have been had they retained their pristine beauty. Nature has been effectually displaced by industry. From the steep cliff on which stands his ancient home a thousand tall chimneys may now be seen, filling the atmosphere with volumes of thick dun-coloured smoke that hang like a pall and drop down soot instead of fatness. The once fair and fertile country is absolutely covered with mighty factories and hives of busy industry, in which tens of thousands of the population find employment. On every hand the ear is assailed with the din and rattle of machinery, and wherever the eye can reach it encounters nothing but steam and smoke and the outward indications of active labour.

The Hall, which is located in the township of Tonge, and distant about a couple of miles from Bolton, is an interesting specimen of the old English mansion of the earlier Tudor period; and, though time has made sad havoc among its beauties and peculiarities, it has happily escaped the assaults of "improvers," and even in its dilapidated and forlorn condition may, in an antiquarian sense, be said to retain its original features comparatively unimpaired. It stands near the edge of a bold rocky steep that rises abruptly from the Eagley Brook—a tributary of the Irwell, that separates the townships of Sharples and Tonge—and commands an extensive view of the surrounding country. It is an irregular pile—a house with many gables—and has evidently been erected at two distinct periods—the older part being in the black and white half-timbered style so frequently met with in the old manor houses of Lancashire and Cheshire; while the more modern portion, though also boasting considerable antiquity, is of stone, with a two-storeyed projecting porch of the same material, erected in 1648, as the date with the initials

N

A A

over the doorway clearly indicates. The mansion does not, however, appear ever to have made any great pretensions to stateliness,

though its possessors were a family boasting considerable ancestral dignity, and one of them, in his pride of lineage, placed his heraldic achievements in an elaborately ornamented panel in one of the rooms, in order that his friends might note his honourable descent. The earliest portion is said, with some show of authority, to date as far back as the year 1483. For some time it was owned by the Brownlows; and over the fireplace in one of the rooms may still be seen the initials of Lawrence Brownlow, with the date 1591, and it is said that an ancient oak bedstead which was removed many years ago from Hall-i'-th'-Wood to Huntroyde has the same initials carved upon it. This part of the house, as we have said, is of timber and plaster, or "post and petrel," as it is locally designated; the walls being composed of a framework of massive timber, with the interstices filled with plaster, and worked in divers quatrefoil and diaper-like patterns. The main structure comprises a long and lofty oblong block, with a short bay projecting at right angles from the further end. The upper chambers overhang the lower, and these again have an overhanging roof springing from a coved cornice; another instance that the mediæval architects who planned and carried out these erections were by no means insensible to the advantage of a varied outline producing that picturesque irregularity which, without any unnecessary sacrifice of domestic comfort, is so favourable to external beauty, as well as to the effect produced by a judicious combination of light and shade—a style infinitely preferable to the dull, dreary uniformities of brick put up in the present day, and which, were it only revived in its original beauty, would enable us to dispense with those Italian forms that were only introduced to satisfy the craving for foreign importations.

Time wrought changes; with the increase of refinement came the necessity for increased accommodation, when, to give additional elbow-room and keep pace with the requirements of the age, the old house, instead of being demolished, as would be the case now-a-days, was added to, a more pretentious structure of stone, with mullioned windows and parapets with ball ornaments, being joined up to it, and from this portion the square porch, which exhibits the same architectural features, projects. The date and the initials show that it was erected by Alexander Norris, son and heir of Christopher Norris, of Tonge-with-Haulgh, whose daughter and heiress, Alice, in 1654, conveyed the place in marriage to John Starkie, of Huntroyde; their descendant in the sixth generation, Le Gendre Nicholas Starkie, of Huntroyde, Esq., being the present possessor. John Starkie must have been an old man when he married, for his death occurred eleven years later at the age of 77, when Alice Starkie, his widow, returned to Hall-i'-th'-

Wood and spent the remainder of her days there, amid the scenes
of her childhood.

After the death of Mrs. Starkie the mansion seems to have
remained unoccupied, and subsequently to have been divided into
small tenements and let to humble occupants, who attached small
import either to its antiquity or the associations connected with it,
content if only they could keep the roof over their heads; and, as
may be anticipated, during those vicissitudes, it was suffered to fall
into a state of decay, until the inroads of dilapidation became only
too painfully visible both within and without.

The greater portion of the mansion is and has been for many
years in the occupancy of a farmer, Mr. James Bromiley, but a
part of the old black and white structure has been divided and sub-
divided into numerous tenements that are now let to small cottagers.
The occasion of our visit was a pleasant autumn afternoon, and
proceeding, as we had been previously advised, from the Oaks
Station, a pleasant walk of a few minutes over the high ground
brought us to the picturesque and interesting old relic. The request
to view the interior was readily complied with, the good woman of
the house cheerfully accompanying us through the wainscoted
parlours and contracted passages, and thence, by a quaintly-carved
black oak staircase, with massive and highly-decorated balusters
and pendants, that leads to the upper chambers and the vacant
lofts above, giving us every facility we could desire in examining
the antiquated dwelling. The dining-hall, a well-proportioned
room, is on the ground floor, but that which most attracts
attention is the chamber above—the only one which seems to
have been treated with any degree of respect—Crompton's room,
the one in which he worked, in which he had his rude bench
and still ruder tools, where he matured his plans and constructed
his primitive models, where for years he laboured on with
anxious hope and enduring perseverance, and where at length—
just one hundred years ago—he triumphed, giving to his country
the invention which has so largely contributed to its wealth and
prosperity. The room is now occupied as a sleeping apartment,

STAIRCASE : HALL-I'-TH'-WOOD.

but in other respects it is little changed since the great inventor's day. It has been subjected to many whitewashings, but the old ornamental plaster cornice still remains ; the old heraldic escutcheon of the Starkies may still be seen ; and there too is the spacious window with its double row of leaded lights extending the entire width, out of which Crompton must so often have wistfully gazed. The attic storey possesses but comparatively little interest, and exhibits only a labyrinth of dark and intricate passages, with small chambers and secret hiding places leading off in every direction. It was here that Crompton, in 1779, on the very eve of the completion of his machine, concealed the various parts after

he had taken it to pieces for safety against the dreaded attack of the machine-breaking rioters of Blackburn, who had driven poor Hargreaves, the inventor of the Jenny, from his home, destroyed nearly every machine within miles of Blackburn, and who, it was feared, would extend their riotous proceedings to Crompton's invention before it had been even put in actual work. The principal entrance to the hall is on the south side, by an arched doorway, over which is a square panel with the initials and date already mentioned. Above this, and separated by a bold moulding, is a porch-chamber, lighted on three sides by square windows, mullioned and transomed, over one of which is a lozenge-shaped

53

sun-dial. Evil days have unhappily fallen upon the building. Where repairs have been attempted they have been made by slovenly hands, and unseemly patches mar the effect of its general appearance; but even in its present condition of neglect and approaching ruin it exhibits much that is architecturally interesting. Apart, however, from such considerations, surely the associations that gather round make it a public duty to protect it from further injury, so that it may be preserved to future generations as a memorial of one of Lancashire's worthiest sons and one of England's greatest benefactors.

Crompton, though himself of humble parentage, could claim a long and respectable lineage, his progenitors, who derived their patronymic from the hamlet of Crompton in Prestwich parish, ranking among the better class of yeomen, and the parent line asserting its gentility by the use of armorial ensigns. His parents resided at Firwood, a farm in the same township, and distant about half a mile from Hall-i'-th'-Wood, that had been owned by their family for several generations, but which Crompton's grandfather had mortgaged to the Starkies, and the father, unable to redeem, had finally alienated to them, continuing the occupancy, however, for some time as tenant, and combining with the business of farming that of carding, spinning, and weaving on a small scale whenever the intervals of farming and daily labour permitted. The couple were honest, hardworking, and religious, but fortune was unpropitious, and during the later years of the elder Crompton's life they appear to have been going down in the world. It was at the farm at Firwood, on the 3rd of December, 1753, that Samuel Crompton first saw the light. Shortly after his birth his parents forsook the old home and took up their abode at a cottage near Lower Wood, in the immediate vicinity. Their stay there was but short, for three or four years after, they removed to the neighbouring mansion of Hall-in-the-Wood, a part of which had been assigned to them by Mr. Starkie, who had become the possessor of Firwood, for the old mansion had, even at that date, been divided into separate holdings, and confided by its owner to the care of somewhat needy occupants.

George Crompton, the father, died shortly after, at the comparatively early age of thirty-seven, from, as is said, a cold taken while helping gratuitously in his over hours to build the organ-gallery in All Saints' Church, Bolton, where he worshipped; and his widow, Betty Crompton, as she was familiarly called, was left to struggle for a livelihood for herself and three children—Samuel, who was then a child of five years, and two girls. She was a woman of superior attainments, industrious, managing, and, withal, strong-minded; energetic in her action, but possessing, with a good deal of outward austerity of manner, much innate goodness of heart. Her good management and business-like habits gained her the confidence and respect of her neighbours, who manifested their appreciation of her abilities by electing her to the office of overseer of the township, an appointment which, though perfectly legal, was of unusual occurrence in days when "Women's Rights" were unthought of; one of the reasons which induced her to accept the office being the desire to compel her son to discharge the duties, which he disliked excessively. Mrs. Crompton abode at the hall after her husband's death, and continued his business with energy and thrift, the produce of her dairy being held in high repute in the neighbourhood, whilst the bees in her old-fashioned garden supplied her with another marketable commodity, added to which she had acquired local fame for her excellent make of elderberry wine, a beverage she hospitably dispensed among her friends and visitors. As may be supposed, she ruled her household with a firm hand, and believing in the wisdom of the proverb that to "spare the rod" is to "spoil the child," she manifested her fondness for her boy by a frequent application of the birch to the unappreciative youngster's breech—as he was wont to say in after years, her practice was to chastise him, not for any particular fault, but because she loved him so well, a mode of training certainly not the best calculated to enable a lad of a naturally diffident and sensitive disposition to engage in the rough battle of life or to make his way successfully in the world. The widow Crompton, notwithstanding, had many good qualities. She did, as she believed, her duty to her fatherless child, and gave him the best education in her power. School boards and board schools were then only in the womb of time, but Lancashire had many excellent schoolmasters, and of the number was William Barlow,* who kept a school at the top of Little Bolton, a pedagogue who worthily upheld the value and dignity of the mathematical sciences, and, on that account, was reputed among his neighbours to be "a witch in figures." Under his tuition young Crompton was placed, and, being of a meditative and retiring disposition, he took kindly to his studies, made satisfactory progress, and was accounted well educated for his station in life.

Of his two sisters little or nothing is known, but residing under the same roof was a lame old uncle, his father's brother, Alexander Crompton; a character in his way, whose peculiarities could hardly fail to have an influence on the mind of the nephew. Like the rest of the family, Uncle Alexander was strict in his religious observances, but being afflicted with lameness was unable to leave his room, in which, in fact, he lived and worked and slept, to attend the services of the sanctuary, and so he compensated himself for the deprivation in a manner that was as original as it was humble and respectful :—

On each succeeding Sunday [says Crompton's faithful biographer, Mr. French], when all the rest of the family had gone to service at All Saints' Chapel, Uncle Alexander sat in his solitary room listening for the first sound of the bells of Bolton Parish Church. Before they ceased ringing, he took off his ordinary working-day coat and put on that which was reserved for Sundays. This done, he slowly read to himself the whole of the Morning Service and a sermon, concluding about the same time that the dismissal bell commenced ringing, when his Sunday coat was carefully put aside,—to be resumed again, however, when the bells took up their burthen for the evening service, which he read through with the same solitary solemnity.

* The author is informed by Dr. Crompton, the grandson of the Inventor of the Mule, that Barlow engraved the plate for Arkwright's bill-heads. The plate itself was found a few years ago amongst a heap of old brass at Messrs. Peel's foundry in Ancoats, and some impressions were then taken from it.

Such was the household then occupying one of the wings of the rambling old mansion. Mrs. Crompton found no happiness in repose; ever doing and ever having much to do was her manner, and that was assuredly the fate of her son. From his earliest childhood the hours that should have been spent in harmless pastime were occupied in rendering such assistance as he could on the farm, or in the humble manufacturing operations carried on in the house, whilst his mother was bargaining and fighting with the outer world. He was put to the loom almost as soon as his legs were "long enough to touch the treddles," and when his day's task was done he was sent to a night school in Bolton to improve his knowledge of algebra, mathematics, and trigonometry. The poor weaver-lad had no playmates or associations with the outer world; he lived a life of seclusion, and his only companion in his brief moments of leisure was his fiddle. His father had been enthusiastically fond of music, and at the time of his death had begun the construction of an organ, leaving behind him a few oak pipes and the few simple tools with which he had made them. The amateur organ-builder's son inherited the father's taste, and made himself a fiddle—the first achievement of his mechanical genius. This was the companion of his solitude, and in after life his solace in many a bitter disappointment.

> With this musical friend [says French] he on winter nights practised the homely tunes of the time by the dim light of his mother's kitchen fire or thrifty lamp; and in many a summer twilight he wandered contemplatively among the green lanes or by the margin of the pleasant brook that swept round her romantic old residence.

And so passed the years of his adolescence—a virtuous, reserved, and industrious youth. The help and stay of a widowed mother—who, if a strict disciplinarian, yet devoted her best energies to the well-being of her family—shunning society, having no companions, and working diligently at his solitary loom, Crompton, if he found little leisure for amusement had at least abundance of time to think, and a thinker he became to his country's advantage.

While young Crompton was assiduously assisting his widowed mother, labouring at his loom by day and amusing himself with his fiddle by night, some of the artisans of his own county were exercising their inventive faculties on the rude appliances of their handicraft, for up to that time there had been little or no improvement on the art of Penelope in spinning and weaving—the distaff was still in common use, every thread being spun singly by the fingers of the spinner, and the machinery in vogue, if by such a name it could be called, was as primitive as that used by the Hindoo. Practical observation enabled them to elaborate their mechanical contrivances step by step, and so a series of progressive inventions followed each other. The invention of the fly-shuttle by Kay, of Bury, and the spinning jenny by Hargreaves, of Blackburn, gave a great impetus to the cotton manufacture, for by the former the productive power of the loom was greatly increased, whilst by the latter the supply of weft kept pace with the requirements of the weaver, but the mule was the real pivot on which its subsequent prosperity turned.

The spinning jenny of Hargreaves is believed to have been invented in the year 1764. It was kept a secret for some time, but before the close of the decade it had got into pretty general use in Lancashire, and was at that time so far perfected that a child could work with it eight spindles at one time. In 1769, Crompton, who was then a lad of sixteen years, spun on one of Hargreaves's machines the yarn which he afterwards wove into quilting, but the machine had many palpable imperfections; the yarn which it turned off had less tenacity than that produced by the old-fashioned single-thread wheel, and much time was lost in piecing the ever-breaking thread; but in Crompton's case the appointed task had to be got through, whatever difficulties might arise, for Mrs. Crompton was inexorable, and to avoid the maternal reproaches much time had to be given to the loom that might otherwise have been spent in pleasant companionship with the fiddle. For five long years the poor weaver lad led this lonesome, uneventful, all work and no play sort of life; no wonder, then, that he became reserved, shy and uncompanionable. For five long years he struggled on, following the dull, unremitting round of labour on his wearisome treadmill, without one single ray of cheering hope to brighten the gloom of his monotonous existence, when his ingenuity was driven to make such improvements in the spinning machine as would ultimately relieve him of the annoyances he was subjected to.

The time was not propitious for inventors. Hargreaves had been persecuted and ruined by the populace, and Arkwright had to remove to Nottingham to escape the popular animosity. Manufacturers were jealous lest their craft should be endangered, and workmen, in their ignorant prejudice against the introduction of new machines, resolved upon their destruction, while, by the common people, those who effected improvements were accounted "conjurors," a name of reproach given to those who were supposed to possess unnatural skill, and to hold commerce with the powers of darkness.

It was in 1774, when he was in his twenty-first year, that the first faint conception of the mule floated through Crompton's brain. The yarn spun by Hargreaves's jenny could only be used for "weft," by reason of its lacking the firmness and tenacity required in the long threads or "warp," while that produced from Arkwright's water frame was too coarse for the manufacture of muslins and other delicate fabrics in imitation of those imported from India. Crompton proceeded silently with the task he had set himself, even the members of the household having little idea of the way in which he occupied his time in the hours stolen from sleep when his day's work was done. Indeed, it was the system of night work that first drew the attention of his family and neighbours to his proceedings. "Strange and unaccountable sounds," says the authority we have previously quoted, "were heard in the Old Hall at most untimely hours, lights were seen in unusual places, and a rumour became current that the place was haunted." On investigation the young mechanical genius was found to be the ghost that had caused so much trouble and alarm to the good people of the locality.

Crompton's difficulty was increased by the fewness of his tools—those he possessed being such as his father had used in his rude attempts at organ building, supplemented by a clasp knife, which is said to have done excellent service; some others he purchased with such cash as he could spare from his slender earnings, and the money he received for his services at the Bolton Theatre, where, during the season, he was content to fiddle for the scanty pittance of eighteenpence a night. Five years of silent, secret, unremitting labour were spent in the realisation of his idea. Wanting in mechanical knowledge, destitute of proper tools, and having to learn the use of the imperfect ones he could procure, it is matter for surprise that in five years he succeeded in making his machine practically useful. His experiences at this time he thus relates in a MS. document he circulated about seventy years ago :

> The next five years had this addition added to my labour as a weaver, occasioned by the imperfect state of cotton spinning, viz., a continual endeavour to realise a more perfect principle of spinning; and though often baffled, I as often renewed the attempt, and at length succeeded to my utmost desire at the expense of every shilling I had in the world.

Neither poverty nor want of mechanical skill was permitted to hinder him. After much trembling and fretting from impecuniousness on the one hand, and the inquisitiveness of interlopers on the other; after matchless patience and unflinching perseverance; after many failures and disappointments, success at length crowned his efforts; his dream had become a reality, the mule* was an accomplished fact. In that same year, 1779, just as he was about to test its merits by putting it into actual work, an outbreak occurred among the Lancashire spinners and weavers; the riotous proceedings which had driven Hargreaves from his home were renewed, and while the storm was raging Crompton, fearing the mob might wreak their vengeance upon his wheel, prudently took

---

* The machine was at first, from the place of its birth, called the "Hall-i'-th'-Wood Wheel," and sometimes, from the fineness of the yarn it produced, the "Muslin Wheel," but subsequently it became more generally known as the "Mule," from the circumstance of its combining the principles of the two inventions of Hargreaves and Arkwright to produce a third much more efficient than either.

it to pieces and hid the parts away in the cocklofts of the old hall.
The incident is thus described by a recent writer :—

Crompton was well aware that his infant invention would be still more
obnoxious to the rioters than Hargreaves's jenny, and appears to have
taken careful measures for its protection or concealment should they have
paid a domiciliary visit to the Hall-in-the-Wood. The ceiling of the
room in which he worked is cut through, as well as a corresponding part
of the clay floor of the room above, the aperture being covered by replac-
ing the part cut away. This opening was recently detected by two visitors,
who were investigating the mysteries of the old mansion ; but they could
not imagine any use for a secret trap-door until, on pointing it out to Mr.
Bromiley, the present tenant, he recalled to his memory a conversation he
had had with Samuel Crompton during one of his latest visits to the Hall
many years ago. Mr. Crompton informed Mr. Bromiley that once, when
he was at work on the mule, he heard the rioters shouting at the destruction of a building at "Folds" (an adjoining hamlet), where there was a
carding engine. Fearing that they would come to the Hall-in-the-Wood
and destroy his mule, he took it to pieces and put it into a skip which he
hoisted through the ceiling into the attic by the trap-door, which had,
doubtless, been prepared in anticipation of such a visit, and which now offers
a curious evidence of the insecurity of manufacturing inventions in their
early infancy. The various parts were concealed in a loft or garret near
the clock, and there they remained hid for many weeks ere he dared to put
them together again. But in the course of the same year the Hall-in-the-
Wood wheel was completed and the yarn spun upon it used for the manufacture of muslins of an extremely fine and delicate texture.

Having succeeded to his utmost desire in solving the problem
on which during five eventful years of his life his mind had been
absorbed, Crompton had leisure to turn his thoughts in another
direction, and the first thing he did was to take to himself a wife.
He had made the acquaintance of an amiable and excellent
woman, Mary Pimlott, the daughter of a quondam West India
merchant, who had come down in the world and, as was said, had
died of a broken heart ; and on the 16th of February, 1780, the
young couple were married in the old church at Bolton. Mary
Pimlott is described as being a handsome dark-haired woman of
middle age and erect carriage, and possessed of remarkable power
in the perception of individual character. She was, moreover, a
"spinster" in the true sense of the word. On her father's death

54

she had gone to reside with friends at Turton, near Bolton, where ample and profitable employment could be obtained in spinning, and it is said that her expertness in the art first attracted young Crompton's attention.

The newly-married pair began housekeeping in a small cottage attached to the old hall, Crompton at the same time retaining one or more workrooms in the mansion where he and his young wife pursued their humble occupation, producing from the new wheel a yarn which both for fineness and firmness astonished the manufacturing community. It does not seem ever to have entered the mind of the young inventor to patent his machine. Accustomed to a quiet, secluded life, without any expensive habits or enjoyments, his highest ambition appears to have been to keep his invention to himself and to·work on in his own simple way in his own home after the fashion of the time, for it was then the idyllic period of cotton manufacturing, organised labour in huge factories being virtually unknown. But the fame of Crompton's yarn spread ; the new wheel was an unmistakable success, and gave promise of realising for its inventor an ample fortune. It was at once seen that the much-admired muslins that had been imported from India, and for which extravagant prices were paid, could now be produced by the English manufacturer, and at a greatly diminished cost. Crompton had his own price, and orders for the wonderful yarn poured in upon him ; the demand was urgent and pressing, and his house was literally besieged with manufacturers anxious to obtain supplies of the much-coveted material, and still more anxious to penetrate the secret of its production, for it soon became noised abroad that he had discovered some novel mode of spinning. People from miles round gathered about his house, anxious to solve the mystery; all kinds of stratagems were practised to obtain admission to his workroom; and when denied, some actually obtained ladders, clambered up to the window of his chamber, and peeped in to satisfy their curiosity. To protect himself from this kind of observation Crompton set up a screen, and then an inquisitive individual, more adventurous than the rest, secreted himself in one of the cocklofts of the hall, and remained there for days watching the operations going on through a gimlet hole he had bored in the ceiling.

There is a well-authenticated tradition that at this time Arkwright, who a few years before had erected a cotton mill at Cromford, in Derbyshire, the nursing place, as it has been called, of the factory opulence and power of Great Britain, made his way to the Hall-in-the-Wood, and contrived to gain access to the house with the object of inspecting the machine of which such wonderful tales were told while the inventor was away collecting rates for his mother, who, as we have said, filled the office of overseer for the township. Arkwright was then in the full tide of his success, and it was an unfortunate circumstance for Crompton that they did not meet. If they had it would probably have led to an arrangement whereby the simple, guileless inventor might have reaped the reward of many years of patient toil and personal sacrifice.

Had Crompton possessed a tithe of the energy and resources of the average Lancashire man he would have triumphed, but, unhappily for himself, these were just the qualities he lacked, and his diffidence and childlike simplicity made him an easy victim in the hands of unscrupulous and crafty traders. Had he bestirred himself there is no reason to doubt but that some capitalist would have been ready to advance the means to patent his invention, but his shyness and morbid sense of independence forbade him to ask for help or co-operation. What Arkwright and Peel did he might have accomplished; but, instead of his succeeding to opulence, he allowed others to reap where he had sown. His very success was the cause of his misfortunes. He was unable to carry on his work in undisturbed privacy, and his moody and sensitive nature could not bear the annoyance to which he was perpetually subjected by prying intruders. It was the crisis in his life. Tormented, worried, driven almost to distraction, he, in a weak moment, yielded to the advice of a well-intentioned but unwise counsellor, and surrendered his invention to an ungrateful community. When relating the story to Mr. G. A. Lee, and Mr. John Kennedy, of Manchester, some years afterwards, Mr. Lee having remarked that "it was a pity he had not kept the secret to himself," he replied "that a man had a very insecure tenure of property which another could carry away with his eyes." He says in the MS. before referred to :—

> During this time I married, and commenced spinning altogether. But a few months reduced me to the cruel necessity either of destroying my machine altogether or giving it up to the public. To destroy it I could not think of; to give up that for which I had laboured so long was cruel. I had no patent nor the means of purchasing one. In preference to destroying it I gave it to the public.

He says he "gave it to the public," and virtually he did ; for, though it was professedly for a consideration, he derived little or no benefit, and only found that he had been made the victim of the greed, and meanness, and sordid treachery of those whom, in his simplicity, he had trusted. Yielding to the deceitful promises of his townsmen and others, he was induced to surrender his much coveted secret on the faith of an agreement that, as it turned out, had no validity in law, and which some of the signatories were base enough to repudiate. The following are the terms in which it was drawn up :—

> Bolton, November 20th, 1780.
>
> We whose names are hereunto subscribed have agreed to give and do hereby promise to pay unto Samuel Crompton, at the Hall-in-the-Wood, near Bolton, the several sums opposite to our names as a reward for his improvement in Spinning. Several of the principal Tradesmen in Manchester, Bolton, &c., having seen his Machine approve of it, and are of opinion that it would be of the greatest utility to make it generally known, to which end a contribution is desired from every wellwisher of trade.

The total sum subscribed was £67 6s. 6d., but even of this miserable amount only about £50 was actually paid, "as much by subscription," says Crompton, "as built me a new machine with only four spindles more than the one I had given up [for he had not only surrendered his secret but the original machine with it]— the old one having forty-eight, the new one fifty-two spindles." Never, certainly, was so much got for so little, and a touch of infamy was added to the merciless transaction by a fact which Crompton thus records :—

Many subscribers would not pay the sums they had set opposite their names. When I applied for them I got nothing but abusive language to drive me from them, which was easily done: for I never till then could think it possible that any man could pretend one thing and act the direct opposite. I then found it was possible, having had proof positive.

These men, as has been truly said, saved their miserable guineas at the expense of their honesty and honour. The treatment to which he was subjected made a lasting impression on his mind. His very integrity increased his mortification at the dishonesty of those he had so generously trusted; his disposition—never a buoyant or cheerful one—was soured, and during the remainder of his life he was moody and mistrustful. While hundreds of manufacturers were accumulating colossal fortunes out of the results of Crompton's skill and ingenuity, the man himself, while so abundantly enriching them, was not able to gather even the smallest grains of the golden harvest, and, but for his energy and frugality, might have lapsed into absolute poverty, a martyr of mechanical invention and another illustration of the scriptural paradox, "Poor, yet making many rich."

It was a bitter disappointment to Crompton to find that the promises so pleasant to the ear were broken to the hope, that he had, in fact, been tricked into giving up the invention that had cost him so many years of anxious thought and toil to a host of selfish manufacturers who were making fortunes out of his simple trust. He became moody, suspicious, and distrustful of everything and everybody; but if he doubted the world he never lost heart in himself. Deprived of his just reward, he removed from the Hall-in-the-Wood to Oldhams, a small cottage across the valley near Astley Bridge, in Sharples, and distant about a mile and a half from Bolton. Here he farmed a few acres, kept three or four cows, and, still adhering to the common Lancashire custom, combined the business of a farmer with that of a manufacturer, and in one of the upper chambers of his house erected his newly-constructed machine. Familiar with the principles of his mule, he was naturally more skilful in the working of it than others; his wife, too, was an expert in spinning, and the yarn they spun was the best and finest in the market, and brought the highest prices; it was supposed, therefore, that he must have made some improvements in his machine, and, as a consequence, he was again pestered with inquisitive visitors anxious to discover the secret of his success, when, to protect himself from the unwelcome intrusion, he is said to have contrived a secret fastening to the door in the upper storey where he worked at the mule.

About this time Crompton invented a new carding-engine, and, anxious to extend his operations, he set up as an employer of labour, but the result was not satisfactory, for the people he engaged to spin under him were continually being bribed to enter the service of other masters, who hoped in this way to gain a knowledge of his secrets, so that eventually he was obliged to fall back upon the labours of his own household, and broke up the carding-engine, remarking that "the devils should not have that." He says :—

> I pushed on, intending to have a good share in the spinning line, yet I found there was an evil which I had not foreseen and of much greater magnitude than giving up the machine, viz., that I must be always teaching green hands, employ none, or quit the country; it being believed that if I taught them they knew the business well, so that for years I had no choice but to give up spinning or quit my native land. I cut up my spinning machines for other purposes.

Whilst residing at Oldhams, Crompton received a visit from Sir (then Mr.) Robert Peel, the first baronet, his object being to offer the inventor a lucrative appointment in his own manufactory, with the prospect of a future partnership, but Crompton's natural infirmity of temper and his quickness to take offence opposed a barrier to his own advancement. He had a prejudice against Peel on account of some imaginary affront,* and so the offer that might have led to his lasting comfort and prosperity was declined.

---

* Peel had bought one of the machines with the intention of causing drawings of it to be made. The affront was that on the occasion of his (Peel's) visit to Crompton's house, he had tendered the Inventor sixpence in consideration of his trouble in showing him the machine.

By this time the mule had become the machine chiefly employed for fine spinning, not only round Bolton but in the manufacturing districts of England, Scotland, and Ireland, and its general appropriation soon changed the neighbourhood of which Manchester was the centre from a country of small farmers to one of small manufacturers. Houses on the banks of streams whose currents would drive a wheel and shaft were eagerly seized upon ; sheds were run up in similar situations ; the clank of wheels and the buzz of spindles were heard in once solitary places in the valleys running off from the Irwell and upon the small streams that flowed down from the barren hills. Crompton's mules, worked by hand, " were erected in garrets or lofts, and many a dilapidated barn or cowshed was patched up in the walls, repaired in the roof, and provided with windows to serve as lodging room for the new muslin wheels," as they were called.

So great was the impetus given to manufacture by the invention of the mule that, within less than six years of its introduction, the number of inhabitants in Bolton had doubled ; whilst in the neighbouring town of Bury, which had " its cotton manufacture originally brought from Bolton," the increase was even more rapid. In order to provide for his increasing family, and, as is said, to escape the annoyance of his being re-elected overseer, Crompton, in 1791, removed from his pleasant little farm at Oldhams to a house in King Street, Bolton, where he enlarged his spinning operations, filling the attics over his own dwelling and those of the two adjoining houses with additional mules and machinery for manufacturing purposes—his elder boys being now able to assist him in his handicraft.

Five years later he had the misfortune to lose the loving and faithful partner of his joys and sorrows. She had been long ailing, and on the 29th of May, 1796, he followed her remains to their last resting place in the old churchyard at Bolton. It is stated that when he returned from the funeral he sat down brokenhearted and in utter despair ; it must have been a sorrowful day for him, for she left him with a family of eight young children.

55

Two of them were lying sick at the time in their cradles, and one died a short time after. The death of his wife made a deep impression on his mind and character. From his childhood he had been imbued with strong religious sentiments, and being of a naturally thoughtful and dreamy disposition, his religion was of a somewhat mystical kind; hence it is not surprising that he should have been led to withdraw from the communion of the Church of England and embrace the tenets of that amiable and philosophic teacher, Emanuel Swedenborg, who at that time had many followers in the town of Bolton. Crompton became a zealous member of the New Jerusalem Church, "taking entire charge of the psalmody," and occupying his leisure hours in composing hymn-tunes for the choir, which was wont to assemble on Sunday evenings at his house to practise.

He struggled manfully to maintain his young family in comfort and respectability, but he was comparatively helpless in the conduct of business, and altogether unfitted to deal with the practical affairs of life. He wrote on one occasion:—

"I found to my sorrow I was not calculated to contend with men of the world; neither did I know there was such a thing as protection for me on earth! I found I was as unfit for the task that was before me as a child of two years old to contend with a disciplined army."

When he did attempt to transact business, to such an extent was this weakness of character manifested that, as is said by his biographer—

"When he attended the Manchester Exchange to sell his yarns and muslins, and any rough-and-ready manufacturer ventured to offer him a less price than he had asked, he would invariably wrap up his samples, put them into his pocket, and quietly walk away."

His countenance was not sufficiently bronzed to enable him to contend successfully with the chafferers on 'Change. Like Watt, who declared he would rather face a loaded cannon than settle an account or make a bargain, he hated that jostling with the world inseparable from the conduct of extensive industrial or commercial operations; but, unlike Watt, he was not fortunate enough in the great crisis of his life to have met with a Boulton who had the quickness of perception to determine when to act and the energy of purpose to carry out the measures which his judgment approved.

It was not until 1800, twenty years after the invention of the mule, that any real attempt was made to recompense him for the sacrifices he had made, and for the inestimable benefits he had conferred upon the community in general and the district in which he laboured in particular. To Manchester belongs the credit of originating the movement. Two manufacturers there, Mr. John Kennedy, one of the founders of the great cotton-spinning firm of M'Connel and Kennedy, and Mr. George Lee, of the firm of Philips and Lee, appreciating the talents of the struggling inventor, started a subscription for the purpose of providing a comfortable competence for him in his declining years. The time was not opportune, and their efforts were in consequence only partially successful. It was the year in which Napoleon's overtures for peace were haughtily and offensively rejected by Lord Grenville; the war with France had imposed additional burdens upon the people, who were already suffering from a prolonged depression of trade; the scarcity caused by a deficiency in the harvest was commonly regarded as a consequence of the war; the country was on the brink of famine; mobs paraded the streets, and the Habeas Corpus Act had to be suspended to avoid the social danger to which a continuance of the rioting must of necessity lead. Comparatively few subscriptions were received; the kindly effort stuck fast, and eventually it had to be abandoned.* Between four and five hundred pounds was all that could be realised, and that was handed to Crompton, who sunk it in his little manufacturing establishment for spinning and weaving. His biographer says—

---

* It is pleasant to note that while so many of those in his own locality who had so largely profited by Crompton's labour either refused to help or gave only very grudgingly, the one who had suffered most by the success of the mule, Richard Arkwright, of Cromford (the second of the name), whose water frame had in a great measure been superseded by it, contributed £30, at the same time generously acknowledging the merits of the invention.

As a consequence of this additional capital, he soon after rented the top storey of a neighbouring factory, one of the oldest in Bolton, in which he had two mules—one of 360 spindles, the other of 220—with the necessary preparatory machinery. The power to turn the machinery was rented with the premises. Here also he was assisted by the elder branches of his family, and it is our duty, though a melancholy one, to record that the system of seducing his servants from his employment was still persisted in, and that one at least of his own sons was not able to withstand the specious and flattering inducements held out by wealthy opponents to leave his father's service and accept extravagant payment for a few weeks, during which he was expected to divulge his father's supposed secrets and his system of manipulating upon the machine.

Aided by the mule the cotton manufacture prodigiously developed itself. The tiny rill which issued from the Hall-i'-th'-Wood had become swollen into a mighty river, carrying wealth and prosperity along its course; and he who had started the stream looked not unreasonably to obtain some small share of the riches that were borne upon its bosom. With this hope, he was induced in 1807 to address a letter to Sir Joseph Banks, the then president of the Royal Society, in which he modestly set forth his grievances, and, describing himself as "a retired man in the country, and unacquainted with public matters," requested the society's advice "to enable him to procure from Government or elsewhere a proper recompense for his invention." There had been some mistake in the address of the letter. It, however, eventually found its way to the Society of Arts, where the application was discussed; but, to Crompton's great disappointment, nothing more came of it.

Four years later he made a survey of all the cotton districts in England, Scotland, and Ireland, and obtained an estimate of the number of spindles then at work on his principle. On his return he laid the results of his inquiries before his friends, Mr. Kennedy and Mr. Lee, with the suggestion that Parliament might "grant him something." It was proved that 4,600,000 spindles were at work upon his mules, using upwards of 40,000,000 pounds of cotton annually; that 70,000 persons were engaged in the spinning, and 150,000 more in weaving the yarn so spun, and that a population of full half a million derived their daily bread from the machinery his skill had devised. This statement, as was afterwards found, fell far short of the actual facts, for it did not include any of the numerous mules used in the manufacture of woollen yarn. The claim was indisputable. With the data before him Mr. Lee entered fully into the case. A Manchester solicitor, Mr. George Duckworth, of Duckworth and Chippindall, Princess Street, offered his gratuitous help, and drew up a memorial to Parliament on his behalf, which was signed by most of the principal manufacturers in the kingdom who were acquainted with his merits. In February, 1812, Crompton proceeded to London with this memorial, and obtained an interview with one of the Lancashire members : and, through the influence of powerful friends who appreciated his merits and sympathised with his misfortunes, he was enabled to place his memorial before Mr. Spencer Perceval, the Chancellor of the Exchequer, who appears to have taken a favourable view of his claim. The matter was referred to a select committee, of which Lord Stanley, the great-grandfather of the present Earl of Derby, was chairman. Evidence was given in favour of the inventor, and, among other information given, it was stated by Mr. Lee that at that time the duty paid upon cotton imported to be spun by the mule amounted to not less than £350,000 a year. The committee reported favourably, and the Chancellor of the Exchequer was ready to propose a vote of £20,000, when Crompton's usual ill-luck intervened in a very shocking manner. It was the afternoon of the 11th May, 1812, and Crompton was standing in the lobby of the House of Commons, conversing with Sir Robert Peel and Mr. John Blackburne, one of the members for Lancashire, when one of them observed, "Here comes Mr. Perceval." The group was instantly joined by the Chancellor of the Exchequer, who addressed them with the remark, "You will be glad to know I mean to propose £20,000 for Crompton. Do you think it will be satisfactory?" Hearing this, Crompton moved off from motives of delicacy, and did not hear the reply. He was scarcely out of sight when there was a great rush of people—Perceval had been shot dead by the madman Bellingham. The frightful catastrophe had in an instant deprived the country of a valuable minister, and lost to Crompton a patron and £15,000. When the new Government had been formed the matter was again brought before the House, and on the 26th of June, on the motion of Lord Stanley, it awarded him £5,000, a sum altogether inadequate for the services he had rendered, as well as out of all proportion to the rewards which Parliament had previously given to other inventors. In an article which appeared some years afterwards in the *Edinburgh Review**, the paltriness of the award was severely commented upon. The reviewer said :—

> To make a lengthened commentary on such a proceeding would be superfluous. Had the House of Commons refused to recognise Mr. Crompton's claim for remuneration they would, whatever might have been thought of their proceedings, have at least acted consistently. But to admit the principle of the claim, to enter into an elaborate investigation with respect to the merit and extensive application of the invention, and then to vote so contemptible a pittance to the inventor, are proceedings which evince the most extraordinary niggardliness on the part of those who have never been particularly celebrated for their parsimonious disposition towards individuals whose genius and inventions have alone enabled Parliament to meet the immense expenses the country has had to sustain.

With the £5,000, or rather with such portion of it as he received—for there were considerable deductions for fees and other charges—Crompton entered into various commercial speculations ; but the fickle goddess did not smile on any of them. Anxious to place his sons in some business, he fixed on that of bleaching, and rented a works at Over Darwen; his eldest and youngest sons, George and James, being admitted as partners. But the unfavourable state of the times, the inexperience and mismanagement of his eldest son, a bad situation, and a tedious and expensive lawsuit with the landlord conspired in a very short time to put an end to this establishment. He was also engaged in cotton spinning and manufacturing, in connection with his sons Samuel and John; but they disagreed, Samuel withdrawing from the concern and going

---

* Vol. xlvi., p. 16, 1827.

to Ireland, leaving his father to carry it on with such help as John could give him. The only business in which he may be said to have been at all successful was that of a cotton merchant, which he carried on in conjunction with his favourite son, William, and a Mr. Wylde. The firm eventually extended its operations to cotton spinning; but young Crompton disliking this branch of the business, the partnership was dissolved, the father and son retiring. The latter afterwards began business on his own account in Oldham, but the fate of the family followed him. He was unsuccessful; a fire consumed his stock, a lawsuit grew out of the fire; and finally, in 1832, he was carried off by an attack of cholera.

Left almost alone in the world, with old age creeping upon him, his sons dead or dispersed, and his only daughter—then a widow—for his housekeeper, Crompton carried on his small original business without assistance, "spending much of his time in devising the mechanism proper for weaving new patterns in fancy muslins." But his lack of business capacity and inability to cope with the common-place incidents of ordinary life destroyed his chances of success, and that unhappy fatality which had accompanied him through life still dogged his steps. To use his own words, he was "hunted and watched with as much never-ceasing care as if he was the most notorious villain that ever disgraced the human form; and if he were to go to a smithy to get a common nail made, if opportunity offered to the bystanders, they would examine it most minutely to see if it was anything but a nail." His patterns were pirated by his neighbours, who reproduced them in fabrics of inferior quality, and thus they were enabled to undersell and beat him out of the market. As he advanced in years his means became more and more straitened, and he was beginning gradually to drift into a state of poverty when, in 1824, Messrs. Hicks & Rothwell, of Bolton, his old friend, Mr. Kennedy, of Manchester, and some other sympathisers, unasked and unknown to Crompton, who had then reached his 72nd year, made a second subscription to purchase a life annuity, and the sum raised yielded a payment of £63 a year. He did not, however, live long to enjoy it. Wearied and worn out with cares and disappointments, but to the last retaining the esteem of his friends and the respect of all who knew him, he died by the gradual decay of nature at his house in King-street, Great Bolton, on the 26th June, 1827, at the age of seventy-three, and a few days later his body, followed by many voluntary mourners, was committed to the dust in the churchyard of Bolton, where a modest flagstone thus perpetuates his name :—

Beneath this stone are interred the mortal remains of Samuel Cromp-ton, of Bolton, late of Hall-i'-th'-Wood, in the township of Tonge, inventor of the spinning machine called the Mule; who departed this life the 26th day of June, 1827, aged 72 years.*

Such is the sad and simple story of the inventor of the spinning mule. Though his life was passed in comparative obscurity and neglect, and he was allowed to end his days in poverty, the name of Samuel Crompton will be held in honoured remembrance so long as the cotton trade endures, for it is to Crompton's mule more than to any other invention we owe that vast Lancashire industrialism which has been the source of untold benefits to his native shire, and has so greatly increased the power and wealth of the nation at large. Looking at the splendid results which his genius accomplished, it must ever be a cause of regret that Lancashire men did so little for him who did so much for them. In the various relations of life Crompton was in all things upright and honourable; he had his failings like other men, but they were those which arose from his simple and unsuspecting nature, and such as should excite commiseration rather than condemnation. The weak point in his character, and that from which nearly all his troubles and misfortunes arose, was the absence of those faculties which enable a man to hold equal intercourse with his fellows. His morbid sense of independence made him averse to the very appearance of favour or patronage, and to ask for even

* The age recorded on his gravestone is clearly an error, Crompton having been born on the 3rd December, 1753, so that he must have been in his 74th year.

that which was his due was always at the cost of acute pain. His manners and actions were at all times guided by a natural politeness and grace, as far from servility as rudeness. By those who knew him in the strength and fulness of his manhood he is described as having been handsome and singularly prepossessing in appearance, and this description is borne out by his portrait, which displays the lineaments of a well-formed head and face that strongly suggests the idea of the thoughtful philosopher and the true gentleman.

Though Crompton's memory remained long neglected, a succeeding generation has happily done something to remove the stain of ingratitude, and to atone in some measure for the shortcomings of his contemporaries. The late Mr. Gilbert James French, a man of energy, intelligence, and culture, first aroused his fellow townsmen to a better appreciation of the value of Crompton's achievements. In two lectures he delivered to the members of the Bolton Mechanics' Institute, and in the handsome volume subsequently issued—"The Life and Times of Samuel Crompton"—a work to which we are indebted for some of the facts here recorded, Mr. French gave a very circumstantial account of the great inventor's career; not content with this tribute to his memory, he set about obtaining subscriptions for the purpose of doing honour to Crompton's name. A sum of £2,000 was raised, and on the 24th Sept., 1862, a bronze statue of the inventor of the mule by Calder Marshall, with bas reliefs of Hall-i'-th'-Wood, and Crompton at work upon his machine, was presented with much pomp and circumstance and many outward manifestations of rejoicing to the Corporation of Bolton. In this tardy recognition of his services Bolton has done something to efface the reproach which the ingratitude of a former generation had stamped upon the town. But Crompton has a more fitting as well as a more enduring monument in those outward indications of active industry which now surround his humble dwelling-place, and borrowing the oft-repeated line from Wren's monument in St. Paul's, it may be said —*Si monumentum requiris—circumspice.*

56

The old dilapidated mansion in which his earlier years were passed still remains. His name has given it an historic importance it never before possessed. To Lancashire men it should be as a very Mecca, and it can never be looked upon with feelings other than those of the deepest interest, for it may be truly said that here the prosperity of the nation hung in suspense as the thoughts and expedients of Crompton's mind came and went, trembled, grew firm, and finally triumphed; and assuredly in no corner of England is the memorable couplet more strongly emphasised than in this now forlorn and weather-beaten abode :—

> Peace hath her victories
> Not less renowned than war.

INDEX.

57

JOHN HEYWOOD, Excelsior Steam Printing and Bookbinding Works,
Hulme Hall Road, Manchester.